GROWTH THEORY AND TECHNICAL CHANGE

ECONOMISTS OF THE TWENTIETH CENTURY

General Editors: Mark Perlman, *University Professor of Economics, Emeritus, University of Pittsburgh* and Mark Blaug, *Professor Emeritus, University of London, Professor Emeritus, University of Buckingham and Visiting Professor, University of Exeter*

This innovative series comprises specially invited collections of articles and papers by economists whose work has made an important contribution to economics in the late twentieth century.

The proliferation of new journals and the ever-increasing number of new articles make it difficult for even the most assiduous economist to keep track of all the important recent advances. By focusing on those economists whose work is generally recognized to be at the forefront of the discipline, the series will be an essential reference point for the different specialisms included.

A list of published and future titles in this series is printed at the end of this volume.

Growth Theory and Technical Change

The Selected Essays of Ryuzo Sato, Volume One

Ryuzo Sato

C. V. Starr Professor of Economics and Director of the Center for Japan–US Business and Economic Studies, New York University, US

ECONOMISTS OF THE TWENTIETH CENTURY

Edward Elgar
Cheltenham, UK • Brookfield, US

HD
82
.S36
1996

Published by
Edward Elgar Publishing Limited
8 Lansdown Place
Cheltenham
Glos GL50 2HU
UK

Edward Elgar Publishing Company
Old Post Road
Brookfield
Vermont 05036
US

A catalogue record for this book is available from the British Library

ISBN 1 85898 494 7

Printed and bound in Great Britain by Hartnolls Limited, Bodmin, Cornwall

Contents

Acknowledgements

The publishers wish to thank the following who have kindly given permission for the use of copyright material.

Academic Press Inc. for articles: 'Stability Conditions in Two-Sector Models of Economic Growth', *Journal of Economic Theory*, **1** (1), June 1969, 107–17; 'A Further Note on a Difference Equation Recurring in Growth Theory', *Journal of Economic Theory*, **2** (1), March 1970, 95–102.

American Economic Association for articles: 'Factor Prices, Productivity, and Economic Growth' with John W. Kendrick, *American Economic Review*, **LIII** (5), December 1963, 974–1003; 'Aggregate Production Functions and Types of Technical Progress: A Statistical Analysis' with Martin J. Beckmann, *American Economic Review*, **LIX** (1), March 1969, 88–101; 'Measuring the Impact of Technical Progress on the Demand for Intermediate Goods: A Survey' with Rama Ramachandran, *Journal of Economic Literature*, **XVIII**, September 1980, 1003–24.

Blackwell Publishers for article: 'The Harrod–Domar Model *vs* the Neo-Classical Growth Model', *Economic Journal*, **LXXIV** (294), June 1964, 380–87.

The Econometric Society for article: 'Optimal Savings Policy when Labor Grows Endogenously' with Eric G. Davis, *Econometrica*, **39** (6), November 1971, 877–97.

Gustav Fischer Verlag for article: 'A Note on Economic Growth, Technical Progress and the Production Function' with Martin J. Beckmann, *Yearbook of Economics and Statistics*, **189** (1/2), 1975, 139–42.

International Economic Review for articles: 'Shares and Growth under Factor-Augmenting Technical Change' with Martin J. Beckmann, **11** (3), October 1970, 387–98; 'The Estimation of Biased Technical Progress and the Production Function', **11** (2), June 1970, 179–208.

Oxford University Press for articles: 'Population Growth and the Development of a Dual Economy' with Yoshio Niho, *Oxford Economic Papers*, **23** (3), November 1971, 418–36; 'Factor Price Variation and the Hicksian Hypothesis: A Micro-economic Model' with Rama Ramachandran, *Oxford Economic Papers*, **39**, 1987, 343–56.

Introduction

Hitotsubashi University
In 1950, just five years after Japan's defeat in World War II, I entered Hitotsubashi University. My first semester there coincided with the beginning of Japan's new university system. Even the school's name was new: it had formerly been called the Tokyo University of Commerce.

Akita Prefecture, where I was born, is at the northernmost tip of Honshu, the main island of Japan, in what is known as the Tohoku region. Perhaps because of the remoteness of the place and the newness of my high school, Yuzawa Prefectural High, no one from there had ever before been accepted by a first-rate Tokyo-based national university directly upon graduation. The only other person from my school to go to Hitotsubashi University before myself was Zosei Ito (now president of Japan Life Co.), who was a year ahead of me.

At first I had considered taking the entrance examination for the University of Tokyo with the intention of specializing in mathematics, but my father promptly vetoed that idea. 'What do you plan to do?' he yelled, 'Teach arithmetic in elementary school? Economics is the subject of the future.' Because I had no confidence in my ability to pay my own way through school, I switched my sights to the Economics Department. My father, who had to deal with MacArthur's land reforms, had a particularly keen interest in economic issues. He instinctively realized that economics would be the key to Japan's postwar reconstruction. When I think about the way I got my start in a field that later came to fascinate me, I can't help being grateful to my father.

It was my father's decision that I take the entrance examination for Hitotsubashi University, because, in those days, Marxist economics was in fashion at the University of Tokyo. Since both the University of Tokyo and Hitosubashi belonged in the first group of national universities, which meant that their entrance examinations were held on the same day, it was impossible to take the examinations for both Universities.

Hitotsubashi University had its own special teaching system known as the 'seminar'. All students, when they reached their third year, would study in small groups under a single professor. Naturally enough, popular professors were swamped with applicants. The screening process consisted of an interview rather than an examination. The seminar I entered was that of Professor Ichiro Nakayama. Professor Nakayama was not only the president of the university but also the chairman of the Japanese government's Central Labour Relations Committee and in that capacity was then resolutely tackling some of the major issues facing postwar Japan. Reflecting the activities of Professor Nakayama, the seminar was extremely lively. In my year, 15 third-year students entered Professor Nakayama's seminar; my compatriot Zosei Ito had entered the previous year. Professor Nakayama was a major figure in politics, whose name was well known throughout Japan. He had the ability and influence to act as an adviser to prime ministers, though he stead-fastly refused to accept a cabinet post. He was also a scholar of great distinction who related the still embryonic trends in economic theory within Japanese academic circles to what was going on in the rest of the world.

In Professor Nakayama's seminar we read Alvin Hansen's *A Guide to Keynes*, J.R. Hicks's *Contribution to the Theory of the Trade Cycle* and *Value and Capital*, Roy Harrod's *Toward a Dynamic Economics*, and *Accumulation of Capital* by Joan Robinson. I also read Keynes's *General Theory*, but found it too difficult; to tell the truth, I couldn't make head or tail of it. *The Economics of John Maynard Keynes* by Dudley Dillard and *The Keynesian Revolution* by Lawrence Klein gave me a sense that I understood something of what Keynes was all about.

Students in the Nakayama seminar in those days generally tended to do research on Keynes, post-Keynesian economics or Schumpeter for their graduation thesis. At Professor Nakayama's suggestion, I wrote my thesis on *The Economics of Control* by Abba P. Lerner. This gave me my first opportunity to look at the problem of how capitalist principles of competition can be introduced into a socialist economic system. Lerner's name was almost totally unknown in Japan at that time. When I later had the chance to meet Professor and Mrs Lerner personally and heard from his own lips how he came to write that famous book, I felt a strange affinity. Compared with the writings of Keynes, Professor Lerner's English style was much easier for me to read back then.

When I was at Hitotsubashi, not much emphasis was given to microeconomic theory. However, I realize now that Professor Nakayama's book *Junsui Keizaigaku* ('Theory of Pure Economics') might well be called the Japanese version of the combined ideas of Walras and Cournot. This work was my introduction to mathematical economics and microeconomics. As I mentioned earlier, at one time I had considered majoring in mathematics, and my interest in the subject remained so great that, in addition to the guidance I received in the Nakayama seminar, I took courses in mathematical economics with Masio Hisatake and Kin'ichi Yamada. It was in these courses that I first came into contact with Paul Samuelson's *Foundations of Economic Analysis*, a book I was subsequently to translate into Japanese. I will discuss mine and Paul's long friendship later on.

In retrospect, I realize that basic education was given short shrift under the Japanese college system, which has the disadvantage of forcing students to specialize in a narrow field of concentration at an early period. Nevertheless, this was the period of confusion after the end of the war, when knowledge of modern economics was surging into Japan, and both Japanese society and the academic world were brimming with energy. With no clearly defined models to pigeonhole me, I spent a fruitful four years at Hitotsubashi absorbing that energy in my own way.

After graduation in 1954, I entered the Mitsui Trust and Banking Co. I was assigned to the Securities Department, but for the most part my work each day consisted of writing drafts of newspaper articles for the manager. There had been some doubt in my mind whether I would go to work for a bank or stay at the university and continue my studies. Japanese universities in those days did not have a well-developed system of graduate education and provided only an uneasy amalgam of an apprentice system and a self-directed learning process. What is more, in the year that I graduated, the boom brought about by the Korean War had ended and the Japanese economy was in a period of recession. Graduates who couldn't find good jobs would stay in school in the hope of finding better ones the following year. In such circumstances, anyone with a bid of confidence aspired to enter a first-rate company. This was the route I chose. I did not give up scholarship, however, or abandon the hope of continuing my study of theoretical economics. While working at Mitsui Trust, I was groping for some practical way to pursue my research and go to the United States to study. It was during this time (1956) that I wrote an article in Japanese entitled 'Growth Rates of Aggregate Supply and Demand: Equilibrium or Dis-equilibrium Growth' for *The Economic Studies Quarterly*, the official publication of the Japanese Economic Association. As I recall, the point of view expressed there was well received. When I later applied for a Fulbright Scholarship, I was able to include this work in my curriculum vitae. I now realize that the basic ideas for the PhD dissertation I submitted to Johns Hopkins are contained in this essay.

Johns Hopkins

When I first went to America as a Fulbright Scholar, I expected to return to Japan in a year and go back to work for the Mitsui Trust and Banking Co. However, I was so impressed by the high quality of graduate school education in the United States that once I had gotten a glimpse of a world of scholarship unimaginable in Japan, especially in the area of theoretical economics, I was determined to remain in America and go on for my PhD degree. In June 1959, I came to an amicable agreement with Mitsui Trust and left the company. That autumn I headed once again to America, this time with my new bride, Kishie Hayashi. The Ise Bay typhoon, which struck while we were on board ship, made a vivid impression on me. With no guarantees for the future, I had burned my bridges; there was no turning back.

My years at Johns Hopkins posed no major problems as far as my studies were concerned. However, life as a graduate student was hard, both because my wife was unused to living in a foreign country and because, to get around the Bank of Japan's currency restrictions then in effect, I had to supplement my meagre scholarship by exchanging yen for dollars with Americans going to Japan. (This was back when the official exchange rate was 360 yen to the dollar, but the going rate on the black market was 400 yen.) To complicate matters further, our son was born.

Because I had kept up with my studies during the five years since my graduation from Hitotsubashi, my background in mathematical economics was not inferior to that of American specialists in this field. On the other hand, the atmosphere at Johns Hopkins in those days was not favourable to the application of mathematics to economics; Professor Fritz Machlup, for example, had the attitude that anything that could be expressed by mathematics ought to be able to be put into words. He would appear at his lectures carrying a compass and a long ruler, carefully draw a graph, and call this a 'theoretical explanation'. In those days it was customary for speakers at the weekly department seminar to begin a theoretical presentation with an apology for using mathematics. That attitude is poles apart from today when economists apologize if they cannot provide neat mathematical proofs for their work.

As part of my PhD programme I took classes with Kuznets and Ed Mills, but the person who made the greatest impression on me was Richard Musgrave. Although not a mathematical economist himself, Musgrave had a deep appreciation of mathematical methods. I became a statistical research assistant for a project of his on tax-shifting that he later published as a book (*The Shifting of the Corporation Income Tax*, Johns Hopkins University Press, 1963) and kindly mentioned my contribution in its preface. Every morning I would input all the data by hand and use an electronic data-processing machine to estimate least square regressions. From today's perspective, when the computer software is available to provide the answers instantaneously, it seems like a completely different world.

As a result of this association, I decided to write my doctoral dissertation under Professor Musgrave – or to be more accurate, such a course of events seemed natural to us both. His book *Public Finance* had just come out, and every day I combed through it in search of a topic to treat in my thesis which hadn't been included.

My interest in growth theory, which had taken shape during my days at Hitotsubashi and which could be glimpsed in my first scholarly work published in *The Economic Studies Quarterly*, became more firmly established at Johns Hopkins. I avidly read Solow's 'Contribution to the Theory of Economic Growth' and Swan's 'Economic Growth and Capital Accumulation', both of which had come out in 1956. These works formed the basis for neoclassical growth theory at that time, and I knew their contents so well that I could take the arguments apart and then put them back together again.

The essence of the neoclassical growth model is this: *the long-run equilibrium growth rate is determined by the population (labour force) growth rate and by the rate of technical progress, but is not dependent on the savings rate.* One day, however, Musgrave said to me: 'If fiscal policy boosts the total savings rate, even in the neoclassical growth model, the growth rate ought to go up.' 'The condition needed for that to happen, I suppose, would be a slow adjustment time for long-run equilibrium,' I replied. This conversation of ours led to the writing of my very first article as a graduate student (the essay that serves as Chapter 1 of this book). As soon as I got home that day, I set to work trying to demonstrate the proposition. I completed the calculations in about a week and showed the results to Musgrave. 'So,' he said with a satisfied look, 'fiscal policy is relevant even in the neoclassical growth model.' He urged me to write up my findings. The resulting article was the first one I had ever written in English. I showed a draft of it to Musgrave, who complained that he couldn't understand what I was trying to say. He pointed out problems with my English sentences and right in front of me helpfully rewrote parts of the introduction.

Professor Musgrave, who had been born in Germany and received his PhD from Harvard, was particularly careful in his use of the English language. He gave useful advice to someone like me who had been born in Japan and was trying to earn a PhD in America. The original version of Chapter 1 first appeared in the *Review of Economic Studies* in 1963, but it had all been completed in 1960. It also became a chapter in my PhD dissertation, which I submitted in 1962. Those are the circumstances under which my article came to be written. In retrospect, I realize the large role played by Professor Musgrave's incomparable scholarly instincts. The controversy over adjustment time continues to this very day in works by Atkinson, King and Rebelo, among others. This theme is also related to the problem of convergence in economic growth as treated, for example, by Barro, Mankiw and Sala-i-Martin.

The actual numerical simulations which I worked out as examples at the time I was writing Chapter 1 were published in the *Economic Journal* and appear as Chapter 2 of this book. The conclusion I reached more than 35 years ago of a long adjustment time in the neoclassical model has been tested and modified but remains unchanged. However, should we regard the fact that Japan has caught up to America in a matter of 50 years as slow or fast? That depends, I suppose, on the criteria used.

There are two points I would like to draw special attention to about my years at Johns Hopkins. The first is the presence of a professor who gave me an interest in history to complement my deep fascination with mathematics. Although Mark Perlman was not my PhD adviser, my fellow students and I all respected him as a good teacher and a kind human being to whom we could talk about even private matters. He was a great asset to Johns Hopkins.

The second point is the freedom I had to pursue my own interest. I imagine that nowadays the PhD programme at Johns Hopkins, as elsewhere, is structured and systematized, but at the time I was there it was extremely flexible. To cite an extreme example, once you took the comprehensive exam, you were then free to do whatever you wanted. After I finished the article mentioned above and while my PhD thesis was beginning to take shape, I used the rest of my time at Johns Hopkins to take courses in advanced mathematics. I studied differential geometry and Lie group theory and became very good friends with Hiroshi Gunji (now a professor of mathematics at the University of Wisconsin), who was then a PhD student in the Maths Department. The training I received at that time was very useful and would serve as the mathematical basis for the book I would later publish, *Theory of Technical Change and Economic Invariance: Application of Lie Groups* (Academic Press, 1981). In those days, however, I had no intention whatsoever of applying mathematics to economics, but studied it in only a general way because I found the subject interesting. It was only later, under the influence of Professors Paul A. Samuelson and Takayuki Nôno, that I came to realize that differential geometry and Lie groups could be applied to economics.

My first job was as an assistant professor at the University of Washington in Seattle. Although I had received better offers from other universities, I went to Seattle because at the time the East Coast offered almost nothing in the way of Japanese food or Japanese culture, and my wife, who was homesick, was eager to move to the West Coast where she could be a little bit closer to Japan. The following year I went to the University of Hawaii and was also affiliated with the East–West Center. As a Fulbright Scholar, I had entered the United States on an exchange visa, but I would need a permanent visa if I was to continue teaching in the US. To get it would require going through special formalities with the American immigration authorities. We moved to Hawaii on the condition that the University of Hawaii would prepare the necessary petition to present to immigration on my behalf. Hawaii had the additional advantage of providing Japanese language education for my son, who was then two years old.

My meeting with Professor John Kendrick, who was then a visiting professor at the University of Hawaii, was to bring about a major change in my subsequent career. Professor Kendrick and I were kindred spirits as far as both our personal and academic interests were concerned. He taught me how to combine an empirical perspective with the theoretical grounding I had already gained. The fruits of our joint research during this period were published in the *American Economic Review* (here, Chapter 3).

Although many of my friends had their doubts as to whether any serious scholarly work could be done in a tropical paradise like Hawaii, the years we spent there, I believe, enabled us to lay the groundwork for our life in both the United States and Japan. Because Hawaii is close to Japan, it was possible for our two children to be enrolled in Japanese schools during the long summer vacations and receive their compulsory education in Japan.

Brown University

I went to Brown University as a vistor in 1965, became a full professor there in 1967, and stayed for nearly 20 years. Most of the essays collected in this volume were written during my period at Brown. I devoted myself exclusively to teaching and research and saw my articles published in journals that are known worldwide.

At Brown, I was fortunate to have such good colleagues as Martin Beckmann and Harl Ryder and to participate with them and others in the Harvard–MIT Mathematical Economics Seminar. When the three of us received our first research grant from the National Science Foundation, the direction of my research moved into a new field. In a joint study with Beckmann (Chapter 11) we were the first to deduce a factor-augmenting type of technical change from the concept of neutrality and establish its theoretical legitimacy. Technical change of this type was independently verified by Hugh Rose in an article in the *Economic Journal* in 1969, a year after our article first appeared. This kind of technical change later became known as the 'Sato–Beckmann neutrality' (Chapter 8), although properly speaking it should be called the 'Sato–Beckmann–Rose type'.

The article I consider a turning point in my thinking was the one that first tested the estimation of the factor-augmenting (Sato–Beckmann–Rose) type of technical change (Chapter 12). Although the article in the *American Economic Review* (Chapter 13) came out before Chapter 12, the latter had been completed in 1965. At a more theoretical level, the article in Chapter 7 analyses whether balanced. growth is possible in a model that posits the existence of the factor-augmenting type of technical change. A more general problem is treated in the article in the *Review of Economic Studies* (Chapter 9).

I subsequently received a Ford Fellowship and a Guggenheim Fellowship and went to Cambridge University and Bonn University to teach and do research. This gave me the opportunity to visit Sir John Hicks. He was interested in difference equations, which he had discussed in his book on *The Trade Cycle*. I was aware of Kakeya's theorem and, as a result of my discussions with Hicks, I was able to write the article that appeared in the *Journal of Economic Theory* (Chapter 10).

The 1960s was a time when growth theory developed rapidly through the application of optimal control theory. The article I wrote with Eric Davis, my first PhD student at Brown, was the first to solve the problem of the golden rule of capital accumulation when labour grows endogenously (Chapter 5). It showed that the 'standard golden rule' had to be modified.

My research then turned to the issues of endogenous growth and endogenous technical change. The joint article on 'endogenous factor augmenting' (Chapter 15) and the survey paper (Chapter 18) that I did with Ramachandran, a brilliant student of mine and now my closest colleague, were extremely useful to my future work. The article I did with Niho (Chapter 6) in the area of the theory of economic development, as well as the one I did with Tsutsui (Chapter 17) that created a model of Schumpeter's hypothesis, are important guideposts to the direction my subsequent research would take.

Two aspects of my life during my years at Brown are worth a special mention. The first was the establishment of a lifestyle that saw us spend four to six months each year in Japan so that my two children could receive a Japanese education. They were thus able to complete their elementary and middle school education simultaneously in both the United States and Japan. During this time, I taught at Japanese universities and did joint research with Japanese scholars. I was also able to keep up my contacts with influential people in Japanese corporations and other sectors of Japanese society. When I later moved to New York University to head the Center for Japan–US Business and Economic Studies, these contacts were to form the basis of a vital pipeline for the Center. The fact that I had not spent my scholarly life exclusively in the United States and had not lost touch with Japan would prove invaluable to my subsequent career.

The second point was that during that 20-year period I was fortunate to meet many of the most famous and influential economists and mathematicians in the world. In particular, my close personal and scholarly relationship with Professor Paul A. Samuelson continues to this very day. I formed a close personal friendship of a different kind with Professor Takayuki Nôno, who came to Brown University as a visiting professor in the Department of Mathematics. My association with him was crucial in my continuing my research into Lie groups. The training in mathematics I received at Johns Hopkins was a valuable tool for this work.

While I was at Hawaii, I published a Japanese translation of Samuelson's *Foundations*. Later, at the Harvard–MIT Mathematical Economics Seminar, I was privileged to have the opportunity to hold many friendly discussions with him. One of the fruits of our joint research from this period is the article entitled 'Unattainability of Integrability and Definiteness Conditions in General Case of Demand for Money and Goods' (*American Economic Review*, September 1984), which will be found in Volume Two (a later volume in this series). In the mid 1970s, by chance I came across an article on conservation laws that Samuelson had published in a non-economics journal (*Proceedings of the National Academy of Science, Applied Mathematics Science, Vol. 67, 1970*). This prompted me to analyse conservation laws and technical progress through the full-scale application of Lie groups; the result was the article on holotheticity that was published in the *Review of Economic Studies* (Chapter 14) and is also in my book *Theory of*

Technical Change. Among the many joint studies I have done with Professor Nono, the one in Chapter 16 solves the difficult problem of optimal endogenous technical change using differential-integral equations.

New York University

As I mentioned earlier, most of the essays in this volume were written before I moved to New York University and the Stern School of Business in 1985. I was given the C.V. Starr Chair in Economics there and became the first director of the Center for Japan–US Business and Economic Studies. In addition, I have continued to hold the teaching position at John F. Kennedy School of Government at Harvard University which I took up towards the end of my stay at Brown.

My responsibilities as director of the Center include organizing research conferences, arranging for monthly panel discussions, and fund-raising. However, these duties have provided me with the quite unexpected incidental benefit of cultivating close personal friendships with an even greater number of distinguished economists in different fields from all over the world than I ever had the opportunity of meeting before. The Center provides a variety of forums in which scholars such as Samuelson, Tobin, Merton Miller, Baumol, Krugman, Gene Grossman, Dixit, Sachs, Zeckhauser and Bhagwati join my NYU colleagues and well known scholars from Japan to discuss topical issues and ongoing research. The year after I moved to NYU, Samuelson joined the Center as the Long-Term Credit Bank of Japan Visiting Professor.

My enthusiasm for writing scholarly articles suitable for publication in academic journals has been, if anything, stronger than ever. Moreover, because of the nature of my job at the Center, my relationship with Japan has deepened and the length of time I spend there has steadily increased. Japan and the United States are the world's two economic superpowers. My recent work has been a theoretical analysis of the economic problems common to them both; one example of this work is an essay in Volume Two that uses differential game theory. But, more than anything else, since taking on the position as Chief Editor for *Japan and the World Economy: International Journal of Theory and Policy*, an academic journal published by North Holland, my interests are no longer confined to mathematical economics, but have broadened in scope. In particular, many of my recent papers have been published under the auspices of the technical research symposium which is held by the Center each year to stimulate interest in scholarly research by bringing together experts from Japan and the US.

Although the move to NYU may appear on the surface to have been a career change, in a sense my having spent a part of each year doing research in Japan ever since my days at Brown can be said to have borne fruit at NYU. It is my modest hope that my contributions to the study of theoretical economics and a better understanding between the United States and Japan may continue to be productive in the years to come.

PART ONE

GROWTH THEORY

[1]

Fiscal Policy in a Neo-Classical Growth Model: An Analysis of Time Required for Equilibrating Adjustment[1]

Solow has shown that, in certain circumstances when substitution between capital and labor is allowed, the warranted rate of growth in the Harrod-Domar model approaches the natural rate of growth [5]. Suppose the economy is in long-run equilibrium growth. Suddenly the savings ratio is increased as a result of fiscal policy. The growth rate of income will rise; but after this initial rise it will decline, moving back towards the equilibrium rate, which is the natural rate of growth. In this " neo-classical " model of growth,[2] we find three main differences from the Harrod-Domar model. First, the equilibrium rate of growth (reference being to true long-run equilibrium, or the natural rate of growth) is now independent of the rate of capital accumulation. It is determined by the growth rate of the labor force and the state of technology. Given these two factors, there is only one rate of capital accumulation that is compatible with equilibrium growth, the one which equates capital growth and income growth. Second, the system is now such that any departure from equilibrium, for instance through an excessive rate of saving, leads to an automatic equilibrating movement back to the natural rate of growth. Third, by using the production function the profit rate, the wage rate and the income per head of the labor force are brought into the model.

When the economy deviates from the natural rate of growth, what factors determine the time length for adjustment from one equilibrium to another? Assuming the neo-classical model, what time period is required for an economy to return to the equilibrium rate with a given amount of adjustment when the approximate values of parameters in the economy are known? What policy implications has the adjustment period with respect to the growth rate of national product and the level of income per head of the labor force? This paper proposes to answer these questions.

[1] I wish to thank Professor Richard A. Musgrave of Princeton University and Professor Edwin S. Mills of the Johns Hopkins University for their encouragement and advice. I also wish to express my appreciation to R. G. Lipsey, Managing Editor, and the referees of this *Review* for their helpful suggestions. I had a chance to discuss this work with Robert M. Solow and Jürg Niehans to whom thanks are due. Donald F. Gordon and Dean A. Worcester of the University of Washington also gave useful comments at various stages of this work. My thanks are due to W. Russell and M. Hansen for their assistance in revising the original paper.

[2] T. W. Swan [7] presents a similar approach to Solow's model. Hahn's model [3] and Tobin's model [8] are also considered to be neo-classical models. Fiscal policy in the Harrod-Domar model has been extensively studied by Professor Musgrave [4, pp. 472-500].

1. A MODEL OF ECONOMIC GROWTH

Let us make the following assumptions: (1) there is only one commodity $Y_{(t)}$ in the society; (2) at any time the production of $Y_{(t)}$ requires two factors of production, capital and labor, $K_{(t)}$ and $L_{(t)}$ respectively; (3) all markets are perfectly competitive; thus, planned investment equals planned saving and the possibility of unemployment is automatically eliminated. The rate of interest and the wage rate adjust to the marginal productivities of capital and labor instantaneously; (4) the natural rate of growth is given outside and independent of fiscal policy; that is, the growth rate of the labor force and technology is independent of fiscal policy. (5) We assume a linear, homogeneous production function; $Y_{(t)}$ is subject to the Cobb-Douglas function multiplied by the neutral technological improvement factor $A_{(t)}$. This production function assures the stability of the long-run equilibrium.[1] Thus,

$$Y_{(t)} = A_{(t)} \ K_{(t)}^a \ L_{(t)}^b \tag{1}$$

where $a + b = 1$. Let $A_{(t)}$ be equal to $A_0 e^{pt}$, that is, technology is improving at p per cent a year, and $L_{(t)} = L_0 e^{nt}$, that is, the labor force is increasing at n per cent a year. Differentiating (1) totally with respect to time, we obtain

$$\frac{\dot{Y}}{Y} = \frac{\dot{A}}{A} + a\frac{\dot{K}}{K} + b\frac{\dot{L}}{L} \tag{2}$$

where $\dot{Y}$ is Newton's notation for $\frac{dY}{dt}$ and so forth. Substituting $\frac{\dot{A}}{A} = p, \frac{\dot{Y}}{Y} = G_Y$ and $\frac{\dot{L}}{L} = n$, we get

$$G_Y = p + a\frac{\dot{K}}{K} + bn \tag{3}$$

Let α be a fraction of total savings (private and public) of the national income. Thus,

$$\alpha = [x + s(1 - x) - g(1 - h)] \tag{4}$$

where x = proportionate income tax rate, s = private saving ratio, g = government expenditures for goods and services as a fraction of national income, and h = governmental capital formation as a fraction of government expenditures. From assumption (3), net investment $\dot{K}$, is equal to the total savings. Thus,

$$\dot{K} = \alpha Y_{(t)} \tag{5}$$

Letting $\frac{Y}{K}$, the output-capital ratio, be equal to r, equation (3) becomes,

$$G_Y = p + a\alpha r + bn \tag{6}$$

When $G_Y = G_K = \alpha r$, the growth rate of capital, r will be constant and remain constant, and the system will be in the long-run equilibrium. In Harrod's model, when r is constant, the warranted rate of growth is equal to the natural rate of growth. Thus r is the stability criterion; divergence of the warranted rate from the natural rate depends on

---

[1] This is one of the examples Solow uses in his analysis of stability in the long-run equilibrium [5, p. 76].

whether r is constant or not.[1] Let us define the constant r as the equilibrium value of the output-capital ratio and designate it by r^*. Then the value of G_Y, when r is equal to r^*, is

$$G_Y^* = \frac{p}{b} + n \tag{7}$$

Thus G_Y^* is the natural rate of growth. It is given by the technological improvement factor p, and the share of labor b, and the growth rate of the labor force n, but by assumption (4), it is independent of the savings ratio and of governmental parameters. G_Y^* is equal to the equilibrium growth rate of income per head of the labor force $\frac{p}{b}$ and the growth rate of the labor force n, because the equilibrium income per head of the labor

force y^* is equal to $A_0^{\frac{1}{b}} \, e^{\frac{p}{b}t} \left(\frac{1}{r^*}\right)^{\frac{a}{b}}$.

Now what happens to G_K and G_Y if the total savings ratio α is changed, be it through fiscal policy or by some other means? Suppose, for instance, the tax rate x is increased. As a result, the growth rate of income defined by equation (6) will rise.[2] But after this initial rise it will begin to decline, moving back towards the natural rate of growth which has remained unchanged. This can be analyzed from the differential equation containing the output-capital ratio. To obtain the differential equation, first differentiate $Y_{(t)} = r_{(t)} \cdot K_{(t)}$ with respect to t and after dividing by Y equate it to equation (6). Since $b = (1 - a)$ the differential equation we obtain is

$$\dot{r} = br \left[\left(\frac{p}{b} + n\right) - \alpha r \right]. \tag{8}$$

This is a Bernoulli equation and thus it can be reduced to a linear differential equation

by setting $\frac{1}{r} = v$. Then since $\dot{v} = -\frac{\dot{r}}{r^2}$, equation (8) becomes a linear equation of the

---

[1] Note that in Solow's model, the stability criterion is $\frac{K}{L}$, the capital-labor ratio, and in general it is

different from our criterion $\frac{Y}{K}$, the output-capital ratio. They are the same only when p, the technological

improvement factor, is zero. But if p is not zero, Solow's criterion $\frac{K}{L}$ cannot be constant in equilibrium,

while our criterion $\frac{Y}{K}$ will be constant. From $Y = A_0 \, e^{pt} \, K^a \, L^b$, $\frac{K}{L} = \left(\frac{A_0 e^{pt}}{r}\right)^{\frac{1}{b}}$. In equilibrium

$G_Y = G_K$; $\frac{Y}{K}$ will be constant, while $\frac{K}{L}$ will be increasing at $\frac{p}{b}$ per cent a year. Therefore we prefer

$\frac{Y}{K}$ to $\frac{K}{L}$ as the criterion.

[2] The impact of a sharp rise in the savings ratio may be of minor importance for the growth rate of income under the assumption of the Cobb-Douglas production function, but we are not interested in the magnitude of increase.

6 Growth Theory and Technical Change

first order, $\dot{v} = b\alpha - (p + bn)v$. Solution is[1] $v_{(t)} = \dfrac{b\alpha}{p + bn} + Ce^{-(p+bn)t}$ or

$$r_{(t)} = \frac{p + bn}{b[\alpha + Be^{-(p+bn)t}]} \tag{9}$$

The above equation shows that during the adjustment period the output-capital ratio r is decreasing from its original value to the new equilibrium value r^* which is equal to $\dfrac{p + bn}{b\alpha}$. Thus during the adjustment period the actual growth rate of income G_Y is higher than the natural rate of growth G_Y^*; as t approaches infinity r will approach r^*. Given sufficient time G_Y will always return to the natural rate G_Y^*.

Although the growth rate of aggregate income G_Y returns to the natural rate of growth G_Y^* which has remained unchanged, the level of aggregate income is now higher than it would have been had the savings ratio not changed. Since we assumed that the growth rate of the labor force has remained constant, the income per head of the labor force must have reached a higher level. If y^* is the equilibrium income per head, it is

equal to $A_0^{\frac{1}{b}} e^{\frac{p}{b}t}\left(\dfrac{1}{r^*}\right)^{\frac{a}{b}}$, but r^* is now lower because $r^* = \dfrac{p + bn}{b\alpha}$ and α is increased,

and therefore y^* is at a higher level though its rate of increase is exactly the same as before.[2] With technology and the share of the labor force given, the equilibrium level of income per head of the labor force depends solely on the total savings ratio and thus on the governmental parameters.

---

[1] The general Bernouli equation $\dfrac{dr}{dt} + Q_{(t)} r = P_{(t)} r^q$ can be reduced to a linear equation by substituting $v = r^{1-q}$. See E. L. Ince [2, pp. 91-103]. Equation (8) can be solved without changing to a

linear form by integrating. Let $\left[\dfrac{p}{b} + n\right]$ be equal to N, then $\displaystyle\int \dfrac{dr}{r(N - \alpha r)} = bt + C$. $\dfrac{1}{N}\left[\displaystyle\int \dfrac{dr}{r} + \right.$

$\left. \alpha \displaystyle\int \dfrac{dr}{N - \alpha r}\right] = bt + C$.

$\dfrac{1}{N}\left[\log_e r - \log_e(N - \alpha r)\right] = bt + C$. $\log_e\left(\dfrac{r}{N - \alpha r}\right) = Nbt + C'$. $\dfrac{r}{N - \alpha r} = Ae^{Nbt}$.

$r = \dfrac{N}{\alpha + A^{-1} \cdot e^{-Nbt}}$. Let $A^{-1} = B$ and since $N = \left[\dfrac{p}{b} + n\right]$, $r = \dfrac{p + bn}{b[\alpha + Be^{-(p + bn)t}]}$.

[2] In equilibrium the wage rate is also at a higher level, but the profit rate is at a lower level, because the wage rate

$$w^* = A_0^{\frac{1}{b}} b \, e^{\frac{p}{b}t}\left(\frac{1}{r^*}\right)^{\frac{a}{b}}$$ and the profit rate $\pi^* = ar^*$. It was pointed out by the referees of

this *Review* that the contrast between values of y^* before and after changes in the savings ratio will depict more clearly what happens when the system moves from one equilibrium to another.

2. ANALYSIS OF THE ADJUSTMENT PERIOD

We showed that if G_Y deviates from G_Y^*, it will return to G_Y^*, given sufficient time. Theoretically when t approaches infinity, then complete adjustment will be achieved. As a practical matter, however, we are interested in knowing how long it will take to achieve virtually complete adjustment, e.g. 90 per cent of the resulting change in the output-capital ratio, or 90 per cent of the return to the natural rate. Once this adjustment is completed, then income per head of the labor force will approach the new level which

is higher than the old one and grow at the constant rate, $\frac{p}{b}$ per cent a year.

Let k be the percentage of the total amount of change in the level of income per head of the labor force y caused by the change in r.[1] Let α_0 and α_1 be the old and new savings ratios respectively. Let r_0^* and r_1^* be the old and new equilibrium values of r corresponding

to α_0 and α_1. Then $r_0^* = \dfrac{p + bn}{b\alpha_0}$ and $r_1^* = \dfrac{p + bn}{b\alpha_1}$. When $t = 0$ equation (9) becomes

$\dfrac{p + bn}{b(\alpha_1 + B)}$ and it must be equal to r_0^*. From this, B is equal to $(\alpha_0 - \alpha_1)$. Thus equation (9) can be written as

$$r_{(t)} = \frac{p + bn}{b[\alpha_1 + (\alpha_0 - \alpha_1)\ e^{-(p + bn)t}]} \tag{10}$$

Let the total amount of adjustment in r from r_0^* to r_1^* be $\triangle r^*$, then it is equal to $r_0^* - r_1^* = \dfrac{(\alpha_1 - \alpha_0)\ (p + bn)}{b\alpha_0\ \alpha_1}$. Suppose that at $t = t_k$ the adjustment in r is k per cent of the total

adjustment. Therefore $\triangle r^* k$ is the amount of adjustment at t_k. Let r_k be the value of r at t_k, then

$$r_k = r_0^* - \triangle r^* k = \frac{(p + bn)\ [\alpha_1 - k(\alpha_1 - \alpha_0)]}{b\alpha_0\ \alpha_1}. \tag{11}$$

But r_k must also be equal to r in equation (10) with $t = t_k$, thus

$$\frac{p + bn}{b[\alpha_1 + (\alpha_0 - \alpha_1)\ e^{-(p \cdot bn)t_k}]} = \frac{(p + bn)\ [\alpha_1 - k(\alpha_1 - \alpha_0)]}{b\alpha_0\ \alpha_1}. \quad \text{From this}$$

$$e^{(p + bn)t_k} = 1 + \frac{\alpha_0\ k}{\alpha_1\ (1 - k)} \quad \text{or}$$

$$t_k = \frac{\log_e\left[1 + \dfrac{\alpha_0\ k}{\alpha_1\ (1 - k)}\right]}{p + bn}. \tag{12}$$

[1] Note that k is not the percentage of the initial value associated with " time constant ".

Equation (12) shows the relationships between the adjustment time of k per cent t_k and other parameters in the system.   Exact relationships can be deduced from the signs of the partial derivatives of t_k with respect to the other parameters.   However, it can be seen by inspecting the above equation that for positive values of all parameters t_k is a monotonically increasing function of α_0 and k, and it is a monotonically decreasing function of α_1, p, b and n.   Therefore the following fundamental results may be stated:[1]

(1) The greater the initial savings ratio, the longer the adjustment period.
(2) The higher the new savings ratio, the shorter the adjustment period.
(3) The higher the productivity increase, the shorter the adjustment period.
(4) The higher the population increase, the shorter the adjustment period.
(5) The greater the share of labor or the smaller the share of capital, the shorter the adjustment period.
(6) The larger the percentage of adjustment, the longer the adjustment period.

Two qualifications to the basic model are in order.   First, consider the general linear, homogeneous production function

$$Y = F(K, L) \tag{13}$$

For simplicity we assume that the neutral technological improvement factor, p, is zero, and the system is stable.   The Cobb-Douglas production function which we used in the previous discussion is a special case when the elasticity of factor substitution is equal to unity, $\sigma = 1$.   If σ can take any value except unity subject to $0 < \sigma < +\infty$, then the shares of capital and labor will change when the system deviates from the natural rate of growth. Dickinson [1, p. 172] has shown that the relationship between the shares of factors and the elasticity of factor substitution is

$$L\frac{\partial a}{\partial L} = K\frac{\partial b}{\partial K} = ab\frac{1 - \sigma}{\sigma} \tag{14}$$

where a and b are the shares of capital and labor respectively.   Thus except when $\sigma = 1$, a and b will change as the system deviates from the natural rate of growth because K and L are increasing at the different rates.[2]   This will not change our conclusion (5) in the last section.   When the system deviates from the natural rate, the adjustment time differs from the case where b is constant, depending upon whether b is increasing or decreasing. If b increases during the adjustment it would shorten the time, but on the other hand if b decreases, it would lengthen the time.[3]

---

[1] The time length of adjustment is independent of the time unit we choose.   From equation (12),

$t_k = \dfrac{\log_e\left[1 + \dfrac{\alpha_0 k}{\alpha_1 (1 - k)}\right]}{p + bn}$.   Suppose that the new unit is m times as long as the old unit, then

p and n will be m times as large as the previous values, but the numerator and b are independent of time.

Thus, the time length measured by the new unit $t'_k = \dfrac{\log\left[1 + \dfrac{\alpha_0 k}{\alpha_1 (1 - k)}\right]}{m(p + bn)} = \dfrac{t_k}{m}$, and therefore the

adjustment time is independent of the time unit chosen.

[2] There are two cases: (1) if $0 < \sigma < 1$, and $G_K > n$, then b will increase and a will decrease, and for $G_K < n$, vice versa; (2) if $1 < \sigma < +\infty$ and $G_K > n$, then a will increase and b will decrease, and for $G_K < n$, vice versa.

[3] It is safe to say that the larger σ, the shorter the adjustment period.   Take two extreme cases.   When $\sigma = 0$, we have the Harrod-Domar case in which there is no adjustment and on the other hand if $\sigma = +\infty$, K and L are no longer different factors, and therefore adjustment is instantaneous.

Second, consider a variable savings ratio and a variable growth rate of the labor force during the adjustment period. Our fundamental results remain the same except that the time of adjustment will be shortened or prolonged depending upon whether s and n increase or decrease during the adjustment period.

Let us apply this model to the American economy to find the approximate length of time for a given percentage of adjustment. We use the Cobb-Douglas production function. Let the neutral technological improvement factor p be 1.3 per cent, the share of labor, b, 65 per cent, the growth rate of the labor force, n, 1.5 per cent, the proportionate income tax rate, x, 17 per cent, the private saving ratio, s, 12 per cent, government expenditures for goods and services as a fraction of the national income, g, 18 per cent, and government capital formation as a fraction of government expenditures, h, 15 per cent, therefore the total savings ratio, α, equals 11.66 per cent and the economy is growing at the natural rate of 3.5 per cent a year.[1] Suddenly x, the tax rate, is increased from 17 per cent to 18 per cent, thus the total savings ratio, α, is increased from 11.66 per cent to 12.54 per cent. Calculation shows that for a 10 per cent adjustment approximately 4 years must pass, and for a 50 per cent adjustment, 30 years, for a 70 per cent adjustment 50 years, and for a 90 per cent adjustment, 100 years. In other words in order to achieve virtually complete adjustment in the output-capital ratio an extremely *long* period is required.

The fundamental results show that the adjustment period can be varied depending upon changes in the values of parameters. But for any small change in the savings ratio, $\dfrac{\alpha_0}{\alpha_1}$ is approximately 1 and t_k is approximately $\dfrac{\log_e\left(\dfrac{1}{1-k}\right)}{p+bn}$. Thus changes in α_0 and α_1 make only minor changes in the adjustment time. Changes in p, b and n have an effect proportional to their effect on $(p+bn)$. For example, when p and n are doubled, the adjustment period is cut in half. From a practical point of view, however, changes in p, b and n have only an insignificant effect for policy. There are two main reasons for this. First, while it is possible under unusual circumstances that technological progress p and the growth rate of the labor force n might double, thereby shortening the adjustment period by one-half, this is impossible in most cases. Second, in the American economy even if p and n are doubled, the adjustment period would only be shortened from 100 to 50 years and this is still a very long period.

Let us briefly state the results of model's application to other economies. The adjustment period is different for different countries because the values of the parameters vary from country to country. The model has been applied to economies representing both underdeveloped and fast growing. For example, to achieve 90 per cent adjustment, with the natural growth rate being 2 per cent, it takes approximately 150 years. To achieve the same adjustment in the fast growing economy, 7 per cent for example, it would take 50 years.

3. Conclusions and Policy Implications

Using a neo-classical growth model we have presented the basic relationships between the adjustment period and values of the parameters, as the economy moves from one equilibrium to another. As a result of applying the model to various economies we have

---

[1] The values are very close to actual values in the American economy estimated by several people including Solow [6].

shown that the adjustment period is extremely *long*. A complete adjustment from one equilibrium to another is virtually never achieved. In our example, it takes from 50 to 150 years to achieve 90 per cent of the total adjustment.

The lengthy adjustment period has the following policy implications. The neo-classical system of variable proportions by no means rules out the use of fiscal policy to affect the actual growth rate. While the natural rate of growth is not affected by capital accumulation, an initial increase in the actual growth rate, due to policy measures, will taper off only slowly, so it will continue for a long period. If the government policy wishes to maintain an increased growth rate, this lengthy period means that effecting changes in the savings ratio is a satisfactory policy. On the other hand if the object of fiscal policy is to raise the level of income per head of the labor force as rapidly as possible, changes in the savings ratio increases the level so *slowly* that the new equilibrium level of income which the higher savings ratio proposes to achieve may not be reached for a very long time; in fact such a long time that a change in the savings ratio is unlikely to be useful as a fiscal policy.

If the government wishes to raise the level of income as quickly as possible, while maintaining a higher growth rate of income, investigation of ways for improving technology in addition to increasing the rate of capital accumulation would be more likely to achieve both of these goals.

Honolulu, Hawaii.   RYUZO SATO.

REFERENCES :

[1]   Dickinson, H. D., " A Note on Dynamic Economics," *Review of Economic Studies.* Vol. 23 (1955), pp. 169-179

[2]   Ince, E. L., *Ordinary Differential Equations*, (London, 1927).

[3]   Hahn, F. H., " The Stability of Growth Equilibrium," *Quarterly Journal of Economics,* Vol. 74 (1960), pp. 206-226.

[4]   Musgrave, R. A., *The Theory of Public Finance : A Study of Public Economy*, (New York, 1959).

[5]   Solow, R. M., " A Contribution to the Theory of Economic Growth," *Quarterly Journal of Economics*, Vol. 70 (1956), pp. 65-94.

[6]   Solow, R. M., " Technical Change and the Aggregate Production Function," *Review of Economics and Statistics*, Vol. 34 (1957).

[7]   Swan, T. W., " Economic Growth and Capital Accumulation," *Economic Record,* Vol. 32 (1956), pp. 334-361.

[8]   Tobin, J., " A Dynamic Aggregative Model," *Journal of Political Economy*, Vol. 62 (1955), pp. 103-115.

[2]

THE HARROD–DOMAR MODEL *vs* THE NEO-CLASSICAL GROWTH MODEL [1]

IT is a well-known characteristic of the simple Harrod–Domar model that even for the long run the economic system is at best balanced on a knife-edge of equilibrium growth. When the economy deviates slightly from the natural growth rate the consequence would be either growing unemployment or prolonged inflation, since the system has no built-in equilibrating force. The shortcomings of this simple model have now been discussed for some time. [2] The underlying assumption of fixed proportions in the combination of capital and labour has been the main object of criticism. In contrast, an alternative model has been developed in which factor proportions are flexible and all rigidities are assumed away. This model is often referred to as the " neo-classical " model.

The basic conclusion of the neo-classical growth model is that, in certain circumstances, when production takes place under the usual neo-classical conditions of variable proportions and constant returns to scale no conflict between the natural and the warranted rates of growth in the Harrod–Domar model is possible; that is, the extreme instability of long-run growth equilibrium is unlikely and, given sufficient time, the actual growth rate can adjust to any given initial condition, achieving balanced growth in the long run.

However, practical implications of the neo-classical growth model hinge heavily on how rapidly adjustment will proceed when the system moves from one equilibrium to another. If the adjustment period is short disequilibrium in the economic system is easily eliminated and balanced growth is promptly achieved. But if the adjustment period is long or if factor substitution takes place at a slow rate disequilibrium, such as unemployment or inflation, may last for a considerable length of time. If adjustment proceeds at a slow rate proportions in the combination of capital and labour may virtually be considered as fixed.

This paper proposes to measure the approximate length of the adjustment period and to show what practical importance the neo-classical growth model has compared with the Harrod–Domar model. Some numerical results are given to demonstrate the approximate length of the adjustment time.

---

[1] The author wishes especially to acknowledge criticism and encouragement from Professor R. A. Musgrave of Princeton University and Professors Edwin S. Mills and Carl F. Christ of the Johns Hopkins University. He has also benefited from comments and suggestions by Professor Robert M. Solow of the Massachusetts Institute of Technology.

[2] Undoubtedly the most important paper is R. M. Solow's " A Contribution to the Theory of Economic Growth," *Quarterly Journal of Economics*, Vol. 70 (February 1956). See also T. W. Swan, " Economic Growth and Capital Accumulation," *Economic Record*, Vol. 32 (1956), and F. Hahn, " The Stability of Growth Equilibrium," *Quarterly Journal of Economics*, Vol. 74 (1960).

I. The Neo-Classical Growth Model

Assume an economy with one product ($Y_{(t)}$) and two factors of production, capital and labour, $K_{(t)}$ and $L_{(t)}$ respectively, capital being an accumulated stock of Y.   Assume neutral technological progress at a constant rate ρ.   We assume further that $Y_{(t)}$ is subject to a linear homogeneous production function, that is, constant returns to scale.   Thus,

$$Y_{(t)} = A_{(t)}F(K_{(t)}, L_{(t)}). \quad . \quad . \quad . \quad . \quad (1)$$

where $A_{(t)}$ is the neutral technological improvement factor and equals $A_0 e^{\rho t}$.

The complete differential of the production function with respect to t gives us

$$\frac{1}{Y}\frac{dY}{dt} = \frac{\partial Y}{\partial K}\frac{K}{Y} \cdot \frac{1}{K}\frac{dK}{dt} + \frac{\partial Y}{\partial L}\frac{L}{Y} \cdot \frac{1}{L}\frac{dL}{dt} + \rho$$

By substituting α and β for the shares of capital and labour, $\dfrac{\partial Y}{\partial K}\dfrac{K}{Y}$ and $\dfrac{\partial Y}{\partial L}\dfrac{L}{Y}$, and letting $\dfrac{1}{Y}\dfrac{dY}{dt} = G_Y$, $\dfrac{1}{K}\dfrac{dK}{dt} = G_K$ and $\dfrac{1}{L}\dfrac{dL}{dt} = \lambda$; the above equation becomes

$$G_Y = \alpha G_K + \beta\lambda + \rho \quad . \quad . \quad . \quad . \quad . \quad (2)$$

Thus the growth rate of income G_Y equals the sum of the technological improvement factor ρ and the weighted mean of the growth rates of capital and labour.   The weight is given to each factor by its respective share in the national income.   Equation (2) can be rewritten in an alternative and, for our purpose, a more convenient form

$$G_Y = \alpha G_K + \beta\left(\lambda + \frac{\rho}{\beta}\right) \quad . \quad . \quad . \quad . \quad (3)$$

If planned investment equals planned saving so that the effective demand is sufficiently large to absorb the effective supply, G_K in the above equation is the warranted, and $\left(\lambda + \dfrac{\rho}{\beta}\right)$ the natural growth rate of income in the Harrod–Domar model.   This is because, at a growth rate equal to G_K, neither surpluses nor deficiencies of capital develop, and at a growth rate of $\left(\lambda + \dfrac{\rho}{\beta}\right)$ the maximum rate of advance is assured with a given rate of population increase and technological improvements.   Replacing G_K and $\left(\lambda + \dfrac{\rho}{\beta}\right)$ by G_w and G_n respectively, equation (3) may be written as

$$G_Y = \alpha G_w + \beta G_n \quad . \quad . \quad . \quad . \quad . \quad (4)$$

In other words, the actual growth rate of income is the weighted mean of the warranted and the natural rates of growth; the weight is given by the shares of capital and labour. If G_w and G_n are identical, then the growth rate of income must be equal to each of them and the economy is in long-run growth equilibrium. But if, for instance, the warranted rate is greater than the natural rate the actual growth rate of income will be equal to neither of them; it lies between G_w and G_n. Thus in Harrod's terms the crucial question of balanced growth boils down to a comparison between G_w and G_n.

Let us now investigate stability of long-run equilibrium. Let $y = \dfrac{Y}{L}$, $v = \dfrac{K}{Y}$ and $k = \dfrac{K}{L}$. From equation (1) we have $y = A_0 e^{\rho t} F(k, 1)$

In equilibrium,

$$\frac{\dot{K}}{L} = \dot{k} + k\lambda = sy$$

or

$$\frac{\dot{k}}{k} = sv^{-1} - \lambda \qquad . \qquad . \qquad . \qquad . \qquad . \qquad (5)$$

where $s =$ the saving ratio. Subtract $\dfrac{\rho}{\beta}$ from either side of equation (5), *i.e.*

$$\frac{\dot{k}}{k} - \frac{\rho}{\beta} = sv^{-1} - \lambda - \frac{\rho}{\beta} = G_w - G_n \qquad . \qquad . \qquad . \qquad (6)$$

But

$$\frac{\dot{v}}{v} = \frac{\dot{k}}{k} - \rho - (F'v)\frac{\dot{k}}{k} \qquad . \qquad . \qquad . \qquad . \qquad . \qquad (7)$$

Combining (7) and (6) gives

$$\frac{\dot{v}}{v} = (1 - F'v)(G_w - G_n) \qquad . \qquad . \qquad . \qquad . \qquad (8)$$

Since $(1 - F'v)$ equals the share of labour, β, which is always positive, G_w must be obviously a diminishing function of v.

Now let v^* be the equilibrium value of v. It is found by solving $G_w = G_n$.

Consider

$$H(v) = (v - v^*)^2 \qquad . \qquad . \qquad . \qquad . \qquad . \qquad (9)$$

$H(v) > o$ if $v \neq v^*$. Also

$$\frac{dH(v)}{dt} = 2(v - v^*)\dot{v} . \qquad . \qquad . \qquad . \qquad . \qquad (10)$$

By equation (8), the above equation is always negative unless $v = v^*$. Hence for all initial conditions for which $v(t)$ is bounded, v approaches v^*. But clearly $v(t)$ is bounded for all $\infty > v(o) > 0$.[1] Thus long-run equilibrium is stable.

---

[1] I am indebted to the referee of this JOURNAL for his suggestion of the above proof, which is an alternative to my original proof derived by the Liapounoff method. Obviously it is assumed that $\lim \sigma \geqslant 1$, where σ is the elasticity of substitution. With regard to this see my paper, " On the Stability of Growth Equilibrium," presented at the 1963 Econometric Society Meeting in Boston, Mass.

We have shown that when G_Y deviates from both the natural rate of growth G_n and the warranted rate G_w it will always come back to G_n by adjustment of supply and demand, achieving $G_Y = G_n = G_w$ given sufficient time. Contrary to the Harrod–Domar growth model, growth equilibrium is stable in the long run. This is the basic result of the neo-classical growth model.

II. Speed of the Adjustment Process

We have seen that when production takes place under the usual neo-classical conditions of variable proportions and constant returns to scale the extreme instability of long-run growth equilibrium in the Harrod–Domar model is unlikely and the actual growth rate of income can adjust to any given initial condition, given sufficient time. Theoretically when t approaches infinity, then complete adjustment will be achieved, but as a practical matter we are interested in knowing how long it will take to achieve a virtually complete adjustment, *e.g.*, 90% of the return of the growth rate of income towards the natural rate of growth.

Let us investigate this problem by assuming further that the production function is the Cobb–Douglas type multiplied by the neutral technological improvement factor.

$$Y = A_0 e^{\rho t} K^\alpha L^\beta \quad . \quad . \quad . \quad . \quad . \quad (11)$$

The Cobb–Douglas production function is extremely useful for computational purposes because the shares of capital and labour are constant. The savings ratio s in the basic model is replaced by the total savings ratio ξ, which is the sum of the private and the public savings. Thus ξ equals $[x + s(1 - x) - g(1 - h)]$, where x = proportionate income tax rate, s = the private savings ratio, g = government expenditures for goods and services as a fraction of national income, and h = government capital formation as a fraction of government expenditures. We shall apply the model to actual economies to find the approximate length of time for a given percentage of adjustment. Since the entire movement of G_Y results from changes in the output–capital ratio, we shall use the output–capital ratio $v^{-1} = r$, the growth rate of income G_Y and the warranted rate of growth G_w.[1]

[1] The tables were prepared from the following equations:

$$r = \frac{\frac{\rho}{\beta} + \lambda}{\xi_2 + (\xi_1 - \xi_2)e^{-(\rho + \beta\lambda)t}} \text{ and } r_m = \frac{\left(\frac{\rho}{\beta} + \lambda\right)[\xi_2 - m(\xi_2 - \xi_1)]}{\xi_2\,\xi_1}$$

where r_m is the value of r with $m\%$ adjustment.
   Setting $r = r_m$ we obtain

$$e^{(\rho + \beta\lambda)t} = 1 + \frac{m\xi_1}{\xi_2(1 - m)}.$$

Example I

In Example I we consider five cases.[1]

Case	ρ	β	λ	x	s	g	h	$\xi = [x + s(1-x) - g(1-h)]$
I	1·3%	65%	1·5%	17%	12%	18%	15%	11·66%
II	,,	,,	,,	18%	,,	,,	,,	12·54%
III	,,	,,	,,	20%	,·	,,	,,	14·30%
IV	,,	,,	,,	17%	,,	19%	,,	10·81%
V	,,	,,	,,	,,	,,	21%	,,	9·11%

Assuming that the system is in long-run equilibrium under Case I, $G_Y = G_n = G_w$ and the economy grows at 3·5% a year. Now suddenly x is raised from 17 to 18% (Case II), thus the total savings ratio is increased from 11·66 to 12·54%. As a result, r starts decreasing from its original value of 0·300171 to its new equilibrium value of Case II, or 0·279106. Table I

TABLE I

Time Length of Adjustment

(From Case I to Case II)

t.	r.	G_w, %.	G_Y, %.	m%.
	0·300171	3·5000	3·5000	
0	0·300171	3·7641	3·5925	0
1	0·299657	3·7577	3·5902	2·44
2	0·299145	3·7513	3·5879	4·87
3	0·298762	3·7465	3·5863	6·67
4	0·298151	3·7388	3·5836	9·59
5	0·297694	3·7331	3·5816	11·76
6	0·297265	3·7277	3·5797	13·80
7	0·296811	3·7220	3·5777	15·95
8	0·296359	3·7163	3·5757	18·10
9	0·296008	3·7119	3·5742	19·76
10	0·295683	3·7079	3·5728	21·31
20	0·292080	3·6627	3·5569	38·41
30	0·289351	3·6285	3·5450	51·36
40	0·287238	3·6020	3·5357	61·40
50	0·285527	3·5805	3·5282	69·52
60	0·284137	3·5631	3·5221	76·21
70	0·283148	3·5507	3·5177	80·81
80	0·282326	3·5404	3·5141	84·71
90	0·281667	3·5321	3·5112	87·84
100	0·281210	3·5264	3·5092	90·01
∞	0·279106	3·5000	3·5000	100·00

shows how r changes as time goes on, to complete the adjustment from the initial position of Case I to the new equilibrium of Case II. The corresponding changes in G_Y and G_w are also shown.

Now let m be the percentage of the initial difference between G_n and G_Y.

---

[1] These values may be very close to actual values in the American economy estimated by several people, including Solow, and Kendrich and Sato. See R. Solow, " Technical Change and the Aggregate Production Function," *Review of Economics and Statistics*, Vol. 39 (August 1957), and J. W. Kendrick and R. Sato, " Factor Prices, Productivity, and Economic Growth," *American Economic Review*, Dec. 1963.

After the first ten years $m = 21\cdot31\%$. After 50 years $m = 69\cdot52\%$ and so forth. For m to reach 90% almost 100 years must pass. Thus when the system deviates from the natural rate it will take almost a century to achieve balanced growth. The values of change in G_w and G_Y in our illustration are very small. Initially G_Y jumps from $G_n = 3\cdot5\%$ to $3\cdot5925\%$, and it gradually comes back to the original value of $3\cdot5\%$. But after the first ten years G_Y still stands at $3\cdot5728\%$.

If, instead, x is raised from 17 to 20% (Case III) we find that the time required for m to reach 90% is shortened (93·4 years) compared to Case I (98·4 years). It, therefore, is clear that a sharp rise in the savings ratio will shorten the time length of the adjustment. Conversely, as shown in Table II, a sharp decrease in the savings ratio will slow the adjustment. In

TABLE II

Comparison of Time Length of Adjustment in Various Cases

$m\%$.	*t* years.			
	Case II.	Case III.	Case IV.	Case V.
10	4·3	3·9	5·1	5·9
20	9·2	8·4	10·3	12·3
30	14·9	13·2	16·7	19·3
40	21·5	19·1	23·7	27·2
50	28·8	26·2	32·1	36·3
60	38·5	35·6	42·4	47·3
70	50·8	46·8	55·6	61·1
80	68·2	63·7	73·4	79·6
90	98·4	93·4	104·4	111·0
100	∞	∞	∞	∞

Case IV for m to reach 90% it take 104·4 years, but in Case V it takes 111 years. The actual growth rate of income and the values of r for different values of m are summarised in Table III.

TABLE III

Comparison of Growth Rate for Various Cases

$m\%$.	Case II.		Case III.		Case IV.		Case V.	
	r.	G_Y, %.	*r*.	G_Y, %.	*r*.	G_Y, %.	*r*.	G_Y, %.
	0·300171	3·5000	0·300171	3·5000	0·300171	3·5000	0·300171	3·5000
0	0·300171	3·5925	0·300171	3·7774	0·300171	3·4107	0·300171	3·2321
10	0·298064	3·5832	0·294629	3·7496	0·302531	3·4196	0·308573	3·2589
20	0·295957	3·5740	0·289087	3·7219	0·304891	3·4286	0·316975	3·2857
30	0·293850	3·5647	0·283545	3·6940	0·307251	3·4375	0·325377	3·3125
40	0·291743	3·5555	0·278003	3·6664	0·309611	3·4464	0·333779	3·3393
50	0·289636	3·5462	0·272461	3·6387	0·311971	3·4553	0·342181	3·3660
60	0·287529	3·5370	0·266919	3·6109	0·314331	3·4643	0·350583	3·3928
70	0·285422	3·5277	0·261377	3·5832	0·316691	3·4732	0·358985	3·4196
80	0·283315	3·5185	0·255835	3·5555	0·319051	3·4821	0·367387	3·4464
90	0·281208	3·5092	0·250293	3·5277	0·321411	3·4911	0·375789	3·4732
100	0·279106	3·5000	0·244755	3·5000	0·323774	3·5000	0·384193	3·5000

Example II

In Example I we assumed a rather low value of ρ and a high value of λ. In this example we put $\rho = 1\cdot7\%$ instead of $1\cdot3\%$ (Solow's estimate is between 1 and 2%) and $\lambda = 1\%$ instead of $1\cdot5\%$, and repeat the same changes in x and g. Table IV illustrates the time length necessary for adjustment in

TABLE IV

Comparison of Time Length of Adjustment

$m\%$.	t (years).			
	Case II'.	Case III'.	Case IV'.	Case V'.
10	4·2	3·8	4·9	5·7
20	8·9	8·1	10·0	11·9
30	14·4	12·8	16·2	18·7
40	20·8	18·5	23·0	26·3
50	27·9	25·3	31·1	35·1
60	37·3	34·4	41·1	45·7
70	49·2	45·3	53·7	59·1
80	66·0	61·7	71·1	77·0
90	95·2	90·4	101·1	107·5
100	∞	∞	∞	∞

various cases. Again four cases are compared. The difference from Example I is that for each case the time required to achieve a given level of adjustment becomes $1\cdot222$ times $\left(\dfrac{1\cdot7\% + 1\% \times 65\%}{1\cdot3\% + 1\cdot5\% \times 65\%} = 1\cdot221978 \right)$ shorter than in Example I.

Example III

In this example, we do not stick to the values of parameters applied to the United States economy, but we will take different possible cases. One case

TABLE V

Time Length of 90% Adjustment

ρ, %.	λ, %.	β, %.	ξ_1, initial total savings ratio, %.	ξ_2, new total savings ratio, %.	G_r, %.	Years to achieve 90% of change.
0	2	75	5	10	2	114
,,	,,	,,	10	5	,,	194
,,	,,	,,	8	10	,,	140
,,	,,	,,	10	11	,,	148
,,	,,	,,	14	16	,,	146
,,	,,	,,	10	15	,,	130
,,	,,	65	10	15	,,	150
1	,,	,,	10	15	3·5	85
2	,,	75	14	16	4·7	62
,,	,,	,,	5	10	,,	49
3	1·5	65	12	15	6·1	52
4	,,	,,	10	18	7·7	36

may apply to under-developed economies, and the others may apply to fast-growing economies.   Table V summarises the time length required for *m* to reach 90%.

III. Conclusion

We have shown that the adjustment process in the neo-classical system of variable proportions takes place only at an extremely slow rate.[1]   When the system deviates from the natural rate of growth it will always come back to the original equilibrium position.   But this is only valid in the *true* long run. Thus the neo-classical growth model may lose its basic foundation unless the time span is extremely long.   For most practical purposes the neo-classical system of variable proportions by no means rules out the use of fixed proportions in the combination of capital and labour which is a characteristic of the Harrod–Domar growth model.   The adjustment process in the dynamic model is so slow that fixed proportions may be a realistic assumption for practical purposes.   The insight of the Harrod–Domar model may still serve as a guiding landmark in theoretical growth analysis, provided that the production side is accounted for in a manner similar to the neo-classical growth model.

RYUZO SATO

University of Hawaii.

[1] The basic relationships between the adjustment period and values of parameters are investigated in my paper, " Fiscal Policy in a Neo-Classical Growth Model: An Analysis of Time Required for Equilibrating Adjustment," *Review of Economic Studies,* February 1963.

[3]

FACTOR PRICES, PRODUCTIVITY, AND ECONOMIC GROWTH

By JOHN W. KENDRICK AND RYUZO SATO*

The recent publication by the National Bureau of Economic Research of consistent estimates of real private product, labor and capital inputs, and factor incomes, prices, and productivity furnishes the statistical basis for analysis in this article of the trends and interrelationships of these variables in the course of U. S. economic development, 1919-60.[1] In particular, the trends in the real prices of the factors and in the quantities of factor services supplied are of interest as determinants of trends in the real incomes of the owners of the factors. To go a step further, changes in the relative prices of labor and capital and in the relative quantities of the factor inputs determine the changes in functional distribution of the national income and influence size distribution. And since the proportion of incomes saved affects the relative growth of the real capital stock and its services, the saving ratio is relevant to factor prices, productivity, and incomes. So also are intangible investment and the associated saving, and the resulting stock of productive capacities, embodied in the tangible factors, which influence the trends in factor productivity as measured. But in the absence of good figures on intangibles, we can only speculate as to their movement and influence.

In the body of the article, we first describe the trends of the key variables in the U. S. private economy, 1919-60, with some reference to the shorter postwar trends, 1948-60. Then we attempt some interpretation and analysis of the trends and interrelationships from several points of view. In Appendix A the precise interrelationships of the variables chosen for study are set forth in mathematical form. Appendix B contains a brief description of the concepts and sources of the

* The authors are, respectively, professor of economics and director, Wealth Study, at The George Washington University, and assistant professor of economics, University of Hawaii. This article was written when Kendrick was visiting professor of economics at the University of Hawaii, fall semester 1962-63. While the article is a joint product, Sato is responsible for the Mathematical Appendix A, and Kendrick for the Statistical Appendix B.

[1] See John W. Kendrick [4, especially Ch. 5] and the *42nd Annual Report* of the National Bureau, [14, p. 40] for an updating through 1960 of the productivity estimates.

estimates, together with tables containing the key variables in index-number form, and their rates of change during the periods 1919-60 and 1948-60. The analysis is confined to the private economy, since this is the sector that reflects the play of market forces, and since, by Commerce Department convention, government product is artificially confined to employee compensation alone.

I. *Summary*

The historical estimates show that there has been little trend in the rate of return on capital over the past 40 years, reflecting a secular standoff between the tendency towards diminishing return to capital and its offsets, primarily technological advance and rising labor input. The relatively constant rate of return has been enough to induce tangible capital formation in excess of the rate of growth of labor input, and a growing intangible investment associated with strong productivity advance. As a result of the increasing relative abundance of capital and the constant rate of return, the real wage rate has risen in excess of the growth of labor productivity, resulting in the capture by labor of almost the entire productivity increment. As a result, the labor share of income has risen, while investment return remained sufficient for continuing growth of the stocks of tangible and intangible capital. There have, of course, been continuing adjustment problems over shorter time periods.

It is sometimes asked if the trends noted are equitable—should labor get all the productivity increment and a rising share of income? One can always reply that economics is neutral on normative questions. But it might be pointed out that the outcome does seem to have been operationally efficient. It is true that a constant rate of return to capital means that property holders do not share the productivity increment. But the rate of return seems to have been sufficient to induce a relatively high rate of total saving and investment and consequent growth of capital stock and productivity. Further, if property returns are largely reinvested, property owners enjoy a rise in their income, even with a constant rate of return. And the rising share of labor in the national income and the associated movement towards somewhat greater equality of the size-distribution of income have probably made somewhat easier the task of finding an adequate market for our increasing productive potential and thus the maintenance of relatively full employment.

The estimates provided in this paper of an elasticity of substitution well under unity support the view that the conventional Cobb-Douglas production function is not an adequate description of the U. S. economy in recent decades. In a concluding section of the paper, we discuss an alternative production function that allows for change in the factor shares in the course of economic growth. A graphic presentation of the rates of growth in the key U. S. macroeconomic variables for recent decades is appended.

II. *Major Trends*

A. *Total Real Factor Income and Input*

The basic economic theorem that the real income and real product of an economy are equal merely says that a nation may consume or add to stock that which it produces. The two are also equal in current as well as constant dollars by the Commerce concept when net national product is valued at factor cost (i.e., exclusive of indirect business taxes less net subsidies).

Since real income and product are equal, it follows that real income per unit of factor input changes in proportion to changes in total factor productivity, defined as the ratio of real product to the sum of real tangible factor inputs. An increase in total factor productivity is distributed to the owners of the factors by means of an increase in average factor prices proportionately greater than the increase in average product prices (unit factor costs). That is, proportionate movements of the ratio of average factor prices to average product prices equal proportionate movements in total factor productivity. This must be so since the factor price index is obtained as the ratio of current-dollar product (income) to real product, and total factor productivity is the ratio of real product to real factor input.[2]

The proposition that real income per unit of factor input can rise only in proportion to total factor productivity is fundamental, but it has less interest than a comparison of real income, productivity, and prices of each of the broad factor classes, human and nonhuman capital—or "labor" and "capital" as we shall call them for short. That is, if the average prices of the two factor input classes show differing movements, changes in the real income per unit of each will differ; and if the real income of each moves differently from the corresponding "partial" productivity ratios (output/labor and output/capital), factor shares of income will change. It is to an analytical description of these

[2] Using and supplementing the symbols given in Appendix A:
Y^* = income and product in current prices
Y = income and product in constant prices
$f(K, L)$ = total factor input (capital and labor)
P_Y = product prices = Y^*/Y
P_f = factor prices = Y^*/f
T = total factor productivity = Y/f
So $Y^*/f \div Y^*/Y = Y/f = P_f/P_Y = T$.

relationships in recent U. S. economic history that we now turn. The analysis is confined to the two major factor classes, but the same framework could be used for multifactor analysis. There is special interest in the two-factor analysis per se, however, due to the relevance of the related functional distribution of income to size distributions and to the importance of the real price of capital in the saving and investment decisions of the community which react back on the relative input quantities and prices of the factors of production.

B. *Relative Factor Prices*

Over the long period, 1919-60, the real price of labor (real labor compensation per hour) in relation to the real price of capital increased by about 1.8 per cent a year, on average. Real average hourly labor compensation alone increased by 2.6 per cent a year, while the real price of capital rose by 0.7, on average over the period as a whole.

The price of capital (i.e., the cost per unit obtained as the quotient of capital compensation and real capital stock) has two main components: the general price level and the rate of return on capital.[3] The average price level of capital goods rose significantly more than the general price level over the period 1919 to 1960, while the rate of return on capital assets showed little or no trend.

Of course the rate of return fluctuated widely over the short business cycle, and to a mild extent from one cycle peak or cycle average to the next, describing what Kuznets would call a "long swing." Between the postwar cycle peaks of 1948 and 1960, the real price of capital fell by about 2 per cent a year on average. This was an unusually sharp drop in an intermediate-term period, reflecting capital shortages, buoyant demand and abnormally high rates of return in the early postwar period, and the gradual reversal of these conditions during the 1950's.

Real average hourly labor compensation showed a larger than average increase of 3.6 per cent a year between 1948 and 1960. Thus, the relative real price of labor rose at an average annual rate of 5.5 per cent a year 1948-60, triple its long-term average.

The average rate of return on capital over the entire period was sufficient to induce enough net investment to cause the real stock of tangible capital to grow 1 per cent a year faster than real labor input, on average—by 1.8 per cent compared with 0.8 per cent. The relative

[3] This can easily be seen in the following formulation, in which K is the real capital stock, P_Y the average prices, π the rate of return on the capital stock in current prices (KP_Y), and C is the current-dollar compensation of capital:

$$\frac{C}{K} = \frac{\pi K P_Y}{K} = \pi P_Y.$$

growth of capital was much greater in the 1948-60 period—3.4 per cent compared with 0.5 per cent, at average annual rates.

C. *Relative Factor Productivity*

Given the average annual rate of growth of real net product (at factor cost) of around 3.2 per cent during both 1919-60 and 1948-60, it is plain that the average output-labor ratio ("labor productivity") increased faster than the average output-capital ratio ("capital productivity") especially during the postwar period. Average labor productivity increased by 2.4 per cent a year over the long period and by 2.8 per cent in the postwar period, on average, compared with increases in capital productivity of 1.3 and —0.1 per cent over the longer and shorter periods. When the two "partial productivity" ratios are combined, the resulting measure of "total tangible factor productivity" shows an increase of approximately 2.1 per cent a year, on average, over both the long period and the shorter postwar period. The total productivity measure is gotten by relating real product to both factor inputs, weighting each by its base-period price, which is assumed to approximate its marginal product at that time (see Mathematical Appendix A, equation 4). This is the same as weighting index numbers of each partial productivity ratio by base-period shares of income.[4] The combined or total productivity measure reflects the *net* saving of tangible inputs per unit of output, and thus the increase in productive efficiency due to intangible investments and changing organization of the economy and its productive units. Each of the partial productivity ratios reflects not only changes in efficiency but also factor substitutions.

D. *Real Unit Factor Costs*

A relationship of interest between factor prices and the partial productivity ratios comes from an analysis of change in unit factor cost (price). Factor cost per unit of output is the sum of unit labor cost and unit capital cost. Each type of factor cost can be further decomposed into factor price and the corresponding partial productivity ratio. (See definitions of α and β at the beginning of Appendix A.) Holding unit factor cost constant between two periods, the real unit cost of each factor remains constant only if the change in its real price is exactly offset by a corresponding change in its average productivity. If the in-

---

[4] If G_T=the rate of technical progress or the rate of total productivity increases, G_k=the rate of growth of the output-capital ratio, or the rate of increase in the partial productivity ratio of capital, and G_l=the rate of growth of the output-labor ratio, or the rate of increase in the partial productivity ratio of labor, then $G_T=\alpha G_k+\beta G_l$, where α and β are the weighting index numbers of the shares of capital and labor respectively. (See equation 7 of Appendix A.)

crease in real price of one factor exceeds its productivity increase, this discrepancy must be offset by an opposite divergence between the real price and productivity of the other factor (with due allowance for the relative weights—factor shares—of each in the base period).

Thus, over the 41-year period, a 2.6 average annual rate of increase in the real price of labor exceeded the increase in labor productivity of 2.4 per cent by 0.2 percentage point; while the increase in the real price of capital of 0.7 per cent a year fell short of the 1.3 per cent increase in capital productivity by 0.6 percentage point. The 0.2 per cent rise in real unit labor cost when weighted by the 0.75 average share of labor is exactly offset by the 0.6 per cent a year decline in unit capital cost weighted by the 0.25 average capital share of national income.[5]

The picture was even more favorable to labor during the postwar period 1948-60. An increase in real average hourly earnings of 3.6 per cent a year exceeded the increase in labor productivity of 2.8 per cent by 0.8 percentage point. The real price of capital dropped by 1.8 per cent a year from the high 1948 level, whereas capital productivity edged down slightly—by 0.1 per cent a year. The 0.8 per cent a year rise in real unit labor cost, weighted by 0.75, approximately equals the 1.7 per cent annual decrease in unit property costs weighted by the factor of 0.25. The substantial decrease in the rate of return on capital 1948-60 was somewhat abnormal, representing a movement from a high rate in the early postwar to a rate in 1960 that was associated with a less-than-full-employment volume of new investment.

To put it somewhat differently—with more relevance for appraisal of the labor productivity criterion for noninflationary wage increases: real average hourly labor compensation can be raised by *more or less* than the increase in labor productivity to the extent of the difference between the rates of change in the output-capital ratio and the real price of capital, weighted by the ratio between the capital and labor shares of income. Thus, the 0.2 percentage-point difference between the rates of increase of real wages and labor productivity is equal to the 0.6 percentage-point difference between the rates of change in capital productivity and the real price of capital reduced by the .25/.75 average income shares of capital and labor.[6]

---

[5] This can be shown mathematically as $\alpha G_\alpha + \beta G_\beta = 0$, where G_α and G_β are the percentage changes of the shares of capital and labor respectively. (See equation 13.)

[6] Using the definitions of G_l, G_k, α, and β, the following relation holds:

$$G_w = G_l + \frac{\alpha}{\beta}(G_k - G_\pi)$$

where G_w and G_π are the percentage changes of the wage rate and the return on capital. (See equation 8.)

E. *Factor Shares of Income*

The lack of pronounced trend in the rate of return on capital over the long run is another way of saying that the total real compensation of capital grew almost in proportion to the real stock of capital. This means that virtually all of the "productivity increment" accrued to labor—when the productivity increment is defined as the difference in a given period between real factor input and net product valued at base-period factor prices and net product prices respectively. If labor obtains a larger proportion of the productivity increment than its income share in the base period, then obviously the labor share of national income is rising.

The rates of change in the income shares of the factors can be quantified in a number of alternative ways. The first has already been introduced in the preceding section: the rates of change in the factor shares can be viewed as the rates of change in the unit real factor costs. Thus, the labor share of national income rose from 72 per cent in 1919 to 77.8 per cent in 1960—an average annual rate of increase of 0.2 per cent, equal to that of unit real labor cost; the drop of the capital share from 28 to 22.2 per cent represents an average annual rate of decline of 0.6 per cent, equal to the rate of decline in unit real capital cost (see Appendix B, Table 1, columns 8 and 9, and Appendix A, equation 13).

A more usual approach is to explain changes in income shares as the product of changes in the relative quantities of input and in the relative prices of the factors. Thus, the average annual rate of decline in labor input relative to total input (a weighted average of labor and capital inputs) was 0.3 per cent 1919-60, while the price of labor rose by 0.5 per cent a year, on average, in relation to the weighted average of the two factor prices. The sum of the two figures, 0.2 per cent, is the rate of increase in the labor share. The corresponding numbers with respect to rates of change in relative capital input and price are 0.8 and −1.4, which explain the 0.6 per cent a year decline in the capital share (see equations 16 and 17).

Since the rate of relative decline in labor input was more than offset by the rate of relative increase in the price of labor, it is apparent that the elasticity of substitution was less than 1. In fact, it was approximately 0.58 over the long period. This can be obtained from the rounded estimates cited in the previous paragraph,

$$\frac{0.3}{0.5} = 0.6 \quad \text{(see Appendix A, footnote 19)},$$

or as the difference between the growth rate of capital and labor inputs, divided by the difference between the growth rates of the real prices of labor and capital (Appendix A, equation 11a):

$$\frac{1.84 - 0.76}{2.56 - 0.71} = 0.58.^7$$

The rates of change in the factor shares can also be expressed in terms of the elasticity of substitution (Appendix A, equations 14 and 15). Thus, the growth of the labor share can be viewed as the difference between the rates of growth of real labor and capital inputs $(0.76 - 1.84 = -1.08)$ times 1 minus the reciprocal of the elasticity of substitution

$$\left(1 - \frac{1}{0.58} = -0.72\right),$$

weighted by the share of capital in income, 0.25. The result is 0.2.[8] The rate of change in the capital share may be obtained as follows (equation 15): $-0.6 = 0.75\ (-0.72)\ (1.08)$.

F. *Saving and Capital Growth*

The growth of population, labor force, and labor input can be regarded as a largely exogenous factor. But the growth of the real tangible capital stock—which influences both relative factor prices, productivity, and thus factor shares—is a function of rates of change in saving ratios and real product, or real investment (see equation 20).

The ratio of real net saving and investment to real net product at factor cost showed a trend rate of decline of approximately 0.6 per cent a year over the long period. This decline is consistent with the declining capital coefficient (rising capital productivity) given the average trend rate of growth of real product. (See equation 18, and Appendix B, Table 1, columns 23, 25, and 5.)

The average annual rate of decline in the saving rate (0.59) falls short of the rate of increase in the output-capital ratio (1.37) by the difference between the rates of growth in real net investment and real capital stock (2.54 and 1.75 per cent, respectively).[9] The faster growth of real net investment than of capital stock was associated with the accelerated rate of growth of capital in the post-World War II period compared with the period as a whole, or even with the 1920's.

Since the growth of capital stock and input depend on the saving

[7] If σ is the elasticity of substitution, and G_K and G_L the growth rates of capital and labor, then

$$\sigma = \frac{G_K - G_L}{G_w - G_\pi}.$$

[8] $G_\beta = \alpha\left(1 - \frac{1}{\sigma}\right)(G_L - G_K)$.

[9] $G_s = G_I - G_K - G_k$, where G_s = the percentage change of the saving ratio and G_I = the growth rate of investment. (See equation 18.)

ratio and consequent growth of real net investment, these variables can be used instead of real capital in some of the previous relationships we have examined. Alternative equations for rates of change in factor shares are developed in Appendix A (equations 24 and 25).

Despite the declining saving ratio, capital formation was large enough to cause the real stock of capital to grow substantially faster than the labor force, as already quantified. It should be further noted, however, that this continuing relative growth of capital was associated with a marked deceleration in the growth of labor input after World War I. If labor input had continued to grow at its pre-1919 rate of over 2 per cent a year, it is questionable if capital accumulation after 1919 would have been sufficient to provide a deepening of capital in relation to labor which explains part of the growth of real labor income.

III. *Interpretation*

These estimates of the trends and interrelationship of some of the chief macroeconomic variables in the course of recent U. S. economic development offer a fascinating scope for explanatory hypotheses.

A. *The Rate of Return*

In the first place, the long-run relative constancy of the rate of return on capital suggests the operation of an important servomechanism. In the absence of technological advance and labor force growth, the accumulation of capital would tend to push down the rate of return. This tendency was apparently offset by technological advance and growth of labor input, on balance. But in periods when the latter forces were strong enough to raise the rate of return, this apparently induced an increasing volume of saving and investment which eventually drove the return back down. Conversely, when the rate of return fell below a percentage adequate to induce a full-employment level of income (as appears to have happened by 1960), a slowdown in capital accumulation reduced the capital-output ratio at full-employment income below its trend level, and set the stage for an increase in the rate of return when demographic and technological forces became favorable enough to produce full-employment demand.

Some mechanism of this sort would seem to underlie the long swing under intensive study by Abramovitz and Kuznets although much further research is necessary. From the viewpoint of secular growth study, the important point is that relative constancy of the long-term rate of return means that most of the productivity increment accrues to labor. The social implications of this tendency with regard to the viability of capitalism are clear.

B. *The Noninflationary Wage Increase*

If a constant long-run rate of return were accompanied by a constant output-capital ratio, the shares of the factors would remain unchanged. The only sustainable means whereby labor may obtain an increase in the output-labor ratio (and thus an increase in the income share) is by technological advances that save capital as well as labor. Over shorter periods a decline in the rate of return—such as occurred during the 1948-60 period both absolutely and in relation to the output-capital ratio—also made possible a faster increase in real wages than in labor productivity. This possibility—and long-term tendency— is of interest particularly in connection with the attempt by the Council of Economic Advisers to formulate a productivity guidepost for noninflationary wage increases. The guidepost should, theoretically, be formulated with allowance for the anticipated divergence between the output-capital ratio and the rate of return on capital consistent with a full-employment inducement to invest (which was not the case prior to an implicit recognition in the 1962 Report). This divergence is not always positive, and thus an upward adjustment to the "labor productivity" guide is not always warranted. When, for example, the rate of return has been depressed to a level inconsistent with a fully employed economy, the required recovery of the rate of return may mean that the real wage rate must rise somewhat less than labor productivity.[10]

But over the long run (two or more long swings), the tendency of the rate of return to relative constancy means that labor tends to get *all* of the productivity increment, regardless of what happens to the output-capital ratio.[11] Rising "capital productivity," other things equal, means that "total productivity," the productivity increment, and real wages all increase more than would otherwise be the case.

The rising output-capital ratio, in conjunction with the constant rate of return, also means that the capital share of national income decreases. Only if the real price of a factor increases proportionately with the corresponding partial productivity ratio does its income share remain constant.

C. *Productivity Advance and Intangible Investment*

The decline in the net saving ratio is often taken at face value, and ascribed in large part to the increasing tax bite out of income. Undoubtedly, the increasing tax ratio reduced saving below the levels it

[10] The practicality of a productivity guideline for noninflationary wage increases is a different issue; here, we merely discuss the formulation.

[11] See Kendrick [4, Ch. 5] in which it is estimated that 99 per cent of the productivity increment 1919–57 accrued to labor.

would have reached with a constant tax ratio. Elsewhere, it has been suggested, however, that despite the larger tax bite, the declining saving ratio holds only if the definition of saving is limited to tangible capital.[12]

If the saving that is associated with intangible investments in research and development and in persons—particularly for health, education and training—are included with conventionally defined saving and investment, it is doubtful if this broader net saving ratio fell at all. Intangible investments appear to be the chief factor behind rising productivity, leaving aside scale economies. The acceleration in productivity advance after 1919 despite the decline in the net tangible investment ratio indirectly confirms other rough evidence that the intangible investment ratio grew substantially after 1919.

The associated increases in capital and labor productivity meant a faster increase in the relative real price of labor than in the period before 1919—enough so to produce the rising share of labor in national income, since the capital-labor ratio showed no acceleration.

If the tangible investment (saving) ratio declined to the point where capital grew less rapidly than labor, this would probably mean an increasing rate of return and at least a temporary reversal in the rising labor share of income (such as occurred in the 1941-46 period). This reverse tendency would be aggravated if intangible investment and saving also declined in relation to income, since this would tend to reduce the rate of growth of labor productivity, which would further dampen the relative increase in the real price of labor.

Once again, a rising rate of return on capital could be expected to set in motion forces that would tend to reverse the direction of the saving ratio. A more rapid growth of the real stocks of both tangible and intangible capital would tend to restore the underlying trends which we have described and attempted to rationalize.

D. *A Production Function for the U. S. Economy*

The following production function would seem to be appropriate for the U. S. economy in recent decades (equation 28):

$$Y = A_0 e^{0.021t} \frac{KL}{(aL^{2/3} + bK^{2/3})^{3/2}}$$

where a and b are the production elasticities in the Cobb-Douglas function (see equation 27).[13] This function differs from the traditional Cobb-Douglas type in two respects. First, the shares of capital and labor are

---

[12] See Volume 9 of the background papers prepared for the Commission on Money and Credit [13].

[13] This is basically the Arrow-Chenery-Minhas-Solow "CES function" [1, pp. 225–50].

no longer constant when capital and labor grow at different rates. Thus, the factor shares can vary depending upon which factor is growing faster. Secondly, the rate of change in the profit rate is no longer equal to the rate of change in the output-capital ratio. Depending upon the proportions of capital and labor, the profit rate can increase more or less than the output-capital ratio. In the same way, changes in the wage rate no longer offset the corresponding changes in the output-labor ratio. Wages can rise more than an increase in the average labor productivity. In short, these differences result from the measured elasticity of substitution being smaller than one, while in the Cobb-Douglas case the elasticity of substitution is well known to be unity. The production function presented above is based on our estimated elasticity of substitution equal to approximately 0.6.[14] Thus, when capital increases faster than labor as seen in the U. S. economy, the share of capital falls. The production function presented here would thus seem to be more realistic under current conditions of growth than the Cobb-Douglas function.

Appendix A—Mathematical Recapitulation

A. *Symbols*

  Y: national income or net national product at factor cost in real terms

  K: real stock of capital goods

  L: labor force in man-hours worked by major industries, weighted by base-period average hourly earnings in each

  π: rate of return on capital

  w: wage rate

  C: total capital compensation $= \pi K$

  W: total labor compensation $= wL$

  α: share of capital in the national income $= \pi(K/Y) = C/Y$

  β: share of labor in the national income $= w(L/Y) = W/Y$

  k: output-capital ratio $= Y/K$

  l: output-labor ratio $= Y/L$

  S: amount of saving

  s: saving ratio as a percentage of the national income $= S/Y$

  I: amount of investment $= dK/dt$

  r: marginal rate of substitution $= \pi/w$

  σ: elasticity of substitution between capital and labor $0 < \sigma < +\infty$

  G_x: growth rate of a variable $x, d \log x/dt$. Thus G_Y is the growth rate of income $= d \log Y/dt$ and so on.

  t: time as an independent variable. Whenever it is clear that the independent variable is time, it will be omitted. For example, income Y is a function of time $Y(t)$, but (t) will be omitted because it is obvious.

---

[14] Our estimate of 0.58 compares with an estimate by I. B. Kravis [6] of 0.64 and with an estimate of 0.57 by Arrow, Chenery, Minhas, and Solow [1].

B. *Basic Assumptions*

We shall make the following assumptions:

1. All markets are highly competitive in the long run. Thus, actual output is closely related to potential output. It is not necessary to assume that actual or realized output is exactly the same as potential output. The above assumption implies that actual output is a constant fraction of potential output and thus the unemployment rate is constant. This assumption may be justifiable, since we are only concerned with the trend of economic growth, but not with cyclical fluctuations.[15]

2. The marginal productivities of capital and labor are approximately equal to the rate of return on capital and the wage rate respectively:

$$\pi = \frac{\partial Y}{\partial K} \quad \text{and} \quad w = \frac{\partial Y}{\partial L}.$$

3. Let us assume that there is an aggregate production function in the economy. By assuming the production function we merely want to seek a good description of the relations among economic variables. The production function is stable in the long run and it may be expressed in the following equation:

(1) $Y = T(t)f(K, L)$

where $T(t)$ is the technological improvement factor and $T(t) \geq 1$. Technical progress is on the average neutral: that is, the technological improvement factor does not enter in determining the shares of factors.[16] In the present study only a constant returns-to-scale function is considered. If the production function is an increasing returns-to-scale function, then it must be the subject of a separate and more ambitious study. We shall define an advance in technology as anything that increases the yield in terms of the real product of a given combination of original factors of production. This definition includes improvements in organization (including scale economies) as well as advances in technique as usually understood. In order to simplify the problem we may assume that a given advance in technology raises the yield of all combinations of production factors in the same proportion. We define technical progress as a process consisting of a series of advances in technique occurring successively in time. Thus, even if the supply of original factors of production were unchanged, the consequence of technical progress would be that the national income steadily increases. $f(K, L)$ represents what the national income would be at any given time if

---

[15] See R. Sato [9] and R. M. Solow [12, pp. 76–86].

[16] It may be somewhat unrealistic to assume that technical progress is neutral. Some technical advance may be applicable to a large volume of production but not to a small one (or vice versa). Some may be applicable to an economy in which the capital-labor ratio is high. Attempts have been made to include "embodied" technology in the production function, but these attempts are still in the formative stage. Especially when one makes an empirical study such as described in this paper, it is not too unrealistic to assume that technical progress is spread over all modes of production and, thus, on the average it is neutral. For detailed discussions of technical progress and economic growth, see "Symposium on Production Functions and Economic Growth" [15].

technology were entirely stationary. From equation (1) we derive:

(2)
$$T(t) = \frac{Y}{f(K, L)}.$$

4. The production function (1) is linear and homogeneous. Thus:

(3)
$$Y(t) = \lambda^{-1} T(t) \cdot f(\lambda K, \lambda L), \quad \lambda > 0.$$

In other words, $T(t)$ is independent of the scale of production:

$$T(t) = \frac{\lambda Y}{f(\lambda K, \lambda L)}.$$

From Euler's theorem,

(4)
$$T(t) = \frac{Y}{\frac{\partial f}{\partial K} K + \frac{\partial f}{\partial L} L}$$

where $\frac{\partial f}{\partial K}$ and $\frac{\partial f}{\partial L}$ are the rate of return on capital, and the wage rate respectively, which would have obtained if there were no technical progress
for the relevant year. We assume that in the base year $T(0)$ is equal to
one. "Total factor productivity" is estimated by equation (4).

5. $f(K, L)$ and $T(t)$ are continuously differentiable with respect to K, L,
and t up to the desirable order.

6. The rate of return on capital π will fall if capital increases relatively
more than labor does and, on the other hand, the wage rate w will fall if
labor increases proportionately more than capital at a given level of technology. Thus:

$$\frac{\partial^2 Y}{\partial K^2} < 0 \quad \text{and} \quad \frac{\partial^2 Y}{\partial L^2} < 0.$$

Assumption 4 implies that the rate of return will rise when labor increases
relatively and the wage rate will rise when capital increases relatively.
Since Y is continuous,

$$\frac{\partial^2 Y}{\partial K \partial L} = \frac{\partial^2 Y}{\partial L \partial K} > 0.$$

C. *Technical Progress and Productivity Increase*

By differentiating equation (2) with respect to t, we obtain

(5)
$$G_T = G_Y - \alpha G_K - \beta G_L.$$

The above equation shows that the rate of increase in total productivity,
i.e., the rate of technological improvement, equals the growth rate of the
national income reduced by the sum of the growth rates of capital and labor
weighted by their respective shares in the national income.

From the homogeneity assumption (assumption 4),

$$Y = \pi K + w L.$$

By taking the total differential of Y, we get:

$$dY = \pi dK + K d\pi + w dL + L dw.$$

Since all variables are functions of time,

$$\frac{dY}{dt} = \pi \frac{dK}{dt} + K \frac{d\pi}{dt} + w \frac{dL}{dt} + L \frac{dw}{dt}.$$

From this we obtain:

$$G_Y = \alpha G_K + \alpha G_\pi + \beta G_L + \beta G_w.$$

By substituting the above equation for equation (5) we obtain:

(6) $$G_T = \alpha G_\pi + \beta G_w.$$

The above result states that the total productivity increase can also be regarded as the weighted mean of the growth rates of the return on capital and the wage rate. The weights to the return on capital and to the wage rate are the shares of capital and labor respectively.

Since $G_k = G_Y - G_K$ and $G_l = G_Y - G_L$, equation (5) may be alternatively written as:

(7) $$G_T = \alpha G_k + \beta G_l.$$

Thus the rate of technical progress is the weighted mean of the rates of growth of the output-capital ratio and the output-labor ratio.

D. *Productivity and Wage Rate*

It is of value to formulate the relationship among variables connected with the growth rate of wages. From equations (6) and (7) the following relation can be readily derived:

(8) $$G_w = G_l + \frac{\alpha}{\beta} (G_k - G_\pi).$$

Thus, average hourly labor compensation can rise percentagewise, by more (or less) than the increase in output per man-hour, to the degree that output per unit of capital input increases more (or less) than the rate of return on capital.[17]

An alternative formulation of the growth of the wage rate may be given in the following way. Since $w = \beta(Y/L)$, we get:

$$G_w = G_\beta + G_Y - G_L.$$

By combining the above equation and equation (5), we obtain:

(9) $$G_w = G_\beta + G_T + \alpha(G_K - G_L).$$

We shall use the above equation in the next section.

E. *Factor Earnings*

From the homogeneity assumption the marginal rate of substitution r

---

[17] This was first formulated (verbally) in Kendrick [5].

is a function of the capital-labor ratio alone. Since the capital-labor ratio equals output per labor input l divided by output per capital input k, the marginal rate of substitution r may be written as:

$$r = \frac{\pi}{w} = \phi\left(\frac{l}{k}\right).$$

On the other hand the ratio of the capital share to the labor share α/β is equal to the marginal rate of substitution r multiplied by the capital-labor ratio or l/k and thus,

$$\frac{\alpha}{\beta} = \frac{l}{k}\phi\left(\frac{l}{k}\right).$$

The share ratio α/β depends solely upon the capital-labor ratio l/k. Differentiating the above equation with respect to l/k, we derive,

(10)
$$\frac{d\left(\frac{\alpha}{\beta}\right)}{d\left(\frac{l}{k}\right)} = r\left(1 - \frac{1}{\sigma}\right)$$

where σ is the elasticity of substitution between capital and labor. Following Hicks, σ is defined as:

(11)
$$\sigma = \frac{\pi w}{Y\dfrac{\partial^2 Y}{\partial K \partial L}}.$$

It may also be written as[18]

(11a)
$$\sigma = \frac{d\left(\frac{l}{k}\right)}{d\left(\frac{1}{r}\right)} \cdot \frac{\frac{1}{r}}{\frac{l}{k}} = \frac{d\left(\frac{K}{L}\right)}{d\left(\frac{w}{\pi}\right)} \cdot \frac{\frac{w}{\pi}}{\frac{K}{L}} = \frac{G_K - G_L}{G_w - G_\pi}.$$

It should be noted that equation (10) is an expression similar to the marginal and average relation in the price theory $[M = P(1 - 1/\xi)]$. Thus

$$-\sigma = \frac{d\left(\frac{l}{k}\right)}{dr} \cdot \frac{r}{\frac{l}{k}}.$$

Thus σ becomes always positive with $\pi > 0$, $w > 0$, and

$$\frac{\partial^2 Y}{\partial K \partial L} > 0.$$

See Hicks [3, pp. 117, 245] and Meade [7]. Meade obtains an expression similar to (11a).

$r = \pi/w$ is considered as an average change in the factor-share ratio and

$$\frac{d\left(\dfrac{\alpha}{\beta}\right)}{d\left(\dfrac{l}{k}\right)}$$

as a marginal change.

Expanding

$$\frac{d\left(\dfrac{\alpha}{\beta}\right)}{d\left(\dfrac{l}{k}\right)},$$

equation (10) may be written as:

$$\frac{\dfrac{\alpha}{\beta}(G_\alpha - G_\beta)}{\dfrac{K}{L}(G_K - G_L)} = \frac{\pi}{w}\left(1 - \frac{1}{\sigma}\right).$$

Since $\alpha = \pi(K/Y)$ and $\beta = w(L/Y)$ the above equation becomes:

(12) $$\frac{G_\alpha - G_\beta}{G_K - G_L} = 1 - \frac{1}{\sigma}.$$

From $\alpha + \beta = 1$ we get:

(13) $$\alpha G_\alpha + \beta G_\beta = 0.$$

By combining equations (12) and (13) the rates of growth of the shares of capital and labor are readily expressed as

(14) $$G_\alpha = \beta\left(1 - \frac{1}{\sigma}\right)(G_K - G_L),$$

and

(15) $$G_\beta = \alpha\left(1 - \frac{1}{\sigma}\right)(G_L - G_K).$$

The above equations show that when $\sigma = 1$, G_α and G_β would be zero and hence the shares of capital and labor are constant regardless of any combinations between capital and labor. When $\sigma > 1$ and capital grows faster than labor, the share of capital increases but the share of labor decreases. If $\sigma < 1$ and capital grows faster than labor, the share of capital decreases, but the share of labor increases.

Using equation (11a), σ is estimated to be approximately 0.58 for the

U. S. economy, 1919–60. Since σ is smaller than one, $G_\alpha < 0$ but $G_\beta > 0$, as $G_K > G_L$.

It is worth noting that G_α and G_β may be respectively considered as real unit capital cost and real unit labor cost, since α equals C/Y and β is equal to W/Y in real terms.

An alternative formulation of the growth rate of the labor share may be derived from equation (9),

$$G_\beta = [G_L - (\alpha G_K + \beta G_L)] + (G_w - G_T).$$

Since $\alpha G_K + \beta G_L$ equals the growth rate of total input or G_f where

$$G_f = \frac{d \log f(K, L)}{dt},$$

the above equation may be written as:

(16) $$G_\beta = (G_L - G_f) + (G_w - G_T).$$

Thus, the growth rate of the labor share equals the annual rate of change in labor input relative to total input plus the growth rate of wages relative to total productivity change. In the same way the growth rate of the capital share may be alternatively written as[19]

(17) $$G_\alpha = (G_K - G_f) + (G_r - G_T).$$

F. *Changes in the Saving Ratio*

We shall now consider the relationship between the saving ratio and the output-capital ratio. From $G_K = sk$, we obtain:

$$G(G_K) = G_s + G_k.$$

Since $G(G_K)$ is also equal to $G_I - G_K$, the above relation becomes $G_s + G_k = G_I - G_K$. Thus,

(18) $$G_s = G_I - G_K - G_k.$$

When capital grows at a constant rate, G_I must be equal to G_K or $G(G_K) = 0$. This implies that

(19) $$G_s = - G_k.$$

Thus the growth rate of the saving ratio must have the opposite sign to the growth rate of the output-capital ratio but numerically must be the same.

When capital grows at an accelerated rate $[G(G_K) > 0]$, G_I must be greater than G_K. The value of G_s may be either positive or negative or equal to zero, depending upon $G_I - G_K \lessgtr G_k$. If, on the other hand, capital grows at a decelerated rate, G_s must be always negative since $G_I < G_K$ and G_k is assumed to be positive.

Next, let us deal with the relations between the saving ratio and the

---

[19] The elasticity of substitution σ may also be equal to:

$$\sigma = \frac{G_L - G_f}{G_T - G_w} = \frac{G_K - G_f}{G_T - G_r}.$$

other variables. Under assumptions 1 and 2, saving must be always equal to investment at any point of time.

Thus,

$$\frac{dK}{dt} = I = S = sY.$$

The growth rate of investment becomes $G_I = G_s + G_Y$.

By using equation (5) we eliminate G_Y in the above equation and obtain:

(20) $G_s = G_I - \alpha G_K - \beta G_L - G_T.$

First we shall assume that the growth rate of capital G_K is constant. Then, since $G_I = G_K$, equation (20) can be simplified to:

(21) $G_s = \beta(G_K - G_L) - G_T.$

In the above equation if G_T is zero, G_s depends solely on the difference between G_K and G_L. If $G_K > G_L$, G_s must be positive and vice versa. When G_T is positive, G_s will not be positive if G_T exceeds the difference between G_K and G_L.

The growth rate of the saving ratio can also be expressed in terms of the elasticity of substitution and other variables. Substituting $G_K - G_L = \sigma(G_w - G_r)$ in equation (21) we have:

$$G_s = \beta\sigma(G_w - G_r) - G_T.$$

Since $G_T = \alpha G_r + \beta G_w$, the equation may be written as

(22) $G_s = \beta(\sigma - 1)(G_w - G_r) - G_r.$

There are three different cases influencing the value of G_s according to the value of σ; (a) $\sigma = 1$, (b) $0 < \sigma < 1$, and (c) $1 < \sigma < +\infty$. In case (a) G_s must be equal to $-G_r$ and thus the growth rate of return on capital must be numerically equal to the percentage change in the saving ratio with the sign of G_r being opposite. Since equation (19) must also be equal to equation (22), G_r must be exactly the same as G_k. In the second case, if σ is less than one, most likely G_s will be negative. In case (c), however, G_s may be positive unless G_r is extremely large.

Let us now assume that G_K is not constant. Since G_I is no longer equal to G_K, equation (20) becomes:

(23) $G_s = (G_I - G_L - G_w) + (1 - \sigma)(G_w - G_T).$

The sign and magnitude of G_s depends on various factors. If $\sigma = 1$, G_s depends on G_I, G_L, and G_w. Most likely G_s is negative because the combined value of G_L and G_w is usually larger than G_I. If $\sigma \neq 1$, total productivity increase G_T must be taken into account. It all depends on how the economy changes in the long run. In the U. S. economy, since $\sigma = 0.58$, $G_I = 2.54$ per cent, $G_w = 2.56$ per cent, $G_L = 0.8$ per cent, and $G_T = 2.08$ per cent, G_s becomes -0.6 per cent.

Another interesting relation may also be found,

$$(24) \qquad G_\alpha = \frac{\beta}{\alpha} \left(\frac{\sigma - 1}{\sigma} \right) (G_I - G_s - G_L - G_T)$$

$$(25) \qquad G_\beta = \left(\frac{1 - \sigma}{\sigma} \right) (G_I - G_s - G_L - G_T).$$

The shares of capital and labor now depend partly on the behavior of the saving ratio. In the U. S. economy, as $\sigma < 1$ and as the value in the second parenthesis in (24) is positive, G_α is negative but G_β is positive.

G. *The Production Function of the U. S. Economy*

Since variables necessary to formulate the production function have been included in the previous sections, it might be well to speculate on the shape of the production function appropriate for the U. S. economy. The following production function,

$$(26) \qquad Y = \frac{T(t)KL}{(aL^\theta + bK^\theta)^{1/\theta}}$$

has the elasticity of substitution $\sigma = 1/(1+\theta)$ as a parameter.

The production function expressed by equation (26) represents a whole family of linear homogeneous production functions containing a constant elasticity of substitution (CES function).[20] If θ approaches zero, σ becomes one. This can be seen by rearranging the above equation and taking the limit of the function as θ approaches zero. Thus,

$$\log Y = \log T(t) - \frac{\log (aK^{-\theta} + bL^{-\theta})}{\theta},$$

$$\lim_{\theta \to 0} \log Y = \log T(t) - \lim_{\theta \to 0} \frac{d}{d\theta} [\log (aK^{-\theta} + bL^{-\theta})],$$

$$\lim_{\theta \to 0} \log Y = \log T(t) + a \log K + b \log L,$$

$$(27) \qquad Y = T(t)K^a L^b$$

where $a+b=1$.

The elasticity of substitution in the U. S. economy is approximately equal to 0.6. The production function most appropriate to the U. S. economy must now look like

$$(28) \qquad Y = A_0 e^{.021t} \frac{KL}{[aL^{2/3} + bK^{2/3}]^{3/2}}$$

since $T(t) = A_0 e^{.021t}$ and $\theta = 2/3$. Although we would not go so far as to say

---

[20] A similar function appears in Solow's article [11]. See also Arrow, Chenery, Minhas and Solow [1] and Frankel [2].

that equation (28) is the best representation of the production function of the U. S. economy for the period, the evidence presented in this study strongly suggests that it is a good description.[21] The purpose of this study was not to find the production function, but we arrived at the above conclusion as a by-product of the productivity study.

H. A Diagrammatic View of U. S. Economic Growth

This section gives a diagrammatic illustration of the U. S. economic growth for the past forty years. Obviously it is not practicable to include all the variables in the diagram and, hence, only the growth rates of capital, labor, and income are selected to show their relations with the changes in the saving ratio, the output-capital ratio, and productivity.

The neoclassical theory of growth asserts that in the long run the growth rates of capital and income tend towards equality.[22] In the U. S. economy, however, we cannot observe this tendency. This may be because the saving ratio is consistently declining and because productivity is increasing, which together disturb the long-run equilibrium adjustment.[23] Although capital has grown at an accelerated rate in the post-1948 period, the saving ratio in 1960 is lower than in 1919. A declining saving ratio and an accelerating growth rate of capital (which latter is not identical with the growth rate of income) are together consistent when technology is improving.

Let us demonstrate this in a diagram based upon the following expression for the growth rate of income:

$$(29) \qquad G_Y = G_T + \alpha s k + \beta G_L.$$

Assume that G_L and s are independent of the output-capital ratio. For simplicity we use the average annual growth rates of labor and technology.

---

[21] An interested reader may test some of the equations set forth in the previous sections. For example

$$\pi = \frac{a}{T_{(t)}^{2/3}} k^{5/3}$$

and

$$w = \frac{b}{(T_{(t)})^{2/3}} l^{5/3}$$

$$\alpha = \frac{a}{(T_{(t)})^{2/3}} k^{2/3}$$

and

$$\beta = \frac{b}{(T_{(t)})^{2/3}} l^{2/3}.$$

The growth rates of shares of capital and labor corresponding to equations (14) and (15) are:

$$G_\alpha = -\frac{2}{3} \frac{b}{(T_{(t)})^{2/3}} l^{2/3}(sk - G_L) = -\frac{2}{3} \beta(G_K - G_L)$$

and

$$G_\beta = \frac{2}{3} \frac{a}{(T_{(t)})^{2/3}} k^{2/3}(sk - G_L) = \frac{2}{3} \alpha(G_K - G_L).$$

[22] See, for example, R. M. Solow [11, pp. 70–73] and Sato [8].

[23] Smithies ponders this possibility [10, p. 201].

The diagram depicts how the U. S. economy moved during the period, 1919–60 (Figure 1).

The output-capital ratio k is measured on the abscissa, and the growth rates on the ordinate. The growth rate of capital with the saving ratio in 1919 ($t=0$) is shown by a line $s_0 k$ through the origin with a slope equal to s_0(8.5 per cent). The growth rate of labor G_L (shown by $k_0 C_0$), which is independent of the output-capital ratio, equals 0.8 per cent. The line G_{Y0} is obtained by adding $\alpha_0 s_0 k$, β_0, G_L and G_T, where α_0 and β_0 are the initial share of capital and labor respectively ($\alpha_0 = 28$ per cent and $\beta_0 = 72$ per cent). G_Y is an increasing function of k because the growth rate of capital is an increasing function in the relevant range. G_Y is convex from below since σ is less than one.[24] The growth rate of income in 1919 is $k_0 A_0$, which is equal to 3.15 per cent, and the growth rate of capital is $k_0 B_0$ and is equal to 1.79 per cent ($s_0 = 8.5$ per cent and $k_0 = 0.21$). The output-capital ratio in 1919 is designated by k_0(0.21). $s_1 k$ and G_{Y1} represent the growth rates in 1960 ($t=41$), and they were derived in the same way as $s_0 k_0$ and G_{Y0} ($s_1 = 6.6$ per cent, $k_1 = 0.38$, $\alpha_1 = 22$ per cent and $\beta_1 = 78$ per cent). If the saving ratio and also technology had remained constant, the economy would have moved along the G_{Y0} line and the growth rates of capital and income would have approached together. But since the saving ratio has declined to s_1(6.6 per cent), concomitantly with improving technology (2.1 per cent), the economy moved in the directions of A_1 and B_1. The growth rate of income remained almost constant, while capital has grown at an accelerated rate from B_0 to B_1. During this period the output-capital ratio has increased from k_0(0.21) to k_1(0.38).

It must be pointed out that if the saving ratio had not declined, both the growth rates of capital and income would have been higher than they are

[24] The diagram is drawn from the production function designated by equation (28). Thus,

$$G_Y = G_T + \frac{a}{(T_{(t)})^{2/3}} s k^{5/3} - \frac{aG_L}{(T_{(t)})^{2/3}} k^{2/3} + G_L.$$

Since G_Y is a function of both t and k, the line G_{Y0} is obtained when $t=0$ and G_{Y1} when $t=41$.

$$\frac{dG_Y}{dk} = \frac{a}{3(T_{(t)})^{2/3}} k^{-1/3}(5sk - 2G_L)$$

which would be positive or negative, or zero depending upon

$$G_K = sk \gtreqless \frac{2}{5} G_L.$$

Since

$$G_K > \frac{2}{5} G_L,$$

G_Y must be an increasing function of k. The second derivative

$$\frac{d^2 G_Y}{dk^2} = \frac{10}{9} \frac{a}{(T_{(t)})^{2/3}} s k^{-1/3} + \frac{2}{9} \frac{a}{(T_{(t)})^{2/3}} G_L k^{-4/3}$$

and, thus, G_Y is convex from below.

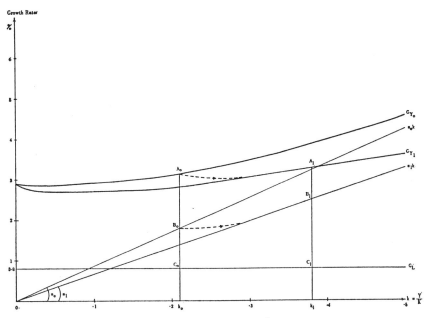

FIGURE 1. U. S. ECONOMIC GROWTH

now. Also wages would have risen higher, but the rate of return on capital would have fallen if the saving ratio had been constant.

APPENDIX B—CONCEPTS AND ESTIMATES

The estimates on which the analysis was based are contained in the tables below. The basic series are those presented in John W. Kendrick [4], extended to 1960 by the same sources and methods described in that volume. Some of the 1960 estimates were published in the *42nd Annual Report* of the National Bureau of Economic Research [14]. In a few instances, minor revisions have been made in the estimates.

Since the concepts underlying the estimates are discussed in some detail in *Productivity Trends in the United States* [4], they will be summarized but briefly in the following notes. The descriptions of the series below will follow the same numbering as the basic tables. All estimates relate to the private domestic economy—the national economy exclusive of general government and the "rest of the world."

(1) *Total factor income* of the private domestic economy is the sum of the compensation accruing to owners of the services of labor and property employed by private industries and government enterprises of the United States. It is derived from the Commerce national income estimates (extrapolated to 1919 by Kuznets estimates), by substracting income originating in general government and in the rest of the world from the total.

TABLE 1—MAJOR MACROECONOMIC VARIABLES—COLUMNS 1-25 U.S. PRIVATE DOMESTIC ECONOMY, SELECTED YEARS, 1919–60

	(1) Total	(2) Labor	(3) Property	(4) Implicit Price Deflator (1)÷(5) Ratio	(5) Total	(6) Labor (2)÷(4)	(7) Property (3)÷(4)	(8) Labor (2)÷(1); (6)÷(5)	(9) Property (3)÷(1); (7)÷(5)
	Factor Income				Real Factor Income			Distribution of Factor Income	
	Current dollars (billions)				Constant, 1929 dollars (billions)			Percentages	
1919	60.85	43.82	17.03	1.075	56.60	40.76	15.84	72.0	28.0
1929	82.67	59.75	22.92	1.000	82.67	59.75	22.92	72.3	27.7
1937	66.43	52.40	14.03	0.789	84.19	66.41	17.78	78.9	21.1
1948	205.10	145.93	59.17	1.507	136.07	96.82	39.25	71.2	28.8
1960	365.92	284.60	81.32	1.814	201.71	156.89	44.82	77.8	22.2
	Index numbers (1929=100)								
1919	73.6	73.3	74.3	107.5	68.5	68.2	69.1	99.6	101.0
1937	80.4	87.7	61.2	78.9	101.4	111.1	77.6	109.1	76.2
1948	248.1	244.2	258.1	150.7	164.6	162.0	171.3	98.4	104.1
1960	442.6	476.3	354.8	181.4	244.0	262.6	195.6	107.6	80.1
	Average annual percentage rates of change								
1948–60	4.94	5.29	2.60	1.58	3.31	3.65	1.11	0.34	−2.21
1919–60	4.47	4.67	3.88	1.28	3.15	3.34	2.57	0.19	−0.57

TABLE 1—(*Continued*)

	(10) Real Factor Input	(11)	(12)	(13) Factor Price	(14)	(15)	(16) Real Factor Price	(17)	(18)
	Total	Labor	Property	Total (1)÷(10)	Labor (2)÷(11)	Property (3)÷(12)	Total (13)÷(4)	Labor (14)÷(4)	Property (15)÷(4)
	Index numbers (1929=100)								
1919	84.9	86.7	80.3	86.7	84.6	92.6	80.7	78.7	86.1
1937	88.9	87.4	93.8	90.4	100.3	65.3	114.6	127.1	82.8
1948	112.3	111.9	113.3	220.9	218.2	227.8	146.6	144.8	151.2
1960	129.1	118.5	169.4	342.8	401.9	209.1	189.0	221.6	115.3
	Average annual percentage rates of change								
1948–60	1.17	0.48	3.43	3.73	5.22	−2.28	2.14	3.61	−1.8
1919–60	1.03	0.76	1.84	3.41	3.87	2.01	2.08	2.56	0.71

Continued overleaf

TABLE 1—(*Continued*)

	(19)	(20) Factor Productivity	(21)	(22) Real Net Investment	(23) Real Net Investment	(24) Real Capital Stock	(25) Real Capital Stock
	Total (5)÷(10)	Labor (5)÷(11)	Property (5)÷(12)	Billions of 1929 dollars	Per cent of real income (22)÷(5)×100	Billions of 1929 dollars	Ratio to real income (24)÷(5)
1919				4.8	8.48	256.5	4.58
1929				7.0	8.47	331.1	4.04
1937				2.4	2.85	315.4	3.76
1948				13.3	9.78	357.5	2.68
1960				13.4	6.64	521.4	2.62
Index numbers (1929=100)							
1919	80.7	79.0	85.3	68.6	100.1	77.5	113.4
1937	114.6	116.5	108.5	34.3	33.6	95.3	93.1
1948	146.6	147.1	145.3	190.0	115.5	108.0	66.3
1960	189.0	205.9	143.8	191.4	78.4	157.5	64.9
Average annual percentage rates of change							
1948-60	2.14	2.84	-0.10	0.07	-3.28	3.19	-0.19
1919-60	2.08	2.36	1.28	2.54	-0.59	1.75	-1.37

(2) *Labor income* is the compensation of employees (wages and salaries plus "supplements") as estimated by the Commerce Department, plus an imputed compensation for the labor services of proprietors. The latter is obtained by multiplying the estimates of numbers of proprietors in each major industry group by the average compensation per full-time equivalent employee in each, based on Commerce estimates. This is only one of a number of possible ways of splitting the net income of proprietors between the labor and property components, but its general reasonableness is indicated by a comparison with corporate income distribution (see items 8 and 9 below).

(3) *Property compensation,* calculated as the difference between (1) and (2), consists of proprietors and corporation profits plus inventory-valuation adjustment, net interest, rents and royalties.

(4) *The implicit price deflator,* obtained as the quotient of (1) and (5), represents the average market prices of the final goods and services comprising net national product, adjusted to eliminate the effects of indirect business taxes less net subsidies. In other words, it is a weighted average of unit factor costs of the various final goods and services, combined by variable quantity weights. (See Kendrick [4, p. 115] for a comparison of market price and unit factor cost indexes. The trends are very similar.)

(5) *Real factor income* is estimated by extrapolating 1929 total factor income in the private domestic economy by an index of the real net national product originating (*cf. ibid.,* Table A-XXII, last column). In effect, this assumes that unit factor cost weights produce the same movements of aggregate real net product as do market price weights.

(6) and (7) *The real income of each factor* class is obtained as the quotient of the current-dollar income and the implicit price deflator (1929 = 100). This procedure is based on the implicit assumption that labor and property compensations are distributed in equal proportions among consumer goods, saving, and direct taxes. While it is probable that saving and taxes absorb a smaller proportion of labor than of property income, estimates do not exist to permit a precise weighting of price indexes of consumer, net investment, and government purchases for each. Moreover, the deflation of each type of income by the same general price index simplifies the analysis. Complications could be introduced by further deflating the real factor income by the ratio of the "appropriate" price index to the general index, if desired.

(8) and (9) *The distribution of factor income* is obtained by computing the percentages accruing to labor and capital, based on the income breakdown. Despite the imputation procedure required to allocate net proprietors income, the distribution of the total shows much the same relative shift as the distribution of factor income originating in the corporate sector where no imputations are necessary, as indicated in the following table. The lower level of the labor share in the total reflects chiefly the fact that agriculture, which is of negligible importance in the corporate sector, comprises almost half the total number of proprietors, while their imputed average compensation is well below the industry average.

Labor Share of Factor Income

	Private Domestic Economy	Corporate Sector
1929	72.3	74.6
1937	78.9	79.9
1948	71.2	74.8
1960	77.8	80.5

The factor shares of income are the same in constant as in current dollars. Thus, the index numbers of the percentage shares are equivalent to index numbers of unit factor costs, (6) ÷ (5) and (7) ÷ (5), and are thus equal to the quotients of real factor prices and factor productivities, (17) ÷ (20) and (18) ÷ (21).

(10) *Total real factor input* is the sum of real labor and capital inputs. It may be thought of as the service-hours made available by the owners of the various factor stocks, combined by the compensation per hour of each. Thus, factor input and factor compensation (cost) are equal in the base period.

(11) *Real labor input* is a weighted aggregate of the man-hours worked in the several industry groups (about 60), combined by the base-period average hourly labor compensation in each. This series rises somewhat faster than an unweighted man-hour aggregate due to the relative shift of workers to higher pay industries.

(12) *Real capital input* is an aggregate of the real capital stock existing in the various industry groups, weighted by the base-period rates of return in each.

(13) *Total factor price*, the quotient of factor income and real input, may also be thought of as an average of the prices of each factor combined by variable input quantity weights. It is the movements of the price ratios indicated by the index numbers that are significant, not the levels.

(14) *Price of labor*, the quotient of labor compensation and labor input, is the mean average hourly labor compensation in the various industries combined by variable man-hour weights.

(15) *Price of property*, the quotient of property (capital) compensation and capital input, in effect is the product of index numbers of capital goods prices and rates of return in the several industries, combined by variable real property input weights.

(16), (17), and (18) *Real factor price* is factor income (total, labor, and property) divided by the implicit price deflator for net national product at factor cost. It represents the purchasing power of factor income per input unit on the assumption that the income of the two major groups is distributed in the same way as the total. As indicated in the text, the real price of capital (property) is its rate of return if the average price of capital goods shows the same movement as the over-all price deflator.

(19) *Total factor productivity*, the quotient of real net product at factor cost (real income) and total real tangible factor input, in effect is a weighted average of the two "partial" productivity ratios. Changes in the total factor

productivity ratio reflect the net saving achieved in the use of factor inputs per unit of output as a result of advances in productive efficiency.

(20) and (21) *Labor and capital productivity* are the quotients of real income (product) and the respective real factor inputs, in index-number form. Each of these "partial" productivity ratios reflects the effects of factor substitutions as well as changing productive efficiency.

(22) and (23) *Real net investment* represents private outlays for new construction, producers' durable equipment and business inventory accumulation, in 1929 dollars, also shown as a percentage of real income or product in the private domestic economy. To ensure consistency, it is estimated as the annual change in the real capital stock (column 24 on a two-year moving average basis to convert from annual averages to end-of-year values).

(24) *The real capital stock* is the total average annual dollar volume, at 1929 prices, of the structures, land, equipment, and inventories in the private domestic economy. The estimates are based largely on those by Goldsmith, and by Kuznets and associates. See [4, Appendix A, and Table IX].

(25) The *"capital coefficient"* is calculated as the ratio of the average annual real capital stock to the annual total real national income or product in the private domestic economy.

REFERENCES

1. K. J. ARROW, H. B. CHENERY, B. MINHAS, AND R. M. SOLOW, "Capital-Labor Substitution and Economic Efficiency," *Rev. Econ. Stat.*, Aug. 1961, *43*, 225-50.
2. MARVIN FRANKEL, "The Production Function: Allocation and Growth," *Am. Econ. Rev.*, Dec. 1962, *52*, 995-1022.
3. J. R. HICKS, *The Theory of Wages.* London 1932.
4. JOHN W. KENDRICK, *Productivity Trends in the United States.* Princeton 1961.
5. ———, "The Wage-Price-Productivity Issue," *Calif. Management Rev.*, Spring, 1962.
6. I. B. KRAVIS, "Relative Income Shares in Fact and Theory," *Am. Econ. Rev.*, Dec. 1959, *49*, 917-49.
7. J. E. MEADE, "The Elasticity of Substitution and the Incidence of an Imperial Inhabited House Duty," *Rev. Econ. Stud.*, Feb. 1934, *1*, 152-53.
8. RYUZO SATO, "Fiscal Policy in a Neo-Classical Growth Model: An Analysis of Time Required for Equilibrating Adjustment," *Rev. Econ. Stud.*, Feb. 1963, *30*, 16-23.
9. ———, "Economic Development and the Growth Rates of Supply and Demand," *Econ. Stud. Quart.* (Riron Keizaigaku), April 1956.
10. A. SMITHIES, "Productivity, Real Wages, and Economic Growth," *Quart. Jour. Econ.*, May 1960, *74*, 189-205.
11. R. M. SOLOW, "A Contribution to the Theory of Economic Growth," *Quart. Jour. Econ.*, Feb. 1956, *70*, 65-94.
12. ———, "Technical Progress, Capital Formation, and Economic Growth," *Am. Econ. Rev., Proc.*, May 1962, *52*, 76-86.

13. The Commission on Money and Credit, "Concepts and Measures of Economic Growth," Research Study Four in *Inflation, Growth, and Employment*, Englewood Cliffs, N.J. 1963.
14. National Bureau of Economic Research, *42nd Annual Report*, June 1962.
15. "Symposium on Production Functions and Economic Growth," *Rev. Econ. Stud.*, June 1962, *29*, 155-266.

[4]

Reprinted from JOURNAL OF ECONOMIC THEORY
All Rights Reserved by Academic Press, New York and London

Vol. 1, No. 1, June 1969
Printed in Great Britain

Stability Conditions in Two-Sector Models of Economic Growth

RYUZO SATO*

Department of Economics, Brown University, Providence, Rhode Island

(1) The important conclusions on the stability of two-sector models of economic growth derived by such well-known works of Uzawa [11], Inada [5], Takayama [10], Shell [7], Drandakis [2], Hahn [4], Amano [1] and others, may be classified into two categories: one, purely technical conditions and the other, purely behavioral conditions. A set of sufficient conditions for stability imposed on the elasticities of substitution by Takayama [10], Drandakis [2] and Amano [1] represents the first type and the factor intensity condition of Uzawa [11], Shinkai [8] and Inada [5] represents the second type of sufficient conditions. The works of Hahn [4] and Inada [5] do take account of both the technical and behavioral conditions by considering the relationship between the momentary and long-run equilibria and also by allowing the different social classes to have different saving behaviors. However, even in these cases a full investigation of the stability conditions has not been carried out by studying the combined effects of both technical and behavioral conditions on stability.

This paper attempts to fill this gap by presenting a set of new stability conditions which combine both technical and behavioral conditions. In this way a wide region of stability is established which includes many plausible cases. Most results obtained thus far may be shown to correspond to the extreme points of this region. Hence, two-sector models of economic growth with plausible values of the parameters will most likely achieve stable balanced growth, unless the models incorporate such extreme assumptions as fixed coefficients, very different saving propensities for different social classes, etc.

(2) Since the essential features of two-sector growth models are well known, we shall simply write down our models without elaborate

* This work was in part supported under the National Science Foundation Grant, G.S. No. 2325. I should like to thank Martin J. Beckmann and Tetsunori Koizumi for stimulating discussions. I have also benefited from the useful comments on an earlier draft by the editor and the referee of this *Journal*.

explanations. We shall discuss two models; one with the classical saving function and the other with nonclassical saving function (Hahn and Matthews [3], pp. 794–801).

MODEL I (CLASSICAL SAVING FUNCTION)

Production Functions ($i = 1$ = Investment Goods, $i = 2$ = Consumption Goods).

$$y_i = f_i(k_i), \quad i = 1, 2 \tag{1}$$

$$f_i > 0, \quad f_i' > 0, \quad f_i'' < 0, \quad f_i(0) = 0, \quad f_i(\infty) = \infty, \quad f_i'(0) = \infty, \quad f_i'(\infty) = 0,$$
$$\forall k_i \in I(0, \infty).$$

Full Employment and Perfect Competition.

$$R = \frac{f_i(k_i) - k_i f_i'(k_i)}{f_i'(k_i)}, \quad i = 1, 2 \tag{2}$$

$$k = \rho_1 k_1 + \rho_2 k_2 \tag{3}$$

$$\rho_1 + \rho_2 = 1. \tag{4}$$

Saving-Investment Behavior (*Classical Assumption*).

$$f_1(k_1) = \frac{s_\pi f_1'(k_1) \cdot k}{\rho_1} \tag{5}$$

$$\frac{\dot{k}}{k} = \frac{\rho_1 f_1(k_1)}{k} - \lambda, \tag{6}$$

where $y_i = Y_i/L_i$ = output–labor ratio in each sector, $k_i = K_i/L_i$ = capital–labor ratio in each sector, $R = w/r$ = wage–rental ratio (marginal rate of substitution), $k = K/L = (K_1 + K_2)/(L_1 + L_2)$ = aggregate capital–labor ratio, $\rho_i = L_i/L$ = fraction of labor in each sector, s_π = the saving ratio from profits, $0 < s_\pi \leqq 1$, λ = sum of the growth rate of the total labor force, $n = \dot{L}/L$, and the depreciation rate, u, i.e., $\lambda = n + u > 0$.

There are eight variables, $y_1, y_2, k_1, k_2, \rho_1, \rho_2, k$ and R to be determined from eight relationships in the model. The time paths of these variables are all dependent on the last equation (equation (6)), which we shall now examine.

In view of $f_i'' < 0$ and $dR/dk_i = -f_i f_i''/f_i'^2 > 0$, we can determine k_i from equation (2) uniquely as a function of R, i.e.,

$$k_i = \Phi_i(R), \quad \Phi_i' > 0, \quad i = 1, 2.$$

Also ρ_1 and ρ_2 can be expressed as

$$\rho_1 = \frac{s_\pi k}{R + \Phi_1(R)} \quad \text{and} \quad \rho_2 = 1 - \frac{s_\pi k}{R + \Phi_1(R)}.$$

Thus, we can write k as,

$$k(R) = \frac{[R + \Phi_1(R)]\Phi_2(R)}{[R + (1 - s_\pi)\Phi_1(R) + s_\pi\Phi_2(R)]}. \tag{7}$$

Substitution of ρ_1 and f_1 into equation (6) gives

$$\frac{\dot{k}}{k} = s_\pi f_1'[\Phi_1(R)] - \lambda. \tag{8}$$

This is the fundamental differential equation expressing the behavior of the model.

It is easy to show that the model has equilibrium solutions for any values of λ/s_π, $0 < \lambda/s_\pi < +\infty$, because of the condition

$$f_1'(\infty) = 0 < f_1'[\Phi_1(R(k^*))] = \lambda/s_\pi < f_1'(0) = +\infty.^1$$

Thus, an equilibrium path exists for any value of the positive aggregate capital–labor ratio k^*. The stability of an equilibrium path depends on the sign of $d(\dot{k}/k)/dk$, i.e., we must have

$$\frac{d(\dot{k}/k)}{dk} = \frac{d(\dot{k}/k)}{dk_1} \cdot \frac{dk_1}{dR} \cdot \frac{dR}{dk} < 0. \tag{9}$$

Since $d(\dot{k}/k)/dk_1$ is equal to $s_\pi f_1'' < 0$ and since $dk_1/dR > 0$, the above condition will be satisfied if and only if

$$\frac{dR}{dk} > 0. \tag{10}$$

The logarithmic differentiation of equation (7) with respect to k yields,

$$\frac{d\log k(R)}{dR} = \frac{1}{\Phi_2(R)} \cdot \frac{d\Phi_2}{dR} + \frac{1 + \dfrac{d\Phi_1}{dR}}{R + \Phi_1(R)} - \frac{1 + (1 - s_\pi)\dfrac{d\Phi_1}{dR} + s_\pi\dfrac{d\Phi_2}{dR}}{R + (1 - s_\pi)\Phi_1(R) + s_\pi\Phi_2(R)}. \tag{10'}$$

If we use the definition of the elasticity of factor substitution $\sigma_i = (d\Phi_i/dR) \cdot (R/\Phi_i)$ ($i = 1, 2$), we can write equation (10') as

$$\frac{d\log k(R)}{dR} = \frac{\sigma_1 s_\pi k_1(R + k_2) + \sigma_2(R + k_1)[R + (1 - s_\pi)k_1] + s_\pi R(k_2 - k_1)}{A}, \tag{11}$$

where

$$A = R \cdot (R + k_1)[R + (1 - s_\pi)k_1 + s_\pi k_2] > 0.$$

The necessary and sufficient condition for global stability of Model I is that expression (11) be positive. For $R > 0$, we can write this as

$$\sigma = \frac{dk}{dR} \cdot \frac{R}{k} > 0.$$

Hence, *the necessary and sufficient condition for global stability is that*

---

[1] The interested reader should refer to alternative conditions in Sato [6].

the aggregate elasticity of factor substitution σ be positive. This condition is satisfied as long as aggregate production is *efficient* in the sense that the reallocation of capital and labor with given input prices cannot increase the aggregate output $Y = pY_1 + Y_2$, where p is the relative price of investment goods in terms of consumption goods.[2]

We shall now derive sets of sufficient conditions for the above, including the well-known results of Uzawa [*11*], Takayama [*10*], Drandakis [*2*], Inada [*5*], Amano [*1*] and others.

(A) *Capital-Intensity Condition* (Uzawa, Shinkai and Inada). From equation (11), it is obvious that as long as

$$k_2 \geqq k_1, \tag{12}$$

the stability condition is satisfied, i.e., as long as the capital intensity in the consumption goods sector is equal to or greater than that in the investment goods sector, the two-sector growth model is globally stable.

(B) *Elasticity of Factor Substitution Conditions* (Takayama, Drandakis and Amano). In view of equation (11), as long as

$$\sigma_1 \geqq 1, \tag{13a}$$

the system is stable. We can also write equation (11) as

$$\frac{d \log k}{dR} = \frac{(R + \sigma_1 k_1)[R + (1 - s_\pi)k_1 + s_\pi k_2] + \\ + (R + k_1)[R(\sigma_2 - 1) + (1 - s_\pi)(\sigma_2 - \sigma_1)k_1]}{A}. \tag{11$'$}$$

Hence, as long as

$$\sigma_2 \geqq 1 \tag{13b}$$

the system is stable. As long as the elasticity of factor substitution in at least one sector is equal to or greater than unity, the two-sector growth model is globally stable.

(C) *Conditions on Substitution and Saving Behavior.* The above two sets of sufficient conditions are either purely technical or purely nontechnical. We shall now derive sufficient conditions consisting of both technical substitutability and saving behavior. Equation (11) will also be positive if

$$Rk_1[\sigma_2(2 - s_\pi) + s_\pi(\sigma_1 - 1)] + s_\pi k_2[R + \sigma_1 k_1] + \sigma_2[(1 - s_\pi)k_1^2 + R^2] > 0. \tag{11$''$}$$

Since the second and third terms are always positive, the above will be positive if

$$\sigma_1 \geqq 1 - \left(\frac{2 - s_\pi}{s_\pi}\right)\sigma_2. \tag{14}$$

---

[2] Note that if aggregate production is efficient, then there exists a unique short-run (or momentary) equilibrium (Hahn [*4*]).

It is seen that both σ_1 and σ_2 can be less than unity to have stability. For example, for $s_\pi = 0.8$, the model can have stable balanced growth even with $\sigma_1 = 0.5$ and $\sigma_2 = 0.333$. As a special case of condition (14), when $s_\pi = 1$, we have

$$\sigma_1 + \sigma_2 \geqq 1. \tag{15}$$

This is the result obtained in Hahn ([4], p. 342). When the saving ratio from profits is less than one, the system can achieve stability even if each of the elasticities of substitution is less than 0.5. *In general, we conclude that the smaller the saving ratio from profits, the more likely can the model achieve stability.*

(D) *Conditions on Technical Substitutability and Relative Shares.* If we assume that s_π is less than unity, we can furthermore derive an interesting condition which relates the relative income shares with technical substitutability. From (11'), we can derive

$$R(\sigma_2 - 1) + (1 - s_\pi)(\sigma_2 - \sigma_1)k_1 \geqq 0$$

as a sufficient condition. If we set $\alpha_1 = k_1 f_1'/f_1 = $ the relative share of capital in the investment goods sector, then the above implies that

$$\alpha_1 \geqq \frac{1 - \sigma_2}{1 - (1 - s_\pi)\sigma_1 - s_\pi \sigma_2}, \quad \begin{matrix} 0 < s_\pi < 1, \\ 0 < \sigma_1 \leqq \sigma_2 < 1. \end{matrix} \tag{16}$$

Even if the elasticities of substitution are both less than unity, *as long as the relative share of capital in the investment goods sector is sufficiently large, the model can achieve stability.*

These are but a few of many other sufficient conditions that one could derive. The essential point, however, is that in general the two-sector growth model with the classical saving function is likely to be stable, unless the *aggregate* elasticity of substitution is zero or negative, which is extremely *unlikely*.

3. MODEL II (NONCLASSICAL SAVING FUNCTION)

We now replace equation (5) of Model I by the nonclassical (or general) saving function:

$$pf_1\rho_1 = s_w y + (s_\pi - s_w)f_2' \cdot k, \tag{17}$$

where $y = pf_1\rho_1 + f_2\rho_2$, $s_w = $ the saving ratio from the wage income. The aggregate capital–labor ratio is now reduced to

$$k(R) = \frac{k_1 k_2 + [(1 - s_w)k_2 + s_w k_1]R}{R + s_\pi k_2 + (1 - s_\pi)k_1}. \tag{18}$$

The process of capital accumulation is expressed by[3]

$$\frac{\dot{k}}{k} = \frac{f_1'}{k}(s_w R + s_\pi k) - \lambda. \tag{19}$$

The necessary and sufficient condition for stability of balanced path (its existence is assumed by the derivative conditions) is that the following inequality be satisfied:

$$\frac{d(\dot{k}/k)}{dk} = \frac{d(\dot{k}/k)}{dR} \cdot \frac{dR}{dk} < 0. \tag{20}$$

Since aggregate production has to be efficient, the above requires that

$$\text{Condition I} \qquad \frac{dR}{dk} > 0 \tag{20a}$$

and

$$\text{Condition II} \qquad \frac{d\dot{k}/k)}{dR} < 0. \tag{20b}$$

Condition I. Let $k(R)$ be equal to $k(R) = m(R)/h(R)$. Then for dk/dR to be positive, we must have $Z(R) = m'(R)h(R) - m(R)h'(R) > 0$. Using $\sigma_i = (dk_i/dR) \cdot (R/k_i)$ $(i = 1, 2)$, $Z(R)$ can be written as

$$Z(R) = (k_2 - k_1)[(s_\pi - s_w)k_1 +$$
$$+ s_\pi(1 - s_w)(k_2 - k_1)] + (R + k_2)(s_w R + s_\pi k_2)\sigma_1 \frac{k_1}{R} +$$
$$+ (R + k_1)\{(1 - s_\pi)k_1 + (1 - s_w)R\}\sigma_2 \frac{k_2}{R} > 0. \tag{21}$$

At glance we can say that if

$$s_\pi = s_w \tag{22}$$

or if

$$s_\pi > s_w \quad \text{and} \quad k_2 \gtreqqless k_1, \tag{23}$$

then $Z(R)$ will be always positive. Hence, *if the saving ratios from profits and wages are the same or if the saving ratio from profits is greater than that from wages, together with the capital-intensity condition, then the aggregate elasticity of substitution* $\sigma = (dk/dR) \cdot (R/k)$ *is always positive.*

There are many other sufficient conditions for σ to be positive. By multiplying $Z(R)$ by R, we get

$$R \cdot Z(R) = Rk_1 k_2[\sigma_2\{2 - (s_\pi + s_w)\} + (s_\pi + s_w)(\sigma_1 - 1) + 2s_\pi s_w] +$$
$$+ R[s_\pi(1 - s_w)k_2^2 + s_w(1 - s_\pi)k_1^2] + \sigma_1 k_1(s_\pi k_2^2 + s_w R^2) +$$
$$+ \sigma_2 k_2[(1 - s_w)k_1^2 + (1 - s_w)R^2]. \tag{21'}$$

---

[3] The reader is asked to refer to Inada [5] for the derivation of (18) and (19).

Thus, another sufficient condition is that the value of the term in the first bracket be nonnegative, i.e.,

$$\sigma_1 \geq 1 - \frac{2s_\pi s_w}{s_\pi + s_w} - \left(\frac{2-(s_\pi + s_w)}{s_\pi + s_w}\right)\sigma_2. \tag{24}$$

This condition contains many interesting results. For instance $\sigma_1 \geq 1$ is a sufficient condition, and also if $s_w = 0$, equation (24) reduces to equation (14) in Model I.

The investigation of equation (24) indicates various sufficient conditions for condition I to be satisfied:

(1) For $s_\pi \to 1$ and $s_w \to 1$, σ can be positive for any $\sigma_1 > 0$.

(2) As long as $s_w \to 0$ and $s_\pi \to 1$ (also $s_\pi \to 0$ and $s_w \to 1$), $\sigma_1 + \sigma_2 \geq 1$ is sufficient for $\sigma > 0$.

(3) When $(s_\pi + s_w) \leq 1$ and $\sigma_2 \geq 1$, then σ is positive. (Obviously there is a case for $\sigma > 0$ with $s_\pi + s_w > 1$.)

(4) If $\sigma_1 \geq 1$, σ is positive regardless of s_π, s_w and σ_2.

(5) For the realistic values of s_π and s_w, each of σ_1 and σ_2 can be less than unity, e.g., $s_\pi = 1$, $s_w = 0.2$, $\sigma_1 = 0.5$ and $\sigma_2 = 0.6$ will do it.

(6) When the two saving ratios, s_π and s_w, are the same (a simple Keynesian assumption), then σ is positive, regardless of σ_i. (See equation (21).)

(7) If the saving ratio from profits is at least equal to the saving ratio from wages, together with the capital-intensity condition, σ is positive.

Condition II and Stability Conditions. We shall now study the implications of the second condition for stability of Model II. Let $\psi(R)$ be equal to $(f_1'/k)(s_w R + s_\pi k)$. The logarithmic differentiation of $\psi(R)$ with respect to R yields

$$\frac{1}{\psi}\frac{d\psi}{dR} = \frac{s_w k_1 k - s_\pi k^2 - s_w R^2 k' - s_w R k' k_1}{k(R + k_1)(s_w R + s_\pi k)}. \tag{25}$$

(A) *Uzawa–Inada Conditions.* If σ is positive, i.e., $k' > 0$, equation (25) will be negative as long as $s_w k_1 - s_\pi k$ is negative. Since $k = \rho_1 k_1 + \rho_2 k_2$, k will be equal to or greater than k_1 as long as $k_2 \geq k_1$. Therefore, if

$$s_\pi \geq s_w \quad \text{and} \quad k_2 \geq k_1 \tag{26}$$

then both Conditions I and II will be satisfied. Hence (26) is a sufficient condition for stable balanced growth. We shall call this set of conditions the Uzawa–Inada conditions.

(B) *Aggregate Elasticity of Substitution Condition.* If in equation (25) we have

$$k_1 k - (R + k_1) R k' \leqq 0, \tag{27}$$

then $d\psi/dR$ is negative. Let α_1 be equal to the relative share of capital in the investment goods sector, i.e., $\alpha_1 = k_1 f_1'/f_1 = k_1/R + k_1$. We can write (27) as

$$k - \frac{R k'}{\alpha_1} \leqq 0 \quad \text{or} \quad \alpha_1 \leqq \sigma = \frac{R}{k} \cdot \frac{dk}{dR}. \tag{27'}$$

Hence, as long as the aggregate elasticity of substitution is equal to or greater than the relative share of capital in the investment goods sector, Model II *is globally stable.*[4]

(C) *Conditions on the Individual Elasticities of Substitution.* To derive sufficient conditions from the elasticity of substitution in each sector we use $Z(R)$ in (21). Equation (27') will be met if

$$\alpha_1 m(R) h(R) - R Z(R) \leqq 0.$$

This condition is equal to

$$Rk_1 k_2 [\alpha_1 \{2 - (s_\pi + s_w) + 2 s_\pi s_w\} - \sigma_2 \{2 - (s_\pi + s_w)\} -$$
$$- (s_\pi + s_w)(\sigma_1 - 1) - 2 s_\pi s_w] + (\alpha_1 - \sigma_1)[s_\pi k_1 k_2^2 + s_w k_1 R^2] +$$
$$+ (\alpha_1 - \sigma_2)[(1 - s_\pi)k_1^2 k_2 + (1 - s_w)k_2 R^2] + (\alpha_1 - 1)[s_\pi(1 - s_w)Rk_2^2 +$$
$$+ s_w(1 - s_\pi)Rk_1^2] \leqq 0. \tag{27''}$$

A sufficient condition for (27'') is

(i) $\sigma_1 \geqq 1 \quad (\Rightarrow \sigma_1 > \alpha_1)$ (28)

(ii) $\sigma_2 \geqq \alpha_1.$

Since (28–i) is already included in Condition I as a sufficient condition, *Model* II *is globally stable if the elasticity of factor substitution in the investment goods sector is equal to or greater than unity, together with the condition that the elasticity of substitution in the consumption goods sector is equal to or greater than the relative share of capital in the investment goods industry.*

(D) *Substitution, Relative Shares and the Saving Behaviors.* As a more general stability condition from equation (27''), in addition to $\sigma_i \geqq \alpha_1$, we can present the condition

$$\sigma_1 \geqq 1 - \left\{ \frac{2 - (s_\pi + s_w)}{(s_\pi + s_w)} \right\} \sigma_2 + \frac{\alpha_1 \{2 - (s_\pi + s_w)\}}{(s_\pi + s_w)} - \frac{2(1 - \alpha_1)s_\pi s_w}{(s_\pi + s_w)}. \tag{29}$$

As long as this condition is met, the aggregate elasticity is positive (com-

---

[4] Note that if (27') is satisfied, then condition I is automatically satisfied.

pared with (24)) and, hence, we have a general stability condition. Fig. 1 shows the stability region derived from (29).[5]

Depending upon the appropriate values of s_π and s_w, we could have the stable case with $\alpha_1 < \sigma_1 < 1$ and $\alpha_1 < \sigma_2 < 1$. Although this condition is not so neat as the other conditions, we can show that the stability

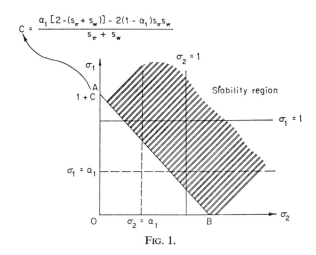

FIG. 1.

condition is satisfied for the most realistic values of s_π, s_w, α_1, σ_1 and σ_2. Consider the case of the Keynesian savings function $s_w = s_\pi = s$. Then, we have

$$\sigma_1 \geq 1 - \left(\frac{1-s}{s}\right)(\sigma_2 - \alpha_1) - (1 - \alpha_1)s.$$

The values of $s = 0.2$, $\sigma_1 = 0.5$, $\sigma_2 = 0.5$ and $\alpha_1 = 0.3$ will certainly meet the stability requirements.

We can also derive another set of sufficient conditions for stability by omitting the last term in equation (29). That is, we have

$$\sigma_1 \geq 1 - \left\{\frac{2 - (s_\pi + s_w)}{s_\pi + s_w}\right\}(\sigma_2 - \alpha_1) \tag{30}$$

$$\alpha_1 \leq \sigma_1, \qquad \alpha_1 \leq \sigma_2.$$

The investigation of (30) and Fig. 2 reveals that:

(a) when $s_\pi + s_w = 1$, $\sigma_1 + \sigma_2 \geq 1 + \alpha_1$ is a sufficient condition for stability (EF);

(b) when $s_\pi + s_w \neq 1$, the stability region may increase as shown by AB in Fig. 2.

---

[5] The stability region indicates the sufficient conditions. Therefore, the region outside the shaded part may not be unstable. This comment also applies to Fig. 2 below.

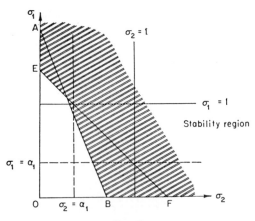

FIG. 2.

We shall summarize the sets of sufficient conditions for stability of the two-sector model with the general saving function:

(1) If the capital intensity condition is satisfied together with the condition that the saving ratio from profits is at least equal to the saving ratio from wages, the system is globally stable (Uzawa and Inada).

$$k_2 \geqq k_1 \quad \text{and} \quad s_\pi \geqq s_w.$$

(2) If the aggregate elasticity of substitution is equal to or greater than the capital share in the investment goods industry, then the system can achieve a stable balanced growth.

$$\sigma \geqq \alpha_1.$$

(3) As long as the elasticity of substitution in the investment goods sector is equal to or greater than unity, the model is stable, provided only that the elasticity of substitution in the consumption goods sector is equal to or greater than the relative share of capital in the investment goods industry

$$\sigma_1 \geqq 1 \quad \text{and} \quad \sigma_2 \geqq \alpha_1.$$

(4) If the following two sets of conditions on the relationship among the elasticities of substitution, the relative shares and the saving ratios from profits and wages are met, Model II is globally stable:

(i) $\sigma_1 \geqq \alpha_1$ and $\sigma_2 \geqq \alpha_1.$

(ii) $\sigma_1 \geqq 1 - \left\{ \dfrac{2 - (s_\pi + s_w)}{(s_\pi + s_w)} \right\} (\sigma_2 - \alpha_1) - \dfrac{2(1 - \alpha_1) s_\pi s_w}{(s_\pi + s_w)}.$

(5) Although the above two sets of conditions appear complicated, the common-sense values of s_π, s_w, α_1, σ_1 and σ_2 will all satisfy the conditions. For example as a Keynesian case if $s = 0.2$, $\sigma_1 = \sigma_2 = 0.5$ and $\alpha_1 = 0.3$, the two-sector model is globally stable. The essential point is that the two-sector growth model is most likely *stable*, unless the model has extreme assumptions concerning its parameters.

REFERENCES

1. AMANO, A., Factor substitution in a two-sector growth model. *Review of Economic Studies.* **32** (1965).

2. DRANDAKIS, E. M., Factor substitution in the two-sector growth model. *Review of Economic Studies.* October, 1963.

3. HAHN, F. H. and MATTHEWS, R. C. D., The theory of growth: a survey. *Economic J.* December, 1964.

4. HAHN, F. H., On two-sector growth models. *Review of Economic Studies.* October, 1965.

5. INADA, K., On a two-sector model of economic growth: comments and a generalization. *Review of Economic Studies.* **30** (1963).

6. SATO, R., A note on scarcity of specific resources as a limit to output: a correction. *Review of Economic Studies.* October, 1967.

7. SHELL, K., Comparative statics for the two-sector model. *Metroeconomica.* May August, 1966.

8. SHINKAI, Y., On equilibrium growth of capital and labor. *International Economic Review.* May, 1960.

9. SOLOW, R. M., Note on Uzawa's two-sector model of economic growth. *Review of Economic Studies.* October, 1961.

10. TAKAYAMA, A., On a two-sector model of economic growth: a comparative static analysis. *Review of Economic Studies.* **30** (1963).

11. UZAWA, H., On a two-sector model of economic growth. *Review of Economic Studies.* October, 1961.

RECEIVED: January 20, 1969.

ECONOMETRICA

VOLUME 39 November, 1971 NUMBER 6

OPTIMAL SAVINGS POLICY
WHEN LABOR GROWS ENDOGENOUSLY

BY RYUZO SATO AND ERIC G. DAVIS[1]

This paper is an attempt to study optimal savings policy in a world where the growth rate of labor responds to economic factors. This modification makes the form of society's social welfare function important—its elasticity affects "real" economic variables. In addition, a rule for direct population control is investigated.

1. INTRODUCTION

THE IMPORTANT QUESTION of the optimal strategy for growth has occupied the minds of economists for some time and has been discussed from many different points of view [5, 6, 7, 8, 11, 17, 18, and 22]. All such studies are based on a highly aggregated view of an economy, with some facets of the real world emphasized with others ignored. But despite the long list of economists who have studied economically-determined population growth, this feature has been often ignored, with some exceptions among growth models not directly concerned with dynamic optimality (Solow [21], Niehans [14], and Davis [7]). This paper is an attempt to study optimal savings in a world where the growth rate of labor is not exogenously determined but rather responds to economic factors. The paper can also be considered as an extension of the work of one of the present authors (Davis [6]) to a study of dynamic optimality under endogenous labor supply.

In the next section we shall first study economic factors affecting population growth. Any attempt to "explain" the growth rate of population is doomed to failure due to the complexity of the interrelationships of the various demographic, economic, and social factors involved. Virtually every action that an individual can undertake has repercussions on one or more of the three components of population growth: birth rates, death rates, and migration rates, so that all spurs to activity are qualitatively, if not quantitatively, significant. With such a diversity of causes there is bound to be variation in the direction of their effects. Hence, at a point in time, the current rate of population growth arises from a matrix of forces, many acting to advance with others acting to impede the increase in numbers. To isolate a single factor, or even one dimension of life, to provide a theory of population growth is clearly a gross simplification of reality, but even the grossest such generalization can contain some interesting insights.

[1] The authors acknowledge the assistance from the National Science Foundation, Grant No. 2325. A part of the present paper was presented at the 1967 Winter Meetings of the Econometric Society, in Washington, D.C. The authors are also grateful to the referee for his useful comments on an earlier version of this paper.

In Section 3 we investigate optimal savings in a world where the growth rate of labor is not exogenously determined but rather responds to economic factors. Allowing population growth to be influenced by economic factors leads to some interesting changes in the rules for optimal investment policy—not only will the "correct" savings rate be altered, but in certain cases, the *form* of society's social welfare function will come into prominence. Section 4 considers the effect of parametric change in the utility function on the steady state values of the economic variables. It will be shown that the wishes of society, as expressed in the utility function it chooses (specifically in the elasticity of its utility function), have meaning in that they affect "real" economic variables, both in the steady state value and in the dynamics on the way to equilibrium. For instance, a sudden decision to evaluate any level of per capita consumption as representing a higher level of utility than previously results in a lower steady state capital-labor ratio.

A rule for direct population control is investigated in Section 5. The basic model in Section 3 is reformulated to study direct optimal policy in combatting population increases. It is shown that the total output must always be kept equal to the total amount of capital multiplied by the responsiveness of the population growth rate to further increases in public expenditures. This in turn implies that the steady state growth rate of population must be kept equal to the savings ratio multiplied by the direct effect of population control. Some aspects of endogenous population growth and optimal investment in human capital are analyzed in the last part of this paper.

2. ECONOMIC FACTORS AFFECTING POPULATION GROWTH

Economists have theorized on population change since the very beginnings of the discipline so it seems appropriate to first briefly mention some of their opinions.

In the eyes of Adam Smith, the size of the population was positively related to the wage level. If wages were high, he felt both birth and death rates would be affected. The argument ran that not only would affluence encourage early marriage and hence higher birth rates, but in addition, children in their role as future workers would be more valuable (as a form of retirement insurance). Since it "pays" to rear more children parents would exhibit greater care and as a result (infant) mortality would decline. David Ricardo concurred, although he emphasized the importance of the workers' environment [1].

However, Malthus [12] was really the first to succeed in systematizing a general theory of population. In its most fatalistic form, Malthus provided not so much an economic theory of population growth as an economic theory of death rates coupled with the postulate that birth rates were biologically determined.

Today, the underdeveloped countries have immediate access to medical techniques and knowledge which evolved gradually over centuries. Thus, specific medical programs aimed at eradicating a particular disease can have a tremendous, almost overnight effect on mortality rates at very low cost. But without an accompanying improvement in the standard of living there are severe limits on what can be done, and hence, it is a valid if somewhat crude hypothesis to postulate that death rates are a decreasing function of per capita income.

On the other hand, birth rates seem to be mostly a non-economic variable, for evidence seems to suggest that they depend more on outside cultural attitudes than on standards of living. This is especially true when applied to underdeveloped countries today. For example, during the decade from 1941 to 1951, India's population grew at an average annual rate of 1.3 per cent but during the following ten-year span the growth rate of population accelerated to an annual rate of two per cent. This increase was due entirely to diminished mortality: The crude death rate (deaths per thousand population per year) fell from thirty in the earlier decade to between twenty-one and twenty-four in the period from 1951 to 1961 (Thompson and Lewis [23, p. 437]).

This, as yet, tentative conclusion that death rates are inversely related to per capita income and that this relationship is a much more significant one than any existing between per capita income and birth rates, has received considerable support from a most comprehensive econometric study by Adelman of the inter-relationships between demographic and economic phenomena [2]. Two conclusions are possible concerning birth rates from this work. Either per capita income has little or no effect on birth rates or there is such a relationship but it is *not* a monotonic one. For an underdeveloped country, it seems likely that the effect on birth rates due to an improved standard of living would be such as to raise the population level. However, as a country becomes more developed, there are rearrangements in the structure of the society which tend to lower the birth rate. The forces of industrialization and urbanization, together with the new higher status of women, all act to lower the average family size and thus the birth rates.

Buttrick [4] has suggested that in fact there exists a third region where once again birth rates are positively related to per capita income. His diagram appears as Figure 1. In his terms, region I represents that stage of development where children are both producers' goods and consumer durables. At a higher stage of development (region II) children cease to be producers' goods while, in addition, costs of child rearing rise. Ultimately a country may move into that stage of relative affluence where children are durable luxury goods and hence birth rates become an increasing function of per capita income (region III).

Of the three components of population growth, migration appears to be the one which bears the closest relationship to economic phenomena, and in particular to per capita income. People have always been willing to move in search of a higher standard of living so long as the interregional differentials were high enough. Certainly no voluntary major migration has ever been isolated where in fact the flow was from a high-income to a low-income country!

The relationship between the growth rate of population and per capita income can be found by adding the migration and birth rate and subtracting the death rate at every level of per capita income. Birth rates introduce some amount of ambiguity as far as the slope of the population function is concerned, for although the migration rate minus the death rate is clearly monotonically increasing in per capita income, in region II birth rates move in the opposite direction. It will be assumed in general that the population function which results is as shown in Figure 2, i.e., the economic effect on birth rates is of a lesser order of magnitude

R. SATO AND E. G. DAVIS

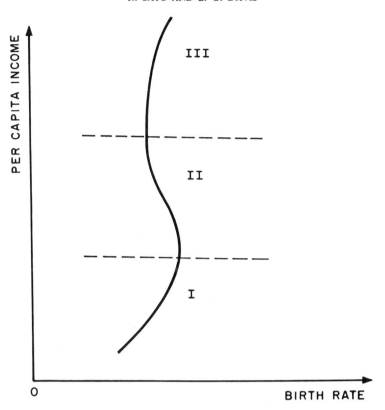

FIGURE 1.—The economic basis for birth rates.

so that the overall relationship between population growth rate and per capita income is monotonic and positive for all levels of per capita income. This is equivalent to assuming that the effect on birth rates is only large enough to alter the second derivative, but never the first derivative of the population function.

3. A MODEL WHERE LABOR GROWS ENDOGENOUSLY

It is now time to study optimal savings in a world where the growth rate of labor is not exogenously determined but rather responds to economic factors.

A single homogeneous output Y is produced with the use of two homogeneous inputs, the capital good K and labor L, subject to a constant returns to scale production function,

$$Y(t) = F[K(t), L(t)].$$

Hence, using the linear homogeneous property of the production function,

(1) $\qquad y = Y/L = f(K/L) \equiv f(k),$

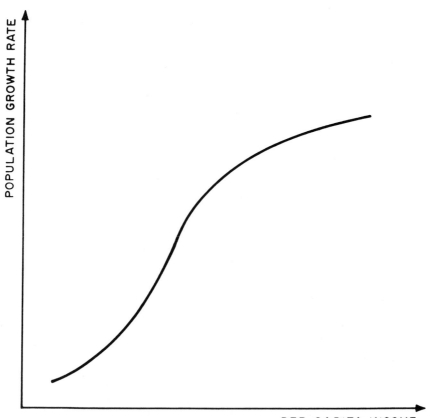

FIGURE 2.—The population function.

where $f(k) = F(K/L, 1)$ and $f'(k) > 0, f''(k) < 0$ for all $0 < k < \infty$. In addition, it is assumed that

$$\lim_{k \to +\infty} \frac{f(k)}{k} = 0 \quad \text{and} \quad \lim_{k \to 0} \frac{f(k)}{k} = \infty,$$

for these are the conditions that guarantee the existence of a golden age for any savings ratio when labor supply grows exogenously.[2] The population grows at a relative rate, n, but here n is a function of per capita income (and it is assumed that the labor supply grows at the same rate, for a constant proportion of the population is productively employed):

(2) $\dot{L} = L(t)n(y).$

[2] A golden age path is defined by $\dot{k} = 0$, and equivalently by $\dot{K}/K = \dot{L}/L = n$. But $\dot{K}/K = sY/K = sf(k)/k$. Thus, the existence of a golden age path requires the existence of a k such that $Y/K = n/s$. If Y/K, as a function of k, ranges from 0 to ∞ as k ranges from ∞ to 0, clearly a golden age path will exist for all possible choices of s and n. See R. Sato [**19** and **20**].

To achieve any unambiguous result it is sometimes necessary that the population function be monotonic. Following Buttrick's analysis presented in Section 2, it will be assumed that $n' \geqslant 0$ (see Figure 2). The second derivative, n'', will be unspecified although it plays a crucial role in the analysis of stability. Thus, $n' \geqslant 0$ but $n'' \gtreqless 0$. However, the case where $n' < 0$ but small will also be discussed.

Also let $c(t)$ be the rate of current consumption per capita, and let $s(t)$ be the current total (public and private) savings ratio. Hence,

(3) $c(t) = [1 - s(t)]y[t]$.

The work by E. Davis [6, 7] has shown that the introduction of endogenous labor growth will "modify" Phelps' golden rule of accumulation that produces maximum consumption per capita among all golden age (balanced growth) paths. The modified golden rule savings ratio must be equal to

(4) $s(t) = \dfrac{kf'(k)}{f(k)}[1 - kn'(y)]$,

where $(kf'(k)/f(k))$ is the relative share of output going to capital. If $n' > 0$, then the optimal savings ratio under endogenous labor supply is less than the relative share of capital (Phelps' golden rule), while on the other hand if $n' < 0$, then it is greater than capital's relative share. (It is assumed that $1 - kn' > 0$ for $n' \geqslant 0$ and the stability conditions are met even when $n' < 0$.) Correspondingly the growth rate of the economy under endogenous labor supply is less than or greater than the marginal productivity of capital depending upon whether n' is positive or negative.

Suppose now that society's task is the more practical one of maximizing the welfare of its citizens starting from arbitrary initial conditions. The choice of an appropriate measure of a welfare stream is no easier here than in the static preserve of welfare economics, but the approach that maximizes the integral over time of the utility of the representative man seems to have historical precedent and will be used here.

There seem to be three objective functions, suitable for integration over time, that have appeared in the literature on dynamic optimality:

CASE 1: Society's welfare is measured by a utility function of per capita consumption with (i) future utility being discounted at a positive rate (Koopmans [11], Cass [5]); (ii) no discounting of future utility (Samuelson [18], Koopmans [11], Ramsey [17]).

CASE 2: Society's welfare over time is measured by weighting the utility index of per capita consumption by numbers; i.e., multiplying the utility function of the representative man by the total population (Cass [5]).[3]

---

[3] It should be noted that when population grows at an exogenously given rate there is no substantial difference between Cases 1(i) and 2 (assuming that the rate of discount is constant over time and for reasons of boundedness exceeds the population growth rate). However, when population grows endogenously the distinction between these two cases is no longer blurred but is very distinct.

The utility index is assumed to be a concave function of per capita consumption, i.e., $U' > 0$ and $U'' < 0$. Also, ρ is defined to be society's discount rate which is assumed constant for all time.

Case 1

The problem is to maximize by choice of $s(t)$

$$\int_0^\infty U[(1 - s(t))f(k)]\, e^{-\rho t}\, dt,$$

subject to $\dot{k} = s(t)f(k) - kn[f(k)]$. The solution is found by applying the Pontryagin maximum principle and maximizing the Hamiltonian function, H, where

$$H \equiv U[(1 - s(t))f(k)]\, e^{-\rho t} + \psi(s(t)f(k) - kn[f(k)]),$$

$$\dot{\psi} = -\frac{\partial H}{\partial k} = -e^{-\rho t}(1 - s)f'U' - \psi(sf' - n - kn'f').$$

Time, t, can be eliminated as an explicit variable by defining q such that $q \equiv e^{\rho t}\psi$. Hence,

$$\dot{q} = e^{\rho t}(\dot{\psi} + \rho\psi) \qquad \text{and} \qquad \dot{\psi} = e^{-\rho t}(\dot{q} - \rho q).$$

Hence,

$$\dot{q} = -(1 - s)f'U' - q(sf' - \rho - n - kn'f').$$

As long as optimality calls for an interior value of s, $0 < s < 1$ (and by the assumption on the utility function only the boundary value, $s = 0$, is possible), the equation $\partial H/\partial s = (-f)U'\, e^{-\rho t} + \psi f = 0$ will apply to yield

(5) $U' = e^{\rho t}\psi = q.$

The optimal time path of the three variables $q(t)$, $k(t)$, and $s(t)$ can thus be found by solving the three equations:

(5) $q = U',$

(6) $\dot{k} = sf - kn[f(k)],$

(7) $\dfrac{\dot{q}}{q} = \rho + n[f(k)] - f'[1 - kn'].$

In the stationary state, $\dot{q} = \dot{k} = 0$, the optimal s^* is equal to

(8) $s^* = \dfrac{k^*n}{f} = \dfrac{k^*}{f}\{f'[1 - k^*n'] - \rho\}.$

The steady state solution to case 1(i) can be found by setting $\rho = 0$ in equation (8), and hence is seen to be simply the modified golden rule of accumulation (equation (4)). (The steady state values of the variables will be denoted q^*, k^*, and s^*.)

Now local stability around this stationary position will be explored by linearizing the differential equations in q and k about the point (q^*, k^*). Equations (6) and

(7) can be approximated by:

(6') $\quad \dot{k} \cong -\dfrac{1}{U''}(q - q^*) + \rho(k - k^*),$

(7') $\quad \dot{q} \cong q^*[2n'f' - f''(1 - k^*n') + k^*f'^2n''](k - k^*).$

The characteristic roots of this system, denoted by λ, can be seen to be

(9) $\quad \lambda = \dfrac{1}{2}\left\{ \rho \pm \sqrt{\rho^2 - 4\dfrac{U'}{U''}[2n'f' - f''(1 - k^*n') + k^*f'^2n'']} \right\}.$

It has been shown in Davis [6] that a sufficient condition for maximum consumption corresponding to the modified golden rule requires the square bracket to be positive. Hence, the two characteristic roots will be real and opposite in sign, i.e., a saddle point solution, and this requirement ensures that there is *no* possibility of complex roots. A saddle point solution simply means that if the economy started from an arbitrary initial position in the (k, q) plane, it would diverge and never achieve the steady state equilibrium unless it started on the "line" that allows an approach to the stationary point. But, in theory this should cause no concern for at a point in time only k is beyond the direct control of the central planners. But s, or equivalently (by equation (13)) q, must be instantaneously "adjusted," given k, by the planning authorities so that the economy "starts" on precisely that path along which it can move to the stationary state. In practice, and in the absence of complete knowledge, this is likely to be an impossible task, but from a simulation one could get some approximation of this "line."

It is seen that Case 1 is essentially the same as the case where labor growth is determined exogenously. An optimal path exists, and it is a saddle point solution. We now proceed to a more interesting and "different" case—Case 2.

Case 2

Suppose now that society is weighted by numbers so that its welfare responds to *total population* as well as per capita consumption.

The problem is to maximize $\int_0^\infty L(t)U[(1 - s)f(k)]\,e^{-\rho t}\,dt$ by choice of $s(t)$, subject to $\dot{L} = L(t)n[f(k)]$ and $\dot{K} = sLf(k)$. This turns out to be a very complicated situation because population grows endogenously, and hence at a nonconstant rate, so that $L(t)$ and $e^{-\rho t}$ cannot be combined as a function only of time. In other words, it is not easy to reduce the problem to one involving only one state variable, the capital-labor ratio. Instead it can be better considered by carrying the calculations through with two separate state variables $L(t)$ and $K(t)$. If one attempts to formulate the objective function in terms of the capital-labor ratio only, one gets

$$\int_0^\infty L(0)\,e^{\int_0^t n[f(k(\tau))]\,d\tau}U[(1 - s)f(k(t))]\,e^{-\rho t}\,dt,$$

which is difficult to handle. If, on the other hand, the problem is treated as one involving two state variables, the computations are simplified. The Hamiltonian function, H, can be defined as:

$$H = LU[(1 - s)f(K/L)] e^{-\rho t} + \psi_1 sLf(K/L) + \psi_2 Ln[f(K/L)],$$

$$\dot{\psi}_1 = -\frac{\partial H}{\partial K} = -e^{-\rho t}(1 - s)f'U' - \psi_1 sf' - \psi_2 n'f',$$

$$\dot{\psi}_2 = -\frac{\partial H}{\partial L} = -e^{-\rho t}U + k e^{-\rho t}(1 - s)f'U' - \psi_1 sf + \psi_1 skf'$$

$$- \psi_2 n + \psi_2 kn'f'.$$

Although the differential equations for the shadow prices, ψ_1 and ψ_2, can be written so as to involve only the capital-labor ratio, the essentially two-state-variable nature of the problem is preserved since there is no way, generally, of combining the shadow prices of capital and labor, ψ_1 and ψ_2 respectively, into a single one for the capital-labor ratio.

Time, t, can be eliminated as an explicit variable by transforming variables with the definitions of $q_1 \equiv \psi_1 e^{\rho t}$ and $q_2 \equiv \psi_2 e^{\rho t}$. If an interior solution is optimal for the control variable, s, $0 < s < 1$, we have

$$\frac{\partial H}{\partial s} = -LfU'e^{-\rho t} + \psi_1 Lf = 0.$$

Thus,

$$U' = \psi_1 e^{\rho t} = q_1.$$

Starting from an initial $k(0)$ and an $s(0)$, or equivalently $q(0)$, so that the economy is on the path to the steady-state position, the optimal time path of the variables is described by the four equations:

(10) $\dot{q}_1 = q_1(\rho - f') - n'f'q_2,$

(11) $\dot{q}_2 = q_1(kf' - sf) + q_2(kn'f' + \rho - n) - U,$

(12) $\dot{k} = sf - kn,$

(13) $q_1 = U'.$

The steady state variables, $q_1^*, q_2^*, k^*,$ and s^*, are found by solving[4]

(14) $s^*f = k^*n,$

(15) $q_1^* = U',$

---

[4] In the case where population grows exogenously ($n' = 0$), equations (14)–(17) simplify and become $s^*f = k^*n$, $q_1^* = U'$, $q_1^*(\rho - f') = 0$, $q_2^*(\rho - n) + q_1^*(k^*f' - s^*f) = U$. The essentially single shadow price nature of this case is seen by noting that the system decomposes into three equations which determine s^*, q_1^*, and k^*, while given these values, the last equation fixes q_2^*. q_2 has no independent role to play!

(16) $q_1^*(\rho - f') = q_2^* n' f'$,

(17) $q_2^*(\rho - n + n' f' k^*) + q_1^*(k^* f' - s^* f) = U$.

There is a *fundamental* difference between the case in which labor grows endogenously and the case in which it grows exogenously. Equations (14)–(17) can be combined to yield one equation in k^* and the parameter ρ only:

(18) $\dfrac{U}{U'} n' = \dfrac{(\rho - n)}{f'}[\rho - f'(1 - k^* n')]$,

where the argument of U and U' is $(f - kn)$. When labor grows exogenously $(n' = 0)$, (18) becomes

(18′) $f'(k^*) = \rho$.

In this case, it is clear that the steady state capital-labor ratio is determined entirely by the society's discount rate—the form of the utility function has no effect at all. But in the endogenous labor case, the utility function itself does play a role. *The wishes of society, as expressed in the utility function it chooses (specifically in the elasticity of its utility function), have meaning in that they affect "real" economic variables (i.e., k^*), both in the steady state value and in the dynamics on the way to equilibrium.*[5]

Since the integral, which is being maximized over infinite time, must converge, it is impossible for ρ to be exceeded by $n[f(k^*)]$. The two remaining cases will be considered, i.e., $\rho > n[f(k^*)]$ and $\rho = n[f(k^*)]$. Assuming first that $\rho > n[f(k^*)]$, it is possible to get an ordering of the steady state values:[6]

(19) $f'(k^*)[1 - k^* n'] > \rho > n$.

This ordering can be used to study the stability about the steady state point s^*, k^*, q_1^*, and q_2^* where $\dot{q}_1 = \dot{q}_2 = \dot{k} = 0$. Now $\dot{q}_1, \dot{q}_2$, and $\dot{k}$ can be approximated in the region about the steady state point to obtain

(10′) $\dot{q}_1 \cong a_{11}(q_1 - q_1^*) + a_{12}(q_2 - q_2^*) + a_{13}(k - k^*)$,

(11′) $\dot{q}_2 \cong a_{21}(q_1 - q_1^*) + a_{22}(q_2 - q_2^*) + a_{23}(k - k^*)$,

(12′) $\dot{k} \cong a_{31}(q_1 - q_1^*) + a_{32}(q_2 - q_2^*) + a_{33}(k - k^*)$,

---

[5] We owe this observation to Professor T. Koopmans. But there are other cases where the utility function "matters" even without endogenous population growth. Suppose that the economy exhibits Harrod-neutral technical change at a constant logarithmic rate, together with exogenous labor growth. Then the form of the utility function, this time expressed by its degree of homogeneity, has a crucial role to play in determining "real" variables and hence in determining the optimal steady state savings ratio. This can also be found in Arrow's paper [3].

[6] The maximum supportable level of utility corresponds to the modified golden rule path (there is no discounting of future utility so that $\rho = n$) which must be defined to be zero from (18), implying that any other feasible level of utility is a negative number. Thus from (18) for $n' > 0$ we have $f'(1 - k^* n) > \rho$.

where a_{ij} are all partial derivatives of $\dot{q}_1$, $\dot{q}_2$, and $\dot{k}$, evaluated at the equilibrium point. The characteristic roots, λ, of this linearized system $A = \{a_{ij}\}$ are found by solving the determinantal equation

$$0 = \begin{vmatrix} \rho - f' - \lambda & -n'f' & -f''q_1^* - q_2^*(n'f'' + f'^2n'') \\ k^*(f' - n) & \rho - n + k^*n'f' - \lambda & k^*f''q_1^* + k^*q_2^*(n'f'' + f'^2n'') \\ -\dfrac{1}{U''} & 0 & f'(1 - k^*n') - n - \lambda \end{vmatrix}.$$

This is not quite as complicated a task as it appears for it does not really require solving a cubic equation. Instead one root can be found by inspection since, when $\lambda = \rho - n$, the first two rows differ only by the multiplicative constant k^*. Thus $\lambda = \rho - n$ is a root, and the variables can be transformed accordingly to reduce the cubic equation to the following quadratic:

$$(20) \qquad \lambda^2 + (n - \rho)\lambda + \frac{a}{U''} - [n - f'(1 - k^*n')][\rho - f'(1 - k^*n')] = 0,$$

where $a \equiv -f''q_1^* - q_2^*(n'f'' + f'^2n'') \equiv -f''q_1^*(\rho/f') - q_2^*f'^2n''$ from (16). Thus, the remaining two characteristic roots are

$$(21) \qquad \lambda = \frac{(\rho - n)}{2} \pm \frac{1}{2}\sqrt{\begin{aligned}&(\rho - n)^2 + \frac{4f''q_1^*}{U''}\cdot\frac{\rho}{f'} + 4[n - f'(1 - k^*n')] \\ &\qquad\qquad \times [\rho - f'(1 - k^*n')] + \frac{4q_2^*f'^2n''}{U''}\end{aligned}}.$$

Recalling that $f'' < 0$, $U'' < 0$, $q_1^* = U' > 0$, and the ordering (19), it is simple to see that the first three terms under the square root sign are all positive. The sign of q_2^* depends on the sign of n', i.e., $q_2^* \gtrless 0$ according to $n' \lessgtr 0$ (equation (16)). Thus when $n' > 0$, the sign of the fourth term has the same sign as n''. Even if n'' is negative and large, it is impossible to have the last term dominate the expression under the square root sign so that the roots would be complex (Davis [6]). Hence, the two roots of (21) both will be real but opposite in sign. (It can be seen also that even when $n' < 0$, together with $n'' > 0$ and large, the system will have real roots.) The entire system then has three roots, all real, with two positive and one negative. In this three dimensional system (q_1, q_2, and k), this is the counterpart to the two dimensional saddle point. It simply indicates that the economy requires a central planning board with the authority to set shadow prices, given initial conditions, so as to successfully direct the time path of the economy towards the stationary state.

The cross-section in the $q_1 - k$ plane is shown in Figure 3, while the other two cross-sections (of the linearized solution) are relegated to the Appendix.

Suppose now that, as a summary, the case of exogenous population growth is contrasted with the endogenous case when there is weighting by total population, the social discount rates are the same, and the exogenously given n equals $n[f(k^*)]$.

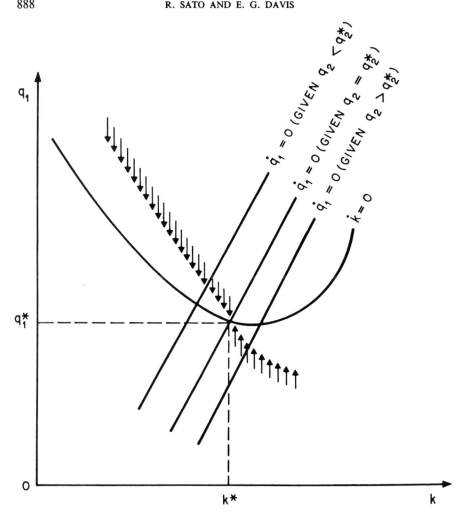

FIGURE 3.—A cross-section of the optimal growth path.

In the exogenous case, the steady state capital-labor ratio, k^*, can be found from $f' = \rho$, while in the endogenous case, it can be found from $f' > \rho$ and thus, in this latter case, equilibrium occurs with a lower capital-labor ratio. In equilibrium the argument of the utility function is $(f - k^*n)$. Clearly, the higher the capital-labor ratio, the higher this argument gets and thus the lower the marginal utility of consumption.

As in the exogenous case when $\rho = n[f(k^*)]$, the steady state value of the variables coincides with the golden (in this case, modified) rule of accumulation derived in (4).

However, the most interesting change is undoubtedly the new importance of the index of utility when population grows endogenously. Now society will be faced with two factors, both of which have a "real" effect: the utility function and the rate at which future utility is discounted. More attention will be paid to the first of these factors in the following section.

4. THE EFFECT OF PARAMETRIC CHANGES IN THE UTILITY FUNCTION

Assume the social utility function

$$U = [(1 - s)f]^{1/a}, \quad \text{where} \quad 0 < \frac{1}{a} < 1.$$

The equilibrium value, k^*, can be found by solving equation (18):

(18') $an'f'(f - k^*n) = (\rho - n)[\rho - f'(1 - k^*n')]$.

Now equation (18') can be totally differentiated by a:

(22) $$\frac{dk^*}{da} = \frac{n'f'(f - k^*n)}{(d/dk^*)[(\rho - n)(\rho - f'(1 - k^*n')) - an'f'(f - k^*n)]}.$$

The numerator of the right-hand side of (22) is obviously positive so it is only necessary to evaluate the sign of the denominator (which will be denoted by D):

$$D = (\rho - n)[-f''(1 - k^*n') + k^*(f')^2n''] + n'f'[f'(1 - k^*n') - n]$$
$$\times [1 + a] + a(f - k^*n)(-n'f'' + (f')^2n'').$$

On the basis of ordering (19) and on the assumption that n'' is never so large as to overturn the sign of the expressions in which it appears, it can be seen that D is positive. Hence,

$$\frac{dk^*}{da} > 0.$$

In other words, as far as parametric changes in the social welfare function are concerned, there is a strong suggestion that *a sudden decision to evaluate any level of per capita consumption as representing a higher level of utility than previously results in a lower steady state labor-capital ratio.*

5. A RULE FOR DIRECT POPULATION CONTROL[7]

By this point it is clear that if the raison d'être of a society is consumption, and in particular per capita consumption, the planning authorities must take into account the induced increase in the population growth rate due to the higher standard of living, and thus the offset to per capita consumption, when settling on optimal investment policy. But realistically, planners have taken much more direct action in combatting population increases. Clearly one of the options available to the planners is to influence directly the population growth function by various public health and education expenditures.

[7] In private comments on the previous draft of Section 3, Professor Jürg Niehans of Johns Hopkins University suggested this introduction of a second control variable, a parameter of the n-function.

Suppose now the population n-function has an additional argument reflecting these government measures:

(23) $\dot{L} = L(t)n[Y/L, e]$,

where e is the fraction of national output that is directed into public health and education expenditures to reduce the population growth rate. It is assumed that $n_1 = (\partial n/\partial(Y/L)) > 0$ but $n_2 = (\partial n/\partial e) < 0$. The rest of the model is the same as before except these new expenditures represent a further subtraction from per capita consumption,

$$C/L = (1 - s - e)Y/L = (1 - s - e)f(k).$$

Suppose that the golden rule problem is again considered. Equivalently, choose s and e as constants so as to maximize C/L subject to $\dot{k} = 0$. The calculations show that the solution becomes

(24) $n_2 = -Y/K$,

(25) $s = \dfrac{kf'}{f}(1 - e - kn_1)$.

Now the "modified"-modified golden rule of accumulation states that *the economy should save an amount less than capital's share, while at the same time engaging in direct population reduction measures until the responsiveness of the population growth rate to further increases in public expenditures is equal to the output-capital ratio.* From the latter condition it can be seen that *the total output must always be equal to the total amount of capital multiplied by the responsiveness of the population growth rate to further increases in public expenditures.* This implies that *in the steady state the equilibrium growth rate of population n^* must be equal to the savings ratio multiplied by the direct effect of population control,* i.e., $n_2 = -Y/K = -n^*/s$.

This rule giving the optimal amount of population control expenditures applies at each point of time, when there is no weighting by numbers. The solution to the problem of maximizing $\int_0^\infty U(C/L)e^{-\rho t}\,dt$ by choice of $e(t)$ and $s(t)$ can be seen to be the four equations:

$$q = U', \qquad n_2 = -\frac{f}{k}, \qquad \dot{k} = sf - kn,$$

$$\frac{\dot{q}}{q} = (\rho + n) - f'(1 - kn_1 - e).$$

Clearly, the steady state position when there is no discounting once again is the modified-modified golden rule.

Some idea of the dynamic behavior of this model was obtained by simulating a model whose equations had the following form:

$$U = [(1 - s - e)f(k)]^\alpha \qquad \text{with} \qquad 0 < \alpha < 1,$$

$$y = k^\beta \qquad \text{with} \qquad 0 < \beta < \tfrac{1}{2},$$

$$n = A(1 - k^{-\beta}) - Be^2 \qquad \text{with} \qquad A, B > 0.$$

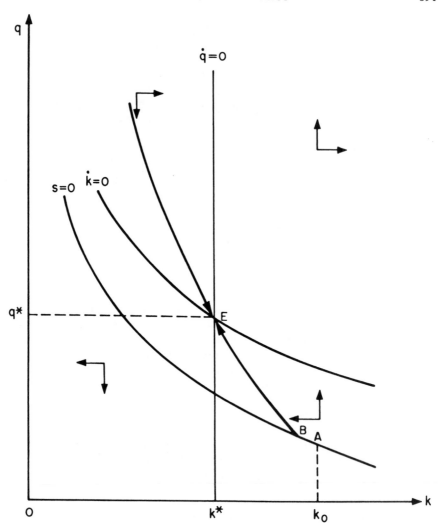

FIGURE 4.—Dynamic behavior of a model with two control variables.

The first two equations are simply the familiar iso-elastic social welfare function and the Cobb-Douglas production function respectively. The justification for the equation for the growth rate of population has no particular basis in demographic terms. It is the simplest form consistent with population growth increasing with respect to per capita income but approaching an upper biological maximum growth rate A. The n-function was made separable in k and e as a computational simplification so that the optimal level of e is determined entirely by k and is independent of s. However, it ought to be noticed that it is not unrealistic to have $(\partial^2 n/\partial e^2) < 0$, for presumably there is a learning process involved in population reduction. Initial expenditures may be more significant in their attack on existing social attitudes, rather than in directly reducing population growth—they prepare the way for further expenditures.

The dynamic behavior is illustrated in Figure 4. Suppose that the initial position of the economy is given by k_0. Then, the optimal choice of q must be Ak_0 with the savings ratio equal to zero. The state variable k will continue to decline while q increases along the path AB. As soon as it reaches the position B, the savings ratio will start rising until all the variables reach their equilibrium values at E.

Until this point in the paper, the words "population" and "labor force," for all practical purposes, have been used interchangeably. However, this is clearly a distortion of reality. To be employed is to be the provider of skilled services. To be skilled requires training. Presumably, the more resources devoted to the inculcation of skills, the more members of the population are potentially employable. Thus, if issues such as frictional unemployment or trade-offs between unemployment and inflation are ignored, the employment (participation) rate depends on the skill level of the population. *The optimal level of training for a population is another variable under the controls of the planning authorities.* In a sense this concept of training costs turns the model into a two-sector economy. Raw population is provided, which in one sector is tranformed into skilled workers, which is used as an input to the other sector where the only "good" in the economy is produced.[8]

Define P as total population, L as the total labor force, $\lambda \equiv L/P$ as the employment (participation) rate, and E as the total training expenses (investment in human capital). Assume further that

$$(26) \qquad \frac{\dot{P}}{P} = n(Y/P).$$

Resources are required both to build up supplies of capital and to make raw population productive. Thus,

$$(27) \qquad \frac{C}{P} = (1 - s)\frac{Y}{P} - \frac{E}{P}.$$

The remaining relationship to be specified is the "production function" for investment in human capital. Assume a simple relationship between λ and E such as

$$(28) \qquad \frac{E}{Y} = R(\lambda),$$

where $R(\lambda)$ satisfies $R'(\lambda) > 0, 1 \geqslant R(\lambda) \geqslant 0, R(0) = 0$, and $R(1) = 1$. The behavior of the capital-population ratio $(k = K/P)$ will be described as before by

$$(29) \qquad \dot{k} = s\lambda f(k/\lambda) - kn[\lambda f(k/\lambda)],$$

where $\lambda f(k/\lambda) = Y/P = F[K, L]/P$.

---

[8] For Dobell and Ho [**8** and **9**], population is provided exogenously, but in the present analysis, in keeping with the general theme, it will be determined by economic variables.

First, the golden rule problem will be considered. Choose s and λ as constant so as to maximize C/P subject to $\dot{k} = 0$. The calculations (see Appendix, Section 2) show that the solution can be arranged to yield

(30) $$s = \frac{kf'}{\lambda f}[1 - R(\lambda) - kn']$$

and

(31) $$\frac{\partial E}{\partial L} = \frac{\partial Y}{\partial L}(1 - kn') = w(1 - kn'),$$

where w is the wage rate of employed workers, equal to marginal productivity. Equations (30) and (31) define the new golden rule. Once again, *the optimal savings ratio is less than the share of capital, while the marginal productivity of capital exceeds the growth rate of the economy. The cost of training an additional worker must be kept equal to the (adjusted) output of one more worker (the adjusted wage rate).*[9] The adjustment can be rationalized by noting that, at a point in time (i.e., given K and P), the marginal product is related to the number of workers, and thus to the total output and hence to the *per capita* output. The lower the marginal product of labor, the higher the per capita output, and as a result the higher the growth rate of population. An increase in population growth rate, induced by an increase in the standard of living, has a retarding effect on per capita consumption through the change in numbers. Because of this effect, optimal behavior requires, not an equalization of cost and output on the margin, but rather a marginal product for workers that is above the marginal training costs.

6. CONCLUDING REMARKS

In this paper we have shown how sensitive the various optimizing rules are to the specification of the model and the objective function. Allowing for endogenous population growth alters the golden rule prescription; weighting the welfare function by total population brings the form of the utility function from insignificance to prominence; the presence of further control variables (and the *way* in which they are introduced into the model) change the optimal rules even more; and so on. We make no claim of expertise in demographic matters and hence certainly do not feel that our models are adequate descriptions of reality, but rather we claim only that we have made an attempt to introduce an economic basis for population growth and have deduced some of the conclusions. Hopefully some demographer with a particular country in mind might be able to fit the relevant equations to his data and carry through the calculations for his specified model,

---

[9] In the case where optimization proceeds from arbitrary initial conditions, this relationship would again show up as one that must be satisfied at each point in time in order that the economy be truly on the correct path. Since neither q nor s are involved in equation (38), it is clear that society's optimal employment ratio is determined entirely by the levels of the capital stock and population with which it finds itself at a point of time.

R. SATO AND E. G. DAVIS

possibly coming up with the loss through non-optimal savings and public expenditures policy.

Brown University
and
Bell Telephone Laboratories

Manuscript received October 1969; revision received March, 1970.

APPENDIX

1. CROSS-SECTIONS IN THE $q_2 - k$ AND $q_1 - q_2$ PLANES IN SECTION 3

From the linearized system of (10′), (11′), and (12′), for given q_1, the $q_2 - k$ plane can be depicted as shown in Figure 5.

(i) $q_2 - k$ plane (given q_1):

$$\frac{\partial q_2}{\partial k}\bigg|_{\dot{q}_2 = 0} = \frac{ak^*}{\rho - n + k^* n' f'} > 0, \qquad a = -f'' q_1^* \left(\frac{\rho}{f'}\right) - q_2^* f'^2 n'' > 0.$$

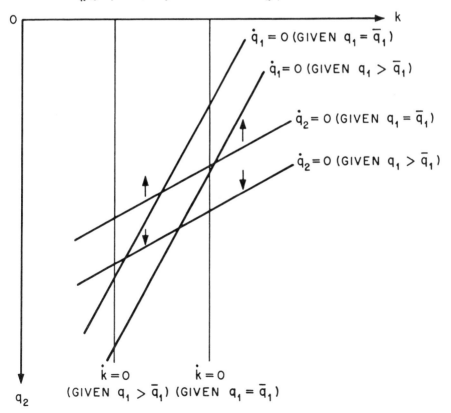

FIGURE 5.—A cross-section in the $q_2 - k$ plane.

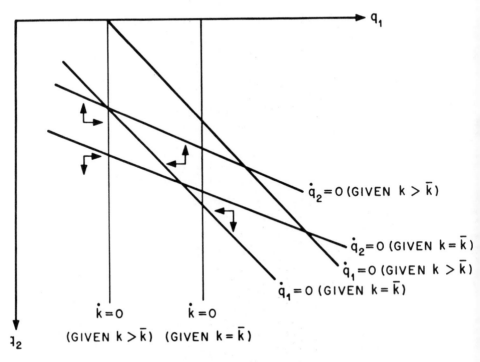

FIGURE 6.—A cross-section in the $q_1 - q_2$ plane.

Suppose that q_1 changes, given k:

$$\left.\frac{\partial q_2}{\partial q_1}\right|_{\dot q_2 = 0} = \frac{k^*(n - f')}{\rho - n + k^*n'f'} < 0, \qquad \left.\frac{\partial q_2}{\partial k}\right|_{\dot q_1 = 0} = \frac{a}{n'f'} > 0,$$

$$\left.\frac{\partial q_2}{\partial q_1}\right|_{\dot q_1 = 0} = \frac{\rho - f'}{n'f'} < 0,$$

$$\left.\frac{\partial q_2}{\partial k}\right|_{\dot q_1 = 0} - \left.\frac{\partial q_2}{\partial k}\right|_{\dot q_2 = 0} = \frac{a(\rho - n)}{(n'f')(\rho - n + k^*n'f')} > 0.$$

(ii) $q_1 - q_2$ plane (given k): In the same way the $q_1 - q_2$ plane for given k can be depicted as shown in Figure 6.

$$\left.\frac{\partial q_1}{\partial q_2}\right|_{\dot q_1 = 0} = \frac{n'f'}{\rho - f'} < 0, \qquad \left.\frac{\partial q_1}{\partial q_2}\right|_{\dot q_2 = 0} = \frac{\rho - n + k^*n'f'}{k^*(n - f')} < 0.$$

Suppose k changes:

$$\left.\frac{\partial q_1}{\partial k}\right|_{\dot q_1 = 0} = \frac{a}{f' - \rho} > 0, \qquad \left.\frac{\partial q_1}{\partial k}\right|_{\dot q_2 = 0} = \frac{a}{f' - n} > 0,$$

$$\left.\frac{\partial q_1}{\partial k}\right|_{\dot q_1 = 0} - \left.\frac{\partial q_1}{\partial k}\right|_{\dot q_2 = 0} = a\left(\frac{1}{f' - \rho} - \frac{1}{f' - n}\right) > 0,$$

$$\left.\frac{\partial q_1}{\partial q_2}\right|_{\dot q_2 = 0} - \left.\frac{\partial q_1}{\partial q_2}\right|_{\dot q_1 = 0} = \frac{(\rho - n)[\rho - f'(1 - k^*n')]}{(f' - \rho)(f' - n)k^*} < 0.$$

R. SATO AND E. G. DAVIS

2. GOLDEN RULE FOR ENDOGENOUS LABOR GROWTH WITH INVESTMENT IN HUMAN CAPITAL

$$\text{Max}_{s,\lambda} M = (1 - s - R(\lambda))\lambda f + \delta(s\lambda f - kn),$$

where δ is a Lagrangian multiplier:

$$\frac{\partial M}{\partial s} = -\lambda f + \lambda f \delta = 0 \Rightarrow \delta = 1;$$

$$\frac{\partial M}{\partial \delta} = s\lambda k - kn = 0 \Rightarrow s\lambda f = kn;$$

$$\frac{\partial M}{\partial k} = (1 - s - R(\lambda))\lambda\left(\frac{1}{\lambda}\right)f' + \delta\left(s\lambda\left(\frac{1}{\lambda}\right)f' - n - k\lambda\left(\frac{1}{\lambda}\right)f'n'\right) = 0$$

$$\Rightarrow (1 - R(\lambda) - kn')f' = n;$$

$$\frac{\partial M}{\partial \lambda} = -\lambda f R' + \left[f + \lambda k\left(\frac{-1}{\lambda^2}\right)f'\right][1 - s - R(\lambda)]$$

$$+ \delta\left\{sf + s\lambda k\left(\frac{-1}{\lambda^2}\right)f' - k\left[f + \lambda k\left(\frac{-1}{\lambda^2}\right)f'\right]n'\right\} = 0$$

$$\Rightarrow \left[f - \frac{k}{f}f'\right][1 - R(\lambda) - kn'] = \lambda f R'.$$

Thus, from $(\partial M/\partial k) = (\partial M/\partial \lambda) = 0$, we get $s = (kf'/\lambda f)[1 - R(\lambda) - kn']$. Also from $(\partial Y/\partial L) = [f - (kf'/\lambda)]$ and $(\partial(RY)/\partial L) = (\partial E/\partial L) = R(\partial Y/\partial L) + \lambda f R'$, $(\partial E/\partial L)$ can be written as (using $(\partial M/\partial \lambda) = 0$): $(\partial E/\partial L) = (\partial Y/\partial L)(1 - kn') = w(1 - kn')$, when $w = (\partial Y/\partial L)$.

REFERENCES

[1] ADELMAN, IRMA: *Theories of Economic Growth and Development.* Stanford University Press, 1961.
[2] ———: "An Econometric Analysis of Population Growth," *American Economic Review* (May, 1963).
[3] ARROW, K. J.: "Applications of Control Theory to Economic Growth," Technical Report No. 2, July 14, 1967, Institute for Mathematical Studies in the Social Sciences, Stanford University.
[4] BUTTRICK, J. A., "A Note on Growth Theory," *Economic Development and Cultural Change* (October, 1960).
[5] CASS, D.: "Optimal Growth in an Aggregative Model of Capital Accumulation," *Review of Economic Studies* (July, 1965).
[6] DAVIS, ERIC G.: "Optimal Savings Policy when Labor Grows Endogenously," unpublished Ph.D. dissertation, Brown University, June, 1968.
[7] ———: "A Modified Golden Rule: The Case with Endogenous Labor Supply," *American Economic Review* (March, 1969).
[8] DOBELL, A. R., AND Y. C. HO: "Optimal Investment Policy: A Control Problem in Economic Theory," Institute of Electrical and Electronic Engineers, Transactions on Automatic Control AC12 (February, 1967).
[9] ———: "An Optimal Unemployment Rate," *Quarterly Journal of Economics* (November, 1967).
[10] EASTERLIN, R. A.: "The American Baby Boom in Historical Perspective," *American Economic Review* (December, 1961).
[11] KOOPMANS, T. C.: "On the Concept of Optimal Economic Growth," *The Econometric Approach to Development Planning*, Pontificia Academia Scientarum, North-Holland Publishing Co., 1965.
[12] MALTHUS, R.: "An Essay on the Principle of Population" (Everyman's Library Edition), vol. 1. New York, 1914.
[13] MERTON, R. C.: "A Golden-Rule for Welfare-Maximization in an Economy with a Varying Population Growth Rate," unpublished manuscript, 1968.

[14] NIEHANS, J.: "Economic Growth with Two Endogenous Factors," *Quarterly Journal of Economics* (August, 1963).
[15] PHELPS, E. S.: "The Golden Rule of Accumulation: A Fable for Growthmen," *American Economic Review* (September, 1961).
[16] PONTRYAGIN, L. S., AND OTHERS: *The Mathematical Theory of Optimal Processes.* New York: Wiley, 1962.
[17] RAMSEY, F. P.: "A Mathematical Theory of Savings," *The Economic Journal* (December, 1928).
[18] SAMUELSON, P. A.: "A Catenary Turnpike Theorem," *American Economic Review* (June, 1965).
[19] SATO, R.: "A Note on Scarcity of Specific Resources as a Limit to Output: A Correction," *Review of Economic Studies* (October, 1967).
[20] ————: *The Theory of Economic Growth.* Tokyo (Keiso-shobo), 1968.
[21] SOLOW, R.: "A Contribution to the Theory of Economic Growth," *Quarterly Journal of Economics* (February, 1956).
[22] SHELL, KARL (EDITOR): *Essays on the Theory of Optimal Economic Growth.* M.I.T. Press, 1967.
[23] THOMPSON, W. S., AND D. T. LEWIS: *Population Problems,* 5th edition. McGraw-Hill, 1965.
[24] UNITED NATIONS (Department of Social Affairs—Population Division): "The Determinants and Consequences of Population Trends," *Population Studies,* No. 17, 1953.

[6]

POPULATION GROWTH AND THE DEVELOPMENT OF A DUAL ECONOMY

By RYUZO SATO *and* YOSHIO NIHO[1]

I. Introduction

THE role of population growth has been a major concern in the theories of developmental economics. In some theories, the growth of population is considered as a contributing factor, in the sense that it provides the human resources for a growing economy. In other theories, however, the growth of population plays a detrimental role for economic development, inasmuch as income growth is always accompanied by population growth; thus leaving the economy with stagnant *per capita* income.

In his path-breaking work, Jorgenson has shown that if population growth of a backward economy is positively related to a level of *per capita* income, more specifically if the growth rate of population is a linear function of *per capita* income, then that economy will necessarily gravitate to a low level equilibrium trap [4, 5]. It is also shown, however, that if the growth rate of population tapers off before the economy reaches this critical level (trap level), and if the population growth rate is no longer affected by changes in *per capita* income at the time when the industrial sector emerges, then the economy can escape the low-level equilibrium trap and develop to a modern industrial nation. In his model the Malthusian type of population growth function prevails only when the backward economy is primarily engaged in agricultural production.

In this paper we shall investigate the working of a different type of economy in which there exist both agricultural and industrial sectors, together with the situation in which the population growth rate is still affected by changes in *per capita* income. Such a model is not entirely unrealistic. In fact, most less developed countries already have acquired an industrial sector, while population control is still a major social and economic problem. It is not difficult to find a country which is still in a less developed stage in terms of the level of *per capita* income, but also has some highly developed industries. (India or Pakistan may be relevant examples.[2]) We shall also study the role of Engel's Law in the process of development, since the assumption of constant *per capita* food consumption seems

[1] This work was in part supported under the National Science Foundation (under Grant No. 2325) and a Ford Foundation Fellowship at the University of Cambridge, England. The authors wish to thank M. J. Beckmann, G. H. Borts, R. Diwan, R. F. Hoffman, T. Koizumi, and G. Suzawa for their useful comments on an earlier draft of this paper.

[2] Since the model is for a closed economy, for precise relevance to the experience of India or Pakistan it would have to be changed to an open economy model.

unrealistic when income is higher than the subsistence level. Thus, we are concerned with a dual economy in which the population growth rate is sensitive to changes in *per capita* income and in which food consumption is governed by Engel's Law.[1]

It will be shown that as long as the actual growth rate of population exceeds the technologically determined maximum rate, capital accumulation and technical progress in industry will have a negligible role in assisting the economy to escape the trap stagnation. A successful development programme must depend on a positive population policy under a sufficiently high rate of technical progress in agriculture.

II. A model of a dual economy

1. Agricultural production

The production process of the agricultural sector in a dual economy, under the assumption of fixity of land, is determined primarily by the amount of labour input and some form of technical progress,

$$Y_a = A(t)F_a(L_a, \overline{N})$$

where Y_a is the amount of agricultural production, L_a is the amount of labour input, $\overline{N}$ is the fixed amount of natural resources such as land, capital, etc., and $A(t)$ represents the technological improvement factor in agriculture. Since the technological factor $A(t)$ can explain any increase of Y_a except the increase due to a simple increase of L_a, this term may represent any increase of production due to irrigation, availability of better fertilizer, spread of technical know-how, such as selection of better seeds, etc., or the creation of any net external economies. The production function Y_a exhibits the usual positive marginal productivities with respect to all factor inputs, and is subject to the law of diminishing marginal rate of substitution. For simplicity we shall assume that agricultural capital is essentially fixed and can thus be included in $\overline{N}$. Although the conclusions by no means depend on a specific form of the production function, provided that the production elasticity of labour is less than unity for all values of labour input, we assume a Cobb–Douglas type production function and constant rate of technological improvement, for the sake of simplicity and computation. Thus,

$$Y_a = A_0 e^{\alpha t} L_a^{1-\beta} \tag{1}$$

where A_0 is a constant determined by the initial level of technique and by the amount of the fixed factor. Without loss of generality we can assume

---

[1] The role of Engel's Law in its relation to the determination of the industrial wage rate is studied by Guha [3] in a different context. His problem is to study whether or not the assumptions of unlimited supply of labour to industry at a constant wage rate (as often assumed in such a work as Fei and Ranis [1]) is theoretically consistent with the existence of Engel's Law.

that the units are chosen such that A_0 is equal to unity. The constant term α is a positive number representing the annual rate of technical progress, and $1-\beta$, positive but less than unity, is the production elasticity with respect to labour input.[1] Consequently, the marginal productivity of labour is positive but diminishing.

2. Industrial production

Production in the industrial sector is represented by the function

$$Y_m = B(t)F_m(K, L_m)$$

where Y_m is the amount of industrial output, K is the amount of capital stock, L_m is the amount of labour employed in industry, and $B(t)$ stands for the technological improvement factor in the industrial sector. We also assume that the marginal productivities of capital and labour are positive and the isoquants are convex. Unlike the agricultural production function, the industrial production function Y_m is a positively homogeneous function of the first degree, i.e. a constant returns to scale production function. This assumption is convenient, since even in a dual economy it is conventionally assumed that perfect competition prevails in the industrial sector. The role of land in manufacturing is assumed to be negligible, and hence, for the sake of simplicity, $\bar{N}$ is not included. Again we employ a special form, i.e. a Cobb–Douglas function. Thus,

$$Y_m = B_0 e^{\lambda t} K^\gamma L_m^{1-\gamma} \tag{2}$$

where $B_0 = $ the initial value of the technological progress factor in industry, conveniently assumed to be also equal to unity, $\lambda = $ the annual rate of technological progress, $\gamma = $ the production elasticity with respect to capital (or the share of capital income), $0 < \gamma < 1$. It will be shown in the next section (Section III) that this function is relevant only after industrial production has been initiated and the economy develops beyond the subsistence level.

3. Wage determination

In regard to the determination of the wage rate in the agricultural sector we employ the traditional assumption that the agricultural real wage rate is determined by institutional forces and is equal to the average productivity of labour employed in agriculture. However, there seems to be no general consensus in the existing literature whether this institutionally determined real wage rate remains fixed or is allowed to vary during the process of development. For example, in their analysis of the labour-surplus economy,

[1] The reader should refer to the works by R. Sato [7 and 8, chap. 6] for specific conditions under which the production elasticities of factor inputs are bounded between zero and one for all values of factor inputs.

Fei and Ranis [1, 2] assume that there exists an institutionally determined real wage rate equal to the initial average productivity of labour, and that this wage rate is held constant as long as there exists surplus labour in agriculture, surplus in the sense that its marginal productivity is less than the real wages. On the other hand, Jorgenson [4, 5] maintains that it is variable, depending upon the changes in the average productivity of the agricultural labour force. Guha [3, equation (8)] has questioned the plausibility of the assumption of a constant wage rate in the Fei–Ranis model and has shown that the wage rate cannot be constant unless the marginal propensity to consume food is zero, i.e. non-existence of Engel's Law.

The constancy of agricultural real wage rate is more compatible with the situation in which the supply of labour is exogenous and food consumption is constant regardless of income change. Since in this model we assume that labour supply is endogenous and that food consumption is positively related to income (Engel's Law), it seems more reasonable to assume that the agricultural wage rate varies. Hence, if w_a is the agricultural wage measured in terms of industrial goods and p is the terms of trade (price of agricultural goods in terms of industrial goods) we have:

$$\frac{w_a}{p} = \frac{Y_a}{L_a}. \tag{3}$$

This equation shows that the total output of agriculture is paid to agricultural workers as wages, and thus there is no rent left for landlords. One interpretation of this equation may be that all the land is owned by cultivators, and hence rent is included in the wages. Another interpretation may be that there is no explicit price of land, since it is owned by the state and the state does not charge any rent.

The industrial real wage rate is determined, under the assumption of competitive market conditions, by the marginal productivity of labour in the production of industrial commodities. Consequently, for the industrial real wages, denoted by w_m, we have:

$$w_m = \frac{\partial Y_m}{\partial L_m}$$

where $\partial Y_m/\partial L_m =$ the marginal productivity of labour employed in industry. For the special case of the Cobb–Douglas production function, we have:

$$w_m = (1-\gamma)\frac{Y_m}{L_m}. \tag{4}$$

Obviously equation (4) is relevant only when the economy is sufficiently developed to have an industrial sector (Stage II).

422 POPULATION GROWTH AND DEVELOPMENT OF DUAL ECONOMY

If we neglect the margin above agricultural wages that is usually assumed to be necessary to induce labour movement to cities, the equality of two money wages requires[1]

$$w_m = w_a. \tag{5}$$

4. Labour supply, the subsistence level of income, and stages of development

We assume that the total supply of labour, i.e. the labour force L, is always a constant fraction of the total population P.[2] Following the Malthusian theory of population it is assumed that the growth rate of population depends upon a level of *per capita* income. Thus, we have:

$$\frac{\dot{P}}{P} = \frac{\dot{L}}{L} = \phi(z), \quad \phi' \geqslant 0, \quad \phi'' \gtrless 0, \tag{6}$$

where $z =$ *per capita* income (in terms of agricultural commodities[3]) defined by

$$z = \frac{Y_a + Y_m/p}{L}.[4] \tag{7}$$

It seems reasonable, for the relevant phase of economic development, to assume that an increase in *per capita* income will have a positive effect (or no effect) on the percentage rate of increase in the total population. It should be noted that the above population growth function is assumed to hold not only when the society is at the primitive stage, but also at the stages where industry emerges and expands.

---

[1] Without changing the conclusions of the analysis we can assume that the money wage rate in one sector, say the industrial sector, is higher than the other sector so that

$$w_a = \mu w_m \ (0 < \mu \leqslant 1).$$

Equation (5) corresponds to the case where $\mu = 1$.

[2] A more realistic model should consider the case of variable participation ratio, such that $L = \theta P$, where θ is a variable. In the actual situation, θ is likely to be a function of $\dot{P}$. The more rapid the rate of growth of population the larger the proportion of young dependants. Offsetting this, however, is the change in proportion of the elderly. But for a particular country at a particular time the relationship is likely to be one way. However, our basic conclusions still hold true as long as $\lim_{t \to \infty} \theta = \theta, 0 < \theta \leqslant 1$.

[3] Measuring population-determining income by current income in terms of agricultural goods may be justified as follows: since we may probably assume that the proportion of non-workers in the total population is negligible, the source of population change may be identified as workers. For the relevant phase of economic development, the standard of living of workers, with which net growth of population is assumed to be associated in Malthusian and demographic population theories, may be represented by the amount of food consumption.

[4] Formally, z represents gross national product per worker measured in terms of agricultural commodities. However, under our assumption that the total labour force is always a constant fraction of the total population, the behaviour of income per head and the behaviour of income per worker become identical. Also, to be more exact, population-determining income may have to be defined in terms of net income. However, defining income in gross terms does not change the behaviour of this model. For these reasons, we employ the definition of z in (7) for the sake of convenience.

We now need a definition of stages. Although the definition is arbitrary, it is convenient to define the stages with respect to the level of *per capita* income, since we assume that the population growth function is a function of *per capita* income only. We first define the 'subsistence level of income' as such a level of income that the percentage growth rate of population becomes zero. Income is just adequate to maintain the present level of the total population. If we denote the subsistence level of income by $\bar{z}$, then we have:

$$\frac{\dot{P}}{P} = \frac{\dot{L}}{L} = \phi(\bar{z}) = 0.$$

Stage I

Stage I is defined as the stage where *per capita* income is below the subsistence level and where the total population is shrinking so that $\dot{P}/P$ is negative.

Stage II

On the other hand, Stage II is defined as the stage where *per capita* income is above the subsistence level and the total population is expanding. Thus, the percentage growth rate of population is positive, $\dot{P}/P > 0$.

The total labour force in a dual economy is divided into the agricultural and industrial labour forces, so that

$$L = L_a + L_m. \tag{8}$$

When the economy is in the first stage, it is inconceivable that the economy will have an industrial sector. Such an economy will most likely be engaged only in the production of basic necessities such as food for self-consumption. The total labour force will be devoted to the production of the agricultural commodities. Thus, $L = L_a$. The industrial sector is assumed to emerge when the economy moves to the second stage (Stage II) where *per capita* income is greater than the subsistence level.

5. Engel's Law and food consumption

Our next behavioural assumption has to do with the society's *per capita* food consumption. In Stage I where there is no industrial production the entire income is spent on consumption of food. Thus, if we let v denote *per capita* food consumption[1]

$$v = \frac{Y_a}{L} \tag{9}$$

then we have $\qquad\qquad v = z \quad \text{for } z < \bar{z}.$ $\qquad\qquad\qquad$ (10)

In traditional theories of development, many economists have treated *per capita* food consumption as constant after the industrial sector emerges.

---

[1] More exactly, v represents food consumption per worker (see p. 422 n. 4).

424 POPULATION GROWTH AND DEVELOPMENT OF DUAL ECONOMY

Our view is that, in fact, *per capita* food consumption increases and that the nature of the increase depends upon the stage of development. Of course, a smaller portion of income will be spent on the food consumption as income rises, since food is considered to be a basic necessity. Hence, for Stage II, we employ a standard assumption regarding the relationship between *per capita* food consumption and *per capita* income, Engel's Law. That is to say, *per capita* food consumption v is positively related to the level of *per*

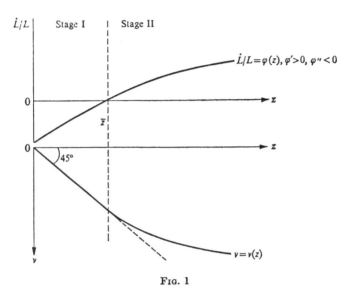

Fig. 1

capita income z, but the rate of increase in food consumption will diminish as z rises. Thus, we have:

$$v = v(z), \quad \text{for } z > \bar{z}$$

and
$$0 \leqslant v' \leqslant 1, \quad v'' \leqslant 0. \tag{11}$$

Since expenditure on food cannot exceed the amount of income, we need the condition $0 \leqslant v' \leqslant 1$, that the slope is less than the 45 degree line.

The relations among the growth rate of population, *per capita* income, and *per capita* food consumption in various stages are illustrated in Fig. 1.

6. Capital accumulation in the industrial sector

On the assumptions (implicit or explicit) of the preceding sections, namely (*a*) that the economy is closed; (*b*) that agricultural products cannot be used as industrial capital; (*c*) that some industrial capital exists; (*d*) that real income can be measured by current income in terms of food; and (*e*) that the elasticity of substitution in the industrial sector is unity, the introduction of Engel's Law enables us to specify the development of in-

come and population without reference to savings behaviour since the quantity of capital affects only the relative price of the two commodities. However, in a more general model (of an open economy or with a non-Cobb–Douglas industrial production function) savings would be important and we therefore specify a savings function to close the model. For the type of economy we are concerned with, the 'classical' savings function seems most appropriate. In this society wage earners do not save, while all profits are automatically saved. Thus, the amount of gross savings is equal to the amount of capital's income in the industrial sector after wages are paid to industrial workers, $Y_m - w_m L_m$. If we let $\dot{K}$ stand for the amount of net capital formation and ηK for the amount of total depreciation, which is assumed to vary according to the amount of the total capital stock K, we have:
$$\dot{K} + \eta K = Y_m - w_m L_m.$$
For the special production function (equation (2)) this relation reduces to:[1]
$$\dot{K} + \eta K = \gamma Y_m. \tag{12}$$

III. Workings of the model

The process of economic development in a dual economy, before it reaches the fully advanced stage of a modern society, may be conveniently described by the stages we defined earlier.

Stage I (stage of a primitive agrarian economy)

We begin with the analysis of a primitive economy where the society is endowed with the initial amount of the labour force, natural resources, and with a given state of technology. This stage is defined as the stage where *per capita* income (*per capita* food consumption) is below the subsistence level and the total population is less than the stationary level of population. The economy at this stage is so primitive that there hardly exists any form of industrial or manufacturing production. The whole labour force is devoted to food production.

Using our definitions and behavioural assumptions, this stage is described by the production function in agriculture (equation (1)), by the behavioural equation for food consumption which is also equal to real wages of workers (equations (3) and (10)), and by the population growth function (equation (6)):
$$Y_a = A_0 e^{\alpha t} L^{1-\beta} \quad (L = L_a), \tag{1}$$
$$\frac{w_a}{p} = \frac{Y_a}{L_a} = v = z, \quad p = 1, \tag{3 and 10}$$
$$\dot{L}/L = \phi(z). \tag{6}$$

[1] The model can be easily extended to the case where savings come from both capital's income and labour's income. In this case (12) becomes $\dot{K} + \eta K = s_\pi \gamma Y_m + s_w (1-\gamma) Y_m$, where s_π = savings ratio out of capital's income and s_w = savings ratio out of labour's income.

With appropriate substitutions and transformations (see Appendix 1) these equations, which describe the development of this primitive society into a more modern society (Stage II), will be reduced to an equation which explains the time path of *per capita* income z,

$$\dot{z}/z = \alpha - \beta\phi(z). \tag{13}$$

This equation tells us that as long as the rate of technical progress is positive *per capita* income z (also *per capita* food consumption v) is always increasing. This is because *per capita* income in this stage is so low that population is declining, while *per capita* agricultural production continues to rise due to

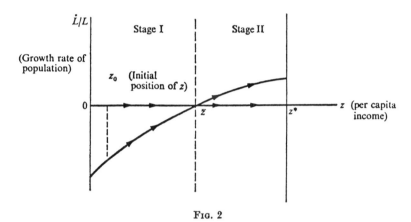

FIG. 2

the positive rate of technical progress. As this progress continues, *per capita* income will increase to the level $\bar{z}$ at which population will cease to shrink and food consumption is sufficient to maintain the present size of total population. However, the agrarian society will *not* stop its development at this level of the subsistence economy, but will continue to advance to a higher level of economic development since $\dot{z}/z = \alpha > 0$ at $z = \bar{z}$. As it passes this point, *per capita* income becomes large enough to induce a positive growth rate of population and a positive rate of surplus of food consumption (see Fig. 2). The society is no longer as primitive as when initial development took place. People are better fed and there is room for savings and accumulation. It is at this stage that their expectations of profit encourage entrepreneurs to create non-agrarian enterprises. The manufacturing sector is bound to emerge. We shall define this stage as the stage of a dual economy (Stage II).

Stage II (stage of dual economy)

The workings and the conclusions of the model do not depend crucially upon the exact position where the second state is defined as starting, as long as as it is after *per capita* income reaches the subsistence level (provided, of course, it occurs before the terminal value of *per capita* income z^* is reached). We shall set the emergence of the second stage at the point where *per capita* income exceeds the subsistence level.

What happens at this stage of economic development depends crucially upon the interactions of the three factors, i.e. the technological improvement factor in agriculture, the population growth function, and the *per capita* food consumption. Depending upon the relationship between the rate of technological progress in agriculture and the rate of population growth, the economy may fall into a trap of stagnation or may achieve a continual increase in *per capita* income. The demand conditions for agricultural output, i.e. the shape of the Engel curve, will be the key factor in determining whether or not in the long run the agricultural and industrial sectors will grow in a balanced fashion.

We now need all the definitions and the behavioural equations set forth in the previous section to analyse the developmental processes of this dual stage (equations (1)–(12)). With appropriate substitutions and transformations (see Appendix 2) this stage of economic development will be explained basically by the behaviour of *per capita* income z;

$$\frac{\dot{z}}{z} = \frac{\alpha - \beta\phi(z)}{\{v'(z)z/v(z)\} + (1-\beta)(1-\gamma s)[1 - \{v'(z)z/v(z)\}]} \tag{14}$$

where s is defined as the proportion of agricultural workers to the total labour force and is given by

$$s = \frac{v(z)}{v(z) + (1-\gamma)[z - v(z)]}, \quad 0 < s \leqslant 1. \tag{15}$$

(See the derivation of this relation in Appendix 2.)

Let us define the concepts of 'development', 'stagnation', and 'degeneration to the primitive agrarian economy' in the following manner:

   (i) We shall define 'development' as the situation in which *per capita* income never ceases to grow. Formally it is the situation in which $\dot{z}/z$ is positive for all levels of z.

  (ii) 'Stagnation' is the situation in which *per capita* income ceases to increase, i.e. $\dot{z}/z = 0$ at $z = z^*$.

 (iii) 'Degeneration to the primitive society' refers to the situation in which per capita income is always decreasing, $\dot{z}/z < 0$, and the dual system eventually returns to the primitive stage of economic development.[1]

---

[1] By development we simply imply that the economy is in such a condition that the standard of living is improving and hence *per capita* income is growing steadily. It will be shown in n. 1, p. 434 that this also implies, under certain conditions, that the proportion of agricultural workers to the total labour force approaches some positive constant.

428   POPULATION GROWTH AND DEVELOPMENT OF DUAL ECONOMY

Since the denominator of equation (14) is always positive, and since we assume that the population growth function (6) is continuous and non-decreasing, $\phi' \geqslant 0$, the sign of the percentage change in *per capita* income $\dot{z}/z$ depends on the numerator of (14), $\alpha - \beta\phi(z)$. *We shall define that level of growth rate of population which is equal to α/β as the 'maximum sustainable rate of population growth'*, i.e.

maximum sustainable rate of
population growth $\bar{\phi} = \phi(z^*) = \alpha/\beta.$ (16)

Thus, the 'maximum sustainable rate' is determined both by the rate of technological progress α and by the production condition (or the elasticity of land) β in agriculture. It refers to that rate of population growth which reduces the growth rate of *per capita* income to zero.

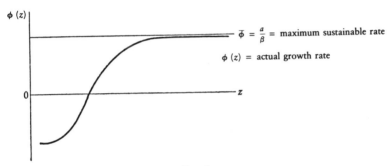

FIG. 3

We can now study the conditions of 'development', 'stagnation', and 'degeneration' of the dualistic economy in terms of the relationship between the 'actual' and 'maximum sustainable' growth rates of population.

Case I: Development: $\alpha/\beta > \phi(z)$

If the actual growth rate of population never exceeds the maximum sustainable rate α/β, then the economy will eventually develop to a modern society. *Per capita* income will increase steadily and the standard of living is constantly improving. This is because the rate at which the society is providing additional income is greater than the rate at which the additional population is claiming agricultural output, generating a surplus which constitutes an addition to *per capita* income. Technological progress in agriculture, under the given production conditions, is sufficiently high for the economy to provide the income necessary for the development of the industrial sector. So long as the actual growth rate $\phi(z)$ is lower than the maximum sustainable rate α/β, the population growth function need *not* be constant in order to achieve the stage of modernization. Consider the population growth function as depicted in Fig. 3. The actual population growth function is always increasing so that ϕ' is always positive. The population growth is affected by increases in *per capita* income, but the actual growth rate never exceeds the maximum sustainable rate. The dualistic economy under these conditions will successfully achieve the steady process of economic development.

Case II: Stagnation: $\alpha/\beta > \phi(z_0)$ *and* $\alpha/\beta \leqslant \phi(z_1)$ *for* $z_0 < z_1$

If the population growth function is such that the actual growth rate is higher than or equal to the maximum sustainable rate α/β for some level of *per capita* income z_1, then the economy will necessarily fall into the trap of stagnation. The reason is that the actual growth rate will become so high that the society's technological and production conditions cannot sustain that level of population growth. If population is expanding at a faster rate than income is growing, the level of *per capita* income decreases until the actual growth rate is reduced to the maximum rate that the society can sustain. Even if the actual growth rate is lower than the maximum sustainable rate at the initial position, increasing *per capita* income will eventually raise the actual growth rate to the level equal to the maximum sustainable rate. Thus, at any rate, the economy will end up in the trap of stagnation in which any additional income provided by the technical progress in agriculture will be eaten up by additional population, leaving no surplus for the increase in *per capita* income and for the development of the industrial sector. It is interesting to note that the economy will fall into the trap of stagnation even if the actual population growth tapers off as income rises.

In Figs. 4a and 4b, the population growth functions taper off at z_1, but *per capita* income will never grow beyond the value z^*. In these cases the actual growth rate will eventually reach the maximum sustainable rate. Hence, again this shows that the 'level' of population growth rate relative to the maximum sustainable rate given in the society will determine whether the society can achieve development or fall into a stagnation.

Case III: Degeneration: $\alpha/\beta < \phi(z)$

There may be a third case in which the economy will degenerate to the primitive agrarian economy. However, as long as we assume the continuity of the population growth function $\phi(z)$, this case may be impossible. Suppose we relax this assumption[1] and assume that we could have

---

[1] We can extend our analysis to include the case in which the function is not monotonic. Even in such a case, the same conditions for 'development', 'stagnation', and 'degeneration' can be applied. Consider the case in which the ϕ function is quadratic. (The following argument is essentially the same as S. C. Tsiang [9].) In case a, since $\alpha/\beta > \phi(z)$ for all the levels of z, the economy will achieve a steady process of development. In case c, since $\alpha/\beta < \phi(z)$ for $z = z_1$, there is at least one point for which $\alpha/\beta = \phi(z^*)$. In this case there are two such points z_1^* and z_2^*. z_1^* is the point of stagnation since the motions of z are toward this

dicontinuity in the ϕ function. If the ϕ function is of such a shape as depicted in Fig. 5, the economy will degenerate to the first stage, i.e. the primitive agrarian economy.

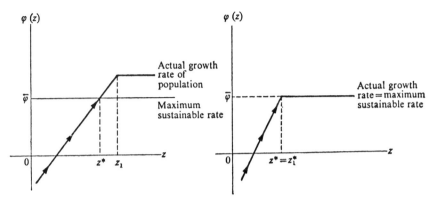

FIG. 4a

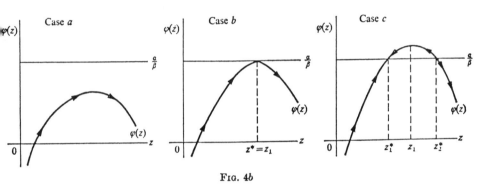

FIG. 4b

IV. Stagnation and development

Let us now investigate how the labour force engaged in agriculture will change during the developmental processes. Let s be the fraction of agricultural workers in the total labour force. As is shown in equation (15), the behaviour of s is solely dependent upon the behaviour of z. Since equation (15) implies

$$\frac{\dot{s}}{s} = -(1-\gamma s)\left[1 - \frac{v'(z)z}{v(z)}\right]\frac{\dot{z}}{z}, \tag{17}$$

the percentage change in the proportion of labour engaged in agriculture is inversely related to the percentage change in *per capita* income (for

point and terminate at this point, unless the initial value is beyond z_2^*. z_2^* is the take-off point since beyond this point z will increase steadily. In case b, $\alpha/\beta = \phi(z^*)$ at $z = z_1$. In this case, if the initial value of z is below this point z^* is the point of stagnation since the motion will terminate at this point, but if the initial position is beyond this point it is the take-off point.

$1-\gamma s > 0$, $1-\dfrac{v'(z)z}{v(z)} > 0$, see Appendix 2). Thus, as *per capita* income rises, the proportion of labour force engaged in agriculture starts to decline. If *per capita* income continues to grow, the labour force will be constantly shifting from agriculture to industry.

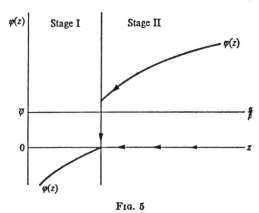

FIG. 5

Stagnation

If the economy falls into a trap of stagnation, labour migration to industry ceases. The growth of *per capita* income comes to an end at $z = z^*$ and the proportion of workers in agriculture to the total labour force becomes constant. That is to say, $\dot{z}/z$ in equation (14) and hence $\dot{s}/s$ in (17) will both become zero. These conclusions will still hold true regardless of the rates of technical progress and capital accumulation in the industrial sector, for high growth rates of these factors will have no effect on the values of z^* and s^*, but will simply cause an increase in the relative price of agricultural commodities. Combined movements of z and s to the stagnation position are depicted in Fig. 6.

It is no exaggerated claim to say that the theoretical analysis of stagnation presented above seems to represent some realistic aspects of today's underdeveloped countries. Take, for instance, India and Pakistan. These countries possess an advanced industrial sector together with a large proportion of workers still in the backward sector of agriculture. *Per capita* income is still very low and the growth rate of population is very high.

We now investigate the role of Engel's Law in the process to stagnation. The level of food consumption in each period under the assumption of Engel's Law will be higher than the case where Engel's Law does not operate.[1] This has two effects in the operations of the model in this stage. First, the

---

[1] As equation (11) indicates, by Engel's Law we imply specifically that $0 < v'(z) < 1$, $v''(z) < 0$. Thus, the case $v(z) = a+bz$ is excluded.

demand for agricultural output in each period will be greater, and thereby retard the movement of labour from the agricultural sector to the industrial sector. This has an effect of slowing down the process of industrialization compared with the case where *per capita* food consumption is assumed to

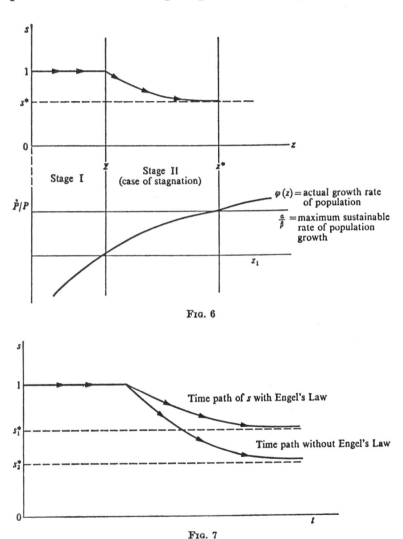

FIG. 6

FIG. 7

be constant. In the second place, the proportion of the labour force engaged in agriculture at this stage will be higher under Engel's Law. At the position of stagnation, the larger proportion of available labour force may still be in agriculture. The comparative effects of Engel's Law in the process of development are shown in Fig. 7.

Development to modern society

If the actual growth rate of population is less than the maximum sustainable rate given in each society by technology and production conditions in agriculture, the dualistic economy will eventually develop to a modern industrialized society. The actual growth rate of population may not

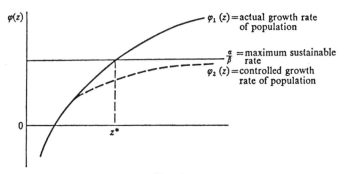

FIG. 8

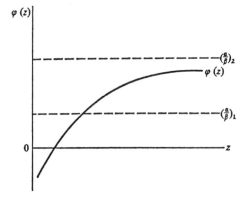

FIG. 9

exceed the maximum sustainable rate due to the natural law of reproduction as exhibited in most advanced countries. On the other hand, if there exists a threat of population explosion it must be controlled by direct or indirect government interventions. In Fig. 8 effect of such a successful population control effort is depicted. If the actual growth rate of population $\phi_1(z)$ tends to exceed the maximum sustainable rate α/β without governmental measures of population control, the society will fall into the trap of stagnation z^*. If, on the other hand, some means are found to suppress this population explosion as depicted by $\phi_2(z)$, the society can achieve the steady process of development ($\alpha/\beta > \phi_2(z)$). The society can *alternatively* achieve modernization if it can raise the maximum sustainable level of population

434 POPULATION GROWTH AND DEVELOPMENT OF DUAL ECONOMY

growth rate higher than the present level of population growth rate by improving technology in agriculture and/or by changing production conditions in agriculture. In Fig. 9 the case of development to modern society is depicted when maximum sustainable rate of population growth is raised from $(\alpha/\beta)_1$ to $(\alpha/\beta)_2$.

The results we have obtained emphasize the importance of positive population policies as well as the policies promoting technical change in the society. Except for the countries where the population growth function already behaves in a reasonable fashion according to the natural demographic law of reproduction, priority must be given to the policies restricting population growth and/or to the policies that promote technological innovations in agriculture.[1]

Brown University, Rhode Island

APPENDIX

1. Derivation of equation (13).

Using equations (1), (3), (6), and (10), and from the production function,

$$Y_a = A_0 e^{\alpha t} L^{1-\beta},$$

we get

$$z = e^{\alpha t} L^{-\beta}.$$

Time derivative of the above equation divided by z is equal to

$$\frac{\dot{z}}{z} = \alpha - \beta \frac{\dot{L}}{L}.$$

Substituting (6) into $\dot{L}/L$, we finally get

$$\frac{\dot{z}}{z} = \alpha - \beta \phi(z). \tag{13}$$

2. Derivations of equations (14), (15), and (17).

First, we define the following ratios: $y_a = \dfrac{Y_a}{L_a}, y_m = \dfrac{Y_m}{L_m}, k = \dfrac{K}{L_m}$. Then, using these ratios, the production functions (1) and (2) and the equations for the wage determinations (3) and (4) can be written as:

$$y_a = e^{\alpha t} L_a^{-\beta}, \tag{A 1}$$

---

[1] As industrialization proceeds, the proportion of agricultural workers to the total labour force s is declining. In the long run the proportion is assumed to reach some constant value s_L^*, $0 < s_L^* < 1$. Both agriculture and industry will then grow in a balanced fashion. In order to satisfy this condition (rather than $s_L^* = 0$) we must place certain restrictions on the demand function for agricultural commodities, i.e. $v(z)$. We have implicitly assumed that $\lim\limits_{z \to +\infty} v'(z) = \xi$, $0 < \xi < 1$. This is the necessary and sufficient condition for $1 > s_L^* > 0$,

for

$$\lim_{z \to \infty} s(z) = \frac{1}{1 + (1-\gamma)\left(\lim\limits_{z \to \infty} z/v - 1\right)}$$

will be positive and less than 1 if and only if

$$\lim_{z \to \infty} z/v(z) = \frac{1}{\lim\limits_{z \to \infty} v'(z)} = \frac{1}{\xi}, \quad 0 < \xi < 1.$$

$$y_m = e^{\lambda t}k^\gamma, \tag{A 2}$$

$$\frac{w_m}{p} = y_a, \tag{A 3}$$

$$w_m = (1-\gamma)y_m. \tag{A 4}$$

If we define the proportion of the labour force engaged in each sector as $s = L_a/L$ and $1-s = L_m/L$, the definitions of z and v (equations (7) and (9)) can be written as

$$z = v+(1-s)\frac{y_m}{p}, \tag{A 5}$$

$$v = y_a s. \tag{A 6}$$

Using (A 3), (A 4), (A 5), (A 6) together with the relation $w_a = w_m$ (equation (5)), y_a can be written as:

$$y_a = \frac{(1-\gamma)z}{1-\gamma s}. \tag{A 7}$$

Substituting (A 6) and (A 7) into the behavioural equation of *per capita* food consumption v (equation (11)), and rearranging the terms, we obtain equation (15) in the text:

$$s = \frac{v(z)}{v(z)+(1-\gamma)(z-v(z))}. \tag{15}$$

Equation (15) has the following properties:

$$0 < s \leqslant 1$$

since

$$1-\gamma > 0, \quad z \geqslant v(z),$$

$$\frac{ds}{dz} = \frac{(1-\gamma)(v'(z)z-v(z))}{[v(z)+(1-\gamma)\{z-v(z)\}]^2} \leqslant 0$$

since $v'(z)z-v(z) \leqslant 0$. (The concavity of $v(z)$ implies this inequality. The equality sign holds when $z = v(z)$, that is, when $z < \bar{z}$, i.e. Stage I.)

Taking the time derivative of (15) and dividing it by s, we obtain equation (17) in the text:

$$\frac{\dot{s}}{s} = -(1-\gamma s)\left(1-\frac{v'(z)z}{v(z)}\right)\frac{\dot{z}}{z}. \tag{17}$$

Substituting (A 7) into the agricultural production function (A 1) and using $s = L_a/L$, we have:

$$\frac{(1-\gamma)z}{1-\gamma s} = e^{\alpha t}(sL)^{-\beta}.$$

Taking the logarithm and then differentiating with respect to time, we get:

$$\frac{\dot{z}}{z}-\left(\alpha-\beta\frac{\dot{L}}{L}\right) = -\beta\frac{\dot{s}}{s}-\frac{\gamma\dot{s}}{1-s}. \tag{A 8}$$

Utilizing the population growth function (6) and the equation (17), we finally obtain the equation (14) in the text:

$$\frac{\dot{z}}{z} = \frac{\alpha-\beta\phi(z)}{\{v'(z)z/v(z)\}+(1-\beta)(1-\gamma s)[1-\{v'(z)z/v(z)\}]} \tag{14}$$

Differentiating equation (14) and evaluating at the point where $\dot{z}/z = 0$ (or $z = z^*$), we obtain:

$$\frac{d(\dot{z}/z)}{dz}\bigg|_{z=z^*} = \frac{-\beta\phi'(z)}{D} < 0, \quad \phi'(z) > 0, \tag{A 9}$$

where D is the denominator of the right-hand side of (14) and is positive for any relevant value of z and s ($z > 0$, $0 < s \leqslant 1$). This inequality tells us that from any initial value z will necessarily move to the value z^*.

436 POPULATION GROWTH AND DEVELOPMENT OF DUAL ECONOMY

REFERENCES

1. FEI, J., and RANIS, G., *Development of the Labor Surplus Economy*, Homewood, Illinois: Irwin, Inc., 1964.
2. —— 'Agrarianism, dualism, and economic development', in *The Theory and Design of Economic Development*, edited by Adelman and Thorbecke, The Johns Hopkins Press, Baltimore, 1966.
3. GUHA, A., 'Accumulation, innovation, and growth under conditions of disguised unemployment', *Oxford Economic Papers*, Nov. 1969.
4. JORGENSON, D., 'The development of a dual economy', *Economic Journal*, vol. lxxi, 1961.
5. —— 'Surplus agricultural labour and the development of a dual economy', *Oxford Economic Papers*, Nov. 1967.
6. LEWIS, W. A., 'Economic development with unlimited supplies of labour', *Manchester School*, vol. xxii, 1954.
7. SATO, R., 'A note on scarcity of specific resources as a limit to output: a correction', *Review of Economic Studies*, Oct. 1967.
8. —— *The Theory of Economic Growth*, Tokyo, Keiso-shobo, 1968.
9. TSIANG, S. C., 'A model of economic growth in Rostovian stages', *Econometrica*, Oct. 1964.

[7]

INTERNATIONAL ECONOMIC REVIEW
Vol. 11, No. 3, October, 1970

SHARES AND GROWTH UNDER FACTOR-AUGMENTING
TECHNICAL CHANGE*

By Ryuzo Sato and Martin J. Beckmann[1]

IT IS WELL KNOWN that in a neoclassical growth model the Hicksian neutral technical progress by itself or in combination with Harrod neutral technical change (factor augmenting technical progress) is not in general consistent with the stable long-run growth equilibrium in the sense that under this type of technical progress there exists, in general, no balanced growth. This implies that technical progress of the Hicks neutral tpye is inconsistent with a golden age where capital, labor (measured in efficiency units) and output all grow at the same rate and the relative shares of capital and labor remain constant (see [5]). However, estimates of technical progress in various countries seem to show that inventions are essentially either Hicks neutral or factor augmenting ([3], [4], [6]).

One remedy frequently suggested to correct the apparent "inconsistency" is to postulate an underlying production function of the Cobb-Douglas form where factor shares are independent of technological bias (unitary elasticity of substitution).

This paper, which deals with factor augmenting technical change in general, intends to show that there is a large family of production functions that behave asymptotically in the same way as the Cobb-Douglas function, although having a very different functional form, and, hence, would not be "inconsistent." These production functions belong to the same class as the Cobb-Douglas function in the sense that they exhibit factor shares which are asymptotically independent of technological bias.

1. By factor augmenting technical change we mean that the production function—assumed as usual to be homogeneous of degree one—can be written

$$Y = f(aL, bK)$$

where

Y is output;
$L(t)$ is labor;
$K(t)$ is capital;
$a(t)$ is an index of labor's productivity;
$b(t)$ is an index of capital's productivity.

We shall say that

* Manuscript received December 4, 1967; revised December 23, 1968.

[1] This is an extension of two papers written independently by the authors. (See M. J. Beckmann [2] and R. Sato [7].) We wish to thank Professors Jerome Stein, Akihiro Amano and the referee for their many illuminating comments during the earlier stages of this work. This work was supported by the National Science Foundation under NSF Grant No. 2325.

$aL = \hat{L}$ is labor measured in efficiency units;
$bK = \hat{K}$ is capital measured in efficiency units.

Sometimes we assume a and b to be growing at constant rates

$$a = e^{\alpha t}, \qquad b = e^{\beta t}.$$

The case where

$$b \equiv 1$$

is known as Harrod neutral technical change, and the case where

$$a \equiv b$$

as Hicks neutral. Factor augmenting technical progress may, therefore, be considered a combination of Harrod and Hicks neutral changes. In that case the Hicksian or Harrodian parts need not by themselves have positive growth rates (See [6]).

2. It is readily shown that with a constant savings ratio, s, capital augmenting progress implies that the labor-capital ratio (when both are measured in efficiency units) declines steadily to zero.

Namely, let

$$\hat{x} = \frac{\hat{L}}{\hat{K}} = \frac{aL}{bK}.$$

Then

(1) $$\frac{\dot{\hat{x}}}{\hat{x}} = \frac{\dot{a}}{a} - \frac{\dot{b}}{b} + n - s\frac{Y}{K}, \qquad 0 < s < 1,$$

where we have assumed $L = L(0)e^{nt}$, i.e., labor grows at a constant rate n. Write $a = a_0 e^{\alpha t}$, $b = b_0 e^{\beta t}$, $\alpha > 0$, $\beta > 0$, and consider

$$\frac{Y}{K} = f\left(\frac{aL}{K}, b\right) = bf\left(\frac{aL}{bK}, 1\right).$$

Now write $f(\hat{x}, 1) = \Phi(\hat{x})$.

By virtue of linear homogeneity

$$\frac{Y}{K} = b\Phi\left(\frac{aL}{bK}\right) \quad \text{say},$$

$$= b\Phi(\hat{x}) \quad \text{say},$$

$$\text{where} \quad \hat{x} = \frac{\hat{L}}{\hat{K}} = \frac{aL}{bK}$$

is the labor-capital ratio in efficiency units and Φ the production function considered as a function of one variable.

Substituting in (1)

$$\frac{\dot{\hat{x}}}{\hat{x}} = \alpha - \beta + n - sb\Phi(\hat{x}).$$

Since $b(t)$ is assumed to be increasing over time without limit, for large t the right-hand side becomes negative, unless $\Phi(\hat{x})$ decreases sufficiently. In either case we have that $\hat{x} \to 0$. Q.E.D.

3. Now the labor-capital ratio in physical units x grows at the rate

$$\frac{\dot{x}}{x} = n - sb\Phi\left(\frac{a(t)}{b(t)}x\right).$$

From the differential equation we infer that either

$$b(t)\Phi\left(\frac{a(t)}{b(t)}x\right)$$

is bounded or

$$x(t) \to 0.$$

At any time t there exists a critical value $x^*(t)$ such that for

$$x > x^*(t), \qquad \dot{x} < 0,$$
$$x < x^*(t), \qquad \dot{x} > 0,$$

and x^* is the solution of

(2) $$b(t)\Phi\left(\frac{a(t)}{b(t)}x^*(t)\right) = \frac{s}{n}.$$

In order for $x^*(t)$ to approach a constant value $x^*(\infty) \neq 0$, a necessary condition is that

$$\lim_{t \to \infty} e^{\beta t}\Phi(e^{(\alpha-\beta)t}) = k$$

exists. Since Φ is a production function with $\Phi' \geq 0$, this is possible only if

$$\alpha < \beta$$

and

$$\Phi(0) = 0.$$

Assume that $\Phi(z)$ may be expanded in a Taylor series at $z = 0$:

$$\Phi(z) = v_1 z + v_2 z^2 + \cdots.$$

Substituting in (2) we have

$$\frac{s}{n} = b_0 e^{\beta t} v_1 \frac{a_0}{b_0} e^{(\alpha-\beta)t} x^* + b_0 e^{\beta t}\left(\frac{a_0}{b_0}\right)^2 e^{2(\alpha-\beta)t} x^{*2} + \cdots$$

$$= a_0 v_1 e^{\alpha t} x^* + 0(e^{2(\alpha-\beta)t}).$$

We conclude that a nonzero equilibrium value $x^*(\infty)$ exists if and only if

$$\alpha = 0.$$

Thus, the labor-capital ratio in physical terms x can approach a finite nonzero equilibrium level only if the technical change is purely capital augmenting, and it will do so if the production function is analytic near zero. The last condition is not satisfied and the result does not apply when the production function is, e.g., Cobb-Douglas.

4. Before turning to the output-capital ratio, let us examine the growth rate

of output.   Differentiating the production function totally with respect to time
we have

$$\dot{Y} = f_1(aL, bK) \cdot [\dot{a}L + a\dot{L}] + f_2(aL, bK) \cdot [\dot{b}K + b\dot{K}]$$

where f_i is the partial derivative with respect to the i-th $(i = aL, bK)$ variable.
Dividing by Y and multiplying the first term by aL, the second by bK, and
dividing, we have

(3)
$$\frac{\dot{Y}}{Y} = \frac{f_1 aL}{Y} \cdot \left(\frac{\dot{a}}{a} + \frac{\dot{L}}{L} \right) + \frac{f_2 bK}{Y} \left(\frac{\dot{b}}{b} + \frac{\dot{K}}{K} \right) .$$

Uuder competitive conditions which will be assumed here, the marginal product
of labor af_1 is the wage rate and $f_1 a \cdot L/Y$ is labor's share equal to λ (say).
Similarly, $f_2 bK/Y$ is the profit share equal to μ, say.   For linear homogeneity
we have by Euler's theorem

$$\mu + \lambda = 1 .$$

Since the production function Φ depends on the capital-labor ratio in efficiency
units only, we have for labor's share

$$\lambda = \frac{L f_1(aL, bK)a}{f(aL, bK)} = \frac{aL f_1 \left(\dfrac{aL}{bK}, 1 \right)}{bK f \left(\dfrac{aL}{bK}, 1 \right)}$$

$$= \frac{\hat{x} \Phi'(\hat{x})}{\Phi(\hat{x})} ,$$

so that share is a function of the factor proportion $\hat{x}$ in terms of efficiency
units only,

$$\lambda = \lambda(\hat{x}) .$$

Now returning to equation (3) we obtain

(3′)
$$\frac{\dot{Y}}{Y} = \lambda(\hat{x})[\alpha + n] + (1 - \lambda(\hat{x})) \left[\beta + \frac{\dot{K}}{K} \right] .$$

Observe that with a constant savings ratio $s, 0 < s < 1$

$$\frac{\dot{K}}{K} = s \frac{Y}{K} = sy,$$

where y denotes the output-capital ratio in physical units.   Substituting in
(3′) and denoting $\dot{Y}/Y = g$

(4)
$$g = \lambda(\hat{x})[\alpha + n] + (1 - \lambda(\hat{x}))[\beta + sy] .$$

5.   Consider now the output-capital ratio in physical terms, y.   We have

$$\frac{\dot{y}}{y} = \frac{\dot{Y}}{Y} - \frac{\dot{K}}{K} = \frac{\dot{Y}}{Y} - s \frac{Y}{K} = g - sy$$

where g, as before, denotes the growth rate of output.

$$\frac{\dot{y}}{y} = \lambda(\hat{x})[\alpha + n] + (1 - \lambda(x))(\beta + sy) - sy \,.$$

(5)

$$\frac{\dot{y}}{y} = \lambda(\hat{x})[\alpha + n - \beta - sy] + \beta \,.$$

Assume that α, β, s, and n are given constants and that $\beta > 0$. Under what conditions does the capital-output ratio in physical units approach a finite nonzero value in time?

At any time there exists a critical value y^*

(6)
$$y^* = \frac{n + \alpha}{s} + \frac{\beta}{s}\left(\frac{1}{\lambda} - 1\right) > 0$$

such that—from (5)—

y is decreasing when $y > y^*$,

y is increasing when $y < y^*$.

A finite limit of y^*—and hence of y—exists if and only if

$$\lim_{x \to 0} \lambda(\hat{x}) > 0$$

exists. If $\lim_{\hat{x} \to 0} \lambda(\hat{x}) = 0$ then

$$\lim_{\hat{x} \to 0} y^*(\hat{x}) = \infty \,.$$

These results are an immediate consequence of (6).

Incidentally, if the output-capital ratio in physical terms approaches some constant value—so that capital and output in physical terms grow at the same rate—then the output-capital ratio in efficiency units will grow at the (constant) rate β of the capital productivity index and hence approaches infinity.

6. The next question is clearly what properties must the production function have in order for labor's share to approach a nonzero limit when the labor-capital ratio falls to zero.

It is well known that constant shares imply a Cobb-Douglas production function. Thus, for small labor-capital ratios, in order for the capital-output ratio to stabilize, the production function must be approximately Cobb-Douglas.

To illustrate, suppose that shares—which must lie between 0 and 1—are a rational function of the labor-capital ratio x.

(7)
$$\lambda(x) = \frac{P(x)}{Q(x)}$$

where $P(x)$ is a polynomial of degree m, $Q(x)$ is a polynomial of degree n. In order for $\lambda(x)$ to be bounded we must have $m \leq n$. Moreover, Q must have no roots on the positive real axis unless they are also roots of $P(x)$. In that case, the order of the root of Q must not exceed that of the roots of P and the factor $(x - r)^q$, where r is the root and q its order in Q, may be cancelled out. Hence, $Q(x)$ may be assumed to have no roots on the positive real axis including zero. $P(x)/Q(x)$ may now be developed in partial fractions.

(8)
$$\frac{P(x)}{Q(x)} = \sum_{i=1}^{v} \sum_{k=1}^{q_i} \frac{c_i}{(x + r_i)^k}$$

where $-r_i$ are the roots of the denominator Q and q_i their order. In particular let all the roots be simple

(9)
$$\frac{P}{Q} = \sum_{i=1}^{n} \frac{c_i}{x + r_i} .$$

By definition of the share function

$$\lambda(x) = \frac{x\Phi'(x)}{\Phi(x)} = \frac{d \log \Phi(x)}{d \log x} = \frac{x d \log \Phi(x)}{dx} .$$

Substituting

$$d \log \Phi(x) = \frac{P(x)}{xQ(x)} \cdot dx .$$

Now develop $P(x)/xQ(x)$ into partial fractions. By assumption all roots are simple.

(10)
$$d \log \Phi = \frac{c_0 dx}{x} + \sum_{i=1}^{n} \frac{c_i dx}{x + r_i}$$

where $-r_i$ are the roots of $Q(x)$. Integrating

$$\log \Phi = \log c + c_0 \log x + \sum_i c_i \log (x + r_i)$$

(11)
$$\Phi = cx^{c_0} \cdot \prod_{i=1}^{n} (x + r_i)^{c_i} .$$

For small x the product terms approach the constant value $c \prod_{i=1}^{n} r_i^{c_i}$ and the function is approximately Cobb-Douglas with $\lambda = c_0$.

Of course, the roots r_i may be complex conjugate. In that case the products of terms in (11) involving complex conjugate roots are of the arctangent type.

Turning to the case of a multiple root let

$$d \log \Phi = \frac{c_0}{x} dx + \sum_{k=1}^{n} \frac{c_k}{(x + r)^k} dx$$

$$\log \Phi = \log c + c_0 \log x + c_1 \log (x + r) - \sum_{k=2}^{n} \frac{c_k}{k + 1} \frac{1}{(x + r)^{k+1}}$$

(12)
$$\Phi = cx^{c_0}(r + x)^{c_1} \exp\left[-\sum_{k=2}^{n} \frac{c_k}{k + 1} \frac{1}{(x + r)^{k+1}} \right] .$$

If several roots, some multiple, occur then the solution is a product of terms (12).

7. Consider finally the share function

$$\lambda(x) = \frac{a + bx^u}{1 - c + cx^u} \qquad u > 0, 0 < \frac{a}{1 - c}, \frac{b}{c} < 1 .$$

It has the property that for $x \to 0$ shares approach $a/(1 - c)$ and for $x \to \infty$ shares approach b/c. The assumption $u > 0$ is no restriction since division of numerator and denominator by x^u generates an expression of the same type with negative u.

Substituting for λ we have

$$d \log \varPhi = \frac{a + bx^u}{(1 - c)x + cx^{u+1}} dx .$$

It is easily verified that the right-hand expression equals

$$\frac{a}{x} + \frac{(b - ac)x^{u-1}}{1 - c + cx^u} .$$

Integrating we have

$$\log \varPhi = \log k + a \log x + \frac{b - ac}{c} \log (1 - c + cx^u)$$

(13)
$$\varPhi = k \cdot x^a (1 - c + cx^u)^{(b-ac)/c}$$
$$\varPhi = k_0 x^a (1 - c_0 + c_0 x^u)^{b/c-a} ,$$

say. In the special case of

$$u = \frac{c}{b - ac} = -\rho$$

the expression in parenthesis is a CES production function (see [1]) provided $\rho = -u > -1$.

The solution (13) is, therefore, the algebraic product of a Cobb-Douglas and a generalized CES production function.

8. We shall now take a general approach to derive conditions for the share of labor λ to approach a value between zero and one, as $\hat{x}$ approaches zero, if in fact such a limit exists. Under point 3 above, it was shown that in fact, the labor-capital ratio in physical terms may approach a finite nonzero value, while the labor-capital ratio in efficiency units always falls to zero. It is, therefore, simpler to base the following analysis on a consideration of the capital-labor ratio in efficiency units.

As demonstrated before we have.

$$\lambda(\hat{x}) = \frac{\hat{x}\varPhi'(\hat{x})}{\varPhi(\hat{x})} .$$

From the definition of the elasticity of factor substitution

$$\sigma(\hat{x}) = \frac{\varPhi'(\hat{x})[\varPhi(\hat{x}) - \hat{x}\varphi'(\hat{x})]}{-\hat{x}\varPhi(\hat{x})\varPhi''(\hat{x})} ,$$

it follows that

(14) $$\frac{1}{\lambda}(\hat{x}) = \frac{1}{\lambda(\hat{x})} = 1 + \frac{B}{\hat{x}} \exp \int_{\hat{x}_0}^{\hat{x}} \frac{d\hat{x}}{\hat{x}\sigma(\hat{x})} , \qquad B > 0$$

where $B > 0$ is a constant of integration. Note that λ, σ and $\varPhi$ are functions of $\hat{x}$ only.

THEOREM 1. *If* $\lim_{\hat{x} \to +0} \lambda(\hat{x}) = \bar{\lambda}$, *then a necessary condition for* $\bar{\lambda}$ *to lie be-*

tween zero and one $(0 < \bar{\lambda} < 1)$ is that:

(15)
$$\lim_{\hat{x} \to +0} \sigma(\hat{x}) = 1 .$$

The necessary and sufficient condition that $\bar{\lambda}$ be $0 < \bar{\lambda} < 1$ is that:

(16)
$$\lim_{\hat{x} \to +0} \int_{\hat{x}}^{\hat{x}_0} \frac{\xi(\tau)}{\tau} d\tau = C , \qquad (C \neq \pm \infty) ,$$

where $\xi(\tau) = 1/\sigma(\tau) - 1$ and the limit points of C are assumed to be bounded.

PROOF.

$$\lim_{\hat{x} \to +0} \lambda(x) = \bar{\lambda}, \, 0 < \bar{\lambda} < 1, \langle=\rangle 1 < \frac{1}{\bar{\lambda}} = 1 + B \lim_{x \to +0} \frac{1}{x} . \qquad \exp \int_{\hat{x}_0}^{\hat{x}} \frac{d\tau}{\tau \sigma(\tau)} .$$

Since $B > 0$,

$$\langle=\rangle \lim_{\hat{x} \to +0} \frac{1}{\hat{x}} \exp \int_{\hat{x}_0}^{\hat{x}} \frac{d\tau}{\tau \sigma(\tau)} = b > 0 .$$

$$b = \lim_{\hat{x} \to +0} \frac{1}{\hat{x}\sigma(\hat{x})} \exp \int_{\hat{x}_0}^{\hat{x}} \frac{d\tau}{\tau \sigma(\tau)} = b \cdot \lim_{\hat{x} \to +0} \frac{1}{\sigma(\hat{x})} .$$

Thus, we obtain $\lim_{x \to +0} \sigma(x) = 1$ as the necessary condition.[2]
On the other hand,

$$\lim_{\hat{x} \to +0} \frac{1}{\hat{x}} \exp \int_{\hat{x}_0}^{\hat{x}} \frac{d\tau}{\tau \sigma(\tau)} = b > 0, \, b < +\infty ,$$

$$\langle=\rangle \lim_{\hat{x} \to +0} \left\{ (-\log \hat{x}) + \int_{\hat{x}_0}^{\hat{x}} \frac{d\tau}{\tau \sigma(\tau)} \right\} = \log b, \, (\neq \pm \infty)$$

$$\langle=\rangle \lim_{\hat{x} \to +0} \int_{\hat{x}}^{\hat{x}_0} \left[\frac{1}{\sigma(\tau)} - 1 \right] \frac{d\tau}{\tau} = C, \, (C \neq \pm \infty) . \qquad \text{Q.E.D.}$$

The above theorem, especially equation (16), is too general. Therefore, we shall present a sufficient condition for equation (16).

THEOREM 2. *If there exists a constant N such that*

(17)
$$\lim_{\hat{x} \to +0} \left| \frac{1 - \sigma(\hat{x})}{\sigma(\hat{x})} \right| (-\log \hat{x})^k = N , \qquad \begin{pmatrix} 0 \leq N < +\infty \\ k > 1; \text{ real} \end{pmatrix} ,$$

then $\lim_{\hat{x} \to +0} \lambda(\hat{x}) = \bar{\lambda}, \, 0 < \bar{\lambda} < 1.$

PROOF. Rewrite (16) as

$$\lim_{t \to +\infty} \int_t^{t_0} \eta(t)(-dt) = C , \qquad (C \neq \pm \infty)$$

where $t = -\log \hat{x}$, $t_0 = -\log \hat{x}_0$ and $\eta(t) = \xi(e^{-t})$. Then equation (16) will converge if

---

[2] It is assumed that the limit points of $\log s(x)$ are to be bounded where

$$\log s(x) - \log s(x_0) = \int_{x_0}^{x} \left[1 - \frac{1}{\sigma(\tau)} \right] d \log \tau .$$

$$^{\exists}N; \lim_{t \to +\infty} \frac{|\eta(t)|}{t^\alpha} = N, \qquad \begin{matrix} 0 \le N < +\infty \\ \alpha < -1 \end{matrix} \, .$$

Setting $-\alpha = k > 1$, we obtain condition (17).[3]   Q.E.D.

9. We shall now discuss the application of the theorems. Theorems 1 and 2 can be utilized to obtain bounds to the actual values of the elasticity of substitution that would guarantee the stable path of a neoclassical growth model of the Solow-Swan type under factor-augmenting technical progress. To have stable balanced growth in such a model, it is sufficient that the share of labor asymptotically approaches a constant value between zero and one, as the labor-capital ratio measured in efficiency units converges to zero. It is easily shown that the production function represented by (13) satisfies the above theorems and, hence, it guarantees a stable balanced path under factor-augmenting technical progress. However, there is a more general class of production functions that would be also consistent with a Golden Age path. We first prove the following theorem.

THEOREM 3.   *The neoclassical growth process with factor-augmenting technical progress will be stable for all positive growth rate of labor $n > 0$ and the constant saving ratio $0 < s < 1$, if the elasticity of factor substitution asymptotically satisfies:*

$$(18) \qquad \frac{1}{1 + \dfrac{c}{(-\log \hat{x})^k}} \le \sigma(\hat{x}) \le \frac{1}{1 - \dfrac{c}{(-\log \hat{x})^k}} \, , \qquad c > 0, \, k > 1 \, ,$$

for all $\hat{x}$ sufficiently small ($\hat{x} < 1$).

PROOF.   Both

$$\sigma(\hat{x}) = \frac{1}{1 + \dfrac{c}{(-\log \hat{x})^k}} \quad \text{and} \quad \sigma(\hat{x}) = \frac{1}{1 - \dfrac{c}{(-\log \hat{x})^k}}$$

satisfy Theorem 2 as long as $k > 1$. For,

$$\lim_{\hat{x} \to +0} \sigma(\hat{x}) = 1$$

and

$$\lim_{\hat{x} \to +0} |\xi(\hat{x})| (-\log \hat{x})^k = N, \qquad\qquad 0 \le N < +\infty \, .$$

Thus,

$$\lim_{\hat{x} \to +0} \lambda(\hat{x}) = \bar{\lambda} \, , \qquad\qquad 0 < \bar{\lambda} < 1 \, ,$$

and also

$$\lim_{\substack{t \to +\infty \\ \text{or} \\ x \to +0}} y = y^* = \frac{n + \alpha}{s} + \frac{\beta}{s}\left(\frac{1}{\bar{\lambda}} - 1\right) > 0 \, ,$$

[3] Note that this condition is similar to, but stronger than, the condition developed for global stability of a neoclassical growth model under no technical progress. That is to say, if this condition is satisfied, then the neoclassical growth model under no technical progress has global stability, but not vice versa. See Sato [7, (422-3)].

which proves the existence and stability of the balanced growth path.

For the inequality parts, we use the definition of $\lambda(\hat{x})$

$$\frac{1}{\lambda(\hat{x})} = 1 + \frac{B}{\hat{x}} \exp \int_{\hat{x}_0}^{\hat{x}} \frac{d \log \hat{x}}{\sigma(\hat{x})} , \qquad B > 0 .$$

Consider $\hat{x}_0$ such that inequality (18) is asymptotically satisfied for $x \leqq x_0 \leqq 1$. Then

(19)
$$1 + B \exp\left[-\frac{c}{1-k} \cdot \frac{1}{(-\log \hat{x})^{k-1}} \right] \leqq \frac{1}{\lambda(\hat{x})}$$
$$\leqq 1 + B \exp\left[\frac{c}{1-k} \cdot \frac{1}{(-\log \hat{x})^{k-1}} \right] , \qquad k > 1 .$$

But both sides of this expression approach

$$1 + B = \frac{1}{\lambda} , \qquad B > 0 \quad \text{as} \quad \hat{x} \to +0 . \qquad \text{Q.E.D.}$$

Figure 1 depicts the stability region of the neoclassical growth model that is consistent with Golden Age paths. It is seen that there is a wide range

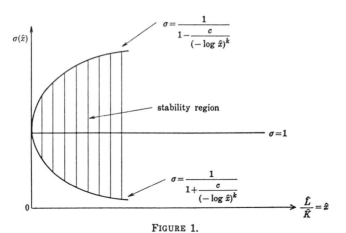

Figure 1.

of values of the elasticity of factor-substitution—thus, a wide variety of forms of production functions—that would be consistent with Golden Age paths. The Cobb-Douglas production function, the production function which combines both a Cobb-Douglas and a CES function (equation (13)) are only special cases of this class of production functions. The most general form of this class of production functions, that we can find thus far, is,

(20) $$\Phi(\hat{x}) = C \exp \left\{ \int_{\hat{x}_0}^{\hat{x}} \left[\frac{d \log \hat{x}}{1 + B \exp\left[\frac{c}{1-k}(-\log \hat{x})^{1-k} \right]} \right] \right\} , \qquad B > 0, C > 0 ,$$

$$k > 1, c > 0 \quad \text{for} \quad \sigma < 1$$
$$k > 1, c < 0 \quad \text{for} \quad \sigma > 1,$$

which is integrated from

$$\sigma(\hat{x}) = \cfrac{1}{1 + \cfrac{c}{(-\log \hat{x})^k}}.$$

10. In conclusion let us recall some well-known implications of an asymptotically constant capital-output ratio $1/y$. First, from $Y/K = y^* = $ constant, it follows at once that $\dot{Y}/K = \dot{K}/K = g$, (say), so that capital and output grow at the same rate. This rate may be determined by substituting for $\dot{K}/K$ in equation (3'),

$$g = \frac{\dot{y}}{y} = \bar{\lambda}(\alpha + n) + (1 - \bar{\lambda})(\beta + g)$$

from which

(21) $$g = \alpha + n + \frac{1 - \bar{\lambda}}{\bar{\lambda}} \beta.$$

It follows that per capita income grows at rate

$$\alpha + \frac{1 - \bar{\lambda}}{\bar{\lambda}} \beta.$$

Consider capital's share $1 - \bar{\lambda} = rK/Y$ where r is the interest rate. From the constancy of K/Y and $\bar{\lambda}$ it follows that $r = (1 - \bar{\lambda})y^*$ is constant. In that case it is possible to define a Golden Rule savings ratio by the condition that asymptotically consumption is maximized. Now

$$C = Y - \dot{K}$$
$$= F(aL, bK) - gK.$$

Differentiation with respect to K implies, $bf_2 - g = 0$ or $r = g$.

Asymptotically, a golden age—even a golden rule—will still exist, and the capital-output ratio, the growth rate and the interest rate will approach constant values, provided that shares approach constant values, i.e., provided that the production function is asymptotically Cobb-Douglas.[4]

Brown University, U.S.A.

REFERENCES

[1]   K. J. ARROW, H. B. CHENERY, B. S. MINHAS, AND R. M. SOLOW, "Capital-Labor Substitution and Economic Efficiency," *The Review of Economics and Statistics,* XLII (August, 1961), 225-50.
[2]   M. J. BECKMANN, "Einkommensverteilung und Wachstum bei Nichtneutralem

---

[4] The above theorem as well as the production function represented by (20) can be directly applied to the optimal control problems with exogenous technical change (see, for example, Karl Shell [8]).

Technischen Fortschritt," *Jahrbücher für Nationalökonomie und Statistik*, CLXXVIII (August, 1965), 80-9.

[3] DAVID, P. A. AND T. VAN de KLUNDERT, "Nonneutral Efficiency Growth and Substitution between Capital and Labour in the U.S. Economy, 1899-1960," *American Economic Review* (June, 1965), 57-94.

[4] DHRYMES, P. J., "A Comparison of Productivity Behavior in Manufacturing and Service Industries," *Review of Economics and Statistics* (February, 1963), 64-9.

[5] PHELPS, E., "Second Essay on the Golden Rule of Accumulation," *American Economic Review*, LV (September, 1965), 793-814.

[6] SATO, R. AND M. BECKMAN, "Neutral Inventions and Production Functions," *Review of Economic Studies* (January, 1968), 57-66. "An Addendum," *Review of Economics Studies* (July, 1968), 366.

[7] ———, "A Note on Scarcity of Specific Resources as a Limit to Output: A Correction," *Review of Economic Studies* (October, 1967), 421-6.

[8] KARL SHELL, ed., *Essays on the Theory of Optimal Economic Growth* (Cambridge: Massachusettes Institute of Technology Press, 1967), Chapter 1.

[8]

Sonderdruck aus den „Jahrbüchern für Nationalökonomie und Statistik"
Band 189, Heft 1/2 (1975)
Gustav Fischer Verlag Stuttgart

A Note on

Economic Growth, Technical Progress and the Production Function

By R y u z o S a t o*) and M a r t i n J. B e c k m a n n*)

1. It is a bit amusing to observe people who take the results of some empirical work so seriously. Professor Bernhard Gahlen's recent contribution [2] to growth theory, especially chapter 6, is a case in point.

Gahlen makes intensive use of the various concepts of "neutrality" of technical change that the present authors have developed in their earlier work [5]. He seems to like the theoretical framework of the analysis, but finds the empirical application [1] of little value and blames the present authors for not applying enough diligence and rigor, when he says, "...As we shall see, the (present) authors did not apply the amount of diligence in their empirical research as seems appropriate [p. 176].

2. Except for a defect in the German data which Professor Gahlen points out (and for which we are grateful), Gahlen's analysis states little more but the fact that empirical work of the sort carried out by us is difficult to interpret.

This everybody knows, and we certainly knew it before we applied the model to the empirical data. As the difficulty of the empirical analysis is brought up, let us mention what we know, but what has completely escaped from Gahlen's criticisms. In other words, Gahlen could have criticized our empirical work more intelligently from the following stand point:

(1) The equations that we are estimating are "differential" equations, and the standard least squares or related methods are illequiped to handle such "differential" equation estimation problem.
(2) There are problems of multicollinearity of "errors in variable" and specification errors.
(3) The equations we are estimating are really simultaneous equations and thus require simultaneous equation estimation techniques e.g. two-stage, or three-stage, least squares or full information methods.

---
*) R y u z o S a t o is Professor of Economics, Brown University, USA and visiting Professor of Economics, University of Bonn, Germany, and M a r t i n B e c k m a n n is Professor of Economics, Brown University, USA and Professor of Applied Mathematics at the Technical Universiy of Munich, Germany.

This amounts to saying, unless econometric methods of estimating s i m u l t a n e o u s d i f f e r e n t i a l equation systems which contain errors in variables, multicollimeridy and specification errors, are perfected, the kind of theoretical analysis that we present can never be tested effectively against any empirical data (good or bad).

Gahlen's observation that "The data used by the authors are wrong; yet to anyone inclined to believe in their results it should appear strange that the results are not greatly changed if the correct data are substituted for the wrong ones" [2, p. 183], shows exactly this point. This is not because the neoclassical theory is useless, but because econometricans up to now are unable to develop more reliable techniques to cope with real world situations.

3. The alternative approach suggested (and estimated) by Gahlen [2], pp. 190—192, is really trivial, because the underlying production-function satisfying three equations (6-3 a, 3 b, 3 c) is nothing but the Cobb Douglas function when σ/α and σ/β are considered to be constant (such as .2533 and .2485 respectively) (see Sato [4]).

4. Gahlen has little use for some of the more esoteric types of neutrality discovered in our analysis. As it turned out, these were also rejected by the data. But this was by no means certain in advance. That Hicks-, Harrod-, Solow-, and Sato-Beckmann-neutrality stand out even on the basis of the rather crude estimates which we performed, is not an entirely trivial result.

5. We can now give a more interesting and hopefully more illuminating interpretation to the various types of neutrality observed in different countries[1]). Consider the following innovation frontier:

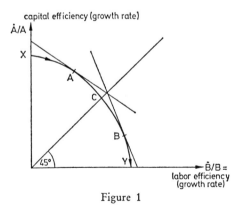

Figure 1

It is known [3] that under the exogenously determined innovation frontier of Sato-Beckmann-neutrality the system will eventually reach the point Y, the Harrod neutral point, starting from any other point with the

---

appropriate value of the elasticity of substitution. The point A is closer to X, the Solow neutral point, while B is closer to Y = the Harrod neutral point. The point C is the Hicks neutral point where $\dot{A}/A \equiv \dot{B}/B$. Different countries may be situated at different points of the diagram depending upon the type of technological frontier, the type of production functions, especially the elasticity of substitution. So it is not surprising to see that Harrod and Solow neutrality may be more realistic than Hicks neutrality. In other words if one country happens to be located at a point closer to X such as A, then the resulting situation would be that Solow neutrality is more favorable than Hicks neutrality.

One can extend this line of reasoning further using the endogenously determined innovation frontier. In figure 2 the innovation frontier is

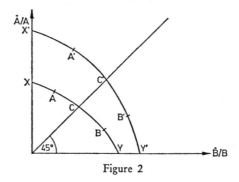

Figure 2

changing over time depending upon the amount of research expenditure of the economy. In this case most of all types of movements including Gahlen's subperiod analysis can be explained by both the position and the curvature of the frontier. Omitting the details we can show that the different types of neutrality may be explained as a result of optimizing behavior:

$$\text{Max} \int_{0}^{\infty} [(1 - \theta_1 - \theta_2)\, P(Y)\, Y - C]e^{-\gamma t}\, dt$$
$$Y, \theta_1 \theta_2$$

$$\text{subject to } \dot{A}/A = h_1\, (\theta_1\, PY)$$
$$\dot{B}/B = h_2\, (\theta_2\, PY)$$

where $P(Y)$ = price, C = cost function (dual to the production function), θ_1 = expenditure ratio for improving efficiency of capital and θ_2 = expenditure ratio for improving labor efficiency (thus θ_1 and θ_2 are expenditure ratios for shifting the frontier). In this way not only the various types of neutrality, but also their movements over time can be explained within a simple framework of optimal control of the Pontryagin type (see [6]).

6. Professor Gahlen seems to have objections to the neoclassical growth theory mainly because the theory in its present form may not be tested effectively against empirical data. Does he have any objection to general equilibrium models of Debreu and Hildenbrand type whose measure theory may have no empirical counterparts? The validity and usefulness of any economic theory does not depend solely on its immediate empirical significance, but depends on how it eventually leads to more understanding of the complex workings of the economy.

Zusammenfassung

Der Aufsatz ist eine Erwiderung auf die Kritik von Bernhard Gahlen in seinem „Der Informationsgehalt der neoklassischen Wirtschaftstheorie für die Wirtschaftspolitik" Mohr, Tübingen 1972, an den früheren Arbeiten von Sato und Beckmann über die Klassifikation des technischen Fortschritts.

Der Aufsatz berührt die Korrektheit der Datenbasis, die Schätzungsmethoden und vor allem die zugrunde liegenden ökonomischen Hypothesen. Es wird eine neue graphische Interpretation der Typen des technischen Fortschritts vorgeschlagen, in bezug auf ihre Auswirkungen auf die „innovation frontier" oder „Fortschrittsgrenzkurve".

Summary

This paper replies to criticism of the authors' previous work on the classification of technical progress made by Bernhard Gahlen in his book: Der Informationsgehalt der neoklassischen Wachstumstheorie für die Wirtschaftspolitik, Mohr, Tübingen 1972.

These deal with the correctness of the data used, the method of estimation applied, and most importantly, with the underlying economic hypotheses. The papers suggest a novel interpretation of neutral types of technical change in terms of their operation on the "innovation frontier", of Sato-Beckmann neutrality.

References

[1] Beckmann, M. J., Sato, R.: Aggregate Production Functions and Types of Technical Progress. American Economic Review, 1969.

[2] Gahlen, B.: Der Informationsgehalt der Neoklassischen Wachstumstheorie für Wirtschaftspolitik. Mohr, Tübingen 1972.

[3] Samuelson, P. A.: A Theory of Induced Innovations along Kennedy-Weizsäcker Lines. Review of Economics and Statistics, 1965, pp. 343—356.

[4] Sato, R.: The Estimation of Biased Technical Progress and the Production Function. International Economic Review, 1970, pp. 179—208.

[5] Sato, R., and Beckmann, M. J.: Neutral Inventions and Production Functions. Review of Economics Studies, 1968, pp. 57—65.

[6] Sato, R., and Ramachandran, R.: Models of Optimal Endogeneous Technical Progress, Discussion Paper. Brown University, 1974 for Econometric Society Meetings.

[7] Stein, J.: Journal of Political Economy, 1972.

9

Reprinted from THE REVIEW OF ECONOMIC STUDIES, Vol. XXXIV (4), October, 1967, R. SATO, pp. 421-426.

A Note on Scarcity of Specific Resources as a Limit to Output: A Correction

1. In the recent issue of this *Review* (February 1963), Ashok Guha [1] studies the asymptotic properties of an isoquant and formulates a theorem for a sufficient condition for the existence and stability of an equilibrium growth rate in a neo-classical growth model of the Solow-Swan type. The theorem states:

"If $\lim_{r \to \infty} \varepsilon \leq 1$ and $\lim_{r \to 0} \varepsilon \geq 1$, our system will converge to an equilibrium where capital and labour both grow at the common rate n, provided only that $n \geq 0$" [1, p. 40].

This theorem has been frequently used,[1] but strictly speaking it is wrong. Consider the following elasticity of factor substitution function:

$$\varepsilon = 1 - \frac{2}{\log\left(\frac{1}{r}\right)}, \quad \lim_{r \to +0} \varepsilon = 1 \text{ and } \lim_{r \to +\infty} \varepsilon = 1, \qquad \text{...(1)}$$

where ε = the elasticity of factor substitution and r = the capital-labour ratio. The production function derived from (1) is

$$\left.\begin{array}{l} \dfrac{Y}{K} = C \exp\left[-\dfrac{1}{\sqrt{B}} \tan^{-1}\left[\sqrt{B}(2+\log r)\right] \right], \\[2mm] \text{for } r \text{ sufficiently large, and} \\[2mm] \dfrac{Y}{K} = C \exp\left[\dfrac{1}{\sqrt{B}} \tan^{-1}\left[\sqrt{B}\left(\log \dfrac{1}{r} - 2\right)\right] \right], \\[2mm] \text{for } r \text{ sufficiently small, } B>0,\ C>0, \end{array}\right\} \qquad \text{...(2)}$$

where $\dfrac{Y}{K}$ = the output-capital ratio.[2] But we have

$$\lim_{r \to +\infty} \frac{Y}{K} = Ce^{-\frac{1}{\sqrt{B}} \cdot \frac{\pi}{2}} > 0$$

$$\lim_{r \to +0} \frac{Y}{K} = Ce^{\frac{1}{\sqrt{B}} \cdot \frac{\pi}{2}} < +\infty. \qquad \text{...(3)}$$

Equation (3) shows that, although Guha's condition (equation (1)) is satisfied, stability is *not* guaranteed for $n \geqq 0$.

2. Since most practical applications of the limiting properties of a production function are to the case of a linear and homogeneous production function, I assume that the production function is linear and homogeneous. Thus, we have that

$$y = f(x), f'(x)>0, f''(x)<0, \forall x \in I(0, \infty), \qquad \text{...(4)}$$

where $y = \dfrac{Y}{K}, x = \dfrac{1}{r} = \dfrac{L}{K}$. Guha's problem is to find the conditions such that

$$\lim_{x \to +0} f(x) = 0$$

$$\lim_{x \to +\infty} f(x) = +\infty. \qquad \text{...(5)}$$

We can formulate the following theorem on the existence and stability condition of the neo-classical growth equilibrium:

Theorem. *Let* $\dfrac{\dot{K}}{K} = s \cdot \dfrac{Y}{K}$, $0<s<1$, $\dfrac{Y}{K} = f\left(\dfrac{L}{K}\right)$ *and* $L(t) = L(0)e^{nt}$, $n \geqq 0$. *Then an equilibrium path exists* $\left(\dfrac{\dot{K}}{K} = n\right)$ *and it is globally stable if the elasticity of factor substitution,*

---

[1] See, for example, D. MacRae [3].
[2] The reader might be tempted to conclude that the example is inadmissable, since the counter-example defined by (1) allows negative ε-values over part of its range. It should be pointed out, however, that only the outer tails of the isoquant are relevant and that (1) is perfectly admissable there. For the details of such discussions, see my paper [4], from which most of this Note was taken.

ε, *satisfies the following conditions*:

$$\exists \varepsilon^*(x); \quad \varepsilon(x) \leqq \varepsilon^*(x), \text{ for } x \text{ sufficiently small, and} \qquad \ldots(6)$$

$$\exists \varepsilon^*(x); \quad \varepsilon(x) \geqq \varepsilon^*(x), \text{ for } x \text{ sufficiently large,} \qquad \ldots(7)$$

where $\varepsilon^*(x)$ *in* (6) *satisfies*

either   (A) $\begin{cases} \lim\limits_{x \to +0} \varepsilon^*(x) = 1 \\ \lim\limits_{x \to +0} \left| \left(\dfrac{1}{\varepsilon^*(x)} - 1 \right) + \dfrac{1}{(-\log x)} \right| (-\log x)^{\lambda} = \gamma, \quad (0 \leqq \gamma < +\infty), \quad \lambda > 1, \end{cases}$

or   (B) $\begin{cases} \dfrac{1}{\varepsilon^*(x)} > 1 + \dfrac{1}{\log x} \\ \lim\limits_{x \to +0} \left| \left(\dfrac{1}{\varepsilon^*(x)} - 1 \right) \right| (-\log x) = \gamma - 1, \qquad (0 \lneqq \gamma \leqq +\infty), \end{cases}$

and $\varepsilon^*(x)$ *in* (7) *satisfies*

either   (A) $\begin{cases} \lim\limits_{x \to +\infty} \varepsilon^*(x) = 1 \\ \lim\limits_{x \to +\infty} \left| \left(\dfrac{1}{\varepsilon^*} - 1 \right) - \dfrac{1}{\log x} \right| (\log x)^{\lambda} = \gamma, \quad (0 \leqq \gamma < +\infty), \quad \lambda > 1, \end{cases}$

or   (B) $\begin{cases} \dfrac{1}{\varepsilon^*} < 1 + \dfrac{1}{\log x} \\ \lim\limits_{x \to +\infty} \left| \left(\dfrac{1}{\varepsilon^*} - 1 \right) \right| (\log x) = \gamma - 1, \qquad (0 \lneqq \gamma \leqq +\infty). \end{cases}$

Proof (outline). As space is limited, I shall simply outline the necessary steps of the proof.

(i) Write $f(x) = \dfrac{Y}{K}$ in terms of $\varepsilon(x)$ as,

$$f(x) = C \exp \int_{x_0}^{x} \frac{v(x)}{x} \, dx, \quad C > 0, \quad x_0 > 0, \qquad \ldots(8)$$

where $v(x) = \dfrac{1}{1 + \dfrac{B}{x} \exp \displaystyle\int_{x_0}^{x} \dfrac{dx}{x\varepsilon(x)}}$, $B > 0$, and $\varepsilon(x) = \dfrac{f'(x)[f(x) - xf'(x)]}{-xf(x) \cdot f''(x)}$.

(ii) In order to prove the equality part of (6): $\varepsilon(x) = \varepsilon^*(x)$, set

$$\lim_{x \to +0} \int_{x}^{x_0} \frac{v(x)}{x} \, dx = +\infty. \qquad \ldots(9)$$

In view of a logarithmic test of convergence ([2], pp. 341-380 and pp. 417-419), the above is satisfied if,

$$\lim_{x \to +0} \frac{1}{v(x)} \Big/ (-\log x) = \bar{p}; \; 0 \leqq \bar{p} < +\infty. \qquad \ldots(10)$$

Using the definition of $v(x)$, (10) can be reduced to

$$\lim_{x \to +0} \left\{ \frac{1}{x(-\log x)} \exp \int_{x_0}^{x} \frac{dx}{x\varepsilon^*(x)} \right\} = p = \frac{\bar{p}}{B}, \; 0 \leqq p < +\infty. \qquad \ldots(11)$$

(iii) Apply the L'Hospital rule to (11) to obtain

$$\lim_{x \to +0} \frac{(-\log x) \cdot \frac{1}{\varepsilon^*(x)}}{(-\log x) - 1} \lim_{x \to +0} \frac{1}{x(-\log x)} \exp \int_{x_0}^{x} \frac{dx}{x\varepsilon^*(x)} = p.$$

The above condition is satisfied if

$$\lim_{x \to +0} \frac{1}{\varepsilon^*(x)} \cdot p = p, \quad (0 \le p < +\infty). \qquad \qquad ...(12)$$

Thus we have two cases: (1) $\lim_{x \to +0} \varepsilon^*(x) = 1$ and $p \ne 0$; (2) $p = 0$.

(iv) Using (11), reduce the first case further to get

$$\lim_{x \to +0} \left\{ \int_{x_0}^{x} \frac{1}{x} \left[\left(\frac{1}{\varepsilon^*} - 1 \right) + \frac{1}{(-\log x)} \right] dx \right\} = \tau, \quad \tau \ne \pm \infty, \qquad ...(13)$$

where $\tau = \log p + \log x_0 + \log(-\log x_0)$. It is known ([2], p. 418) that (13) will be satisfied if

$$\lim_{x \to +0} \left| \left(\frac{1}{\varepsilon^*(x)} - 1 \right) + \frac{1}{(-\log x)} \right| (-\log x)^\lambda = \gamma, \quad (0 \le \gamma < +\infty, \lambda > 1). \qquad ...(14)$$

Equations (12) and (14) imply the sufficient condition for (A) in the theorem.

(v) In the same way, reduce the second case, $p = 0$, to the condition

$$\lim_{x \to +0} \left\{ \int_{x}^{x_0} \frac{1}{x} \left[\left(\frac{1}{\varepsilon^*} - 1 \right) + \frac{1}{(-\log x)} \right] dx \right\} = +\infty. \qquad ...(15a)$$

The above will be met if

$$\frac{1}{\varepsilon^*} > 1 + \frac{1}{\log x} \quad \text{and} \quad \lim_{x \to +0} \left| \left(\frac{1}{\varepsilon^*} - 1 \right) \right| (-\log x) = \gamma - 1, \quad (0 < \gamma \le +\infty), \qquad ...(15b)$$

which proves the second part (B) in the theorem.

(vi) For the inequality part of (6), $\varepsilon(x) < \varepsilon^*$, use equation (8) and choose x_0 such that $\varepsilon(x) < \varepsilon^*$ for $x \le x_0$. Then, for

$$z \le x_0, \ H[\varepsilon(z)] = B \exp \left[\int_{x_0}^{z} \frac{dt}{t\varepsilon(t)} \right] < H[\varepsilon^*(z)],$$

and also

$$\int_{x_0}^{x} \frac{v[\varepsilon(z)]}{z} dz = \int_{x_0}^{x} \frac{dz}{z + H[\varepsilon(z)]} < \int_{x_0}^{x} \frac{dz}{z + H[\varepsilon^*(z)]}.$$

Hence, we have

$$f[\varepsilon(x)] < f[\varepsilon^*(x)]. \qquad \qquad ...(16)$$

The right-hand side of this expression goes to zero when $x \to +0$, i.e.

$$0 \le \lim_{x \to +0} f[\varepsilon(x)] < \lim_{x \to +0} f[\varepsilon^*(x)] = 0, \quad {}^\forall \varepsilon(x) < \varepsilon^*(x). \qquad ...(17)$$

(vii) As a final step, apply a similar argument to the condition $\lim_{x \to +\infty} f(x) = +\infty$ in order to obtain $\varepsilon(x)$ which satisfies (7) in the theorem.

3. The above theorem should be interpreted with care. I shall make the following observations:

(i) The existence of limits of $\varepsilon(x)$ as $x \to +0$ and $x \to +\infty$ are *not* required. Consider the function $\varepsilon(x) = \dfrac{1}{2} + \dfrac{1}{3}\sin\dfrac{1}{x}$. $\varepsilon(x)$ has no limit as $x \to +0$, but $\varepsilon(x) < \varepsilon^*$ and hence this function satisfies the theorem.

(ii) The most general $\varepsilon^*(x)$ function that I can find thus far which satisfies the theorem is

$$\varepsilon^*(x) = \cfrac{1}{1 + \cfrac{1}{\log x}} + 0(x). \qquad \qquad ...(18)$$

In particular, if

$$\varepsilon^*(x) = \cfrac{1}{1 + \cfrac{1}{\log x}}, \qquad \qquad ...(19)$$

then the production function is

$$f(x) = \left(A + \frac{B}{C}\log x\right)^{\frac{1}{B}}, \quad \begin{array}{l} A > 0,\ C > 0 \\ B < 0 \text{ for } x \text{ small} \\ B > 0 \text{ for } x \text{ large} \\ B \to 0 \text{ for all } x > 0 \text{ (Cobb-Douglas).} \end{array} \qquad ...(20)$$

(iii) When $\varepsilon^*(x) = \cfrac{1}{1 + \cfrac{a}{\log x}}$ and $a > 1$, it does not satisfy the theorem. The counter-example to Guha's theorem that I have used in equation (1) belongs to this class of $\varepsilon^*(x)$.

(iv) As a corollary to our theorem, we can formulate a theorem similar to Guha's.

Corollary : *A neo-classical growth system with a given s, $0 < s < 1$, and a given $n \geq 0$, will converge to the balanced growth rate if :*

$$\varepsilon(r) \leq 1, \text{ for sufficiently large } \frac{K}{L} = r, \qquad \qquad ...(21)$$

and

$$\varepsilon(r) \geq 1, \text{ for sufficiently small } \frac{K}{L} = r. \qquad \qquad ...(22)$$

Proof. This is a special case of the above theorem: i.e. $\varepsilon^*(x) = 1$. Q.E.D.

(v) As I have proved elsewhere [4], if we set up the conditions that $\lim\limits_{x \to +0} v(x) = a$, $0 < a < 1$ and $\lim\limits_{x \to +\infty} v(x) = b$, $0 < b < 1$ ($v(x) =$ labour's share), then the above theorem is automatically satisfied. Also, $\lim\limits_{x \to +0} \varepsilon(x) < 1$ and $\lim\limits_{x \to +\infty} \varepsilon(x) > 1$ satisfy the requirements.

(vi) From the above remarks we can provide a correct interpretation of Guha's theorem, which is as follows:

"If $\lim\limits_{x \to +0} \varepsilon \leq 1^-$ and $\lim\limits_{x \to +\infty} \geq 1^+$,

the neo-classical growth model of the Solow-Swan type will converge to an equilibrium where capital and labour both grow at the common rate n, provided only that $n \geq 0$."

4. K. Inada ([3], p. 120) formulates so-called derivative conditions as a sufficient condition for the existence of an equilibrium path in the two-sector growth model. He also shows that these conditions are sufficient for the existence and stability of an equilibrium

growth rate in the one-sector growth model of the Solow-Swan type. The derivative conditions are:

$$\lim_{x \to +0} f'(x) = +\infty \qquad \qquad ...(23)$$

and

$$\lim_{x \to +\infty} f'(x) = 0. \qquad \qquad ...(24)$$

In addition to the above conditions, Inada assumes that

$$\begin{cases} f(x)>0, \ f'(x)>0, \ f''(x)<0, \ ^\forall x \in I(0, \infty), \ \text{and} \\ \lim_{x \to +0} f(x) = 0, \ \lim_{x \to +\infty} f(x) = +\infty. \end{cases} \qquad ...(25)$$

Since, as shown by equations (4) and (5), a sufficient condition for the stability of the one-sector growth model requires only (25), it is obvious that the derivative conditions are more than sufficient for stability of the one-sector model. Hence, our main theorem is more general than Inada's derivative conditions. The derivative conditions are essentially for the two-sector model.[1]

Brown University   R. SATO.

REFERENCES

[1] Guha, Ashok. " Scarcity of Specific Resources as a Limit to Output ", *Review of Economic Studies*, **30**, (1963).

[2] Hardy, G. H. *A Course of Pure Mathematics*, 7th ed. (London, 1938).

[3] Inada, Ken-ichi. " On a Two-Sector Model of Economic Growth: Comments and a Generalization ", *Review of Economic Studies*, **30**, (1963).

[4] Sato, Ryuzo. " Some Theorems on the Asymptotic Properties of Production Functions and their Applications ", presented at the 1966 Econometric Society Meetings.

[5] MacRae, Duncan. " A Small Country in a Large World ", presented at the Harvard-MIT Mathematical Economics Seminar, 1965.

[1] It may be of interest to formulate the derivative conditions in terms of the elasticity of factor substitution. Using

$$v(x) = \frac{xf'(x)}{f(x)}, \frac{1}{f'(x)} = \frac{x}{f(x)} + \frac{B}{f(x)} \exp \int_{x_0}^{x} \frac{dx}{x\varepsilon(x)}.$$

For $\lim_{x \to +0} f'(x) = +\infty$, we must have

$$\lim_{x \to +0} \frac{1}{f'(x)} = \lim_{x \to +0} \left[\frac{x}{f(x)} + \frac{B}{f(x)} \exp \int_{x_0}^{x} \frac{dx}{x\varepsilon(x)} \right] = 0.$$

Using the L'Hospital rule, the above may be reduced to

$$\lim_{x \to +0} \frac{1}{f'(x)} = \lim_{x \to +0} \left[\frac{1}{f'(x)} + \frac{B \frac{1}{x\varepsilon(x)} \exp \int_{x_0}^{x} \frac{dx}{x\varepsilon(x)}}{f'(x)} \right] = 0.$$

The results of somewhat involved computations show that a sufficient condition for a derivative condition, $\lim_{x \to +0} f'(x) = +\infty$, requires that $\lim_{x \to +0} [\varepsilon(x) + x \varepsilon'(x)] = 1$.

In the same way, we can find the condition for $\lim_{x \to +\infty} f'(x) = 0$. I will leave the computation to the reader.

10

Reprinted from JOURNAL OF ECONOMIC THEORY
All Rights Reserved by Academic Press, New York and London

Vol. 2, No. 1, March 1970
Printed in Belgium

A Further Note on a Difference Equation Recurring in Growth Theory

RYUZO SATO*

Department of Economics, Brown University
Providence, Rhode Island 02912

Received: October 8, 1969; Revised January, 1970.

In the recent issue of this Journal (June, 1969), Knut Sydsaeter [11] makes some interesting observations on the characteristic roots of a difference equation recurring in many branches of modern economic growth theory (see, e.g., Domar [2, 3], Neisser [9], Hicks [5], Johansen [6], Beckmann [1]). The difference equation under investigation is

$$z_t - (a_1 z_{t-1} + a_2 z_{t-2} + \cdots + a_n z_{t-n}) = 0, \tag{1}$$

and the characteristic equation corresponding to (1) is

$$x^n - (a_1 x^{n-1} + a_2 x^{n-2} + \cdots + a_n) = 0 \tag{2}$$

where $a_i \geqslant 0$ for $1 \leqslant i \leqslant n$.

It is well-known that Eq. (2) for $a_i \geqslant 0$ has a simple positive root, ρ, with the largest modulus and that this root lies between 1 and $A = \sum_{i=1}^{n} a_i$. (See, e.g., [1, 5, 11].) This largest root and its relation to the other $(n - 1)$ roots of Eq. (2) will determine the growth process of the difference equation. The following theorem summarizes Sydsaeter's analysis on the other $(n - 1)$ roots.

THEOREM 1.

The characteristic equation (2) *under the condition*

$$a_1 > a_2 > \cdots > a_n > 0 \tag{3}$$

or under the condition

$$a_i = a > 0, \qquad 1 \leqslant i \leqslant n \tag{4}$$

* This work was partially supported by the National Science Foundation. The author wishes to thank Martin J. Beckmann and the editor and the referee of this Journal for their useful comments.

has at least $(n - 1)$ *roots in the interior of the unit circle. Consequently, the cyclical components in the solution of the corresponding difference equation* (1) *under either the condition* (3) *or* (4), *are damped.*

However, as noted [11, p. 106], Sydsaeter has *not* proved that all $(n - 1)$ roots are in the interior of the unit circle in the case where the coefficients satisfy the relation,

$$a_1 \geqslant a_2 \geqslant \cdots \geqslant a_n > 0, \tag{5}$$

with some, but not all the a_i's equal.

In many practical cases, one cannot *a priori* set the condition that the a_i's are nonincreasing. For instance, if the a_i's represent the net returns on an investment project at the time t $(=i)$, then a_i's can take any non-negative values—it can even take negative values for some i. (See Beckmann [1, p. 34].) (A plantation of fruit trees or coffee trees may be a case in point.) Thus, it will be useful to study Sydsaeter's problem under more realistic and more general conditions.

The purpose of this note is to derive several useful theorems which are more general than the results given in Sydsaeter's paper (his results being a special case), and to show that the growth process represented by the difference equation (1) can generate a stable exponential path under more general assumptions. Also, as a special case of a theorem, it will be shown that all $(n - 1)$ roots of (2) are in the interior of the unit circle in the case where the coefficients satisfy (5), with some, but not all the a_i's equal.

We first prove the following lemma:

LEMMA 1   (Kakeya's Theorem [7][1]).

(1) *If the coefficients* b_i $(0 \leqslant i \leqslant m)$ *of the polynomial,*

$$f(x) = b_0 x^m + b_1 x^{m-1} + \cdots + b_{m-1} x + b_m = 0, \qquad b_0 = 1, \tag{6}$$

satisfy the condition,

$$b_0 > b_1 > b_2 > \cdots > b_m > 0, \tag{7}$$

then the moduli of all the roots of (6) *are less than unity, i.e.,*

$$|\beta_j| < 1 \qquad (1 \leqslant j \leqslant m). \tag{8}$$

---

[1] Kakeya's Theorem [7] was published in *Tôhoku Mathematical Journal* (Japan, 1912), but sometimes it is referred to as the Eneström–Kakeya Theorem (see, e.g., Marden [8, p. 106, Exercise 1]), since G. Eneström [4] had already shown in a Swedish article of 1893, whose French translation appeared also in *Tôhoku Mathematical Journal* (1920), that when b_i satisfy condition (7), the moduli of the roots of (6) lie between the maximum and minimum values of b_i/b_{i-1}, i.e., $\min (b_i/b_{i-1}) < |\beta_j| < \max (b_i/b_{i-1})$, $(1 \leqslant i, j \leqslant m)$. For an economic application of Kakeya's Theorem, see Beckmann [1, p. 41].

(2) *If the coefficients b_i satisfy the condition*

$$b_0 \geqslant b_1 \geqslant b_2 \geqslant \cdots \geqslant b_m > 0, \tag{7'}$$

then the moduli of all the roots of (6) do not exceed unity,[2] i.e.,

$$|\beta_j| \leqslant 1 \qquad (1 \leqslant j \leqslant m). \tag{8'}$$

Proof. We use the properties of a nonnegative matrix. In view of Descartes' rule, Eq. (6), under condition (7), has no roots which are real and positive. Thus, the equation

$$(x - 1) \sum_{i=0}^{m} b_i x^{m-i} = 0, \quad b_0 = 1, \quad b_i > b_{i+1}, \qquad (0 \leqslant i \leqslant m - 1) \tag{9}$$

has only one positive real root equal to unity. The remaining m roots of (9) are the same as those of (6). Let c_i be equal to

$$c_i = \begin{cases} b_i - b_{i+1} & (0 \leqslant i \leqslant m - 1) \\ b_m & (i = m). \end{cases} \tag{10}$$

Then by condition (7)

$$c_i > 0.$$

Using c_i, Eq. (9) can be written as

$$x^{m+1} - \sum_{i=0}^{m} c_i x^{m-i} = 0. \tag{9'}$$

Define the companion matrix of (9') as

$$B = \begin{bmatrix} 0 & 1 & 0 & & 0 \\ 0 & 0 & 1 & & 0 \\ \vdots & \vdots & \vdots & & \vdots \\ & & & & 1 \\ c_m & c_{m-1} & c_{m-2} & \cdots & c_0 \end{bmatrix}, \qquad B \geqslant 0.$$

The roots of (9) or (9') are the same as the characteristic roots of B. Since B is a nonnegative, indecomposable (or irreducible), and primitive matrix (at least one diagonal element being positive), it has a positive root

---

[2] It is easy to show that if the coefficients b_i satisfy the condition $0 < b_0 < b_1 < \cdots < b_m$, then the roots are greater than unity in absolute value, i.e., $|\beta_j| > 1$, and also if b_i satisfy the condition $0 < b_0 < b_1 < \cdots < b_m$, then $|\beta_j| > 1$ for $1 < j < m$.

which is simple and is greater than any other root of B in absolute value (the Perron–Frobenius theorem). In Eq. (9), the largest simple positive root is unity and, hence, all the other roots of B, which are the roots of (6), are less than unity in absolute value.

If, instead, the coefficients b_i satisfy (7'), then B may no longer be primitive and, hence, $|\beta_j|$ may be equal to the largest root, i.e., $|\beta_j| \leqslant 1$.

Q.E.D.

Going back to Eq. (2), we can now derive a more general theorem using the above lemma. Since Eq. (2) has the largest simple positive root, say ρ, by factoring out the term $(x - \rho)$ we can rewrite (2) in the form of

$$(x - \rho)(b_0 x^{n-1} + b_1 x^{n-2} + \cdots + b_{n-2} x + b_{n-1}) = 0, \quad b_0 = 1 \quad (2')$$

where the coefficients of the two equations, a_i's and b_i's, are related as $a_{i+1} = \rho b_1 - b_{i+1}$ $(0 \leqslant i \leqslant n - 1)$. The left-hand side of this *reduced* equation (2') is identical with that of the *original* equation (2) and, hence, Eqs. (2) and (2') have the same roots. Thus, we can obtain the conditions of the roots of the original equation (2) by studying the roots of the *reduced* equation (2').

THEOREM 2. *By factoring out the term $(x - \rho)$, Eq. (2),*

$$x^n - (a_1 x^{n-1} + a_2 x^{n-2} + \cdots + a_n) = 0 \tag{2}$$

can always be reduced to (2')

$$(x - \rho)(b_0 x^{n-1} + b_1 x^{n-2} + \cdots + b_{n-2} x + b_{n-1}) = 0, \quad b_0 = 1 \quad (2')$$

where ρ is the greatest simple positive root of (2) and the coefficients of the two equations, a_i's and b_i's, are related as

$$a_{i+1} = \rho b_i - b_{i+1}, \quad \rho > 0, \quad (0 \leqslant i \leqslant n - 1). \tag{11}$$

The equation (2) $(a_i \geqslant 0)$ has at least $(n - 1)$ roots in the interior of the unit circle if the coefficients of the reduced equation (2') satisfy:

(i) $b_i > 0,$ $(0 \leqslant i \leqslant n - 1)$ \hfill (12)

(ii) $b_i > b_{i+1},$ $(0 \leqslant i \leqslant n - 2).$ \hfill (13)

Hence, the cyclical components in the solution of the corresponding difference equation under the conditions (12) and (13) are damped.

Proof. We assume that some a_i's are positive such that the largest real root ρ is positive. Otherwise, the problem becomes trivial when $\rho = 0$.[3] It can be seen from the assumptions (12) and (13) that the coefficients of the reduced equation (2′), i.e., b_i's of $f(x) = \sum_{i=0}^{n-1} b_i x^{n-i-1} = 0$, satisfy Lemma 1 (Kakeya's Theorem) when $n - 1$ is equal to m, and, hence, at least $(n - 1)$ roots of equation (2) have the moduli less than unity. Q.E.D.

As a special case of Theorem 2, we can derive the results given in Sydsaeter's paper. Using relationship (11), we can write the b_i's as,

$$b_i = \frac{\sum_{k=i}^{n-1} \rho^{n-k-1} a_{k+1}}{\rho^{n-i}}, \qquad 0 \leqslant i \leqslant n - 1,$$

and, hence, $(b_i - b_{i+1})$ will be equal to

$$b_i - b_{i+1} = \frac{\sum_{k=i}^{n-1} \rho^{n-k-1}(a_{k+1} - a_{k+2})}{\rho^{n-i}}, \qquad 0 \leqslant i \leqslant n - 2, \quad (a_{n+1} = 0).$$
$$(13')$$

Then, we have,

COROLLARY 1.

(= *Theorem* 1).

Proof. If the condition (3) is met, each term in the numerator of (13′) will be positive, as seen from,

$$(a_{k+1} - a_{k+2}) > 0, \qquad (0 \leqslant k \leqslant n - 1).$$

Also if condition (4) is met, then $(a_{k+1} - a_{k+2})$ will be zero for $0 \leqslant k \leqslant n - 2$, but since the last term a_n is positive, (13′) will be positive. Hence, Theorem 2 is automatically satisfied under either the condition (3) or (4). Q.E.D.

In the case where some, but not all the a_i's are equal, $b_i - b_{i+1}$ will still be all positive and, hence, we have

---

[3] If the companion matrix of (2) is indecomposable, then ρ will be positive. An $n \times n$ matrix is indecomposable if there exists no $n \times n$ permutation matrix P such that

$$PAP^T = \begin{bmatrix} A_{11} & 0 \\ A_{21} & A_{22} \end{bmatrix}$$

where A_{11} and A_{22} are square nonvoid submatrices. Otherwise, A is called decomposable and, if $A_{21} = 0$, completely decomposable.

COROLLARY 2.

If the coefficients a_i of Eq. (2) satisfy the condition,

$$a_1 \geqslant a_2 \geqslant \cdots \geqslant a_n > 0 \tag{5}$$

with some, but not all the a_i's equal, then at least $(n-1)$ roots of (2) lie in the interior of the unit circle.

Theorem 2 does not require the condition that

$$a_i - a_{i+1} \geqslant 0.$$

Consider, as examples, the following two equations:

$$x^3 - (1.1x^2 + 1.14x + 1.32) = (x-2)(x^2 + 0.9x + 0.66) = 0 \tag{14.i}$$

$$a_i - a_{i+1} < 0 \qquad \text{for all} \quad 1 \leqslant i \leqslant 2,$$

and

$$x^3 - (1.1x^2 + 1.3x + 1) = (x-2)(x^2 + 0.9x + 0.5) = 0 \tag{14.ii}$$

$$a_1 - a_2 < 0, \qquad a_2 - a_3 > 0.$$

These equations do not satisfy Theorem 1 nor Corollary 2 but their $(n-1)$ roots (in this case each two roots) are in the interior of the unit circle, since these equations satisfy Theorem 2.

Since the coefficients b_i of equation (2') are nonnegative as long as the a_i's of the original equation (2) are nonnegative, this may be as far as one can carry the analysis under the condition $a_i \geqslant 0$. However, as mentioned earlier, the coefficients a_i of Eq. (2) need not be nonnegative. Sometimes we encounter the situation in which some a_i's are negative. For instance, if a_i represents the return after wages on an investment project at time $t = i$, the net returns for several initial periods may be negative, followed by positive returns for some time and again negative thereafter (Beckmann [1, p. 34]). Even under these conditions, it is conceivable for Eq. (2) to have a simple positive real root with the largest modulus, ρ. If there exists such a root, then Theorem 2 may perhaps be applied in certain cases.

If, for instance, the coefficients a_i are such that the companion matrix of Eq. (2) is a power-positive matrix of odd exponent, then there *always* exists a simple positive real root with the largest modulus. (See Sato [10].)[4] That is to say, if A satisfies the condition:

$$A^q > 0, \qquad q = \text{odd integer,}$$

[4] See R. Sato [10] for comprehensive analyses of power-positive and related matrices and their applications to economic dynamics. Theorem 2 is extended to cover the case of a power-positive matrix.

where

$$A = \begin{bmatrix} 0 & 1 & 0 & \cdots & 0 \\ 0 & 0 & 1 & \cdots & 0 \\ \vdots & \vdots & \vdots & & \vdots \\ & & & & 1 \\ a_n & a_{n-1} & a_{n-2} & \cdots & a_1 \end{bmatrix},$$

then there exists ρ such that $\rho > |\alpha_j|$.

As a matter of fact, as long as there exist transformations (11) in Theorem 2, such that

$$a_{i+1} = \rho b_i - b_{i+1}, \qquad \rho \geqslant |\alpha_j|, \tag{11}$$

then neither a_i nor b_i need be all nonnegative, for one can provide a still more general theorem.[5] [For example, if (11) is satisfied together with the condition $|b_0| > \sum_{i=1}^{n-1} |b_i|$, then Eq. (2) has $(n-1)$ roots less than unity in absolute value.] However, if one pushes the analysis still further, the resulting theorems will become too complicated for practical applications.

REFERENCES

1. M. J. BECKMANN, Capital and interest in a one-commodity world with unlimited labor, *Econ. Stud. Quart.* **17** (1966), 33–44.
2. E. D. DOMAR, Depreciation, replacement and growth, *Econ. J.* **63** (1953), 1–32.
3. E. D. DOMAR, Depreciation, replacement and growth—and fluctuations, *Econ. J.* **67** (1957), 655–658.
4. G. ENESTRÖM, Remarque sur un théorème relatif aux racines de l'équation $a_n x^n + \cdots + a_0 = 0$ où tous les coefficients sont réel et positifs, *Tôhoku Math. J.* **18** (1920), 34–36. (Translation of a Swedish article of 1893.)
5. J. R. HICKS, "A Contribution to the Theory of Trade Cycle," pp. 171–198, Oxford Univ. Press, London/New York, 1950.
6. L. JOHANSEN, Some theoretical properties of a two-sector model of optimal growth, *Rev. Econ. Stud.* **34** (1967), 125–142.

[5] We have taken for granted that one is interested in *absolute* stability of growth processes, but sometimes in growth theory one's interest lies only in *asymptotic* (or *relative*) stability (see Beckmann [1]). In this case the existence of a root ρ such that $\rho > |\alpha_j|$ is necessary and sufficient for relative stability. (If a_i satisfy the condition of a power-positive matrix with odd exponent, then relative stability is always guaranteed.) Also, if one is interested in the damping of only *cyclical* components, then a sufficient condition is that

$$\max (a_{i+1}/a_i) < 1, \, a_i > 0 \quad (1 \leqslant i \leqslant n-1),$$

for the moduli of complex roots of Eq. (2) are less than the greatest of the quotients, a_{i+1}/a_i.

7. Sôichi Kakeya, On the limits of the roots of an algebraic equation with positive coefficients, *Tôhoku Math. J.* **2** (1912–1913), 140–142.
8. M. Marden, "The Geometry of the Zeros of a Polynomial in a Complex Variable," Mathematical Survey No. III, *Amer. Math. Soc.* Providence, R.I., 1949.
9. H. Neisser, Depreciation, replacement and regular growth, *Econ. J.* **65** (1955), 159–161.
10. R. Sato, On the stability properties of dynamic economic systems, Presented at the 1969 Winter Econometric Society Meetings in New York.
11. K. Sydsaeter, Note on a difference equation occurring in growth theory, *J. Econ. Th.* **1** (1969), 104–106.

PRINTED IN BELGIUM BY THE ST. CATHERINE PRESS, TEMPELHOF, 37, BRUGES, LTD.

PART TWO

TECHNICAL CHANGE

[11]

Neutral Inventions and Production Functions[1]

1. Technical progress plays a crucial part in the process of economic growth, and its analysis occupies a central place in contemporary growth models (cf. e.g. v. Weizsäcker [15]). In one general and widely used approach, technology appears as a parameter of the neo-classical production function. Assume as usual that there are two productive factors, capital K and labour L, and one output Y which is subject to the following linear homogeneous production function:

$$Y = F(K, L, t) \qquad \qquad ...(1)$$

where t denotes time, or alternatively, an index of the state of technology.

However, in this form, the role of technology is much too general to permit a thorough-going analysis. It is essential to specify the way in which technology enters the production function. The usual procedure has been to formulate certain hypotheses concerning the way in which technical progress has affected certain important variables that are derived from the production function. These variables include: (1) the capital-output ratio; (2) the output per man; (3) the factor proportions; (4) the marginal productivities; and (5) the marginal rate of substitution. Thus one might postulate that technical progress has affected any one of these characteristics in a predetermined way; for instance that it has left a certain variable invariant. However, since these variables will depend not only on technology but also on input proportions, it is necessary to neutralize the effect of any changes in inputs. Thus one arrives at one famous criterion of so-called technical neutrality, that technical progress is neutral—in the sense of Hicks—if the marginal rate of substitution is invariant under technical change as long as the factor proportions are unchanging. By contrast technical progress is called Harrod neutral whenever the capital-output ratio is unchanging as long as the interest rate does not change.

The implications of the two types of technical progress are well-known and indeed far reaching (Uzawa [14]). If we intend to clarify the nature of the specification of technical change, the following three questions deserve close examination.

(1) Are there alternative ways of describing—and hopefully of justifying theoretically —the known types of technical progress? We might include among the known types purely capital augmenting progress and also a combination of Hicks and Harrod neutrality, the so-called factor augmenting technical progress.

(2) Are there any other economic variables which might be considered to be invariant under technical change, such as the elasticities of output with respect to an input or the elasticity of factor substitution? Or are there any other meaningful combinations of the usual variables considered so far?

(3) As a result of alternative specifications, how many pure types of technical progress can be distinguished, and what is their functional form? An answer to a very special case is given by Uzawa [14] for Harrod and Hicks neutrality.

[1] The authors wish to express their appreciation to Robert Solow, Hirofumi Uzawa, the members of the Harvard-MIT Mathematical Economics Seminar and the referees of this *Review* for their constructive criticisms. We should also like to acknowledge the assistance of Mr L. Weinert of the University of Bonn who carried out the statistical regression.

Another purpose in setting up alternative specifications of technical change is, of course, to obtain hypotheses about technical change which might be tested and (in all but a few cases) refuted. The critical nature of technical progress requires that a theoretical analysis be made of the principal ways in which the functional relation between output, input, and technical progress can be specified. Suppose one wishes to analyze the long-run behaviour of some crucial economic variable, such as the return to capital, the wage rate, or their ratios in terms of other variables; then what variables should be selected depends on the type of technical progress one has postulated. For instance if we assume Harrod neutrality, then the major variable that would explain the return to capital must be the capital-output ratio; moreover *t* which refers to the state of technology should not be included among the explanatory variables—by definition. Contrariwise if technical progress is Hicks neutral, then the long-run behaviour of the ratio of marginal productivities, that is the marginal rate of substitution, should be dependent only on the capital-labour ratio and not on time. Suppose, however, that tests show that the marginal rate of substitution is better correlated with some other variable and/or with time, what should then be our conclusion as to the way in which technology enters into the production function? The object of this paper is to explore all possible hypotheses and to classify the resulting types of relationship. Following the usage of Harrod and Hicks, we shall label these classes as types of " technical neutrality ".

In section 3 Hicks and Harrod neutrality are re-examined. Section 4 introduces capital augmenting, "Solow" neutrality, and some extensions. Section 5 explores variants of Hicks neutrality, and section 6 introduces new types of neutrality that are based on the elasticity of factor substitution. These production functions which contain two parameters of technical progress are particularly interesting for econometric analysis. In section 7 factor augmenting progress is obtained, and section 8 shows that sometimes neutrality implies that there is no technical progress at all. Section 9 presents a table of all the types of technical progress discovered so far. Section 10 finally presents a summary of some econometric evidence from the United States, Japanese, and German data as to the prevailing types of technical progress. In this way, the paper will re-examine the justification for the so-called impossibility theorem, which asserts that it is impossible to estimate both the efficiencies of capital and labour and the form of the production function at the same time. Against this we shall set our own " possibility theorem " stating that it can be done using our broader framework, viz., one which also justifies factor augmenting technical progress.

2. Define the output-capital ratio $Y/K = y$, the labour-capital ratio $L/K = x$, the output-labour ratio $Y/L = z = y/x$, and the capital-labour ratio $K/L = k = 1/x$, then

$$y = f(x, t) \qquad \text{...(2)}$$

$$z = \phi(k, t) \qquad \text{...(3)}$$

where $f(x, t) = F(1, L/K, t)$ and $\phi(k, t) = F(K/L, 1, t)$. The marginal productivities of capital and labour, $\partial F/\partial K = r$ and $\partial F/\partial L = w$, are respectively written as,

$$r = f - x f_x = \phi_k \qquad \text{...(4)}$$

and

$$w = \phi - k \phi_k = f_x. \qquad \text{...(5)}$$

We further assume that the marginal productivities of both factors are positive and the marginal rate of substitution is diminishing:

$$f_x > 0 \quad \phi_k > 0 \qquad \text{...(6)}$$

and

$$f_{xx} < 0 \quad \phi_{kk} < 0. \qquad \text{...(7)}$$

3. We shall start with a considerably simplified proof of Uzawa's results on Hicks neutrality.

NEUTRAL INVENTIONS AND PRODUCTION FUNCTIONS 59

Case I. *Hicks Neutrality.* Inventions are classified as Hicks neutral if the marginal rate of substitution between capital and labour remains constant at a constant capital-labour ratio [7]. We interpret this as *technical progress is Hicks neutral if the marginal rate of substitution is independent of technical progress $A(t)$.* Define the marginal rate of substitution between capital and labour as:

$$R(x, t) = r(x, t)/w(x, t). \qquad \text{...(8)}$$

Then Hicks neutrality implies that

$$R(x, t) = \bar{R}(x), \qquad \text{...(9)}$$

and therefore $\partial R(x, t)/\partial t = 0$. Since $\bar{R}(x) = \dfrac{f - xf_x}{f_x} = \dfrac{f}{f_x} - x$ using (4) and (5), we obtain

$\dfrac{\partial f}{f} = \dfrac{\partial x}{\bar{R}(x) + x}$. Integrating with respect to f and x we get

$$\log f(x, t) - \log A(t) = \int \frac{\partial x}{\bar{R}(x) + x}$$

where $\log A(t)$ is the arbitrary constant arising from integrating $\partial f/f$, which measures the technical progress factor. From this we derive $f(x, t) = A(t) \exp \displaystyle\int \frac{\partial x}{\bar{R}(x) + x}$. If we put

$f(x) = \exp \displaystyle\int \frac{\partial x}{\bar{R}(x) + x}$, then we obtain the following production function which expresses Hicks neutral inventions:

$$f(x, t) = A(t) \cdot f(x),$$

that is

$$F(K, L, t) = A(t)F(K, L), \qquad \text{...(10)}$$

a well-known result.

Case II. *Harrod Neutrality. Inventions are Harrod neutral if the output-capital ratio remains constant at a constant rate of return to capital.* This implies that the rate of interest r is a function of the output-capital ratio y alone: i.e.,

$$r = \psi(y). \qquad \text{...(11)}$$

Using (4) we obtain the differential equation

$$y - xy_x = \psi(y) \qquad \text{...(11a)}$$

which may be " solved " along the same lines to yield the well-known result,

$$F(K, L, t) = F(K, B(t) \cdot L). \qquad \text{...(12)}$$

Upon substitution in (1) it is seen that (12) is also sufficient for Harrod neutrality.

4. This representation of Harrod neutral technical progress suggests an exactly opposite symmetric case, i.e. the " mirror-image ", in which the output-labour ratio is undisturbed at a constant wage rate. We shall call this *Solow Neutrality*, since R. M. Solow [13] first made use of this form of production functions in order to estimate embodied technical progress (cf. also Hahn and Matthews [6, p. 830]).

Case III. *Solow Neutrality. Inventions are Solow Neutral if the output per worker is invariant at a constant wage rate.* Thus,

$$w = \phi(z), \qquad \text{...(13)}$$

i.e., $z - kz_k = \phi(z)$. As in the case of Harrod neutrality, an integration of (13) will give us

$$F(K, L, t) = F(B(t) \cdot K, L). \qquad \text{...(14)}$$

This type of purely capital augmenting progress has been used by Diamond [3] and by Fei and Ranis [4] in their analysis of production in underdeveloped countries: the return to capital is rising while the wage rate and the output per worker remain constant in the early stages of development (cf. also W. A. Lewis [10]). This form of technical progress permits also the aggregation of capital in the presence of embodied technical progress (F. Fisher [5]).

The idea of neutral technical progress may now be extended in a number of ways by letting one economic variable be unaffected by technical change as long as some other variable(s) remain constant. For example, if neutrality requires constancy of the relative shares, then Hicks neutrality satisfies this requirement because these shares are undisturbed at a constant capital-labour ratio. Also, Harrod neutrality satisfies the above requirement since the relative shares are constant at a constant interest rate. Furthermore in the Solow case, the relative shares are constant at a constant wage rate.

Two other cases resemble these, and we shall discuss them: the output-capital ratio is undisturbed at a constant wage rate (Case IV); and the output-labour ratio is undisturbed at a constant interest rate (Case V).

Case IV. *Inventions are neutral in the sense that the output-capital ratio is unaffected at a constant wage rate.* This implies

$$w = y_x = h(y), \qquad \qquad ...(15)$$

whose integral is $y = f(x + C(t))$. Hence the production function has the form

$$F(K, L + C(t)K). \qquad \qquad ...(16)$$

A special case is that of $F(L + C(t)K)$. When capital and labour are perfect substitutes, this production function is also Solow neutral. The function (16) may be interpreted in the following way: labour is no longer an independent factor; since the output-capital ratio is undisturbed at a constant $x + C(t)$, this implies $dx/dt = -dC/dt$. Therefore, at a constant capital-output ratio a decrease in the labour-capital ratio is always compensated by technical advance. This amounts to saying that technical progress is always compensated—though not necessarily stimulated—by technological advance. As one referee has suggested, neutrality of this type is impossible for arbitrary changes in the capital-labour ratio.

Case V. *Inventions are neutral in the sense that the output-labour ratio is invariant at a constant interest rate.* This is the symmetric case to the previous one:

$$r = z_k = g(z), \qquad \qquad ...(17)$$

which yields the production function

$$F(K + C(t) \cdot L, L). \qquad \qquad ...(18)$$

And the same comments apply *mutatis mutandis*. The possibility that technical progress is stimulated by an increase in the labour-capital ratio, is likely to occur only in those underdeveloped countries where labour grows faster than capital.

5. Two cases which we take up in this section are variants of Hicks neutrality since they involve the marginal rate of substitution, but in combination with (1) the output-capital ratio and (2) the output-labour ratio.

Case VI. *Inventions are neutral in the sense that the marginal rate of substitution is undisturbed at a constant output-capital ratio.* (*Anti-Hicks.*) That is

$$r/w = \frac{y}{y_x} - x = \phi(y). \qquad \qquad ...(19)$$

NEUTRAL INVENTIONS AND PRODUCTION FUNCTIONS 61

This differential equation may be solved by changing the variables $\dfrac{\partial x}{\partial y} - \dfrac{1}{y}x = \phi(y)/y$, to

give a solution $x/y = \displaystyle\int \dfrac{\phi(y)}{y^2}\,\partial y + C(t)$. In general it is not possible to write y as an explicit

function of x. But since $x/y = 1/z$, y may be explicitly expressed in terms of $1/z$ as

$$1/z = N(y) + C(t), \text{ or more symmetrically}$$

$$g(K/Y) + L/Y = C(t). \qquad \ldots(20)$$

And $Y = F(K, L, t)$ is the implicit solution of (20).

In the same way if,

Case VII. *Inventions are neutral in the sense that the marginal rate of substitution is unaffected at a constant output-labour ratio*, then

$$w/r = \frac{z}{z_k} - k = \phi(z). \qquad \ldots(21)$$

It turns out that the solution of (21) is identical with (20), which we had labelled Anti-Hicks.

Case VIII. *Inventions are neutral in the sense that the capital-labour ratio remains unchanged as long as the wage rate is constant.* That is, the wage rate is a function of the labour-capital ratio alone,

$$y_x = \phi(x). \qquad \ldots(22)$$

Integration yields at once $y = \Phi(x) + C(t)$ or

$$Y = C(t)K + F(K, L) \qquad \ldots(23)$$

where F does not contain time explicitly. This may be termed the capital additive case. Here technical progress has the form of an extra bonus in proportion to capital stock. In the same way,

Case IX. *Inventions are neutral in the sense that the capital-labour ratio remains unchanged as long as the interest rate is constant.*

$$z_k = \phi(k) \qquad \ldots(24)$$

$$z = \Phi(k) + C(t)$$

$$Y = C(t)L + F(K, L). \qquad \ldots(25)$$

This is the labour additive case where technical progress has the form of a bonus proportional to the employment of labour. Write (25) as

$$\frac{Y}{L} = C(t) + f(K/L). \qquad \ldots(26)$$

It is then demonstrated that, under this type of neutrality, output per man is basically a function of the capital intensity of production K/L, and over time is augmented through an increase in efficiency quite independent of factor use.

Introduce now factor shares (say labour's share β) as a variable to be considered invariant in its relation to the capital-labour, capital-output, and labour-output ratio. It turns out that we then obtain Hicks, Harrod and Solow neutrality again so that this is an alternative characteristic of these principal types.

6. A somewhat different approach to the concept of neutrality is obtained if we use the elasticity of factor prices, or the elasticity of factor substitution itself as a criterion. In empirical studies it is often true [12] that we know something about the long-run value

of the elasticity of substitution; and if neutrality is defined in terms of the elasticity of factor substitution, then this makes possible the formulation of an appropriate production function and the estimation of technical progress.

Case X. *Inventions are neutral in the sense that the elasticity of factor substitution is unaffected at a constant capital-labour ratio.* That is,

$$\sigma(x) = \frac{y_x(y - xy_x)}{-xyy_{xx}}, \quad \partial\sigma(x)/\partial t = 0, \qquad \qquad \ldots(27)$$

where $\sigma(x) = $ the elasticity of factor substitution. In order to integrate the above equation we define $u = y/y_x$, so that

$$\sigma(x) = -\frac{y_x}{xy_{xx}} + \frac{y_x^2}{yy_{xx}} = \frac{u}{x(1 - u_x)} + \frac{1}{1 - u_x}.$$

Now setting $u - x = v$, then $1/x\sigma(x) = v_x/v$, whose integral is

$$\frac{y}{y_x} - x = v = B(t) \cdot \exp\left[\int \frac{\partial \log x}{\sigma(x)}\right]$$

where $B(t) > 0$. Integrating again we get

$$y = A(t) \exp \int_{x_0}^{x} \frac{\partial\eta}{\eta + B(t) \exp\left[\int_{\eta_0}^{\eta} \frac{\partial \log \varepsilon}{\sigma(\varepsilon)}\right]}. \qquad \ldots(28)$$

The production function (28) represents a generalized form of Hicks neutrality; *for Hicks neutrality is sufficient, but not necessary in order that the elasticity of substitution be constant at a constant capital-labour ratio.* When $B(t) = B$, then (28) reduces to the Hicks neutral case.

As an example, consider the case where σ is constant, i.e. $\sigma(x, t) = \bar{\sigma}$. From

$$v = B(t) \exp\left[\frac{1}{\bar{\sigma}} \int \partial \log x\right]$$

we obtain $y(x, t) = A(t)[x^{-\left(\frac{1 - \bar{\sigma}}{\bar{\sigma}}\right)} + B(t)]^{-\left(\frac{\bar{\sigma}}{1 - \bar{\sigma}}\right)}$, which is a CES production function with technical progress in the efficiency parameter A and in the distributive parameter B. When $\bar{\sigma} = 1$, we have [1] $y(x, t) = A(t)x^{\frac{1}{1 + B(t)}}$, yielding a Cobb-Douglas production function where relative shares $\frac{B(t)}{1 + B(t)}$ and $\frac{1}{1 + B(t)}$ are affected by technical progress.

In a similar way a generalized concept of Harrod neutrality can be obtained. That is,

Case XI. *Inventions are neutral in the sense that the elasticity of factor substitution is undisturbed at a constant output-capital ratio* (Generalized Harrod Neutral).

Since σ can be alternatively defined as

$$\sigma(y) = \frac{\partial r/r}{\partial y/y}, \qquad \qquad \ldots(29)$$

we assume that $\sigma = \sigma(y)$ and $\partial\sigma(y)/\partial t = 0$. Integration of (29) gives

$$r = B(t) \exp\left[\int \sigma(y)\partial \log y\right],$$

---

[1] In order for this to be considered a genuine technical progress, we must set the condition, $\partial \log y/\partial t > 0$. Thus, for $y = A(t)x^{\frac{1}{1 + B(t)}}$, the following relation must hold: $\partial \log y/\partial t = \frac{A}{A} - \frac{B}{(1 + B)^2} \log x > 0$.

NEUTRAL INVENTIONS AND PRODUCTION FUNCTIONS 63

and from (11) and (11a) we obtain

$$x = A(t) \exp \left[\int \frac{\partial y}{y - B(t) \exp \left[\int \sigma(y) \partial \log y \right]} \right]. \qquad \ldots(30)$$

Thus, if $B(t) = B =$ constant, we have the Harrod neutral case.
Exactly the same thing can be true for the Solow case.

Case XII.

$$k = A(t) \exp \left[\int \frac{\partial z}{z - B(t) \exp \left[\int \sigma(z) \partial \log z \right]} \right]. \qquad \ldots(31)$$

Notice that (30) and (31) are implicit representations of the production functions involved.

Case XIII. In the same way one can show that when *the elasticity of substitution depends on the marginal rate of substitution*, the production function has the form

$$y = A(t) \exp \int \frac{\partial x}{x + \phi(B(t)x)}. \qquad \ldots(32)$$

7. The so-called impossibility theorem [12] states that technical progress is not identifiable when it appears as a combination of Harrod and Hicks neutrality (the factor augmenting case to be considered as Case XIV below), unless the form of the production function is known, or alternatively, the elasticity of factor substitution is known. The reason given is that there are three unknowns, namely the efficiencies of capital and labour as well as the elasticity of factor substitution, while there are only two independent equations. However, if we are willing to assume Case X (or XI or XII) it follows by definition that the elasticity of factor substitution may be estimated independently from the capital-labour ratio (or the output-capital ratio, or output-labour ratio).

Consider finally the possibility that the elasticity of substitution depends only on factor shares.

Case XIV. *Inventions are neutral in the sense that the elasticity of substitution remains unchanged as long as the income shares of factors are constant (Factor Augmenting Technical Progress).*

$$\partial \log \left(\frac{y - xy_x}{y_x} \right) \Big/ \partial \log x = \phi(xy_x/y). \qquad \ldots(33)$$

Letting $xy_x/y = u$ we have $x \dfrac{\partial}{\partial x} \log \left[x \left(\dfrac{1}{u} - 1 \right) \right] = \phi(u)$. From this we obtain $\partial x/x = \partial u/\phi(u)$

which yields $\log x + \log B(t) = g(u)$, or $u = G(B(t)x)$.

In view of (33)

$$xy_x/y = G(B(t)x),$$

$$\int \frac{\partial y}{y} = \int \frac{\partial x}{xG(B(t)x)},$$

$$y = A(t) \exp \int^x \frac{B(t)\partial v}{B(t)vG(B(t)v)}.$$

Substituting $B(t)v = s$ we obtain

$$y = A(t) \exp \int^{B(t)x} \frac{\partial s}{sG(s)}$$

(where the integration is carried out at constant t),

$$y = A(t)f(B(t)x) \text{ so that}$$

$$Y = F(A(t)K, A(t)B(t)L). \qquad \ldots(34)$$

This is the case of factor augmenting technical progress. For an alternative but more involved characterization compare the result with the work by Phelps [11]. Factor augmenting progress plays an important part in the recent works on " biased " technical progress (Diamond-McFadden [2] and Sato [12]), and on asymptotically balanced growth (Beckmann [1]).

8. In certain cases, requiring that one variable be unchanged as long as some other variable is constant excludes technical progress altogether. Thus, *suppose that the interest rate is unchanged as long as the wage rate is constant* (Case XV), then

$$y - xy_x = \phi(y_x). \qquad \qquad ...(35)$$

An analysis of the solution of this equation (a Clairaut equation) shows that the constant of integration is independent of time and that there is no technical change. This can be easily checked by the following equation:

$$\frac{\partial F/\partial t}{F} = (1-\beta)\frac{\dot{r}}{r} + \beta \frac{\dot{w}}{w}$$

where β = labour's share. If $\dot{r}/r = 0$ whenever $\dot{w}/w = 0$, the factor frontier does not move over time and there is no technical progress.

9. The contents of this paper are summarized in the table on page 65.

10. To test the alternative hypotheses regarding the types of technical progress the regression analysis was applied to the data for the United States, Japan, and Germany.[1] Since the space is limited, the results may be briefly summarized as follows:

(1) Although the basic three types of neutral technical progress, i.e., Hicks, Harrod and Solow neutral, are, on the average, the meaningful empirical assumptions in all three countries, some new definitions of neutral technical progress are proved to be better empirical assumptions than the three previously mentioned types. For example, in Japan the types of Generalized Hicks and Solow neutral technical progress (Case X, XII) are more suitable than the standard definitions of neutrality. In these cases it is found that by introducing t in the equation the value of R^2 is increased, and also the regression coefficient of t is significant at the 99 per cent level.

(2) Also in the U.S. economy, such new definitions as Labour Combining (Case IV) and Capital Combining (Case V) are better or as good as the standard Hicks neutral technical progress, while these definitions have very little empirical relevance in either the Japanese and German economies.

(3) Anti-Hicks ranked very high in the case of Germany together with the Capital Additive type.

(4) Most of the other new definitions are also proved to be useful concepts in all three countries.

(5) Referring briefly to the case of Factor Augmenting Technical Progress (Case XIV), it is shown that the separate study [12] confirms the hypothesis that the elasticity of factor substitution remains unchanged as long as the income shares are constant, more particularly that $\sigma = 1 \cdot 558 \, \alpha$ where α = capital's share. The implication of this result is far reaching, since equation (33) not only justifies the theoretical basis for factor augmenting technical progress, but also makes it " possible " to estimate both the efficiencies of capital and labour, and the form of the underlying production function simultaneously, which is quite contrary to the so-called Impossibility Theorem.

Brown University   R. Sato
                                                            M. J. Beckmann

[1] The data on the U.S. economy are from John Kendrick's work [9]. The data on the Japanese economy are computed from *Japan Statistical Yearbook, 1949-1962*, except the capital series which is obtained from the addition of the net private capital formation (non-primary) to the value of capital stock in 1930. The German data are taken from W. G. Hoffmann [8].

NEUTRAL INVENTIONS AND PRODUCTION FUNCTIONS 65

SUMMARY OF CLASSIFICATIONS

is invariant with respect to		1 L/K	2 Y/K	3 Y/L	4 R	5 r	6 w	7 β
1	$\dfrac{L}{K}$							
2	$\dfrac{Y}{K}$	No						
3	$\dfrac{Y}{L}$	technical	progress					
4	R	I Hicks	VI	VII				
5	r	IX	II Harrod	V	XV			
6	w	VIII	IV	III Solow	No technical	progress		
7	β	I	II	III	I	II	III	
8	σ	X	XI	XII	XIII	not integrable by quadrature		Factor Augmenting XIV

L labour w wage rate r interest rate β labour share
K capital R marginal rate of substitution
Y output σ elasticity of substitution

Case I. Hicks Neutral   IX. Labour Additive
    II. Harrod Neutral   X. Generalized Hicks Neutral
    III. Solow Neutral   XI. Generalized Harrod Neutral
    IV. Labour Combining   XII. Generalized Solow Neutral
    V. Capital Combining   XIII. Quasi-Hicks
    VI. Anti-Hicks   XIV. Factor Augmenting
    VII. Anti-Hicks   XV. No Technical Progress
    VIII. Capital Additive

Cases I-IX will be essentially reduced to the following four types:

1. Product Augmenting: Hicks (I) and Anti-Hicks (VI and VII)
2. Augmenting one factor: Harrod (II) and Solow (III)
3. Additive to product: Labour or capital additive (VIII and IX)
4. Additive to one factor: Labour or capital (IV and V).

Cases X-XIV use the elasticity of factor substitution as a criterion of neutrality.[1]

REFERENCES

[1] Beckman, M. J. "Einkommensverteilung und Wachstum bei nichtneutralem technischen Fortschritt", *Jahrbücher für Nationalökonomie und Statistik*, **178** (1965), 80-89.

[1] In cells 8-5 and 8-6, which are the same, only a special solution could be obtained by assuming the relationship to be a special linear one. The result was a special case of the CES function.

E

[2]   Diamond, P. and McFadden, D.   " Identification of the Elasticity of Substitution and the Bias of Technical Change: An Impossibility Theorem ", *Working Paper* No. 62.   Inst. of Business and Economic Research, University of California, Berkeley.

[3]   Diamond, P. A.   " Technical Change and the Measurement of Capital and Output ", *Review of Economic Studies*, **32**, No. 92 (1965), 289-298.

[4]   Fei, J. and Ranis, G.   " Innovational Intensity and Factor Bias in the Theory of Growth ", *International Economic Review*, **6** (1965), 182-198.

[5]   Fisher, F. M.   " Embodied Technical Change and the Existence of an Aggregate Capital Stock ", *The Review of Economic Studies*, **32** (1965), No. 92, 263-288.

[6]   Hahn, F. H. and Matthews, R. C. O.   "The Theory of Economic Growth: A Survey", *Economic Journal* (Dec. 1964), pp. 781-902.

[7]   Hicks, J. R.   *Theory of Wages*, 2nd edition (1965), Ch. VI.

[8]   Hoffmann, W. G.   *Das Wachstum der deutschen Wirtschaft seit der Mitte des* 19. *Jahrhunderts* (Springer Verlag, Berlin, Heidelberg, New York, 1965).

[9]   Kendrick, J. W.   *Productivity Trends in the United States* (Princeton, 1961).

[10]   Lewis, W. A.   " Economic Development with Unlimited Supplies of Labour ", *Manchester School of Economics and Social Studies*, **22** (1954), 139-191.

[11]   Phelps, E. S.   " An Axiomatic Approach to Technical Progress ", *Cowles Foundation Discussion Paper*, 1965.

[12]   Sato, R.   "The Estimation of Biased Technical Progress and the Production Function ", Presented at the 1965 Econometric Meetings.

[13]   Solow, R. M.   " Technical Progress, Capital Formation, and Economic Growth ", *American Economic Review*, Proceedings (May, 1962), 76-86.

[14]   Uzawa, H.   "Neutral Inventions and the Stability of Growth Equilibrium ", *Review of Economic Studies*, **28** (1961), 117-124.

[15]   v. Weizsäcker, C. C.   *Zur ökonomischen Theorie des technischen Fortschritts* (Göttingen, 1966).

ERRATA

On page 62, equation (29) should read:-

$$\sigma^* \,(y) \,=\, 1/\sigma(y) \,=\, \frac{\partial r/r}{\partial y/y},$$

and in the last expression on page 62 and equations (30) and (31) on page 63 should read σ^* for σ.

Reprinted from The Review of Economic Studies, Vol. XXXV (3), July 1968, R. Sato and M. Beckmann, p. 366.

Neutral Inventions and Production Functions: an Addendum

In our paper in this *Review*, Vol. XXXV (1), January, 1968, pp. 57-66, two cases were described as not integrable by quadrature, viz., when the elasticity of substitution $= \dfrac{y'(y-xy')}{-xyy''}$ is a function of only the interest rate $y-xy'$ or the wage rate y' (p. 65). This blemish may now be removed. In order to integrate

$$\frac{y'(y-xy')}{-xyy''} = \phi(y-xy') \qquad \qquad ...(1)$$

we set
$$y(x) = u(\log x)$$
$$= u(q),$$

$$y'(x) = u'(q).\frac{1}{x} \quad \text{and} \quad y''(x) = \frac{u''(q)-u'(q)}{x^2}.$$

Substituting in (1),

$$\frac{u'.(u-u')}{-u(u''-u')} = \phi(u-u')$$

we have a second order equation which does not involve q. It may be integrated by standard methods to yield

$$\log u(q) = \int^{u-p} \frac{\phi(\xi)}{\xi}\, d\xi - \log C(t), \qquad \qquad ...(2)$$

where $p = \dfrac{du}{dq}$.

Solving (2) for $\dfrac{1}{p} = \dfrac{dq}{du}$ we obtain

$$\frac{dq}{du} = \frac{1}{u+\Phi(Cu)},$$

$$\log x = q = \log A(t) + \int^{u} \frac{dv}{v+\Phi[C(t)v]},$$

$$x = A(t)e^{\int^{y} \frac{dv}{v+\Phi(C(t)v)}}. \qquad \qquad ...(3)$$

Observe that equation (3) is identical with equation (32) (p. 63) in our paper with x and y interchanged. Therefore, the present production function is the inverse of the production function for Case XIII when the elasticity of substitution depends on the marginal rate of substitution.

The case where σ is a function of the wage rate y' reduces to the same equation with $z = \dfrac{Y}{L}$ and $k = \dfrac{K}{L}$ in place of y and x, and the same conclusions apply *mutatis mutandis*.

Brown University

R. Sato
M. Beckmann

[12]

INTERNATIONAL
ECONOMIC
REVIEW

June, 1970
Vol. 11, No. 2

THE ESTIMATION OF BIASED TECHNICAL PROGRESS AND THE PRODUCTION FUNCTION*

By Ryuzo Sato[1]

1. Introduction

Production functions and technical progress play a crucial role in the modern theory of economic growth. A production function specifies a long-run relationship between inputs and outputs, and technical progress is an essential factor of underlying forces of the growth of per-capita income. At the purely theoretical level, it is entirely possible to conjecture a model of economic growth based on the general form of production functions and general types of technical progress, but for empirical analysis such a model would be too broad to allow for a thorough analysis. There are a number of ways to approach the estimation of production function and technical progress in economic growth, but from the standpoint of empirical analysis the following two seem the most appropriate: (1) Assume that the elasticity of substitution is constant (*CES* production function) and technical progress is neutral, and (2) assume that the production function has a variable elasticity of substitution, together with nonneutral technical progress.

Following the publication of Paul Douglas' *Theory of Wages*, 1933, and more recently the publication of the well-known articles by Solow [13] and Arrow, *et al.* [1], considerable attention has been paid to the first type of approach; subsequently there have been a number of illuminating works by Domar [4], Dhrymes [5], Johansen [7], Kendrick and Sato [9], and others.

The second type of approach may be justified by considering the so-called Hicksian mechanism of technical progress. In the *Theory of Wages*, first published in 1932, Hicks presents what is essentially a theory of income distribution with biased technical progress wherein he treats the elasticity of factor substitution as a variable. Hicks notes that inventions over the last few centuries have generally been of a labor-saving nature and suggests that the relative increase of capital to labor may have served as a stimulus to such biased inventions. Not only have inventions been biased, but the elasticity of substitution has changed with the changes in factor proportions. "Capital increases $\cdots$ and in consequence a labor-saving invention is made and

* Manuscript received August 26, 1967; revised July 15, 1968.

[1] The author is indebted to John Wise, Ronald Hoffman, Yeong-Her Yeh, George H. Borts and Martin J. Beckmann for their helpful comments on an earlier draft of this paper. The author also acknowledges the statistical assistance rendered by Gilbert Suzawa and Atsumi Kawasaki.

adopted ⋯ increasing the elasticity of substitution," [6, (124–6)]. Thus Hicks was concerned with the way technical progress affected the distribution through its effects on the elasticity of substitution. However since Hicksian analysis is made in the context of a very broad static approach, it is not directly applicable to empirical data which requires a detailed analysis in a dynamic context.

The present paper intends to reformulate the Hicksian mechanism of technical progress by using a specific form of bias, i.e., the factor augmenting technical progress. The paper consists of a theoretical and an empirical part. In the theoretical part a factor augmenting hypothesis is justified and the elasticity of substitution with biased technical progress is defined; the fundamental relations among the elasticity of substitution and the efficiencies of capital and labor are derived; the so-called "Impossibility Theorem" is discussed; and a new type of production function (constant elasticity of derived demand, i.e., *CEDD*), which has a particular significance in that it makes the estimation of bias possible, is presented. In the empirical part the model is applied to the data from the U. S. nonfarm sector, 1909–1960; tests of neutral technical progress and tests of the Cobb-Douglas function are performed; the efficiencies of capital and labor are estimated from the assumptions of *CES* functions as well as *CEDD* functions; and several forms of these prodution functions are estimated that would explain the long-run behavior of the U. S. private sector for the past 50 years. Among these forms the *CEDD* production function in which the elasticity of substitution is variable ($\sigma = 1.558\alpha$; $\alpha =$ capital's share) proves to be more explanatory than *CES* functions.

2. THE THEORY OF BIASED TECHNICAL PROGRESS

2.1. *The factor augmentation hypothesis.* There are various ways of incorporating the bias of technical change into the production function, but the following formulation seems the easiest since the properties of linear homogeneity can still be maintained.

$$(1) \qquad\qquad Y(t) = F[A(t)K(t), B(t)L(t)]$$

where $Y(t)$ is output at time t; $K(t)$, capital; $L(t)$, labor; and $A(t)$ and $B(t)$ are the "efficiencies" of $K(t)$ and $L(t)$ respectively. In addition to the linear and homogeneous assumption, it is assumed that Y is continuously differentiable with respect to K, L, A, B and t up to the desired order. Both factor and commodity markets are assumed highly competitive so that factors of production are paid their marginal products.

One justification for the formulation of equation (1) has been made by Sato and Beckmann [12]. They show that if technical progress is such that the elasticity of factor substitution is unaffected as long as income shares are constant, equation (1) can be derived from the assumption

$$(2) \qquad\qquad\qquad \sigma = \phi(\alpha)$$

where σ is the elasticity of substitution and α, the share of capital. Discussion of the empirical implications of this assumption will be postponed until we come to the estimation of production functions.

In equation (1), if $A(t)$ and $B(t)$ are identical, technical progress is neutral in the Hicksian sense; and when $B(t) > A(t) = 1$, technical progress is neutral in the Harrod sense.

Our first task is to establish a method for isolating both $A(t)$ and $B(t)$ from the production function. Totally differentiating equation (1) with respect to time we get:

$$\frac{\dot{Y}}{Y} = \frac{\partial F}{\partial(AK)} \cdot \frac{\partial(AK)}{\partial K} \cdot \frac{K}{Y} \cdot \frac{\dot{K}}{K} + \frac{\partial F}{\partial(AK)} \cdot \frac{\partial(AK)}{\partial A} \cdot \frac{A}{Y} \cdot \frac{\dot{A}}{A}$$

$$+ \frac{\partial F}{\partial(BL)} \cdot \frac{\partial(BL)}{\partial L} \cdot \frac{L}{Y} \cdot \frac{\dot{L}}{L} + \frac{\partial F}{\partial(BL)} \cdot \frac{\partial(BL)}{\partial B} \cdot \frac{B}{Y} \cdot \frac{\dot{B}}{B}.$$

Since

$$\frac{\partial F}{\partial A} = K \cdot \frac{\partial F}{\partial(AK)}, \quad \frac{\partial F}{\partial K} = A \cdot \frac{\partial F}{\partial(AK)}, \quad \frac{\partial F}{\partial B} = L \cdot \frac{\partial F}{\partial(BL)}$$

and $\partial F/\partial L = B \cdot (\partial F/\partial(BL))$, the following relations must hold:

$$\frac{\partial F}{\partial A} \cdot \frac{A}{Y} = \frac{\partial F}{\partial K} \cdot \frac{K}{Y} = \frac{AK}{Y} \cdot \frac{\partial F}{\partial(AK)}$$

and

$$\frac{\partial F}{\partial B} \cdot \frac{B}{Y} = \frac{\partial F}{\partial L} \cdot \frac{L}{Y} = \frac{BL}{Y} \cdot \frac{\partial F}{\partial(BL)}.$$

Letting $\partial F/\partial K \cdot (K/Y) = \alpha$ and $(\partial F/\partial L) \cdot (L/Y) = 1 - \alpha = \beta$, $\dot{Y}/Y$ may be written as:

$$\frac{\dot{Y}}{Y} = \alpha\left(\frac{\dot{K}}{K} + \frac{\dot{A}}{A}\right) + \beta\left(\frac{\dot{L}}{L} + \frac{\dot{B}}{B}\right).$$

If we further assume that $x = L/K = 1/k$ and $z = Y/L$, then:

$$(3) \qquad \frac{\dot{z}}{z} = \alpha\frac{\dot{A}}{A} + \beta\frac{\dot{B}}{B} - \alpha\frac{\dot{x}}{x}.$$

If the efficiencies of capital and labor are the same $\dot{A}/A = \dot{B}/B = \dot{T}/T$ (where T is total technical progress), equation (3) reduces to the original equations derived by Solow [13] and also by Kendrick and Sato [9] for the estimation of neutral technical progress because (3) becomes:

$$(3a) \qquad \frac{\dot{z}}{z} = \frac{\dot{T}}{T} - \alpha\frac{\dot{x}}{x}.$$

When $\dot{A}/A \neq \dot{B}/B$, the Solow-Kendrick method breaks down since it measures the weighted mean of the two efficiencies.

Equation (3) contains two unknowns, $\dot{A}/A$ and $\dot{B}/B$; hence, we need an additional independent equation to estimate the two unknowns. In order to derive this additional relationship, however, we must first define the elasticity of factor substitution.

2.2. *Definition of the elasticity of substitution with biased technical progress.* Let w and r stand for the wage rate and the return on capital respectively. Then

$$(4) \qquad\qquad w = Bf'(Cx)$$

and

(5) $r = Af(Cx) - xBf'(Cx)$,

where $f(Cx) = F(1, BL/AK)$ and $C = B/A$. If technical progress is nonneutral, the value of the elasticity itself is influenced by the efficiencies of capital and labor. Therefore, we need to introduce a new definition of the elasticity. In equation (1) if $AK = K'$ and $BL = L'$, the elasticity of substitution between K' and L' is defined by:

(6)
$$\sigma = \frac{d\left(\dfrac{K'}{L'}\right)\Big/\dfrac{K'}{L'}}{d\left(\dfrac{\partial F/\partial L'}{\partial F/\partial K'}\right)\Big/\dfrac{\partial F/\partial L'}{\partial F/\partial K'}} \cdot$$

Since $\partial F/\partial K' = r/A$ and $\partial F/\partial L' = w/B$, σ is also equal to

$$\sigma = \frac{d\left(\dfrac{AK}{BL}\right)\Big/\dfrac{AK}{BL}}{d\left(\dfrac{Aw}{Br}\right)\Big/\dfrac{Aw}{Br}} \cdot$$

Another way of expressing the above is

(6a)
$$\sigma = \frac{\dfrac{\dot{A}}{A} - \dfrac{\dot{B}}{B} - \dfrac{\dot{x}}{x}}{\dfrac{\dot{A}}{A} - \dfrac{\dot{B}}{B} - \dfrac{\dot{r}}{r} + \dfrac{\dot{w}}{w}} ,$$

because A, B, x, r and w are all functions of time. If $A = B$ or if technical progress is neutral, equation (6) reduces to the definition given by Hicks [6]. Also, if $\dot{A}/A = \dot{B}/B$, σ becomes the expression derived by Kendrick and Sato [9, (989)].

Using the definition $y = Y/K$, equation (6) can also be written as

(6b)
$$\sigma = \frac{w \cdot r}{-xy\dfrac{\partial w}{\partial x}} ,$$

since σ may be alternatively defined as

(6c)
$$\sigma = \frac{\dfrac{\partial Y}{\partial L'} \cdot \dfrac{\partial Y}{\partial K'}}{Y \cdot \dfrac{\partial^2 Y}{\partial K'\partial L'}} = \frac{w \cdot r}{Y \cdot \dfrac{\partial w}{\partial K}} \cdot$$

To prove the equality of (6b) and (6c), we use

$$w = Bf'(Cx) \text{ and } \frac{\partial w}{\partial K} = -\frac{B^2}{AK} \cdot x \cdot f''(Cx) ,$$

and obtain $Y \cdot \partial w/dK = -B^2/A \cdot x \cdot y \cdot f''(Cx)$. Since $\partial w/\partial x = B^2 f''(Cx)/A$, we also get

$$-x \cdot y\frac{\partial w}{\partial x} = -\frac{B^2}{A} \cdot x \cdot y \cdot f''(Cx) ,$$

which proves that

$$-x \cdot y \frac{\partial w}{\partial x} = Y \cdot \frac{\partial w}{\partial K} \ .$$

2.3. *The Fundamental Relations.* The above results can now be used to derive expressions for $\dot{A}/A$ and $\dot{B}/B$ in terms of the elasticity of substitution. Differentiating equation (4) with respect to time we obtain

$$\frac{dw}{dt} = f'(Cx)\frac{dB}{dt} + \frac{B^2}{A} \cdot f''(Cx)\left[\frac{x}{B}\frac{dB}{dt} - \frac{x}{A}\frac{dA}{dt} + \frac{dx}{dt} \right].$$

Division of the above equation by w gives:

$$\frac{\dot{w}}{w} = \frac{\dot{B}}{B} + \frac{Cxf''(Cx)}{f'(Cx)}\left[\frac{\dot{B}}{B} - \frac{\dot{A}}{A} + \frac{\dot{x}}{x} \right].$$

Using the expressions $\partial w/\partial x = B^2 f''(Cx)/A$ and $r/y = \alpha$ and equation (6b), we can write

(7)
$$\frac{\dot{w}}{w} = \frac{\dot{B}}{B} - \frac{\alpha}{\sigma}\left(\frac{\dot{B}}{B} - \frac{\dot{A}}{A} + \frac{\dot{x}}{x} \right).$$

In a similar fashion we can write

(8)
$$\frac{\dot{r}}{r} = \frac{\dot{A}}{A} + \frac{\beta}{\sigma}\left(\frac{\dot{B}}{B} - \frac{\dot{A}}{A} + \frac{\dot{x}}{x} \right).$$

We also have the expression, derived in Section 2.1,

(3)
$$\frac{\dot{z}}{z} = \alpha\frac{\dot{A}}{A} + \beta\frac{\dot{B}}{B} - \alpha\frac{\dot{x}}{x} \ .$$

Solving equations (3) and (7) and using (8), we get the fundamental equations for estimating $\dot{A}/A$ and $\dot{B}/B$:

(9)
$$\frac{\dot{A}}{A} = \frac{\sigma\dfrac{\dot{r}}{r} - \dfrac{\dot{y}}{y}}{\sigma - 1}, \quad \sigma \neq 1$$

and

(10)
$$\frac{\dot{B}}{B} = \frac{\sigma\dfrac{\dot{w}}{w} - \dfrac{\dot{z}}{z}}{\sigma - 1}, \quad \sigma \neq 1 \ .$$

Two remarks are in order regarding the properties of equations (9) and (10).
Remark 1: The Cobb-Douglas Case. Equations (9) and (10) suggest that in order to estimate A and B, σ cannot be equal to unity. As is well known, when $\sigma = 1$, i.e., in the case of the Cobb-Douglas, there is no method to separate A and B from the function. This can be observed from equation (7) which may also be written as

$$\sigma\frac{\dot{w}}{w} + \alpha\frac{\dot{x}}{x} = (\sigma - \alpha)\frac{\dot{B}}{B} + \alpha\frac{\dot{A}}{A} \ .$$

If $\sigma = 1$, then $\dot{w}/w = \dot{z}/z$; thus the above equals

$$\frac{\dot{z}}{z} + \alpha\frac{\dot{x}}{x} = \alpha\frac{\dot{A}}{A} + \beta\frac{\dot{B}}{B}$$

which is exactly the same as equation (3). Hence, there is only one equation for two unknowns $\dot{A}/A$ and $\dot{B}/B$. I shall come back to this point later, when I set up a method to test the validity of the assumption that σ equals unity.

Remark 2: The "Impossibility Theorem." Even assuming that σ is not equal to unity, there is still a serious problem. We have no knowledge of the value of σ which must be known beforehand according to (9) and (10) in order to estimate $\dot{A}/A$ and $\dot{B}/B$. There are actually three unknowns, σ, $\dot{A}/A$ and $\dot{B}/B$ with only two independent equations as can be seen by check-ing the Jacobian determinant. The Jacobian determinant of equations (3), (7) and (8) is equal to:

(11)
$$J = \begin{vmatrix} \alpha & \beta & 0 \\ (\sigma - 1) & 0 & \left(\dfrac{\dot{A}}{A} - \dfrac{\dot{r}}{r}\right) \\ 0 & (\sigma - 1) & \left(\dfrac{\dot{B}}{B} - \dfrac{\dot{w}}{w}\right) \end{vmatrix}$$

which turns out to be equal to zero.[2] This proposition, that $\dot{A}/A$ and $\dot{B}/B$ cannot be estimated unless σ is known *a priori*, is later referred to as the "Impossibility Theorem" by Diamond and McFadden [3] since in general there is no way of identifying σ (i.e., the form of the production function) and hence, it is *impossible* to estimate A and B.

However, the problem is not so bad as the above would indicate. First of all, under certain conditions, there is a definite method of identifying the elasticity of factor substitution through its relation to the shares of capital and labor. Second, as John Wise suggests, one could determine the long-run reliability of the various estimates of A and B obtained from assumed values of σ by testing the short-run variability of output per unit of labor. These various methods of identifying the underlying production function will be discussed in later sections.

I shall now derive the other relationships which will be of great importance, not only in investigating the changes in the relative shares, but also in testing the neutrality assumption of technical grogress. The percentage changes in the shares of capital and labor, α and β, are equal to

(12)
$$\frac{\dot{\alpha}}{\alpha} = -\beta\left(1 - \frac{1}{\sigma}\right)\left(\frac{\dot{B}}{B} - \frac{\dot{A}}{A} + \frac{\dot{x}}{x}\right)$$

and

---

[2] Strictly speaking, what we have proved is that three equations cannot be solved for $\dot{A}/A$ and $\dot{B}/B$ and σ.

(13)
$$\frac{\dot{\beta}}{\beta} = \alpha\left(1 - \frac{1}{\sigma}\right)\left(\frac{\dot{B}}{B} - \frac{\dot{A}}{A} + \frac{\dot{x}}{x}\right).$$

The above equations show that although technical progress is not neutral, α and β (the shares of capital and labor) can be constant, even if $\sigma \neq 1$. Thus, constancy of α and β does not necessarily imply that the underlying function is the Cobb-Douglas. Note also that if technical progress is neutral, i.e., $\dot{A}/A = \dot{B}/B = \dot{T}/T$, then (12) and (13) will be reduced to the equations derived by Kendrick and Sato [9, (990)].

It is now appropriate to discuss the effect of technical progress; that is, whether technical progress is labor-saving or capital-saving. Hicks [6, (121–2)] defines "labor-saving" inventions as those whose initial effects, at constant capital-labor ratio, are to increase the ratio of the marginal product of capital to that of labor; he defines "capital-saving" inventions as those whose initial effects are to diminish that ratio. In the context of the present analysis, these definitions can be expressed in the following manner; Let $\omega = r/w$, then by subtracting equation (7) from (8) we obtain

(14)
$$\frac{\dot{\omega}}{\omega} = \frac{\dot{r}}{r} - \frac{\dot{w}}{w} = \left(\frac{\dot{A}}{A} - \frac{\dot{B}}{B}\right)\left(1 - \frac{1}{\sigma}\right) + \frac{1}{\sigma}\frac{\dot{x}}{x}.$$

There are three cases: $\sigma = 1$; $\sigma > 1$; and $\sigma < 1$.

  (1) $\sigma = 1$: $\dot{\omega}/\omega = 0$ at a constant x; hence technical progress always appears neutral.
  (2) $\sigma > 1$: If A grows faster than B, i.e., $\dot{A}/A > \dot{B}/B$, shifts are "labor-saving," but if B grows faster than A, $\dot{B}/B > \dot{A}/A$, shifts are "capital-saving."
  (3) $\sigma < 1$: In this case, if A grows faster than B, technical progress is "capital-saving," but if B grows faster than A, it is "labor-saving."

The effects of inventions on the relative income shares are now determined by both the elasticity of factor substitution and the biasedness of inventions. Equations (12) and (13) suggest that, when $\sigma < 1$, "labor-saving" inventions $(\dot{A}/A < \dot{B}/B)$ raise the share of capital, reducing the share of labor, whereas "capital-saving" inventions reduce the capital share, increasing the labor share. Of course, when $\sigma > 1$, the converse relationships hold true.

  2.4. *The elasticity of factor substitution and the factor augmenting hypothesis.* We are now in a position to show how factor augmenting technical progress as represented in equation (1) is derived from equation (2). Equation (2) states that the elasticity of factor substitution is directly related only to the factor shares, and that technical progress does not disturb this relationship, i.e.,

(2)
$$\sigma = \psi(\alpha, x, t) = \Phi(\alpha), \quad \frac{\partial \psi}{\partial x} = 0, \quad \frac{\partial \psi}{\partial t} = 0.$$

What I wish to show is that if technical progress leaves the elasticity of substitution undisturbed so long as the income shares are constant, then such a shift must be factor augmenting. From the definition of the elasticity of factor substitution given in Section 2.1., we may write the inverse of σ in equation (2) as,

$$(15) \qquad \frac{\partial \log \left(\dfrac{y - xy_x}{y_x} \right)}{\partial \log x} = \phi \left(\frac{xy_x}{y} \right) .$$

Letting $xy_x/y = 1 - \alpha = \beta$ we have $x(\partial/\partial x) \log [x((1/\beta) - 1)] = \phi(\beta)$ or

$$\partial \log x = \partial \beta / u(\beta) ,$$
$$\log x + \log C(t) = g(\beta), \quad \beta = G(C(t)x) .$$

Since $\beta = xy_x/y$, we get,

$$\frac{xy_x}{y} = G(C(t)x) , \qquad \frac{\partial y}{y} = \frac{\partial x}{xG(C(t)x)} ,$$

$$\log y = \log A(t) + \int^x \frac{\partial \xi}{\xi \cdot G(C(t)\xi \Gamma} ,$$

$$y = A(t) \exp \int^x \frac{C(t)\partial \xi}{C(t)\xi \cdot G(C(t)\xi)} .$$

Substituting $C(t)\xi = v$, we obtain

$$y = A(t) \exp \int^{C(t)x} \frac{\partial v}{vG(v)}$$

where integration is carried out at constant t. Thus, we get, $y = A(t)f(C(t)x)$, i.e.,

$$(1) \qquad Y = F[A(t) \cdot K, B(t) \cdot L]$$

which justifies the introduction of the factor augmenting technical progress.

Although full justification of equation (2) itself is given in the article by Sato and Beckmann [12], it is intuitively quite natural to assume equation (2) from the definition of the elasticity of factor substitution; for, letting $f = e^F$ and $x = e^x$, we can write α and σ simply as

$$(16) \qquad \alpha(e^x) = \frac{\partial F}{\partial X}$$

and

$$(17) \qquad \frac{1}{\sigma} = 1 + \frac{\dfrac{\partial \alpha}{\partial X}}{\alpha(1 - \alpha)} .$$

Equation (17) suggests that equation (2) (σ is a function of α alone) is a natural expression, since σ does not involve x directly but involves only α and its derivative.

In view of the "Impossibility Theorem" referred to in the previous section, we must now set up an additional relationship to estimate the rate of technical progress ($A(t)$ and $B(t)$). Since equation (2) implies the factor augmenting hypothesis, it seems best to set up the additional independent relationship by utilizing equation (2). That is to say, we first assume the specific form of the elasticity of substitution function (as a function of the income shares) and then use (9) and (10) to estimate $\dot{A}/A$ and $\dot{B}/B$. Two special (simple) forms of equation (2) are of particular interest from the empirical point of view.

(18) $$\sigma = c; \ c = \text{constant} \ (c > 0)$$

and

(19) $$\sigma = \gamma_1 \alpha \quad \text{or} \quad \sigma = \gamma_2 \beta$$

where γ_1 and γ_2 are constants, $\gamma_1 > 0$, $\gamma_2 > 0$, and $\beta = 1 - \alpha$. The first case (equation (18)) is, of course, the *CES* production function and the second case may be referred to as the constant elasticity of derived demand production function (*CEDD*) for reasons given later.[3]

a. *CES functions.* Since *CES* production functions have been frequently used in recent works [1], [2], [9] and [13], it is not necessary to describe them in this paper. I shall simply write the general form of the function with the biased technical progress factors $A(t)$ and $B(t)$ as

(20) $$Y = [a(A(t)K(t))^{-\rho} + b(B(t)L(t))^{-\rho}]^{-1/\rho}$$

where $\sigma = 1/(1 + \rho)$.

b. *CEDD functions.* The assumption of constant elasticity of substitution is a useful device for estimating $\dot{A}/A$ and $\dot{B}/B$ from equations (9) and (10) as it is empirically manageable. However, the value of the elasticity of substitution may vary in the course of the expansion and contraction of an economy. A device (equation (19)) that permits variation in the elasticity of substitution while still being empirically manageable is the *CEDD* production function. There are two reasons for using the *CEDD* function when one wants a production function with a variable elasticity of substitution. Firstly, equation (19) is the simplest form of the factor augmentation hypothesis (equation (2)). Secondly, equation (19) assumes that the elasticities of derived demand for the factors are constant and thus a simple regression analysis may be applied to estimate these elasticities.

Assume for the moment that there is no technical change, i.e., $A(t) = B(t) = 1$, then E_k, the elasticity of derived demand for capital per unit of labor, is defined as

---

[3] One might be tempted to formulate a more general production function such as $\sigma = a + b\alpha$, $a \neq 0$, which combines both *CES* and *CEDD* functions. Unfortunately this formulation, in general, gives no explicit integration. However, one positive approach is to set $1/\sigma = a + b/\alpha$, which can be integrated to get a production function.

$$y = [A(t)x^{1-a} + (1 - a)B(t)x^b]^{1/(1-a)} .$$

This function can be looked at as a combination of *CES* and *CEDD* and also *CES* and *C–D* (Cobb-Douglas) functions. The function was also derived independently by M. J. Beckmann from

$$\alpha(x) = \frac{a + bx^u}{1 + cx^u}, \quad u > 0 .$$

$$(21) \qquad E_k = -\frac{dk}{dr}\frac{r}{k} \ .$$

This can be treated as the demand elasticity of capital per unit of labor with respect to the return to capital or as the elasticity of the marginal productivity curve of k. If we consider an aggregate economy in which the price of income P_Y is fixed (say $P_Y = 1$), then E_k must be equal to $-(\partial Y/\partial K)/(K \cdot \partial^2 Y/\partial K^2)$, which is nothing but the elasticity of derived demand for capital for and given value of labor input. Thus,

$$(22) \qquad E_k = \frac{f(x) - xf'(x)}{-x^2 f''(x)} \ .$$

Since σ in equation (6c) with $A(t) = B(t) = 1$ can alternatively be written as

$$\sigma = \frac{xf'(x)}{f(x)} \cdot \frac{f(x) - xf'(x)}{-x^2 f''(x)} \ ,$$

one sees that

$$(23) \qquad \sigma = \beta E_k \ .$$

In words, the elasticity of factor substitution equals the product of the share of labor and the elasticity of derived demand for capital per unit of labor.

A symmetrical relationship will hold between α and β, and between E_k and E_z, if E_z is defined as the elasticity of derived demand for labor per unit of capital input

$$(24) \qquad E_z = -\frac{dx}{dw}\frac{w}{x} = \frac{z(k) - kz'(k)}{-k^2 z''(k)} \ .$$

Thus

$$(25) \qquad \sigma = \alpha E_z \ .$$

Obviously a *CES* function assumes $\sigma = \beta E_k = \alpha E_z = $ constant. Although we have no a priori knowledge as to the values of E_k and E_z, it is not entirely arbitrary to assume that one or both of these derived demand elasticities may be constant—which is the assumption of equation (19). As mentioned above, we can call a production function with constant E_k and/or E_z a "constant elasticity of derived demand production function." Since $E_k = \sigma/\beta$ and $E_z = \sigma/\alpha$, the ratio of the elasticity of substitution to the factor share must be constant when the elasticity of derived demand is constant. However, E_k and E_z cannot be constant at the same time unless σ, α, and β are constant. Hence, only when the function is the Cobb-Douglas will both E_k and E_z be constant. Also, only when a *CES* function is the Cobb-Douglas function can it be at the same time a *CEDD* function. Since, in general, only one of the two elasticities of derived demand can be constant, *CEDD* functions may be divided into two categories: (1) *CEDD* with E_k constant and (2) *CEDD* with E_z constant.

Now let us derive a general form for *CEDD* functions with E_k constant. If the elasticity of the marginal productivity curve of $k(E_k)$ is constant, then

$$f(x) - xf'(x) = a_1 x^{\delta_1},$$

where $a > 0$ and $1/\delta_1 = E_k$. Integrating the above equation we get

(26)
$$f(x) = \frac{a_1}{1 - \delta_1} x^{\delta_1} + b_1 x, \; \delta_1 \neq 1,$$

where b_1 is an arbitrary constant. Thus

(26a)
$$Y = \frac{a_1}{1 - \delta_1} K^{1-\delta_1} L^{\delta_1} + b_1 L,$$

which is the general form of *CEDD* functions with $E_k = 1/\delta_1 = \sigma/\beta$. In the same way, if the elasticity of the marginal productivity curve of x is constant we obtain

(27)
$$z(k) = \frac{a_2}{1 - \delta_2} k^{\delta_2} + b_2 k, \;\; \delta_2 \neq 1$$

and

(27a)
$$Y = \frac{a_2}{1 - \delta_2} K^{\delta_2} L^{1-\delta_2} + b_2 K,$$

which is the general form of *CEDD* functions with $E_x = 1/\delta_2 = \sigma/\alpha$.

If we introduce the condition that $A(t) \neq B(t) \neq 1$, then (26a) and (27a) can be written respectively as

(28)
$$Y(t) = \frac{a_1}{1 - \delta_1}[A(t)K(t)]^{1-\delta_1}[B(t)L(t)]^{\delta_1} + b_1(B(t)L(t))$$

and

(29)
$$Y(t) = \frac{a_2}{1 - \delta_2}[A(t)K(t)]^{\delta_2}[B(t)L(t)]^{1-\delta_2} + b_2(A(t)K(t)).$$

It is easy to show that *CEDD* functions have a *linear* elasticity of substitution, a linear function of L/Y, or a linear function of K/Y. If $z = a_1 k^{1-\delta_1}/(1 - \delta_1) + b_1$, then $\sigma = 1 + b_1((1 - \delta_1)/\delta_1)(L/Y)$. If $y = a_2 x^{1-\delta_2}/(1 - \delta_2) + b_2$, then $\sigma = 1 + b_2((1 - \delta_2)/\delta_2)(K/Y)$. This linearity permits relatively easy empirical work, a good property of the *CEDD* function mentioned above.[4]

c. *Unitary elasticity of derived demand production functions: "Bernoulli" production functions.* The cases of $E_k = 1$ and $E_x = 1$ are of special interest from an empirical point of view. If the elasticity of derived demand for K/L is equal to unity, then

(30)
$$\sigma = \beta,$$

and if the elasticity of derived demand for L/K is equal to unity, then

---

[4] Thus, if E_k is constant, factor augmenting technical progress implies also generalized Harrod neutral inventions and if E_x is constant it coincides with generalized Solow neutral inventions. See Sato and Beckmann [12].

(31) $$\sigma = \alpha .$$

Therefore, if $E_k = 1$, σ can be directly estimated from β, and if $E_x = 1$, by α. The production function with $E_k = 1$ becomes

(32) $$z(k) = a_1 \log k + b_1 ,$$

and the production function with $E_x = 1$ becomes[5]

(33) $$y(x) = a_2 \log x + b_2 .$$

Thus, in general, with $A(t) \neq B(t) \neq 1$,

(34) $$Y(t) = a_1 B(t) L(t) \left(\log \frac{A(t)K(t)}{B(t)L(t)} \right) + b_1 B(t) L(t), \quad \sigma = \beta$$

and

(35) $$Y(t) = a_2 A(t) K(t) \left(\log \frac{B(t)L(t)}{A(t)K(t)} \right) + b_2 A(t) K(t), \quad \sigma = \alpha .$$

An interesting property of equation (32) is that this production function always has a *constant* profit per unit of labor input. For this reason production function (32), the unitary elasticity of derived demand production function, may be termed the "constant profit (per labor) production function." In the same way, since $\sigma = \alpha$, production function (33) will provide a *constant* wage per-capital input and may be termed the "constant wage (per capital) production function."

Since equations (32) and (33) have the same properties as the so-called *Bernoulli* equations in utility theory, they belong to a family of what may be called the "Bernoulli production functions."[6]

3.   TESTS OF NEUTRAL TECHNICAL PROGRESS AND THE COBB-DOUGLAS FUNCTION

We have come to the point where the model can be applied to an actual economy. I shall apply the model to the private nonfarm sector of the

---

[5] When $\delta_1 \to 1$ or $\delta_2 \to 1$, then (26) will reduce to (32) and (27) will reduce to (33). This can be observed in Taylor's expansion of (32) and (26) at a point k°:

(32)' $$z(k) = a_1 \log k^\circ + b_1 + a_1(k - k^\circ)k^{\circ -1}$$
$$- \frac{a_1(k - k^\circ)^2 k^{\circ -2}}{2!} + \frac{2a_1(k - k^\circ)^3 k^{\circ -3}}{3!} + \cdots$$

and

(26)' $$z(k) = \frac{a_1}{1 - \delta_1} k^{\circ 1 - \delta_1} + b_1 + a_1(k - k^\circ)k^{\circ -\delta_1}$$
$$- \frac{a_1 \delta_1 (k - k^\circ)^2 k^{\circ -\delta_1 -1}}{2!} + \frac{a_1 \delta_1 (1 + \delta_1)(k - k^\circ)^2 k^{\circ -\delta_1 -2}}{3!} + \cdots .$$

By taking $\lim_{\delta_1 \to 1} z$ of (26)' we get (32)', if b_1 in the second equation is equal to $a_1 \log k^\circ + b_1$ of the first equation. In the same way when $\delta_2 \to 1$ then (27) will reduce to (33).

[6] For example Marshall called this type of equation the Bernoulli equation.

U. S. economy, 1909–1960, with Kendrick's data [8] which is summarized in Appendix I. I begin with the test of Hicksian neutrality and the text of the Cobb-Douglas function, since we must show that technical progress is *not* Hicks neutral and that the production function is *not* the Cobb-Douglas.

3.1.   *Test of neutral technical progress.* There is no one method to test the neutrality assumption, but the usual approach has been to test $\dot{T}/T$ against k and to be satisfied with the fact that $\dot{T}/T$ and k are independent. Certainly if $\dot{T}/T$ is completely independent of k, then technical progress is neutral. However, when the variations of the capital share are not as great as the variations of k, $\dot{T}/T$ may not be heavily dependent on k even if technical progress is not neutral. Resek [10] deserves the credit for questioning the usual assumption of neutral technical progress and for providing a method of testing its validity.

Let us apply his test. A comparison of the marginal rate of substitution with the capital-labor ratio will, under certain circumstances, provide a test of neutrality. If technical progress is not neutral, then a relationship between r/w and L/K such as $r/w = \phi(L/K)$ will shift upward or downward, *provided* that the shares of capital and labor are not extremely stable.[7]

Figure 1 shows the observations for 1909–1960. Since the points do not fall on a single line, the technical change may be nonneutral. In order to see the change over time, the points are divided into four groups, 1909–1929, 1930–1939, 1940–1948, and 1949–1960. The points belonging to these groups can be distinguished on the graph. Each of these time periods shows a distinctive pattern.

Another test can be applied. Suppose technical progress is, on the average, neutral; then, from equations (7) and (8):

(7a)
$$\frac{\dot{w}}{w} = \frac{\dot{T}}{T} + \frac{\alpha}{\sigma}\frac{\dot{k}}{k}$$

and

(8a)
$$\frac{\dot{r}}{r} = \frac{\dot{T}}{T} - \frac{\beta}{\sigma}\frac{\dot{k}}{k}$$

where $\dot{T}/T = \dot{A}/A = \dot{B}/B$, and $\dot{k}/k = -\dot{x}/x$. If we estimate $\dot{T}/T$ from the above two equations by the regression analysis between $\dot{r}/r$ and $\dot{k}/k$, and between $\dot{w}/w$ and $\dot{k}/k$, the two estimates should be the same. The results of the regression equations using the data in Appendix I are shown below:

---

[7] The condition that the shares are not extremely stable is very important, because if the shares are absolutely constant, the above test cannot be applied, a fact which Resek fails to understand. He states that if $r/w = \theta(L/K)$, where θ is constant, then the production function is the Cobb-Douglas. This is wrong; it may or may not be the Cobb-Douglas and technical progress may or may not be neutral, but this method simply suggests that the shares are constant. David and Van de Klundert [2] also recognize the possibility of nonneutral technical progress, but assume *CES* functions.

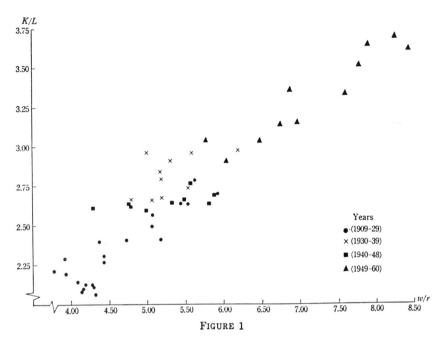

FIGURE 1

(36) $\dfrac{\dot{w}}{w} = \underset{(.00891)}{.01667} + \underset{(.23107)}{.64198}\,\dfrac{k}{k},\quad R = .36891,\quad F = 7.7190$
$T = 1.87093\quad T = 2.77830\,,$

and

(37) $\dfrac{\dot{r}}{r} = \underset{(.01148)}{.01141} - \underset{(.29771)}{.47484}\,\dfrac{k}{k},\quad R = .222,\quad F = 2.5439$
$T = .9939\quad T = 1.59495\,.$

$\dot{T}/T$ obtained from (37) is much lower than $\dot{T}/T$ obtained from (36). Thus, technical progress may be nonneutral.

3.2. *Test of the Cobb-Douglas function.* As I have already shown, if $\sigma = 1$, then there is no method that can be applied to separate $A(t)$ and $B(t)$ because

$$Y = (AK)^{\alpha}(BL)^{1-\alpha} = A^{\alpha}B^{1-\alpha}K^{\alpha}L^{1-\alpha}\,,$$

and $A^{\alpha}B^{1-\alpha}$ cannot be separated into A and B. I now test whether the underlying production function in the U. S. private nonfarm sector is of the Cobb-Douglas form, that is, whether the elasticity of substitution is unity. I use two methods: (1) average elasticity of substitution method, (2) regression equation method.

a. *Average elasticity of substitution method.* This method uses the average of the estimated values of the elasticity of substitution. Define $R(z/w)$ to be equal to the ratio of $\dot{z}/z$ to $\dot{w}/w$, then from (10), we get

(38)
$$R\left(\frac{z}{w}\right) = \frac{\sigma}{1 + (\sigma - 1)\dfrac{\dot{B}/B}{\dot{z}/z}} .$$

Also, if $R(y/r)$ and $R(x/\omega)$ are equal to the ratio of $\dot{y}/y$ to $\dot{r}/r$, and to the ratio of $\dot{x}/x$ to $\dot{\omega}/\omega$ respectively. Then

(39)
$$R\left(\frac{y}{r}\right) = \frac{\sigma}{1 + (\sigma - 1)\dfrac{\dot{A}/A}{\dot{y}/y}}$$

and

(40)
$$R\left(\frac{x}{\omega}\right) = \frac{\sigma}{1 + \dfrac{(\sigma - 1)\left(\dfrac{\dot{A}}{A} - \dfrac{\dot{B}}{B}\right)}{\dfrac{\dot{x}}{x}}} .$$

If, in an actual situation, $\sigma = 1$, then $R(z/w)$, $R(y/r)$ and $R(x/\omega)$ should be, on the average, the same and equal to unity, regardless of whether A and B are the same or not. That is,

(41)
$$\bar{R}\left(\frac{z}{w}\right) = \bar{R}\left(\frac{y}{r}\right) = \bar{R}\left(\frac{x}{\omega}\right) = 1$$

where – indicates the average value of R's. Thus, (41) may be used as a test of the Cobb-Douglas function. Note, however, that even if (41) holds true, it still does not prove that the function is definitely the Cobb-Douglas, but it *does* prove that the shares are absolutely constant because if the shares are constant $\dot{B}/B = \dot{z}/z$, $\dot{A}/A = \dot{y}/y$, and $\dot{x}/x = \dot{A}/A - \dot{B}/B$.

The results of this test are shown in Appendix II. The considerable differences among these values indicate that σ is *not* equal to unity. Theoretically σ must be positive, but $R(z/w)$, $R(y/r)$, and $R(x/\omega)$ can be negative depending upon the values of $\dot{A}/A$ and $\dot{B}/B$ in relation to $\dot{y}/y$, $\dot{z}/z$, and $\dot{x}/x$. If we compute the averages of $R(z/w)$, $R(y/r)$, and $R(x/\omega)$, then

$$\bar{R}\left(\frac{z}{w}\right) = 1.0801 \, ,$$

$$\bar{R}\left(\frac{y}{r}\right) = .2784 \, ,$$

$$\bar{R}\left(\frac{x}{\omega}\right) = .7490 \, .$$

Thus, not only for each year, but also for the average values, all three estimates are *very different*. From this we may conclude that the underlying production function is *not* the Cobb-Douglas function. It is interesting to note that the only one of these three tests which makes no use of figures on capital and rate of return to capital is the one that approximately satisfies the Cobb-Douglas requirement $(\bar{R}(z/w) = 1.080)$.

b. *Regression equation method.* The second method that can be applied to estimate the elasticity of substitution depends on regression equations fitted to the percentage changes of the wage rate and the return to capital (equations (7) and (8)). We have already estimated these regression equations in the previous section obtaining equations (36) and (37). For the reader's convenience, the regressions are reproduced here:

$$(36) \qquad \frac{\dot{w}}{w} = \underset{(.00891)}{.01667} - \underset{(.23107)}{.64198} \frac{\dot{x}}{x}, \qquad R = .3689, \qquad F = 7.7190 \,,$$
$$T = 2.77830$$

$$(37) \qquad \frac{\dot{r}}{r} = \underset{(.01148)}{.01141} + \underset{(.29771)}{.47484} \frac{\dot{x}}{x}, \qquad R = .2222, \qquad F = 2.5439 \,,$$
$$T = 1.59495$$

where $\dot{x}/x = -\dot{k}/k$. The coefficients of $\dot{x}/x$ in equations (36) and (37) are respectively equal to the averages of $-\alpha/\sigma$ and β/σ. Since the values of $\bar{\alpha}$ and $\bar{\beta}$ are 0.337 and 0.663, $\bar{\sigma}$ is estimated from (36) as

$$\bar{\sigma} = .524938 \,,$$

and from (37) as

$$\bar{\sigma} = 1.3962 \,.$$

The estimate obtained from (37) is not as good as the estimate obtained from (36). The T value in (37) is equal to 1.59495 and is not as high as 2.77831 which is the T value in (36). We conclude from this that σ is not equal to unity, and most likely is less than unity.

4. ESTIMATION OF $A(t)$ AND $B(t)$

We are now in a position to estimate the rates of factor augmenting technical progress, since we have evidence that the technical progress is not neutral and that the underlying production function is not of the Cobb-Douglas type.

4.1. *CES functions.* Various estimates have been made with respect to the value of σ under the assumption of neutral technical progress, using the U. S. data. Arrow, *et al.* [1] suggests that σ is approximately equal to .569. Kravis estimates σ as .64. The estimate of Kendrick and Sato [9] suggests that σ is approximately equal to .58. Equation (36) of this paper suggests that σ is approximately equal to .525. As I have assumed that σ is probably greater that .5 but less than .8, I have chosen three values of σ for the estimation of $\dot{A}/A$ and $\dot{B}/B$: $\sigma = .5$, $\sigma = .6$, and $\sigma = .7$. Since I have only discrete values of $r(t)$, $w(t)$, $z(t)$, and $y(t)$, the estimates of $\dot{A}/A$ and $\dot{B}/B$ are substituted by $\Delta A(t)/A(t)$ and $\Delta B(t)/B(t)$. The results of the computation are shown in the Appendix III. In all three cases, the average values of $\Delta A/A$ are different from those of $\Delta B/B$, suggesting that technical progress is non-neutral. In all three cases the average values of $\Delta A/A$ are smaller than those of $\Delta B/B$. The average values of $\Delta A/A$ and $\Delta B/B$ (for 51 years) are respectively equal to .0127 and .0199 for $\sigma = .5$. When σ is increased from

.5 to .6, then the average of $\Delta A/A$ increases slightly to .0145, while it does not significantly affect the average value of $\Delta B/B$ (.0193). This tendency continues when σ is changed from .6 to .7, increasing the average value of $\Delta A/A$ to .0174. However, if we exclude the 1942–1945 (war period) estimates of $\Delta A/A$ and $\Delta B/B$, then for the different values of σ all the averages of $\Delta A/A$ and $\Delta B/B$ are values in the neighborhood of .7 percent for $\Delta A/A$ and 2 percent for $\Delta B/B$. The difference between the average value of $\Delta A/A$ and that of $(\Delta B/B)$ $(\Delta B/B - \Delta A/A)$ ranges from approximately 1.3 to .2 percentage points depending on which values are selected and also on which years are included for the computation of the averages.

Since σ is smaller than unity and $\dot{B}/B$ is greater than $\dot{A}/A$, technical progress is on the average "labor-saving," meaning the share of capital will increase if the capital-labor ratio remains constant.

The last column of Appendix III is provided for the purpose of comparing these estimates with a series of the "total productivity" change $\Delta T/T$ which were derived from Solow's method. If technical progress is neutral, then $\Delta A/A$, $\Delta B/B$, and $\Delta T/T$ should be the same. On the contrary they differ greatly from one another, not only on the average but also for each year.

4.2. *CEDD functions.* I have used essentially three *CEDD* functions to estimate $\Delta A/A$ and $\Delta B/B$: (1) a Bernoulli production function (unitary elasticity of derived demand production function; (2) a production function with a constant $E_k > 1$; and (3) a production function with a constant $E_x > 1$. One obvious justification for using the Bernoulli equation with $E_k = 1$ is that we can use the share of labor β as the elasticity of factor substitution σ. The value of β varies from year to year and so does the value of σ, but it stays in the neighborhood of .66, which may not be far from the true value of σ.

The main reason for employing the function with $E_k > 1$ is to consider the possibility that entrepreneurs may tend to increase profit per labor as the capital-labor ratio increases. The production function

$$Y = \frac{a_1}{1 - \delta_1}(AK)^{1-\delta_1}(BL)^{\delta_1} + b_1(BL)$$

must be subject to the restrictions $a_1 > 0$, $b_1 < 0$, and $\delta_1 < 1$. I have chosen, more or less arbitrarily, the value of E_k to equal 1.2, i.e., $\delta_1 = .833$. Thus $\sigma(t)$ is estimated from 1.2 $\beta(t)$.

The third equation I have used here has a constant elasticity of the marginal productivity of labor per unit of capital input ($E_x = $ constant). It is

$$Y = \frac{a_2}{1 - \delta_2}(AK)^{\delta_2}(BL)^{1-\delta_2} + b_2(AK), \ a_2 > 0, \ b_2 < 0, \ \delta_2 < 1 \ .$$

A strong justification for this function comes from the regression equation shown by (36). In equation (36) the coefficient of $\dot{x}/x$, .64198, must be equal to α/σ. This implies that E_x equals 1.558. The reliability of this estimate is assured because the T value of the coefficient is sufficiently high (2.7783) and in the long run E_x can be considered as fixed.

The last assumptions employed are that $\sigma = \beta$ and that β is, on the average, constant. Since the average value of β is equal to .663, I assumed that $\sigma = .663$. This imposes an extra assumption on the relationship between $\dot{A}/A - \dot{B}/B$ and $\dot{x}/x$. In equation (13), β would be constant with $\sigma \neq 1$, if $\dot{A}/A - \dot{B}/B = \dot{x}/x$. I have used this assumption in view of the fact that α and β are relatively constant.

The results for the estimates of $\Delta A/A$ and $\Delta B/B$ are shown in Appendix IV. Most estimates are similar to those obtained under the assumption of *CES* functions. $\Delta B/B$ is, on the average, higher than $\Delta A/A$, except in the second case ($\sigma = 1.2\,\beta$) where the average value of $\Delta A/A$ is 3.77 percent, while the value of $\Delta B/B$ is only .46 percent. The magnitude of the average values of $\Delta A/A$ and $\Delta B/B$ seems very reasonable except in the case of ($\sigma = 1.2\,\beta$). $\Delta A/A$ varies from .74 percent to 1.7 percent, while $\Delta B/B$ varies from 1.9 percent to 2.3 percent.

5. ESTIMATION OF THE PRODUCTION FUNCTIONS

5.1. *Explanation of the short-run variations of output per labor in terms of long-run models.* The final stage of work is to estimate the production function. Since the values of each $\Delta A/A$ and $\Delta B/B$ are estimated from a particular assumption regarding the elasticity of factor substitution, in view of the Impossibility Theorem the same values should *not* be used to test the validity of that assumption. This situation is avoided by not using each year's $\Delta A(t)/A(t)$ and $\Delta B(t)/B(t)$, but instead using the *average values* for constructing $A(t)$ and $B(t)$ series. Thus, the estimation of the production function involves the testing of the "usefulness" of long-run models for the explanation of the short-run variations. I owe this method to John Wise.

Let us show how this method would be applied, using an example. Suppose we wish to test the reliability of both $\Delta A/A$ and $\Delta B/B$ estimated from a *CES* function, say $\sigma = .6$, and also to test the reliability of that *CES* function. Then the method requires that we: (1) compute the average $\Delta A/A$ and $\Delta B/B$; (2) construct the series of $A(t) = A(0)(1 + \mu)^t$ and $B(t) = B(0)(1 + \gamma)^t$ where μ and γ are the averages of $\Delta A/A$ and $\Delta B/B$; (3) estimate the regression equation of the *CES* function, using those $A(t)$ and $B(t)$; (4) test the reliability of the estimate in terms of such statistics as correlation coefficient, T value, and standard errors. If we apply this method to the different estimates of $\Delta A/A$ and $\Delta B/B$, this provides a basis for a comparison of the various production functions.

The results of the computation are shown in Table 1. I have used income per labor ($z = Y/L$) as a dependent variable for the regression analysis. The different average values of $\Delta A/A$ and $\Delta B/B$, which were derived by excluding the war period 1942-1945, are applied for some production functions.

Although the results of the regression analysis are remarkable in terms of the correlation coefficient, the *CEDD* functions in general provide better statistical estimates in terms of the regression coefficients and their standard errors. Specifically, the *CEDD* production function with $E_z = 1.558$ has the best explanatory power since both the regression coefficients are significantly

TABLE 1

ESTIMATION OF THE PRODUCTION FUNCTIONS

	CES Functions $z = [a(Ak)^{-\rho} + bB^{-\rho}]^{-1/\rho}$, $\sigma = \dfrac{1}{1+\rho}$				CEDD Functions $z = aB \log\left(\dfrac{A}{B}k\right) + bB,\ E_k = 1,$ $z = \dfrac{a_2}{1-\delta_2}(Ak)^{\delta_2}B^{1-\delta_2} + b_2(Ak),$ $E_z = \text{constant} = \dfrac{1}{\delta_2}$		
	$\sigma = .5$	$\sigma = .6$		$\sigma = .7$	$E_k = 1$ $\sigma = \beta$	$E_k = 1$ $\sigma = \beta = .663$	$\sigma = 1.558\ \alpha$
μ	.0127	.0145	.0073*	.0174	.0123	.0167	.0074
$\hat{\gamma}$	.0199	.0193	.0206	.0194	.0189	.0195	.0227
$\hat{a}$	.02352	−.03622	−.03271	−.07703	.12437	.12995	$1.26943 = \left(\dfrac{a_2}{1-\delta_2}\right)$
$S_{\hat{a}}$	.38864	.23868	.21686	.17735	.13198	.12104	.07590
T	.06052	.15176	.15082	.43432	.94232	1.10736	16.72460
$\hat{\delta}$	1.73665	1.55136	1.54422	1.45400	.82636	.72686	−.66019
$S_{\hat{\delta}}$	.19798	.16823	.12023	.16331	.05931	.06915	.06696
T	8.77170	9.22185	12.84385	8.90349	13.93314	10.51085	9.85920
F	1071.42	1285.25	1291.16	1329.36	1575.77	1647.85	1838.2301
R	.9888	.9914	.9908	.9906	.9923	.9926	.9934
R^2	.9776	.9822	.9819	.9814	.9847	.9853	.9868

* excluding 1942–1945.

different from zero. The results of this production function are

$$
\begin{aligned}
z &= \underset{(.07590)}{1.26943}\ (A(t)k)^{\delta_2}B^{1-\delta_2} - \underset{(.06696)}{.66019}\ (A(t)k) \\
T &= 16.7260 \qquad\qquad\qquad T = 9.85920 \\
F &= 1838.2301 \qquad\qquad\quad R = .9934
\end{aligned}
\tag{38}
$$

where $A(t) = A(0)\,(1 + .0074)^t$, $B(t) = B(0)\,(1 + .0227)^t$ and $\delta_2 = 1/E_z = .64198$. An interesting aspect of (38) is that the first part of the equation has the Cobb-Douglas form. The coefficient of the second part, −.66019, is statistically very significant ($T = 9.85920$), which implies that the second part of (38) is not equal to zero.

Good estimates are also obtained from the "Bernoulli" production function, where the elasticity of factor substitution is approximately equal to the share of labor. The following Bernoulli production function with $E_k = 1$ has strong explanatory power for the U. S. private nonfarm sector:

$$
z = .124\left[B(t)\log\left(\frac{A(t)}{B(t)}k\right)\right] + .826B(t)
\tag{39}
$$

where $A(t) = A(0)\,(1 + .0123)^t$ and $B(t) = B(0)\,(1 + .0189)^t$.

On the other hand, none of the CES functions provide satisfactory results in terms of individual regression coefficients; the sign of the first coefficient,

a, is generally wrong. The *CES* function that yields the best estimate is
the one with the elasticity of substitution equal to .6, but here also the

FIGURE 2

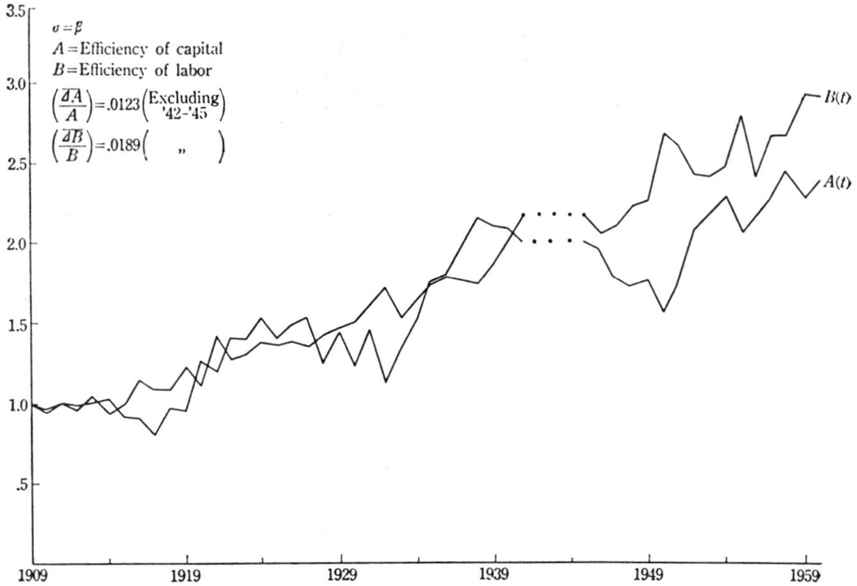

FIGURE 3

sign of α is negative. This is the value of the elasticity estimated by Solow, Kravis, and Kendrick and Sato.

The $A(t)$ and $B(t)$ series corresponding to the two *CEDD* functions (equations (38) and (39) with $E_x = 1.558$ and $E_k = 1$) are constructed from each year's $\Delta A/A$ and $\Delta B/B$, and are shown in Figures 2 and 3. It seems that these two estimates of $A(t)$ and $B(t)$ represent the two extreme values and that the true values of $A(t)$ and $B(t)$ lie somewhere between these; approximately, $\dot{A}/A = 1$ percent and $\dot{B}/B = 2$ percent.

5.2. *CES vs. CEDD functions*[3]. Although we have seen that the *CEDD* functions are a better approximation than the *CES* from the statistical inference on the regression coefficients, one hardly knows what to make of the difference between an R of .991 (*CES*) and one of .993 (*CEDD*). However, the point is not to decide whether *CES* or *CEDD* or $C-D$ (Cobb-Douglas) is "true." The point is that some of these functions have rather special implications, and one really wants to know whether to believe (approximately) these implications.

The significance of the Cobb-Douglas is that it implies that as capital increases relative to labor, the rate of profit behaves in such a way as to keep the share of profits about constant. The significance of concluding that σ is less than one is that it implies that the rate of return will fall even farther so that the share of profits will fall. The *CEDD* production function has quite different implications from the *CES*. In the case of the *CEDD* function the share of profits will fall even more rapidly than in the case of the *CES* unless technical progress is labor-saving.

The different implications of various production functions are illustrated in Figure 4 using: (1) the Cobb-Douglas, $\sigma = 1$; (2) a *CES* where $\sigma = .6$; and (3) a *CEDD* (equation (38)) where $\sigma = 1.558\ \alpha(k, t)$ and

$$\alpha = \frac{1.26943 \times .64198(A(t)k)^{.64198}B(t)^{.35802} - .66019(A(t)k)}{1.26943(A(t)k)^{.64198}B(t)^{.35802} - .66019(A(t)k)}.$$

If the production function is a *CES* or a $C-D$ function, technical progress of any kind will have no effect on σ by definition (two straight lines at $\sigma = 1$ and $\sigma = .6$). On the other hand, if technical progress is Hicks neutral and the production function is the *CEDD*, the value of σ will fall over time, along σ_1 line, forcing the return to capital and the share of capital to zero. In order to prevent this decline of the profit rate and capital's share, entrepreneurs must introduce biased (labor-saving) technical progress, which shifts σ_1 curve to σ_2 curve, thus maintaining the relatively constant profit rate and capital share at a higher capital-labor ratio.

For example, σ in 1909 was equal to .52139 (PP'). If technical progress had been entirely Hicks neutral, then σ in 1960 would have been approximately .15 (QQ'). However, since technical progress was in fact biased

---

[3] The interested reader should compare the results of the present paper with those of David and van de Klundert [2], who assume that the underlying production function is only of the *CES* type. Their estimates of the efficiencies are almost identical with the present estimates.

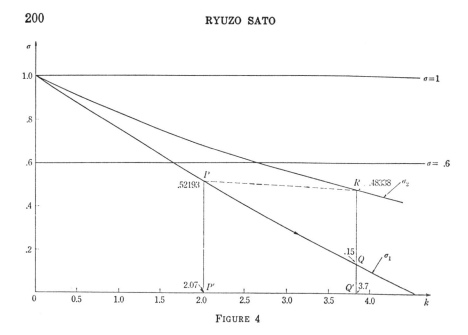

FIGURE 4

(labor-saving), the σ_1 function shifted to the σ_2 function during this period, explaining the fact that the U. S. economy maintained a relatively high value of σ (.48338 $= RQ'$) as well as a relatively constant value of the profit share α. Thus, if one allows for technical progress of the biased kind, it is more natural to assume that the economy is operating under a production function with a *variable* elasticity of substitution rather than with a fixed elasticity.

6. SUMMARY

This paper has attempted a theoretical as well as empirical analysis of the Hicksian mechanism of technical progress and economic growth. It has set forth a simple way of separating the efficiencies of capital and labor, $A(t)$ and $B(t)$, and of estimating the aggregate production functions. The method rests on the values of the elasticity of substitution, combined with the original Solow method. Listed below are some of the conclusions which emerge from a rough application of the model to the U. S. data 1909-1960.

1. The elasticity of factor substitution is most likely less than unity (between 0.5 and 0.7). The Cobb-Douglas production function is not appropriate for the explanation of the U. S. private nonfarm sector behavior for recent decades.

2. Technical progress is, on the average, nonneutral. The labor efficiency tends to rise faster (2 percent) than the capital efficiency (1 percent).

3. Since the elasticity of factor substitution is less than unity, technical progress is *labor-saving*.

4. The constant elasticity of derived demand production (*CEDD*) functions have more explanatory power than the *CES* functions applied to the data:

1) $z = 1.26943\,(A(t)k)^{\delta_2}B(t)^{1-\delta_2} - .66019\,(A(t)k)$ where $A(t) = A(0)(1 + .0074)^t$, $B(t) = B(0)(1 + .0227)^t$ and $\delta_2 = 1/E_z = .64198$, and;

2) $z = .124[B(t)\cdot\log\,((A(t)/B(t))k)] + .826B(t)$ where $A(t) = A(0)(1 + .0123)^t$ and $B(t) = B(0)(1 + .0189)^t$.

5.   As capital deepening proceeds, the share of capital declines if technical progress is neutral. The reason for the introduction of biased technical progress by entrepreneurs comes from this consideration. Whenever the share of capital tends to fall, entrepreneurs introduce labor-saving inventions which prevent the capital share from declining.

6.   The relative constancy of the capital share is partly due to the adjustment of a variable elasticity of factor substitution. In order to maintain its constancy, the factor shares must be related to the elasticity of factor substitution in such a way that the elasticity increases when the share of capital declines or when the share of labor increases; that is,

$$\sigma = \phi(\alpha)\,.$$

7.   The simplest relationship of $\phi(\alpha)$ is represented by *CEDD* functions. This is one justification for the use of the *CEDD* production functions.

8.   As can be observed from the estimation of $\Delta A/A$ and $\Delta B/B$, they (especially $\Delta A/A$) are very sensitive to the values of the elasticity of factor substitution. This implies that inventions first affect the elasticity, which in turn affects the relative shares. If the production function is of the *CEDD* type, the effects of technical progress on the relative shares are immediate. This is a second justification for the use of these functions.

Brown University, U. S. A.

RYUZO SATO

APPENDIX I

TIME SERIES FOR U.S. PRIVATE NONFARM SECTOR

Year	Private nonfarm GNP Y	Capital K	Man hours L	Share of capital α	Return of capital r	Wage rate w
1909	44,664	138,436	66,563	.335	.108	.446
10	44,910	145,520	68,831	.330	.102	.437
11	47,195	146,167	70,102	.335	.108	.448
12	48,226	153,595	72,786	.330	.104	.444
13	51,937	156,659	73,839	.334	.112	.468
14	45,886	147,066	71,210	.325	.101	.435
15	46,676	151,603	70,859	.344	.106	.432
16	56,293	171,325	78,007	.358	.118	.463
17	52,695	175,687	79,459	.370	.111	.418
18	56,365	180,011	78,283	.342	.107	.474
19	58,985	180,546	75,422	.354	.116	.505
20	59,734	184,298	76,336	.319	.103	.533
21	58,698	155,887	68,167	.369	.139	.543
22	62,084	168,694	74,269	.339	.125	.553
23	71,285	197,128	81,994	.337	.122	.576
24	74,284	197,560	79,197	.330	.124	.628
25	75,481	211,265	82,429	.336	.120	.608
26	81,366	226,996	86,127	.327	.117	.636
27	81,833	227,826	86,508	.323	.116	.640
28	83,097	235,339	87,083	.338	.107	.632
29	88,562	249,382	89,467	.332	.118	.661
30	79,817	242,728	81,854	.347	.114	.637
31	73,021	215,616	72,386	.325	.110	.681
32	60,665	183,450	62,069	.397	.131	.589
33	57,772	174,308	61,248	.362	.120	.602
34	65,041	181,611	62,366	.355	.127	.673
35	74,221	184,713	66,023	.351	.141	.730
36	83,278	195,770	73,426	.357	.152	.729
37	90,884	207,780	77,568	.340	.149	.773
38	83,743	192,708	70,460	.331	.144	.795
39	91,530	199,232	75,131	.347	.159	.796
40	101,313	210,558	79,694	.357	.172	.817
41	116,415	232,213	89,276	.377	.189	.812
42	127,434	254,535	97,056	.356	.178	.846
43	136,274	263,965	101,633	.342	.177	.882
44	146,470	263,740	100,124	.332	.184	.977
45	145,052	255,976	94,920	.314	.178	1.048

(*Continued on next page*)

APPENDIX I

(Continued)

Year	Private nonfarm GNP Y	Capital K	Man hours L	Share of capital α	Return to capital r	Wage rate w
1946	140,288	255,196	96,671	.312	.172	.998
47	142,022	266,942	100,072	.327	.174	.955
48	149,895	279,048	101,304	.332	.178	.988
49	147,122	281,433	96.784	.326	.170	1.025
50	163,260	294,869	100,352	.363	.201	1.036
51	173,398	317,629	104,801	.345	.188	1.084
52	178,864	332,480	106,168	.317	.171	1.151
53	186,264	343,207	109,195	.311	.169	1.175
54	184,482	344,371	103,523	.305	.163	1.238
55	200,993	362,673	107,954	.329	.182	1.249
56	205,730	376,986	124,341	.319	.174	1.127
57	210,125	389,533	111,104	.311	.168	1.303
58	205,700	383,892	106,250	.301	.161	1.353
59	221,385	402,047	110,732	.316	.174	1,368
1960	227,593	412,304	111,881	.309	.171	1.406

Note: Y and K are in millions of 1929 dollars.

APPENDIX II

DATA FOR A TEST OF THE COBB-DOUGLAS PRODUCTION FUNCTION

Year	$R\left(\dfrac{z}{w}\right)$	$R\left(\dfrac{y}{r}\right)$	$R\left(\dfrac{x}{\omega}\right)$	Year	$R\left(\dfrac{z}{w}\right)$	$R\left(\dfrac{y}{r}\right)$	$R\left(\dfrac{x}{\omega}\right)$
1910	1.3786	.7721	.4378	25	.7416	1.5706	56.4000
11	1.2480	.7968	.4398	26	.6977	− .1211	.4102
12	1.7778	.7351	.4247	27	.2222	− .2558	− .1566
13	1.1306	.7395	− .3062	28	− .6772	1.5493	.3803
14	1.2069	.5739	− .8907	29	.8223	1.1266	− .5474
15	−3.1449	− .2818	− .6855	30	.4032	2.2792	−29.6818
16	1.3015	.6195	− .6735	31	.5170	− .8022	.0286
17	.8180	1.5166	− .1594	32	.2055	− .1510	.0218
18	.6681	−1.1283	.2209	33	−1.6806	− .0229	− .3201
19	1.2932	.5361	−2.3391	34	.9062	1.3539	.4405
20	.0095	.0634	.0506	35	.9257	1.0957	1.8937
21	4.9620	.5375	.2137	36	−6.2857	.7666	.6266
22	−1.6630	.2063	− .0512	37	.5624	−1.3632	.0651
23	.9649	.7195	.8742	38	.5090	.1844	.2881
24	.8829	2.3789	.4915	39	18.8462	.5726	.3074

(Continued on next page)

RYUZO SATO

APPENDIX II

(Continued)

Year	$R\left(\frac{z}{w}\right)$	$R\left(\frac{y}{r}\right)$	$R\left(\frac{x}{\omega}\right)$	Year	$R\left(\frac{z}{w}\right)$	$R\left(\frac{y}{r}\right)$	$R\left(\frac{x}{\omega}\right)$
1940	1.6226	.5992	.0499	51	.3770	.2069	.2496
41	−4.0484	.4461	.1653	52	.3076	.1479	.2142
42	.1716	.0194	.0721	53	.6078	− .7373	.0893
43	.5074	−5.3929	− .2321	54	.8409	.3560	.6216
44	.8591	1.8526	.1910	55	4.8750	.3199	− .1053
45	.6307	− .5905	.2295	56	1.6965	.3391	1.8690
46	1.0599	.8854	1.8190	57	1.3437	.3277	.8148
47	.5000	−2.8957	− .1949	58	.8919	.1533	.3440
48	1.2246	.4311	2.9820	59	4.2267	.3601	− .1159
49	.7368	.5837	.6548	1960	.9198	− .1437	.3610
50	6.1887	.3619	− .0818	*Average*	1.0801	.2784	.7490

APPENDIX III

ESTIMATION OF $\dot{A}/A$ AND $\dot{B}/B$ FROM CES FUNCTIONS
$(\sigma = .5, \; \sigma = .6, \; \sigma = .7)$

Year	$\sigma = .5$		$\sigma = .6$		$\sigma = .7$		% Change of total productivity $\frac{\dot{T}}{T} = \frac{\dot{z}}{z} + \alpha\frac{\dot{x}}{x}$
	$\dfrac{\dot{A}}{A}$	$\dfrac{\dot{B}}{B}$	$\dfrac{\dot{A}}{A}$	$\dfrac{\dot{B}}{B}$	$\dfrac{\dot{A}}{A}$	$\dfrac{\dot{B}}{B}$	
1910	− .0320	− .0362	− .0253	− .0400	− .0140	− .0467	− .0340
11	.0330	.0368	.0273	.0398	.0180	.0450	.0356
12	− .0180	− .0230	− .0130	− .0265	− .0043	− .0323	− .0202
13	.0342	.0646	.0250	.0680	.0093	.0737	.0559
14	− .0160	− .1072	.0070	− .1153	.0457	− .1283	− .0829
15	− .0738	.0504	− .1040	.0440	− .1543	.0883	.0092
16	.0242	.1074	.0050	.1175	− .0273	.1343	.0777
17	− .1282	− .0684	− .1445	− .0588	− .1717	− .0423	− .0905
18	.1218	.0396	.1615	.0200	.2280	− .0127	.0655
19	.0056	.0974	− .0125	.1065	− .0423	.1213	.0650
20	.1102	− .0516	.1693	− .0775	.2677	− .1210	− .0026
21	.0194	.1642	− .0405	.2008	− .1403	.2613	.1107
22	.0658	− .0784	.1103	− .1025	.1843	− .1427	− .0278
23	− .0108	.0370	− .0073	.0365	− .0017	.0353	.0191
24	.0604	.0634	.0715	.0585	.0900	.0503	.0608
25	− .0712	− .0158	− .0808	− .0118	− .0967	− .0047	− .0339
26	.0318	.0174	.0463	.0108	.0700	− .0003	.0212
27	.0130	− .0036	.0185	− .0060	.0273	− .0100	.0022

(Continued on next page)

APPENDIX III

(Continued)

Year	$\sigma = .5$ $\frac{\dot{A}}{A}$	$\sigma = .5$ $\frac{\dot{B}}{B}$	$\sigma = .6$ $\frac{\dot{A}}{A}$	$\sigma = .6$ $\frac{\dot{B}}{B}$	$\sigma = .7$ $\frac{\dot{A}}{A}$	$\sigma = .7$ $\frac{\dot{B}}{B}$	% Change of total productivity $\frac{\dot{T}}{T} = \frac{\dot{z}}{z} + \alpha \frac{\dot{x}}{x}$
1928	$-.1764$	.0300	$-.1995$	.0405	$-.2380$	.0583	$-.0005$
29	.1168	.0282	.1225	.0245	.1327	.0180	.0259
30	$-.1248$	.0074	$-.1473$	.0185	$-.1847$	.0373	$-.0379$
31	.0948	.0022	.1275	$-.0135$	.1823	$-.0393$	.0324
32	$-.2088$	.0920	$-.3010$	.1540	$-.4547$	.2573	$-.0298$
33	.0960	$-.0942$	.1428	$-.1233$	.2210	$-.1713$	$-.0229$
34	.0940	.0856	.1038	.0808	.1200	.0723	.0873
35	.1182	.0664	.1230	.0635	.1310	.0587	.0861
36	.0386	.0190	.0303	.0240	.0160	.0327	.0259
37	.0750	.0070	.0988	$-.0053$	.1383	$-.0260$	.0302
38	.0220	.0004	.0360	$-.0063$	.0597	$-.0177$	.0078
39	.0136	.0476	$-.0065$	.0593	$-.0400$	.0787	.0346
40	.0150	.0576	$-.0003$	.0658	$-.0253$	.0790	.0426
41	$-.0098$	.0564	$-.0345$	.0720	$-.0760$	.0980	.0310
42	.0594	$-.0264$	.0898	$-.0430$	.1403	$-.0707$	.0041
43	.0660	.0006	.0840	$-.0095$	.1137	$-.0263$	.0243
44	.1028	.0698	.1190	.0630	.1460	.0517	.0791
45	.0736	.0176	.1003	.0053	.1450	$-.0157$	.0351
46	$-.0268$	$-.0560$	$-.0250$	$-.0575$	$-.0217$	$-.0600$	$-.0465$
47	$-.0782$	$-.0002$	$-.1005$	.0113	$-.1380$	.0300	$-.0260$
48	$-.0032$	.0484	$-.0095$	.0523	$-.0203$	.0583	.0299
49	$-.0078$	.0170	.0020	.0123	.0183	.0043	.0086
50	$-.0426$	.1206	$-.0918$	.1480	$-.1737$	.1940	.0613
51	.0406	$-.0110$	.0680	$-.0248$	.1137	$-.0477$	.0062
52	.0700	$-.0224$	.1123	$-.0425$	.1830	$-.0760$	.0070
53	.0292	.0044	.0395	.0005	.0567	$-.0063$	.0114
54	.0106	.0346	.0225	.0308	.0423	.0240	.0256
55	$-.0376$	.0770	$-.0730$	.0940	$-.1323$	.1223	.0396
56	.0148	$-.1420$	.0300	$-.1505$	.0553	$-.1647$	$-.0943$
57	.0124	.1150	.0243	.1100	.0443	.1017	.0760
58	.0304	.0092	.0488	.0023	.0797	$-.0093$	.0144
59	$-.0210$	.0524	$-.0448$	.0628	$-.0847$	.0800	.0291
60	.0224	.0074	.0323	.0025	.0490	$-.0057$	.0126
Average	.0127	.0199	.0145	.0193	.0174	.0194	.0159
Average Excl. '42 to '45	.0073	.0203	.0073	.0206	.0073	.0223	

RYUZO SATO

APPENDIX IV
ESTIMATION OF $\dot{A}/A$ AND $\dot{B}/B$ FROM CEDD FUNCTIONS
$(\sigma = \beta,\ \sigma = \bar{\beta},\ \sigma = 1.2\,\beta,\ \sigma = 1.558\,\alpha)$

| Year | $\sigma = \beta$ | | $\sigma = \bar{\beta} = .663$ | | $\sigma = 1.2\,\beta$ | | $\sigma = 1.558\,\alpha$ | |
	$\dfrac{\dot{A}}{A}$	$\dfrac{\dot{B}}{B}$	$\dfrac{\dot{A}}{A}$	$\dfrac{\dot{B}}{B}$	$\dfrac{\dot{A}}{A}$	$\dfrac{\dot{B}}{B}$	$\dfrac{\dot{A}}{A}$	$\dfrac{\dot{B}}{B}$
1910	−.0182	−.0442	−.0190	−.0436	.0097	−.0602	−.0313	−.0366
11	.0218	.0427	.0220	.0427	−.0005	.0550	.0320	.0374
12	−.0076	−.0303	−.0083	−.0297	.0138	−.0449	−.0175	−.0235
13	.0156	.0713	.0163	.0712	−.0209	.0846	.0327	.0652
14	.0338	−.1243	.0288	−.1226	.1353	−.1584	−.0150	−.1077
15	−.1288	.0762	−.1323	.0780	−.2366	.1272	−.0832	.0547
16	−.0064	.1235	−.0131	.1270	−.0665	.1548	.0143	.1127
17	−.1511	−.0546	−.1599	−.0496	−.1967	−.0275	−.1401	−.0616
18	.1953	.0035	.1988	.0018	.3414	−.0686	.1330	.0343
19	−.0240	.1121	−.0291	.1148	−.0822	.1413	−.0027	.1016
20	.2442	−.1107	.2246	−.1018	.5197	−.2317	.1087	−.0509
21	−.0656	.2160	−.0964	.2347	−.2342	.3185	−.0228	.1899
22	.1501	−.1242	.1519	−.1249	.3174	−.2150	.0763	−.0841
23	−.0042	.0356	−.0042	.0356	.0093	.0328	−.0101	.0371
24	.0833	.0533	.0819	.0540	.1296	.0332	.0617	.0628
25	−.0899	−.0077	−.0896	−.0077	−.1271	.0089	−.0732	−.0151
26	.0621	.0037	.0596	.0045	.1240	−.0255	.0328	.0169
27	.0248	−.0090	.0234	−.0083	.0489	−.0197	.0131	−.0036
28	−.2207	.0503	−.2211	.0504	−.3083	.0908	−.1818	.0323
29	.1286	.0205	.1282	.0208	.1530	.0045	.1176	.0277
30	−.1646	.0271	−.1682	.0291	−.2431	.0708	−.1329	.0113
31	.1655	−.0314	.1582	−.0279	.3089	−.0995	.0964	.0014
32	−.3045	.1564	−.3872	.2122	−.5083	.2935	−.3239	.1696
33	.1674	−.1384	.1866	−.1501	.3090	−.2256	.1234	−.1124
34	.1101	.0777	.1131	.0763	.1416	.0615	.0987	.0834
35	.1265	.0615	.1276	.0608	.1421	.0520	.1203	.0653
36	.0249	.0272	.0223	.0288	−.0018	.0434	.0342	.0378
37	.1197	−.0165	.1208	−.0169	.2082	−.0630	.0811	.0038
38	.0508	−.0133	.0493	−.0128	.1091	−.0411	.0238	−.0004
39	−.0219	.0683	−.0252	.0700	−.0921	.1088	.0065	.0519
40	−.0092	.0706	−.0142	.0733	−.0575	.0961	.0074	.0617
41	−.0422	.0769	−.0579	.0866	−.1075	.1179	−.0308	.0695
42	.1084	−.0534	.1181	−.0588	.2053	−.1066	.0744	−.0346
43	.0991	−.0178	.1006	−.0190	.1648	−.0548	.0711	−.0021
44	.1355	.0560	.1341	.0567	.2015	.0278	.1052	.0687
45	.1369	−.0118	.1252	−.0065	.2689	−.0734	.0712	.0188

(Continued on next page)

BIASED TECHNICAL PROGRESS   207

APPENDIX IV

(*Continued*)

Year	$\sigma = \beta$		$\sigma = \bar\beta = .663$		$\sigma = 1.2\,\beta$		$\sigma = 1.558\,\alpha$	
	$\dfrac{\dot A}{A}$	$\dfrac{\dot B}{B}$	$\dfrac{\dot A}{A}$	$\dfrac{\dot B}{B}$	$\dfrac{\dot A}{A}$	$\dfrac{\dot B}{B}$	$\dfrac{\dot A}{A}$	$\dfrac{\dot B}{B}$
1946	−.0221	−.0596	−.0231	−.0591	−.0121	−.0672	−.0270	−.0560
47	−.1254	.0239	−.1214	.0217	−.2219	.0724	−.0798	.0008
48	−.0160	.0560	−.0154	.0558	−.0419	.0712	−.0039	.0439
49	.0129	.0071	.0110	.0080	.0555	−.0136	−.0732	.0169
50	−.1168	.1620	−.1365	.1739	−.2627	.2436	−.0726	.1373
51	.0899	−.0357	.0935	−.0377	.1869	−.0846	.0496	−.0154
52	.1678	−.0691	.1519	−.0614	.3711	−.1656	.0680	−.0215
53	.0540	−.0055	.0490	−.0033	.1069	−.0260	.0280	.0049
54	.0410	.0243	.0335	.0270	.1060	.0018	.0084	.0354
55	−.1116	.1125	−.1062	.1101	−.2595	.1836	−.0415	.0789
56	.0492	−.1611	.0442	−.1585	.1202	−.2005	.0145	−.1413
57	.0415	.1029	.0356	.1053	.1029	.0451	.0109	.1157
58	.0791	−.0093	.0662	−.0042	.1863	−.0491	.0260	.0109
59	−.0766	.0766	−.0671	.0724	−.1922	.1268	−.0195	.0518
1960	.0469	−.0049	.0415	−.0021	.0988	−.0298	.0210	.0081
Average	.0208	.0169	.0167	.0195	.0377	.0046	.0074	.0227
Average Excl. '42 to '45	.0123	.0189	.0079	.0218	.0230	.0094	.0011	.0236

REFERENCES

[1] ARROW, K., et al., "Capital-Labor Substitution and Economic Efficiency," *Review of Economics and Statistics*, (August, 1961), 225-50.

[2] DAVID, P. A. AND VAN DE KLUNDERT, T., "Biased Efficiency Growth and Capital-Labor Substitution in the U. S. Economy, 1899-1960," *American Ecomomic Review*, LV (June, 1965), 357-94.

[3] DIAMOND, P. A. AND MCFADDEN, D., "Identification of the Elasticity of Substitution and the Bias of Technical Change: An Impossibility Theorem," Berkeley: University of California, 1965. (Mimeographed).

[4] DOMAR, E. D., "On the Measurement of Technological Change," *Economic Journal*, LXXI (December, 1961), 709-29.

[5] DHRYMES, P. J., "A Comparison of Productivity Behavior in Manufacturing and Service Industries," *Review of Economics and Statistics*, XLV (February, 1963), 64-9.

[6] HICKS, J. R., *The Theory of Wages*, 2nd edition (New York: St. Martin's Press, 1963).

[7] JOHANSEN, L., "A Method for Separating the Effects of Capital Accumulation and Shifts in Production Functions upon Growth in Labor Productivity," *Eco-*

nomic Journal, LXXI (December, 1961), 775-82.

[8] KENDRICK, J. W., *Productivity Trends in the United States* (Princeton: Princeton University Press, 1961).

[9] ――――, AND SATO, R., "Factor Prices, Productivity and Economic Growth," *American Economic Review*, LIII (December, 1963), 974-1003.

[10] RESEK, R., "Neutrality of Technical Progress," *Review of Economics and Statistics*, XLV (February, 1963), 55-63.

[11] SATO, R., "A Note on Scarcity of Specific Resources as a Limit to Output: A Correction," *Review of Economic Studies*, XXXIV (October, 1967), 421-6.

[12] ――――, AND BECKMANN, M. J., "Neutral Inventions and Production Functions," *Review of Economic Studies*, XXXV (January, 1968), 57-65. Addendum, XXXV (July, 1968), 366.

[13] SOLOW, R. M., "Technical Change and the Aggregate Production Function," *Review of Economics and Statistics*, XXXIX (August, 1957), 312-20.

13

Aggregate Production Functions and Types of Technical Progress: A Statistical Analysis

By Martin J. Beckmann and Ryuzo Sato*

The problem of estimating the rate and type of technical progress continues to be a major concern to economists. One of the difficulties encountered is that of accurate specification both of the aggregate production function and of the type of technical progress. There are different specifications of the production function and there are different assumptions regarding the way technological advance changes the production function. In recent work the type of production function most commonly applied is the CES function. We refer specifically to the works of Arrow, *et al.* [1], David, *et al.* [3], Domar [5], Dhrymes [6], Kendrick and Sato [8], and Jorgenson and Griliches [7]. With regard to technology, exogenous or endogenous forms may be assumed. In the exogenous case which we wish to examine in this paper, it has been customary for reasons of theoretical and technical convenience to assume "neutrality" usually in the sense of Hicks or Harrod. However, as we have shown in a theoretical paper on this subject, a number of other types of "neutrality" are possible and plausible (Sato and Beckmann [10]). By "neutrality" we mean the neutrality of the effects of technical change, that is to say, relationships between certain economic variables are *invariant* under technical change [10, p. 57].

A further complication arises from the

fact that these problems of specification of the form of a production function and the form of technical progress are not independent, for some forms of a production function necessarily preclude some types of technical progress. For other types of production functions certain distinctions do not arise. Consider, for example, the case of a production function of the Cobb-Douglas type. Technological change can shift the production function in any of a variety of ways, including changing the coefficients of labor and capital. But if technical change is not to change these coefficients, the change must "enter multiplicatively" and thus be either Hicks-neutral or Harrod-neutral (or their combination-factor-augmenting technical progress), but there is no way of distinguishing the two types. In other cases shown below, the choice of a specific form of a production function necessarily excludes certain types of technical progress. But the main point is that, in picking the type of technical progress, there is no reason to concentrate solely on the standard (Hicks and Harrod) forms of neutral technical progress. There are many other meaningful types of "neutral" technical progress.

In our article [10] already referred to we have systematically studied the problems mentioned above from a theoretical point of view. The paper discusses the close connection between the form of a production function in general and the type of technical progress of exogenous type, that would be consistent with a

* The authors are both professors of economics at Brown University. They wish to acknowledge the assistance of Diplomvolkswirt Lothar Weinert in performing the regressions. This work was in part supported by the National Science Foundation.

given form of a production function. It is also shown that various new types of "neutral" technical progress can be meaningfully determined and that the standard definitions of Hicks and Harrod are re-classified in a more general framework.

The present paper examines some of these results by presenting statistical evidence on the forms of production functions and on the types of technical progress. The model is applied to three countries, the United States, Japan, and Germany.

I. *The Model*

The following standard notation will be used:

Y = output
K = capital
L = labor
$y = Y/K$ = output-capital ratio
$x = L/K$ = labor-capital ratio
$z = Y/L = y/x$ = output-labor ratio
$k = K/L = 1/x$ = capital-labor ratio
r = return to capital
w = wage rate
$R = r/w$ = marginal rate of substitution
$\alpha = r/y$ = capital's relative share of income
$\beta = 1 - \alpha = w/z$ = labor's relative share of income
t = time, also used as the index of exogenous technical progress.

Our general assumptions are as follows: (1) A production function of Y is homogeneous of degree one in the two-factor inputs, capital K and labor L; (2) the factor as well as commodity markets are both perfectly competitive in the long run and, hence, the factors are paid according to their marginal productivities; and (3) technical progress is purely exogenous, i.e., technical change enters in a production function simply in the form of time t.

We define a production function as:

$$(1) \qquad Y(t) = F[K(t), L(t), t]$$

or alternatively,

$$(2) \qquad y = F\left(1, \frac{L}{K}, t\right) = f(x, t)$$

and

$$(3) \qquad z = F\left(\frac{K}{L}, 1, t\right) = \phi(k, t).$$

The marginal productivities of capital and labor are equal to their respective prices and hence

$$(4) \qquad r = \frac{\partial F}{\partial K} = f - xf_x = \phi_k$$

$$(5) \qquad w = \frac{\partial F}{\partial L} = \phi - k\phi_k = f_x.$$

We assume that the production function is continuous, and that the marginal productivities of both factors are positive, but that their ratio (the marginal rate of substitution) is diminishing:

$$(6) \qquad f_x > 0 \qquad \phi_k > 0$$

$$(7) \qquad f_{xx} < 0 \qquad \phi_{kk} < 0.$$

In the production function (equation (1)), we introduced t as an index of the state of technology. However, in this form, the role of technology is much too general to permit a thoroughgoing analysis. It is essential to specify the way in which technology enters the production function. The usual procedure has been to formulate certain hypotheses concerning the way in which technical progress has affected relationships between certain important variables that are derived from the production function. These variables include: (1) the capital-output ratio; (2) the output per man; (3) the factor proportions; (4) the marginal productivities; and (5) the marginal rate of substitution. Thus, one might postulate that technical progress has affected any one of these characteristics in a predetermined way; for instance, that it has left a certain variable invariant. However, since these variables will depend not only on technology but also on input proportions, it is necessary to neutralize the effect of any changes in inputs. This is the reason for considering not how variables, but how relationships between variables are affected by technical change. In particular if relationships are postulated to be invariant under technical change, one obtains the famous criteria of technical neutrality. Technical progress is Hicks-neutral when the relationship between the marginal rate of substitution and the factor proportion is unchanged. By contrast technical change is called Harrod-neutral when the relationship between the capital-output ratio and the interest rate does not change, and Solow-neutral, when the relationship between output per worker and the wage rate is invariant. In the notation above Hicks-neutrality means

$$(8) \qquad R = R(x)$$

whereas with general technical progress we would have

$$R = R(x, t).$$

It is easy to show that (8) can be integrated to yield

$$Y = A(t)F(K, L)$$

where Hicks-neutral technical progress is seen to be product augmenting. In the same way we can derive the production functions which express Harrod-neutrality or Solow-neutrality.

We have generalized this concept of technical neutrality by formulating and extending this principle of invariance to all other relationships between variables: a technical progress is neutral in some sense when the relationship in which a certain economic variable stands to some other variable remains unchanged through time, that is, through technical progress (Sato and Beckmann [10]).

This principle not only yields a number of interesting new types of technical change, but suggests a more effective way of estimating production functions and technical progress: by estimating this relationship (usually a differential equation) rather than the production function in integrated form which would involve the technical progress term as a constant of integration. Of course, in making such estimates, it is necessary to specify the form of the relationships involved. We have followed the usual procedure of assuming linear and log linear relationships. (Other forms are not ruled out but would require special argument.) We examine relationships between the following seven variables: output/capital ratio; output/labor ratio; labor/capital ratio; interest rate; wage rate; marginal rate of substitution; and labor's share.

Readers of our earlier paper will note that we have dropped the elasticity of factor substitution from our list, even though it yields some of the most intriguing types of production function and of technical progress. The reason is that the approximations used to measure this elasticity from available data are too crude to allow meaningful estimates. A large percentage of the empirical elasticities of factor substitution did, in fact, turn out negative. (The presence of these errors is, in part, explained by the "impossibility theorem" of Diamond and McFadden [4].) However, there is an alternative way of introducing factor augmenting technical progress—the *pièce de résistance* among types of progress that can be defined with the aid of the elasticity of factor substitution—e.g., by letting the interest rate be a log linear function of both the capital-output ratio and of time. In fact, there are several other similar ways.

There are $7 \cdot 6/2 = 21$ relationships that are possible between pairs of variables between which one can assume invariant relationships. Among these, time invariant relationships between the capital-output ratio, the capital-labor ratio, and the output-labor ratio do not allow any technical change at all. Similarly an invariant relationship between pairs from the interest rate, the wage rate, and the marginal rate of substitution is inconsistent with technical change [10, p. 64]. Hicks-, Harrod-, and Solow-neutrality can each be generated in three different ways. For instance in the case of Harrod-neutrality, if the relationship between the interest rate and the capital-output ratio is invariant under technical change (Table 1, col. 1, row 1), this happens to imply that the relationship between labor's share and the output-capital ratio is also invariant (Table 1, col. 1, row 4), and that the relationship between labor's share and the interest rate is invariant (Table 1, col. 4, row 4).[1]

The types of technical progress that are thus generated fall into the following four classes:

1. *Product augmenting*

1.1 Hicks neutrality

$$Y = A(t)F(K, L)$$

where Y = output, K = capital, L = labor, and $A(t)$ = technical progress term (Cases 3-6, 3-7, 6-7). Here product is increased in proportion to the output that would be obtained in the absence of technical change.

1.2 Labor additive

$$Y = A(t)L + F(K, L)$$

The increase in product is here proportional to the amount of labor used (Case 3-4).

1.3 Capital additive

$$Y = A(t)K + F(K, L)$$

The increase in product is proportional to the amount of capital used (Case 3-5).

2. *Labor augmenting*

2.1 Harrod neutrality (Cases 1-4, 1-7, 4-7)

$$Y = F(K, AL)$$

2.2 Labor combining

$$Y = F(K, A(t)K + L)$$

The augmentation of labor—as measured in efficiency units—is proportional to the amount of capital used (Case 1-5).

3. *Capital augmenting*

3.1 Solow neutrality (Cases 2-5, 2-7, 5-7)

$$Y = F(AK, L)$$

3.2 Capital combining

$$Y = F(K + A(t)L, L)$$

The augmentation of capital is proportional to the amount of labor used (Case 2-4).

4. *Input decreasing*[2]

4.1 Labor decreasing

1. The inverse production function is of the form

---

[1] Let the interest rate be an invariant function of the output-capital ratio. In the notation above

$$y - xy' = \phi(y), \quad \text{where } \phi \text{ denotes the invariant relationship.}$$

Rearranging terms

$$\frac{xy'}{y} = \frac{y - \phi(y)}{y} = \psi(y) \quad \text{say.}$$

This says that labor's share is an invariant function of the output–capital ratio.

Eliminating y between the above two relations we obtain

$$\frac{xy'}{y} = \xi(y - xy')$$

i.e., the relationship between the share and the interest rate is invariant.

[2] Readers should note that following the suggestion of the referee we have changed Anti-Hicks in the previous article [10, p. 60] to Input Decreasing.

TABLE 1—TYPES OF TECHNICAL PROGRESS IMPLIED BY ALTERNATIVE INVARIANT RELATIONSHIPS

	1 $\dfrac{\text{output}}{\text{capital}}\ y$	2 $\dfrac{\text{output}}{\text{labor}}\ z$	3 $\dfrac{\text{labor}}{\text{capital}}\ x$	4 interest r	5 wage w	6 MRS R
4 interest r	Harrod II	capital combining V	labor additive IX			
5 wage w	labor combining IV	Solow III	capital additive VIII	No		
6 MRS R	labor VI decreasing	capital VII decreasing	Hicks I	technical progress		
7 share β	Harrod II	Solow III	Hicks I	Harrod II	Solow III	Hicks I

$$L = G(K, Y) + C(t)Y \qquad \frac{dC}{dt} < 0$$

where $C(t)$ is decreasing with time. The reduction of the labor input is thus proportional to output Y (Case 1-6).

4.2 Capital decreasing

2. This is the symmetric case when the inverse production function is of the form

$$K = H(K, Y) + C(t)Y \qquad \frac{dC}{dt} < 0$$

Here the reduction of capital is proportional to output (Case 2-6).

Thus, technical progress may operate on the input side or on the product side and its effect may be proportional to any of the basic magnitudes: output, labor, or capital input. Combinations of these types may also arise. The invariance principle will generate certain of these when the elasticity of factor substitution is added to our list of variables, so that second order differential equations arise which involve two time terms as "constants" of integration.

Alternatively, such combinations arise when a time term is entered into the postulated relationships to express the null hypothesis that the relationship is *not* invariant with respect to time. The most important of these combinations is:

5. *Factor augmenting technical progress*

$$Y = F[A(t)K, B(t)L]$$

This combination of Harrod and Hicks, or Solow and Hicks neutrality is obtained in Case 1-7 when the capital-output ratio is a separable function of labor's share and of time[3]

$$\frac{Y}{K} = A(t)\phi(\text{share}).$$

Among the types of technical progress that we have obtained in this way are several which are well known in the literature: Hicks, Harrod, Solow, and factor augmenting technical change. The less obvious new types are all of the kind where the augmentation (reduction) of one variable is proportional to some other variable.

II. *Statistical Analysis*

We have applied regression analysis to time series data for the U.S., Japanese, and German private nonfarm sectors (see the table in the Appendix). Linear and log-linear regression equations are estimated for the relationships in Table 1—specifica-

---

[3] Factor-augmenting technical progress can be obtained in a more general way from the invariant relationship between the share and the elasticity of factor substitution (See our article [10, p. 63]).

tion in terms of two economic variables—rather than from the implied production functions. The direct estimation of production functions is in general more difficult because of nonlinearity of the functions. Also by using these relationships it becomes unnecessary to estimate the constants of integration that enter the production functions.

It should be noted that by specifying the alternative formulations as linear or log-linear functions we have at the same time specified the form of the production functions. For example, to test Harrod neutrality we applied,

$$r = \text{interest rate}$$

$$(9) \quad r = a + by + u(t) \qquad y = \frac{\text{output}}{\text{capital}}$$

and

$$(10) \quad \log r = a + b \log y + u(t)$$

where $u(t)$ is a random variable satisfying $E[u]=0$ and $E[uu']=\sigma^2 I$. By assuming r as a linear function of y, we have specified that the production function must be equal to:

$$y = \frac{1}{1-b}(A(t)x)^{1-b} + \frac{a}{1-b}, \quad 0 < b < 1,$$

which is a combination of the Cobb-Douglas type with a linear function in terms of K.[4] This follows by integration of the differential equation (9). Also the assumption of a log-linear form, $\log r = a + b \log y$, implies a production function of the CES type:

$$y = [\alpha + (A(t)x)^{1-b}]^{1/(1-b)}, \quad \log \alpha = a$$

Table 2 summarizes the implied specification of production functions corresponding to a linear and (whenever integration is possible) log-linear alternative form of alternative specifications.

[4] This function is the same as the one obtained in the article [12] as a CEDD (constant elasticity of derived demand) production function.

The overall conclusion to be drawn from Table 2 is that in virtually every case the implied production function turns out to be a modification of the Cobb-Douglas or CES production functions. In fact, the estimated values of the coefficients in these functions tend to make the approximation to Cobb-Douglas usually quite close. This is yet another confirmation of the robustness of the Cobb-Douglas function for empirical work. It also removes to a large extent the difficulty of controlling the form of the production function while testing for the type of technical progress, since the production function turns out to be very much the same in every case. Certain of the new functional forms obtained may be of interest in themselves as generalizations of Cobb-Douglas and/or CES and may merit further empirical exploration.

III. Results

The linear and log-linear equations in the second column of Table 2 were estimated in the form:

$$q(t) = a + bp(t) + u(t) \quad \text{or}$$

$$\log q(t) = a + b \log p(t) + u(t),$$

where $p(t)$ and $q(t)$ stand for the economic variables listed in Table 2, such as R and x for the case of Hicks neutrality. To test the invariance of these relationships with respect to technical change, i.e., time, we compared the fit as measured by R^2 with that obtained when a time term is added:

$$q(t) = a + bp(t) + ct + u(t) \quad \text{or}$$

$$\log q(t) = a + bp(t) + ct + u(t).$$

In Table 3, the values of R^2 are computed and ranked for different definition of "neutrality" in three countries. It is interesting to note that Solow Neutral Technical Progress ranks first in both the United States and Germany, and third in Japan. Harrod neutrality ranked

TABLE 2—IMPLIED PRODUCTION FUNCTIONS CORRESPONDING TO LINEAR (OR LOG-LINEAR) FORMS OF ALTERNATIVE SPECIFICATIONS

Types	Forms	Alternative Specifications	Implied Production Functions
I. Hicks	Linear	$R = a + bx$	$y = A(t)[a + (1+b)x]^{1/(1+b)}$
	Log-linear	$\log R = a + b \log x$	$y = A(t)[\alpha + x^{1-b}]^{1/(1-b)}$, $\log \alpha = a$ CES
			$b = 1$ (United States and Germany)
			$y = A(t)x^{1/(1+a)}$ CD
			$b = 3$ (Japan),
			$y = A(t)\dfrac{x}{\sqrt{1 + \alpha x^2}}$
II. Harrod	Linear	$r = a + by$	$y = \dfrac{(A(t)x)^{1-b}}{1-b} + \dfrac{\alpha}{1-b}$, $0 < b < 1$
	Log-linear	$\log r = a + b \log y$	$y = [\alpha + (A(t)x)^{1-b}]^{1/(1-b)}$
III. Solow	Linear	$w = a + bz$	$z = \dfrac{(A(t)k)^{1-b}}{1-b} + \dfrac{\alpha}{1-b}$, $0 < b < 1$
	Log-linear	$\log w = a + b \log z$	$z = [\alpha + (A(t)k)^{1-b}]^{1/(1-b)}$
IV. Labor-combining	Linear	$w = a + by$	$y = A(t)e^{bx} - \dfrac{a}{b}$, $b < 0$,
	Log-linear	$\log w = a + b \log y$	$y = [\alpha(1-b)x + A(t)]^{1/(1-b)}$ $\log \alpha = a$,
			$b < 0$ (Germany and Japan)
			$b \neq 1$
V. Capital-combining	Linear	$r = a + bz$	$z = A(t)e^{bk} - \dfrac{a}{b}$, $b < 0$,
	Log-linear	$\log r = a + \beta \log z$	$z = [\alpha(1-b)k + A(t)]^{1/(1-b)}$, $\substack{b \neq 1, \\ \log \alpha = a}$
VI. Labor-decreasing	Linear	$R = a + by$	$x = -a + A(t)y + by \log y$
	Log-linear	$\log R = a + b \log y$	$x = \dfrac{\alpha}{b-1}y^{b-1} + A(t)y$, $\substack{b \neq 1 \\ \log \alpha = a}$
VII. Capital-decreasing	Linear	$R = a + bz$	$k = -a + A(t)z + bz \log z$
	Log-linear	$\log R = a + b \log z$	$k = \dfrac{\alpha}{b-1}z^{b-1} + A(t)z$, $\substack{\beta \neq 1 \\ \log \alpha = a}$
VIII. Capital-additive	Linear	$w = a + bx$	$y = ax + \dfrac{b}{2}x^2 + A(t)$
	Log-linear	$\log w = a + b \log x$	$y = \dfrac{\alpha}{1+b}x^{1+b} + A(t)$, $\log \alpha = a$
IX. Labor-additive	Linear	$r = a + bk$	$z = ak + \dfrac{b}{2}k^2 + A(t)$
	Log-linear	$\log r = a + b \log k$	$z = \dfrac{\alpha}{1+b}k^{1+b} + A(t)$, $\log \alpha = a$

first and second in Japan and the United States, but did not rank well in Germany (Rank 7). Hicks neutrality does not rank as high as the Solow or Harrod types.

Capital-Additive Neutrality ranks very high in Germany (Rank 2), but not in the United States and in Japan. It is understandable to have such high

BECKMANN AND SATO: AGGREGATE PRODUCTION FUNCTIONS 95

TABLE 3—COMPARISONS OF R^2 IN LOG-LINEAR REGRESSIONS AMONG THREE COUNTRIES

Type	United States		Japan		Germany	
	R^2	Rank	R^2	Rank	R^2	Rank
I. Hicks	.831	4	.785	2	.708	4
II. Harrod	.933	2	.855	1	.422	7
III. Solow	.944	1	.758	3	.980	1
IV. Labor-combining	.897	3	.021	8	.770	3
V. Capital-combining	.818	5	.039	7	.272	9
VI. Labor-decreasing	.466	8	.755	4	.692	5
VII. Capital-decreasing	.702	7	.001	9	.653	6
VIII. Capital-additive	.779	6	.473	6	.950	2
IX. Labor-additive	.411	9	.633	5	.347	8

ranks in the Solow and Harrod neutral cases, since the log-linear relations imply that the production functions are of the CES type. Thus, Solow and Harrod neutral types are cast in a particularly favorable position. In order to offset this effect of the form of the production function, we might consider imbedding the various types of neutrality in CES functions and covering these estimates. However, this method becomes feasible only as further progress is made in nonlinear econometric estimation.

The above observation (Table 3) is made by comparing only the log-linear estimates. Our findings may now be summarized as follows:

(1) Among the unconventional types of neutral technical progress several perform well in one or the other country, but none is leading. In the United States, labor-combining and capital-combining technology; in Japan, labor-decreasing and labor-additive technology; in Germany, both labor and capital decreasing, and capital-additive technology. Such a phe-

nomenon, however, might well be expected when fitting a number of different forms to different time series.

(2) The traditional types of Hicks, Harrod, and Solow neutrality are for all countries at least as good as the unconventional types of neutrality. It is noteworthy that Solow (i.e., capital augmenting) technical change performs particularly well.

(3) When in the equations for Hicks, Harrod, and Solow neutrality, time is entered as an additional explanatory variable, a closer fit can be expected. Interestingly enough, this effect is quite small. We conclude that general factor-augmenting technical progress does not give a substantially improved explanation of observed data when compared with technical progress that augments only one factor.

(4) No matter how technical change is specified, the estimated production function turns out to be close to a Cobb-Douglas or CES function in every case.

TABLE 4—SUMMARY OF REGRESSION ANALYSIS

Case	Form	United States a	United States b	United States u	United States R²	Japan a	Japan b	Japan u	Japan R²	Germany a	Germany b	Germany u	Germany R²
I	A	−.026,389	.580,145 (.121,335)		.811,588	−.254,093	.796,724 (.046,880)		.908,754	.058,087	.276,869 (.008,406)		.926,549
	B	−.485,458	1.198,325 (.076,493)		.830,747	.383,005	2.237,489 (.277,063)		.784,587	−1.380,571	1.085,609 (.071,132)		.708,263
	C	.013,551	.504,116 (.090,435)	−.000,322 (.000,344)*	.814,856	−.375,492	.858,207 (.095,078)	.001,805 (.002,420)*	.910,532	.817,057	.175,457 (.028,842)	−.009,775 (.002,549)	.936,691
	D	−.538,890	1.107,802 (.172,822)	−.001,026 (.001,759)*	.831,920	−2.331,131	4.005,844 (.433,596)	.055,876 (.017,387)	.842,632	3.475,582	−1.008,516 (.541,317)	−.069,990 (.017,942)	.752,562
II	A	.013,864	.302,251 (.012,080)		.926,041	−.030,018	.479,584 (.039,861)		.833,096	.001,823	.224,966 (.014,461)		.737,879
	B	−1.168,961	.911,675 (.034,449)		.933,367	1.793,163	2.693,458 (.206,203)		.854,724	−1.518,591	1.295,658 (.163,260)		.422,751
	C	.009,807	.323,825 (.032,859)	−.000,149 (.000,211)	.926,784	.017,492	.395,445 (.035,432)	−.000,789 (.000,172)	.904,616	.052,942	.189,708 (.046,813)	−.000,442 (.000,506)*	.740,153
	D	−1.106,066	.955,426 (.095,211)	−.000,710 (.001,438)*	.933,696	1.966,091	2.617,725 (.228,667)	−.007,194 (.009,116)*	.857,885	−1.466,777	1.181,552 (.496,687)	−.007,604 (.006,590)*	.423,153
III	A	−.036,839	.697,252 (.007,673)		.993,982	−.026,839	.875,767 (.075,674)		.822,242	.010,752	.746,239 (.014,016)		.970,554
	B	−.414,634	1.031,527 (.011,106)		.944,237	.137,289	1.103,453 (.115,775)		.758,013	−.265,134	.994,800 (.015,308)		.980,042
	C	−.063,478	.821,924 (.033,149)	−.003,455 (.000,908)	.995,374	.069,000	.577,292 (.707,585)	.002,451 (.000,457)	.912,358	.002,807	.654,477 (.027,732)	.001,058 (.000,281)	.974,740
	D	−.297,913	1.194,377 (.086,169)	−.002,011 (.002,011)*	.994,642	−1.407,621	.705,585 (.109,861)	.014,953 (.002,745)	.882,517	.642,899	.801,519 (.066,744)	.004,132 (.001,392)	.981,917
IV	A	−.397,308	2.771,952 (.155,091)		.864,662	.208,065	−.242,226 (.213,943)		.042,331	.763,165	−.487,095 (.046,784)		.557,616
	B	1.021,123	1.514,068 (.072,189)		.897,937	−2.025,586	−.115,743 (.115,940)		.021,229	−1.500,712	−1.385,858 (.081,748)		.769,682
	C	−.000,182	.660,232 (.272,677)	.014,598 (.001,752)	.944,028	.141,036	.368,657 (.112,215)	.005,789 (.000,542)	.811,569	−.771,899	.571,675 (.067,269)	.013,280 (.000,794)	.896,873
	D	−.657,637	.346,295 (.088,964)	.018,950 (.001,344)	.979,812	−2.747,259	.200,311 (.080,733)	.003,022 (.003,218)	.761,732	−2.413,575	.624,482 (.092,287)	.028,264 (.001,224)	.968,307
V	A	.067,161	.054,158 (.005,125)		.755,093	.054,108	−.065,174 (.079,121)		.022,862	.281,014	−.184,381 (.026,082)		.367,537
	B	−2.026,375	.552,497 (.036,890)		.817,724	−2.189,412	.919,042 (.846,102)		.039,094	−2.404,576	−.661,721 (.116,591)		.272,492
	C	.078,873	.009,346 (.023,955)	.001,533 (.000,656)	.782,372	.106,872	.308,362 (.060,601)	−.003,068 (.000,357)	.731,342	.311,397	.166,519 (.035,548)	−.004,044 (.000,358)	.746,764
	D	1.914,342	.710,726 (.295,951)	−.003,722 (.006,907)	.818,795	7.889,027	4.074,027 (.722,973)	−.118,631 (.018,064)	.621,728	3.159,768	2.185,240 (.430,130)	−.060,864 (.008,971)	.528,056

TABLE 4 (continued)

Case	Form	US a	US b	US c	US R^2	Japan a	Japan b	Japan c	Japan R^2	Germany a	Germany b	Germany u	Germany R^2
VI	A	.305,742	-.262,962 (.039,162)		.474,163	-.244,581	3.539,219 (.487,176)		.645,376	.966,664	2.131,526 (.073,539)		.907,141
	B	-2.190,085	-.652,395 (.091,272)		.465,582	3.818,745	2.809,199 (.297,411)		.754,690	-.017,879	2.681,516 (.192,718)		.692,422
	C	.210,313	.244,507 (.073,321)	-.003,508 (.000,471)	.753,400	.442,668	2.336,622 (.364,200)	-.011,413 (.001,760)	.858,254	.564,030	1.075,771 (.182,100)	-.013,242 (.002,150)	.935,798
	D	-.448,352	-.609,184 (.171,508)	-.015,661 (.002,592)	.754,245	4.713,351	2.417,409 (.282,963)	-.037,217 (.011,280)	.823,361	.946,798	.557,070 (.533,273)	-.029,854 (.007,075)	.745,722
VII	A	.282,890	-.075,764 (.006,762)		.715,145	.577,124	-1.360,882 (.621,724)		.141,789	1.774,939	-1.972,929 (.182,406)		.576,330
	B	-1.611,741	-.479,029 (.044,105)		.702,315	-2.052,128	-.184,414 (.957,427)*		.001,278	-2.139,442	-1.656,522 (.130,218)		.652,985
	C	.279,586	-.060,345 (.033,245)*	-.000,432 (.000,910)*	.716,453	.981,497	1.501,815 (.505,887)	-.023,509 (.002,980)	.733,693	2.029,136	.902,844 (.146,791)	-.033,832 (.001,492)	.939,873
	D	-1.616,149	-.485,254 (.354,881)*	-.000,146 (.008,282)*	.702,315	9.296,663	3.368,245 (.824,213)	-.133,584 (.020,594)	.600,941	3.802,668	1.383,721 (.491,430)	-.064,996 (.010,249)	.764,430
VIII	A	2.426,093	-4.328,043 (.306,632)		.741,247	.272,995	-.152,912 (.030,229)		.468,743	.532,799	-.064,474 (.005,779)		.591,430
	B	-2.368,070	-2.099,567 (.158,346)		.778,575	-2.060,528	-.542,902 (.106,499)		.472,600	.750,778	-.615,976 (.015,408)		.948,940
	C	.020,847	.230,605 (.409,138)*	.019,397 (.001,558)	.937,812	-.138,094	.055,285 (.042,097)	.006,113 (.001,072)	.754,092	-.755,220	.109,309 (.008,507)	.016,589 (.000,781)	.935,175
	D	-1.121,793	.011,833 (.124,014)*	.023,930 (.001,258)	.973,577	-3.028,126	.032,434 (.144,630)*	.027,753 (.005,800)	.709,868	-1.565,577	-.264,609 (.114,248)*	.011,743 (.003,787)	.954,130
IX	A	.024,233	.043,923 (.008,179)		.365,768	.100,242	-.035,127 (.002,382)		.882,303	.265,131	-.102,244 (.012,358)		.443,169
	B	-2.853,472	.901,195 (.152,493)		.411,244	-2.443,550	-2.304,631 (.325,759)		.633,148	-2.131,350	.469,633 (.069,528)		.346,625
	C	.189,751	.058,582 (.006,127)	.003,222 (.000,170)	.924,151	.094,765	-.003,797 (.003,797)	.000,218 (.000,258)*	.885,229	.329,986	.070,766 (.020,959)	-.003,841 (.000,422)	.718,105
	D	-1.660,905	-1.119,328 (.124,636)	.021,902 (.001,265)	.923,467	-5.359,488	-4.038,470 (.447,677)	.083,634 (.017,951)	.793,343	1.910,007	1.273,127 (.509,318)	-.058,247 (.016,886)	.426,858

Note: 1. The values in parentheses are t / statistics.
2. ( )* indicates that the coefficient is not significantly different from zero.
3. Form: A $q = a+bp+u$
   B $\log q = a+b \log p+u$
   C $q = a+bp+cd+u$
   D $\log q = a+b \log p+cd+u$
4. The data in the appendix are constructed by the authors from the articles [11] [12] and also from W. G. Hoffmann, *Das Wachstum der deutschen Wirtschaft seit der Mitte des 19. Jahrhunderts,* New York 1965.

APPENDIX

TIME SERIES FOR THE UNITED STATES, JAPAN, AND GERMAN FEDERAL REPUBLIC PRIVATE NON-FARM SECTORS

	United States (Y and K are measured at 1929 dollars)					Japan (Y and K are measured at 1930 Yen)				
Year	$y=\dfrac{Y}{K}$	$z=\dfrac{Y}{L}$	$x=\dfrac{L}{K}$	r	w	$y=\dfrac{Y}{K}$	$z=\dfrac{Y}{L}$	$x=\dfrac{L}{K}$	r	w
1909	.3226	.6710	.4808	.108	.446					
1910	.3086	.6525	.4730	.102	.437					
1911	.3229	.6732	.4796	.108	.448					
1912	.3140	.6626	.4739	.104	.444					
1913	.3315	.7034	.4713	.112	.468					
1914	.3120	.6444	.4842	.101	.435					
1915	.3079	.6587	.4674	.106	.432					
1916	.3286	.7216	.4553	.118	.463					
1917	.2999	.6632	.4523	.111	.418					
1918	.3131	.7200	.4349	.107	.474					
1919	.3267	.7821	.4177	.116	.505					
1920	.3241	.7825	.4142	.103	.533					
1921	.3765	.8611	.4373	.139	.543					
1922	.3680	.8359	.4403	.125	.553					
1923	.3616	.8694	.4159	.122	.576					
1924	.3760	.9380	.4009	.124	.628					
1925	.3573	.9157	.3902	.120	.608					
1926	.3584	.9447	.3794	.117	.636					
1927	.3592	.9460	.3797	.116	.640					
1928	.3531	.9542	.3700	.107	.632					
1929	.3551	.9899	.3588	.118	.661					
1930	.3288	.9751	.3372	.114	.637	.1846	.200	.9229	.0593	.1358
1931	.3387	1.0088	.3357	.110	.681	.1896	.206	.9202	.0531	.1483
1932	.3307	.9774	.3383	.131	.589	.1871	.198	.9451	.0575	.1372
1933	.3314	.9432	.3514	.120	.602	.1891	.195	.9697	.0594	.1338
1934	.3581	1.0429	.3434	.127	.673	.2030	.206	.9854	.0654	.1397
1935	.4018	1.1242	.3574	.141	.730	.1942	.201	.9663	.0689	.1296
1936	.4254	1.1342	.3751	.152	.729	.1925	.203	.9482	.0670	.1324
1937	.4374	1.1717	.3733	.149	.773	.2000	.216	.9259	.0800	.1296
1938	.4346	1.1885	.3656	.144	.795	.1874	.210	.8922	.0665	.1355
1939	.4594	1.2183	.3771	.159	.796	.1787	.204	.8758	.0609	.1344
1940	.4812	1.2713	.3785	.172	.817	.1612	.196	.8225	.0584	.1250
1941	.5013	1.3040	.3845	.189	.812	.1665	.207	.8044	.0574	.1356
1942	.5007	1.3130	.3813	.178	.846	.1490	.196	.7605	.0525	.1270
1943	.5163	1.3408	.3850	.177	.882	.1390	.192	.7241	.0489	.1244
1944	.5554	1.4629	.3796	.184	.977	.1180	.179	.6590	.0408	.1171
1945	.5667	1.5282	.3708	.178	1.048	.1025	.192	.5337	.0349	.1265
1946	.5497	1.4512	.3788	.172	.998	.0540	.123	.4392	.0032	.1156
1947	.4320	1.4192	.3749	.174	.955	.0595	.160	.3720	.0011	.1570
1948	.5372	1.4797	.3630	.178	.988	.0698	.195	.3580	.0021	.1892
1949	.5228	1.5201	.3439	.170	1.025	.0815	.230	.3542	.0101	.2015
1950	.5537	1.6269	.3403	.201	1.036	.0984	.266	.3700	.0160	.2226
1951	.5459	1.6545	.3299	.188	1.084	.1066	.247	.4316	.0193	.2023
1952	.5380	1.6847	.3193	.171	1.151	.1148	.261	.4397	.0165	.2234
1953	.5427	1.7058	.3182	.169	1.175	.1191	.267	.4461	.0197	.2229
1954	.5357	1.7820	.3006	.163	1.238	.1193	.256	.4659	.0175	.2184
1955	.5542	1.8618	.2977	.182	1.249	.1275	.271	.4705	.0199	.2287
1956	.5457	1.6546	.3298	.174	1.127	.1414	.293	.4827	.0266	.2379
1957	.5394	1.8912	.2852	.168	1.303	.1452	.291	.4989	.0184	.2540
1958	.5358	1.9360	.2768	.161	1.353	.1482	.294	.5040	.0280	.2384
1959	.5506	1.9993	.2754	.174	1.368	.1659	.342	.4850	.0390	.2616
1960	.5520	2.0342	.2714	.171	1.406	.1825	.380	.4802	.0478	.2804

BECKMANN AND SATO: AGGREGATE PRODUCTION FUNCTIONS 99

GERMAN FEDERAL REPUBLIC

Year	Y (GNP) Prices of 1913 (Million Mark)	K Capital Stock Prices of 1913 (Mrd. Mark)	L Labor Force in Hours Worked (Billion hours)	$\beta = 1 - \alpha$ Share of Labor Income
1850	9,449	7.16	56.7	.819
1851	9,390	7.19	56.7	.819
1852	9,578	7.38	56.7	.819
1853	9,565	7.50	56.7	.819
1854	9,793	7.63	56.7	.778
1855	9,657	7.79	58.4	.778
1856	10,442	7.98	58.4	.778
1857	10,948	8.10	58.4	.778
1858	10,888	8.33	58.4	.778
1859	10,938	8.48	58.4	.778
1860	11,577	8.65	58.4	.753
1861	11,364	8.89	58.4	.753
1862	11,872	9.22	58.4	.753
1863	12,729	9.55	58.4	.753
1964	13,127	8.85	58.4	.753
1865	13,167	10.00	58.4	.750
1866	13,293	10.20	58.4	.750
1867	13,318	10.30	60.9	.750
1868	14,099	10.60	60.9	.750
1869	14,188	10.90	60.9	.750
1870	14,169	11.70	60.9	.778
1871	14,653	12.50	60.9	.778
1872	15,683	13.10	60.9	.778
1873	16,347	13.70	60.9	.778
1874	17,545	14.20	60.9	.778
1875	17,651	14.60	68.8	.800
1876	17,548	14.80	68.8	.800
1877	17,438	15.00	68.8	.800
1878	18,257	15.20	68.8	.800
1879	17,839	15.50	68.8	.800
1880	17,679	16.05	68.8	.766
1881	18,122	16.80	68.8	.766
1882	18,441	17.40	68.8	.766
1883	19,427	18.50	68.8	.766
1884	19,923	19.70	68.8	.766
1885	20,417	20.80	73.7	.762
1886	20,548	22.20	73.7	.762
1887	21,362	23.50	73.7	.762
1888	22,266	25.00	73.7	.762
1889	22,859	26.60	73.7	.762
1890	23,589	28.30	73.7	.741
1891	23,579	29.20	73.7	.741
1892	24,539	29.80	73.7	.741
1893	25,760	31.30	73.7	.741
1894	26,383	32.90	73.7	.741
1895	27,621	34.60	80.7	.731
1896	28,615	37.40	80.7	.731
1897	29,437	40.50	80.7	.731
1898	30,703	44.40	80.7	.731
1899	31,813	47.50	80.7	.731

GERMAN FEDERAL REPUBLIC (Continued)

Year	Y (GNP) Prices of 1913 (Million Mark)	K Capital Stock Prices of 1913 (Mrd. Mark)	L Labor Force in Hours Worked (Billion hours)	$\beta = 1 - \alpha$ Share of Labor Income
1900	33,169	49.80	80.7	.726
1901	32,406	51.20	80.7	.726
1902	33,142	52.00	80.7	.726
1903	34,979	54.00	80.7	.726
1904	36,405	57.00	80.7	.726
1905	37,189	60.10	80.7	.712
1906	38,283	63.40	90.2	.712
1907	39,993	67.00	90.2	.712
1908	40,665	69.10	90.2	.712
1909	41,482	71.80	90.2	.712
1910	42,981	74.30	90.2	.709
1911	44,478	77.90	90.2	.709
1912	46,388	82.00	90.2	.709
1913	48,480	85.20	99.0	.709
1925	45,515	76.63	89.0	.873
1926	43,688	77.63	89.0	.873
1927	51,806	81.92	89.0	.873
1928	52,969	85.40	89.0	.873
1929	53,596	86.60	89.3	.873
1930	50,326	86.70	89.3	.971
1931	45,226	83.81	89.3	.971
1932	41,011	82.27	89.3	.971
1933	45,068	82.41	89.3	.971
1934	49,395	83.96	89.3	.971
1935	53,856	86.62	89.3	.781
1936	59,511	88.86	89.3	.781
1937	63,098	96.03	89.3	.781
1938	67,967	103.22	92.9	.781
1950	40,052	69.54	52.9	.740
1951	44,151	74.03	52.9	.740
1952	46,278	78.98	52.9	.740
1953	49,090	83.28	52.9	.740
1954	53,828	89.31	52.9	.740
1955	59,393	97.54	52.9	.728
1956	62,283	104.86	52.9	.728
1957	64,363	112.25	52.9	.728
1958	66,613	118.87	60.2	.728
1959	71,008	126.70	60.2	.728
1960			60.2	.771
1961			60.2	.771
1962			60.2	.771
1963			60.2	.771
1964			60.2	.771

REFERENCES

1. K. J. ARROW, H. B. CHENERY, B. MINHAS, AND R. M. SOLOW, "Capital-Labor Substitution and Economic Efficiency," *Rev. Econ. Stat.*, Aug. 1961, *43*, 225–47.

2. M. J. BECKMANN, "Einkommensvertei-

BECKMANN AND SATO: AGGREGATE PRODUCTION FUNCTIONS 101

lung und Wachstum bei Nichtneutralem Technischen Fortschritt," *Jahrb. Nationalök. und Stat.*, Aug. 1965, *178*, 80–89.

3. P. A. DAVID AND T. VAN DE KLUNDERT, "Nonneutral Efficiency Growth and Substitution between Capital and Labor in the U.S. Economy, 1899–1960," *Am. Econ. Rev.*, June 1965, *55*, 357–94.

4. P. DIAMOND AND D. McFADDEN, "Identification of the Elasticity of Substitution and the Bias of Technical Change: Impossibility Theorem," *Working Paper* 62, Institute of Business & Economic Research, University of California, Berkeley 1965.

5. E. D. DOMAR, "On the Measurement of Technological Change," *Econ. Jour.*, Dec. 1961, *71*, 709–29.

6. P. J. DHRYMES, "A Comparison of Productivity Behavior in Manufacturing and Service Industries," *Rev. Econ. Stat.*, Feb. 1963, *45*, 64–69.

7. D. W. JORGENSON AND Z. GRILICHES, "The Explanation of Productivity Change," *Rev. Econ. Stud.*, July 1967, *34*, 249–84.

8. J. W. KENDRICK AND R. SATO, "Factor Prices, Productivity and Economic Growth," *Am. Econ. Rev.*, Dec. 1963, *53*, 974–1004.

9. R. R. NELSON, "Aggregate Production Function and Medium-Range Growth Projections," *Am. Econ. Rev.*, Sept. 1964, *54*, 575–606.

10. R. SATO AND M. J. BECKMANN, "Neutral Inventions and Production Functions," *Rev. Econ. Stud.*, Jan. 1968, *35*, 57–67.

11. R. SATO, "Technical Progress and the Aggregate Production Function of Japan (1930–1960)," *Econ. Stud. Quart.*, March 1968, *19*, 15–24.

12. ———, "The Estimation of Biased Technical Progress and the Production Function," *Internat. Econ. Rev.*, forthcoming.

13. R. M. SOLOW, "Technical Change and the Aggregate Production Function," *Rev. Econ. Stat.*, Aug. 1957, *39*, 312–20.

14

Review of Economic Studies (1980) XLVII, 767–776

0034-6527/80/00540767$02.00

The Impact of Technical Change on the Holotheticity of Production Functions

RYUZO SATO

Brown University

1. INTRODUCTION AND MOTIVATION

In recent years many economists have attempted to study technical progress and production functions in order to investigate the impact of technical changes under different assumptions on such economic variables as prices of factor inputs, their distributive shares, factor requirements and the degree of scale effect, etc. (Samuelson (1965), Sato (1970), Sato and Beckmann (1968) and Wolkowitz (1970)). Many new concepts have been introduced, such as " homothetic " production functions (Sato (1977) and Wolkowitz (1970)), " neutrality " of inventions (Sato (1970) and Sato and Beckmann (1968)) and " optimal returns to scale " (Sato (1980)), etc.

Motivation for this research topic is derived from the so-called Solow–Stigler controversy. Solow (1957) shows that a substantial portion of the increase in per capita output in U.S.A. cannot be explained by growth in the capital–labour ratio. The unexplained portion is attributed to technical progress. Solow (1957) notes that he is " . . . using the phrase 'technological change' as a shorthand expression for any kind of shift in the production function. Thus slowdowns, speedups, improvements in education of the labour force, and all sorts of things appear as 'technical change'." Solow assumes that technical progress is Hicks neutral and that the production function is linear homogeneous.

Stigler (1961) criticizes the latter assumption. This is followed by an exchange of comments between Stigler (1961) and Solow (1961). After rejecting the possibility of estimating the extent of increasing returns by fitting cross-sectional production functions to numerous industries within country, Stigler attempts to fit an international cross-sectional production function, using U.S. and British data. He also uses Cobb–Douglas production function in his statistical analysis. His conclusion deserves quotation:

> " The conclusion to be drawn, aside from the inevitable one that more work should be done, is that economies of scale are potentially of the same order of magnitude as technical progress. I consider the problem of establishing the approximate magnitudes of these economies a major one, not merely of productivity calculations, which are not especially important, but of the theory of economic growth. "

In his reply, Solow holds that he considers the attempt to separate increasing returns to scale from technical progress difficult on econometric grounds and that as economic theorist he would prefer to stick to the assumption of constant returns.

The economies of scale can manifest itself in many ways. It may generate a homogeneous but nonlinear production function with constant scale elasticity. It may underlie a homothetic production function with variable scale elasticity. It may even generate a non-homothetic production function.

It is obvious that Solow and Stigler are both right in this controversy. Consider a cost-minimizing firm producing output under a homothetic production function:

$$Y = F[f(K, L)] \qquad \qquad ...(1)$$

where Y = output, K = capital and L = labour and f = continuously differentiable function of homogeneous degree one with respect to K and L, with

$$f_i > 0 \quad \text{and} \quad f_{ii} < 0 \qquad (i = K, L),$$

and F = any strictly monotone increasing (or homothetic) function of f. Suppose that the firm adopts the exogenous technical progress of " the uniform and equal multiplication type " so that capital and labour measured in the efficiency unit, $\bar{K}$ and $\bar{L}$, are expressed as:

$$\bar{K} = T(t)K = e^{\alpha t}K, \quad \bar{L} = T(t)L = e^{\alpha t}L, \quad \alpha \geqq 0. \qquad ...(2)$$

The production function after the introduction of technical progress of the uniform multiplication type is:

$$\bar{Y} = F[f(\bar{K}, \bar{L})] = F[f(e^{\alpha t}K, e^{\alpha t}L)] = F[e^{\alpha t}f(K, L)]$$
$$= G_{(t)}[f(K, L)]. \qquad ...(3)$$

The impact of such a type of technical change is, of course, " neutral " in the sense of Hicks. This means that in terms of isoquants, the characteristics are unchanged or *invariant* (using the concept of the group theory which we plan to employ) before and after the technical progress, except for the labelling of isoquants, and that there exists always some other homothetic function G which has the same labelling as the production function with that type of technical progress. Thus, *the impact of the type of technical progress (2) can always be represented by another member of the same family of homothetic production functions.* That is to say, *the impact of technical progress on the production function is transformed to a scale effect.*

The Solow–Stigler controversy occurs because the type of technical progress (2) is completely transformed to a Hicks neutral type and the Hicks neutral type is undistinguishable from the homotheticity (or returns to scale). In order to empirically identify both the scale and (unobservable) technical progress effects, one must know what type of technical progress is completely separable from the scale effect. When the impact of technical progress on the production function is transformed to a scale effect, then the production function is said to be *holothetic* under a given type of technical progress. (A more precise definition of holotheticity will be given in the next section.) Thus, to avoid the Solow–Stigler type of controversy we must use a production function *not holothetic under a given type of technical progress* (see Theorem 2). This is the obvious reason why we are interested in the general conditions of holotheticity. We intend to study the holotheticity of production functions by the Lie theory of continuous groups of transformations.

2. HOLOTHETICITY AND THE GROUP PROPERTIES OF TECHNICAL PROGRESS FUNCTIONS

Consider a general quasi-concave and continuously differentiable neoclassical production function with the usual properties,

$$Y = f(K, L). \qquad ...(4)$$

Assume that, when exogenous technical progress t is introduced,[1] it will not change the form of the production function f, but change the output level by affecting the way in which the factor inputs are combined, i.e.

$$Y = f(K, L, t). \qquad ...(4')$$

Definition 1 (Technical Progress Functions). When exogenous technical progress t is introduced it will change the way in which the K and L are combined. The functions which combine factor inputs through the technical progress parameter t may be called the technical progress functions of K and L, i.e.

$$T_t: \quad \bar{K} = \phi(K, L, t), \quad \bar{L} = \psi(K, L, t) \qquad \qquad ...(5)$$

where $\bar{K}$ and $\bar{L}$ are " effective " capital and " effective " labour and

$$(\phi, \psi) = \text{a vector of } \textit{technical progress functions.}$$

ϕ and ψ are independent and generally analytic functions.

Following the example of homothetic production functions under the uniform factor-augmenting technical progress, we present,

Definition 2 (Holotheticity of a Production Function Under a Given Type of Technical Progress). When the whole effect of technical progress T_t, working through the technical progress functions ϕ and ψ in f, is represented by some strictly monotone transformation F, then the production function is said to be " holothetic " (complete-transforming type) under a given T_t, i.e.

$$Y = f(K, L, t) = f(\phi, \psi, 0) = f(\bar{K}, \bar{L}) = f[\phi(K, L, t), \psi(K, L, t)]$$
$$= g(h(K, L), t) = F_{(t)}[f(K, L)],$$

$$\text{where } h(K, L) = f(K, L, 0) = f(K, L). \quad ...(4'')$$

We present several interpretations of the holotheticity condition. First, we observe that when the *total effect of a given type of technical progress working through the technical progress functions is completely transformed into a scale effect of production without changing the shape of the isoquant map,* then the production function is said to be *holothetic* under a given type of technical progress T_t. The *impact* of technical progress is completely absorbed by the production function as a *scale effect.* Hence, *the isoquant map of a production function is not affected by a given type of technical progress.*

The second interpretation of the holotheticity condition is closely related to the concept of separability of technical progress. From condition (4''), it is seen that as t affects Y through the technical progress functions ϕ and ψ, t is separated from the basic technology $f(K, L)$. When the total effect of technical progress is *transformed* to a weakly separable production function through the technical progress functions, then the production function is said to be holothetic under ϕ and ψ.[2] Care must be taken to note that we are not assuming a weakly separable function, but the continuous transformation of t through ϕ and ψ results in the weakly separable form if f is holothetic under ϕ and ψ.[3]

Thirdly, from the right-hand side of equation (4''), $Y = F_{(t)}[f(K, L)]$, if the production function is *holothetic* under T, each function is transformed into another function of the same family by the operation of technical progress.[4] Thus, the family of curves may be *invariant* as a whole under the transformation of ϕ and ψ. Thus the concept of holotheticity is closely related to the concept of *invariance* under the technical progress transformation T. This last interpretation enables us to use the analysis of invariance, central to the Lie theory of transformation groups.

The last interpretation of holotheticity as the invariance condition of the Lie group theory suggests that we must impose certain restrictions on the technical progress transformation T. We assume the following conditions:

Assumptions (The Lie Group Properties (Campbell (1966) and Eisenhart (1933) Sato (1980))). The technical progress functions ϕ and ψ satisfy:

(A) The result of the successive performance of two transformations

$$T_t: \bar{K} = \phi(K, L, t), \bar{L} = \psi(K, L, t) \quad \text{and} \quad T_{\bar{t}}: \bar{\bar{K}} = \phi(\bar{K}, \bar{L}, \bar{t}), \bar{\bar{L}} = \psi(\bar{K}, \bar{L}, \bar{t})$$

is the same as that of the single transformation (Composition),

$$T_{t+\tilde{\imath}}: \overline{K} = \phi(K, L, t+\tilde{\imath}), \overline{L} = \psi(K, L, t+\tilde{\imath}),$$

i.e.

$$T_t T_{\tilde{\imath}} = T_{t+\tilde{\imath}}. \qquad \qquad \dots(6.1)$$

(B) The value $-t$ determines the transformation inverse to that obtained by using t (Inverse):

$$T_t^{-1} = T_{-t}, \quad \text{or} \quad T_t^{-1}: K = \phi(\overline{K}, \overline{L}, -t), L = \psi(\overline{K}, \overline{L}, -t) \qquad \dots(6.2)$$

and

(C) $t = 0$ gives the identical transformation, $t_0 = 0$ (Identity), i.e.

$$T_0 = I, \text{ or } T_0: \overline{K} = \phi(K, L, t_0) = K, \overline{L} = \psi(K, L, t_0) = L. \qquad \dots(6.3)$$

When ϕ and ψ satisfy the Assumptions A, B, and C, then the type of technical progress T is said to possess the *Lie group properties* (see Appendix). This type of technical progress may be referred to as a *Lie type of technical progress* or simply a " *holothetic* " *technical change*.[5]

Economic Interpretation of the Lie Group Properties. The group properties of the technical progress functions can be given a simple and straightforward economic interpretation. We may assume that the technical progress parameter t also represents the year t in which technical progress takes place. Thus $\overline{K}$ and $\overline{L}$ may be considered as the " effective capital " and " effective labour " at year t. Assumption A implies that if the " effective capital " and " effective labour " at year t, say $t = 1$, and the " effective capital " and " effective labour " at year $\tilde{\imath}$, say $\tilde{\imath} = 2$, are expressed as the same functions ϕ and ψ of the previous year's values, then any year's " effective capital " and " effective labour " will be expressed only by the changes $(t+\tilde{\imath})$ in the technical progress parameter. Assumption B implies that the initial capital and labour can also be expressed by the same technical progress functions by using $-t$ of the process of technical change. Finally Assumption C implies that the initial capital and labour will always be equal to " effective " capital and " effective " labour if there is no technical progress $(t = 0)$.[6]

Definition 3 (Invariant Family of Curves). A family of curves $f(K, L) = C$ is said to be *invariant* under a group G_1, if every transformation of the group transforms each curve into some curve of the family, i.e.

$$g = F(f) \qquad \qquad \dots(7)$$

where $g(K, L, t) = f[\phi(K, L, t), \psi(K, L, t)]$.

Lemma (Fundamental Lemma of Holotheticity). *A family of production functions is holothetic under a given type of technical progress if and only if it is invariant under a group.*

Proof. If a family of production functions is holothetic, we have from Definition 2,

$$Y = f(K, L, t) = f(\overline{K}, \overline{L}) = f[\phi(K, L, t), \psi(K, L, t)]$$

$$\equiv g[f(K, L), t] = F_{(t)}[f(K, L)]. \qquad \dots(4'')$$

Hence the production function after technical progress $F_{(t)}$ is always a function of the production function before technical progress f. But this is exactly the condition of the invariance of a family of curves under a group. Conversely, writing the equation of the family in the form $f(K, L) = C$, it will be invariant, if $f(\overline{K}, \overline{L}) \equiv g(K, L, t) = C'$ is the equation of the same family of curves for every value of t, C and C'. ‖

3. EXISTENCE OF GENERAL CLASS OF HOLOTHETIC TECHNOLOGY

We are now in a position to show the existence of the general class of holothetic technology under technical progress T.

Theorem 1 (Existence). *If the technical progress functions* T

$$T: \quad \bar{K} = \phi(K, L, t), \quad \bar{L} = \psi(K, L, t) \qquad \qquad ...(5)$$

satisfy the Lie group properties (6.1), (6.2) *and* (6.3), *then there exists one and only one holothetic technology under* T, *such that*

$$Y = f(K, L, t) = f[\phi(K, L, t), \psi(K, L, t)] = g[f(K, L), t] = F_{(t)}[f(K, L)].$$

Hence, there exists a general class of production functions under which the total effect of technical progress T *is completely transformed to returns to scale.*

Proof. By the fundamental existence theorem (Appendix and Eisenhart (1933)), the problem is reduced to that of finding a general solution to the Lagrange linear partial differential equation of the type

$$\xi(K, L)\frac{\partial f}{\partial K} + \eta(K, L)\frac{\partial f}{\partial L} = G(f) \neq 0.$$

($G(f)$ may be zero. This equation is known to have a unique general solution (up to monotonicity), say $Y = f(K, L)$ (F. John (1971)). ‖

Estimation of Technical Progress and the Scale Effect

The above theorem will answer the basic question related to the Solow–Stigler controversy. Using the above theorem we can now find the condition under which both the scale economies and technical change may be identified. As the converse of the above theorem we formulate the following:

Theorem 2 (Possibility Theorem of Estimation of Technical Progress). *The effect of technical change* T *and the scale effect of* f *are independently identifiable if and only if the production function is not holothetic under a given type of technical change* T.

Proof. This follows immediately from the basic property of the holothetic technology under a given technical progress transformation. ‖

The above theorem makes it *possible* to estimate both the technical progress effect and scale effect of a production function, provided that the production function is not holothetic under the assumed type of technical progress.

4. EXISTENCE OF A LIE TYPE OF TECHNICAL PROGRESS

The next question is: Can we conversely show whether or not a given production functions is holothetic under some type of technical progress functions? That is to say, is there always any T such that the given isoquant map is unaltered? The answer is affirmative.

Theorem 3 (Existence of a Lie Type of Technical Progress). *Given an isoquant map, there exists at least one Lie type of technical progress function under which the production function is holothetic.*

Proof.[7] First, we want to know whether

$$f(x^1, t) = f(x^2, t) \text{ implies } f(x^1, s) = f(x^2, s) \qquad \text{for all } s,$$

where x^1 and x^2 are the different values of (K, L). Now this implies that there exist transformations $F(s, t)$ satisfying:

$$f(x, s) = F_{(s, t)} \circ f(x, t) \quad \text{(all } s, t, x).$$

Suppose that $s - t = s' - t'$ and $f(x^1, t) = f(x^2, t')$. Then $s' - s = t' - t = h$ (say) and so it follows that $f(x^1, s) = f(x^2, s')$. But

$$f(x^1, s) = F_{(s, t)} \circ f(x^1, t) \quad \text{and} \quad f(x^2, s') = F_{(s', t')} \circ f(x^2, t').$$

Therefore, $F_{(s, t)} = F_{(s', t')}$ and we can write $F_{(s, t)}$ as F_{s-t}. It now follows that the transformation F_u form an additive Lie group, because:

(a) $F_u \circ F_v \circ f(x, t) = F_u f(x, t+v) = f(x, t+u+v) = F_{u+v} \circ f(x, t) = F_{v+u} \circ f(x, t)$;

(b) the associative law $F_{(u+v)+w} = F_{u+(v+w)}$ is satisfied;

(c) F_0 is the identity mapping;

(d) F_{-u} is defined by $F_{-u} \circ f(x, t) = f(x, t-u)$.

So the Lie group exists and the additive group can be transformed to any other non-additive group. ‖

The concepts of " holothetic " production functions under a Lie type of technical change and the " neutrality " of technical progress in the sense of Hicks are closely related.

Corollary to Theorem 3 (Product-Augmenting Type of Technical Progress). *For any production function, there exists at least one type of technical progress functions such that they can always be reduced to a " Hicksian neutral product-augmenting type " of technical progress, i.e.*

$$f(K, L, t) = f(\bar{K}, \bar{L}) = A(t)f(K, L). \qquad \text{...(8)}$$

Proof. This is a special case of Theorem 3 when the transformation is log-additive. ‖

5. AN ALTERNATIVE APPROACH BY " INFINITESIMAL TRANSFORMATION " OF THE GROUP

We shall briefly discuss an alternative formulation of holothetic technology by Lie's infinitesimal transformations. The usefulness of this approach lies in making it possible to *construct* the classes of holothetic technologies. Since the technical progress functions ϕ and ψ are assumed to be analytic functions we have

$$\begin{cases} \bar{K} = \phi(K, L; \delta t), \\ \bar{L} = \psi(K, L; \delta t), \end{cases} \qquad \text{...(9)}$$

where $t = 0$ is the value of the parameter determining the identical transformation (6.3). Then we write

$$\begin{cases} \delta K = \bar{K} - K = \xi(K, L)\delta t \\ \delta L = \bar{L} - L = \eta(K, L)\delta t \end{cases} \qquad \text{...(10)}$$

where

$$\left. \frac{\partial \phi}{\partial t} \right|_{t=0} = \xi \quad \text{and} \quad \left. \frac{\partial \psi}{\partial t} \right|_{t=0} = \eta.$$

We shall call (10) an *infinitesimal transformation of technical change* and write this with Lie (Appendix) as

$$U = \xi(K, L) \frac{\partial}{\partial K} + \eta(K, L) \frac{\partial}{\partial L}. \qquad \text{...(11)}$$

Then the necessary and sufficient condition for holotheticity under a given T is simply stated as

$$Uf = \xi \frac{\partial f}{\partial K} + \eta \frac{\partial f}{\partial L} = G(f) \neq 0,$$

which has a general solution yielding the class of holothetic technology. It may be best to illustrate this by the following examples:

Example a. If technical progress is the uniform (neutral) factor-augmenting type, i.e. $T: \bar{K} = e^{\alpha t}K, \bar{L} = e^{\alpha t}K, \alpha \geqq 0$, then the holotheticity technology is nothing but the *homothetic* technology (Shephard (1970)), derived from

$$Uf = \alpha K \frac{\partial f}{\partial K} + \alpha L \frac{\partial f}{\partial L} = G(f) \neq 0,$$

i.e.

$$Y = g[f(K, L)], \quad \lambda f = (\lambda K, \lambda L), \quad g' > 0.$$

Hence, after technical progress, we have

$$Y = g[f(\bar{K}, \bar{L})] = g(e^{\alpha t}f(K, L)) = F_{(t)}[f(K, L)].$$

In order to estimate both the uniform rate of technical progress and the scale effect, we should *never* use the homothetic technology under the neutral type of technical change (to avoid the Solow–Stigler controversy).

Example b. On the other hand, if the underlying assumption of technical change is the non-uniform, biased type, i.e.

$$U = \alpha K \frac{\partial}{\partial K} + \beta L \frac{\partial}{\partial L},$$

the holothetic technology is the " almost homothetic " family of production functions (Houthakker (1960), Kolm (1976), Lau (1972) and Sato (1977)), derived from

$$U = \alpha K \frac{\partial f}{\partial K} + \beta L \frac{\partial f}{\partial L} = G(f) \neq 0, \quad \text{i.e. } Y = f\left[K^{1/\alpha}Q\left(\frac{L^{\alpha}}{K^{\beta}}\right)\right].$$

Any other families including the " homothetic " family should be used in order to isolate the effect of that type of technical progress from the scale economies.

To supplement the understanding of Theorem 3 we use the following examples:

Example c. Given a homothetic Cobb–Douglas function, $Y = F(K^{\alpha}L^{\beta})$, the differential equation and an integrating factor are

$$\alpha L dK + \beta K dL = 0 \quad \text{and} \quad I = \frac{1}{KLQ(Y)}.$$

Thus from the definition of the integrating factor I,

$$KLQ = \xi \alpha L + \eta \beta K.$$

By setting $\xi = a(Y)K$, we can immediately obtain

$$\eta = b(Y)L, \quad b(Y) = \frac{Q(Y) - \alpha a(Y)}{\beta}.$$

Hence, it is holothetic under

$$U = a(Y)K \frac{\partial}{\partial K} + b(Y)L \frac{\partial}{\partial L}.$$

If a and b are constants, we obtain the biased factor-augmenting type.

Example d. For homothetic CES functions, $Y = F[\alpha K^{-\rho} + \beta L^{-\rho}]$, we have

$$\alpha K^{-(1+\rho)} dK + \beta L^{-(1+\rho)} dL = 0 \quad \text{and} \quad I = \frac{1}{Q(Y)}.$$

A Lie type of technology is immediately obtained as

$$U = a(Y) K^{(1+\rho)} \frac{\partial}{\partial K} + b(Y) L^{(1+\rho)} \frac{\partial}{\partial L}.$$

If $Q(Y)$ in I is set equal to $\alpha K^{-\rho} + \beta L^{-\rho}$ and ξ to K, so that

$$\alpha K^{-\rho} + \beta L^{-\rho} = \xi \alpha K^{-(1+\rho)} + \eta \beta L^{-(1+\rho)}$$

and $\eta = L$, we get

$$U = K \frac{\partial}{\partial K} + L \frac{\partial}{\partial L},$$

which is the neutral type of technical progress.

A multi-factor extension may be briefly commented on. Although the actual calculations will be immensely complicated, we can extend the basic results to the general case of n-factor production functions. Thus, given a type of technical progress functions in terms of their infinitesimal transformation

$$T: \quad U = \sum_{j=1}^{n} \xi_j \frac{\partial}{\partial X_j},$$

then it can be shown that there exists one and only one family of production functions holothetic under T, i.e. $Y = f(X, t) = F_{(t)}[f(X)]$, $f(\overline{X}, 0) = f(\phi) = f(\phi(X, t))$, where $\overline{X} = \phi(X, t)$ is a vector of technical progress functions resulting from U. Conversely, it can be proved that, for any given isoquant map, there exists at least one type of T under which it is holothetic. We shall leave the proof of these assertions to the interested reader (or see Sato (1980)).

APPENDIX

Basic Concepts of Continuous Groups of Transformations

Groups and Groups of Transformations

Let T_a represent a transformation scheme,

$$T_a: \quad \bar{x}_i = f^i(x:a) \qquad 1 \leqq i \leqq n, \qquad \qquad \text{...(A.1)}$$

where $x = (x_1, ..., x_n)$ and $a = (a_1, ..., a_r) = $ a vector of r *essential* parameters. Let T_b represent substitution, $T_b: \bar{x}_i = f^i(\bar{x}:b)$ $1 \leqq i \leqq n$. Then $f(x:a)$ is said to form a r-parameter (Lie) group G_r, if, in addition to the associative law:

(1) T_a, $T_b \in G_r$, and $T_c = T_a \cdot T_b \in G_r$, where $c = c(a, b)$;

(2) $T_{a^\circ} = I \in G_r$ and $T_a \cdot T_{a^\circ} = T_a = T_{a^\circ} \cdot T_a$, where $a^\circ = $ a particular set of values of a;

(3) There exists $-a$ such that $T_{-a} \cdot T_a = T_a \cdot T_{-a} = T_{a^\circ} = I$ $\therefore T_{-a} = T_a^{-1} \in G_r$.

Infinitesimal Transformation of a Group

The transformation $\bar{x}_i = f^i(x; a_1^\circ + \delta a_1, ..., a_r + \delta a_r)$, determines,

$$\bar{x}_i - x_i = \delta x_i = \sum_{j=1}^{r} \frac{\partial f^i(x:a^\circ)}{\partial a_j} \delta a_j = \sum_{j=1}^{r} \xi_{ij} \delta a_j, \qquad 1 \leqq i \leqq n. \qquad \text{...(A.2)}$$

Let $\delta a_j = e_j \delta a$, $e_j = $ constant, then (A.2) is,

$$\delta x_i = (\sum_{j=1}^{r} e_j \xi_{ij}) \delta a = \xi_i \delta a, \qquad (1 \leqq i \leqq n). \qquad \text{...(A.2')}$$

(A.2') is called the *infinitesimal transformation* of the group. Using Lie's symbol

$$U = \sum_{i=1}^{n} \xi_i \frac{\partial}{\partial x_i},$$

the action of U on f is written as

$$Uf = \sum_{i=1}^{n} \xi_i \frac{\partial f}{\partial x_i}. \tag{A.3}$$

Theorem. (The Fundamental Existence Theorem of the Invariant Differential Equation).

(i) *The necessary and sufficient condition that the differential equation*

$$M_1(x, y)dx + M_2(x, y)dy = 0$$

be invariant under the group U is $[U, R]f = \lambda(x, y)Rf$, where $[U, R]$ = a Lie bracket defined by $[U, R]f \equiv (UM_2 - R\xi)(\partial f/\partial x) - (UM_1 + R\eta)(\partial f/\partial y)$, $U = \xi(\partial/\partial x) + \eta(\partial/\partial y)$ and $R = M_2(\partial/\partial x) - M_1(\partial/\partial y)$.

(ii) *The necessary and sufficient condition that there exists a general differential equation $f(x, y, y') = 0$ invariant under the group U is $U'f \equiv 0$ whenever $f = 0$, where $U'f$ is defined by*

$$U'f = \xi(x, y)\frac{\partial f}{\partial x} + \eta(x, y)\frac{\partial f}{\partial y} + \left(\frac{d\eta}{dx} - p\frac{d\xi}{dx}\right)\frac{\partial f}{\partial p}, \, p = \frac{dy}{dx} = y'.$$

(iii) *If the family of integral curves of the differential equation*

$$M_1(x, y)dx + M_2(x, y)dy = 0$$

is left unaltered by the group $U = \xi(x, y)(\partial/\partial x) + \eta(x, y)(\partial/\partial y)$, then $(\xi M_1 + \eta M_2)^{-1}$ is an integrating factor of the differential equation.

A proof of the theorem (i) may be found in Eisenhart (1933), pp. 80–89, especially Theorems 23.3 and 25.1. A proof for (ii) is found in Eisenhart (1933), pp. 90–108, especially Theorem 27.2. Also see Sato (1980), Appendix.

First version received October 1975; final version accepted January 1980 (Eds.).

The author wishes to acknowledge helpful comments on earlier drafts by Paul A. Samuelson, T. Nôno and P. J. Hammond. This work was partly supported by a NSF grant.

NOTES

1. For the utility and demand analysis, the exogenous change may be identified as " taste change ". Needless to say that everything we say about production technologies will carry over to preference orderings by substituting " technical change " with " taste change ".

2. I owe this interpretation to Paul A. Samuelson in his private correspondence. In fact in (4') $Y = g[h(K, L), t] = g[f(K, L), t]$ is exactly the weakly separable form.

3. Thus, the so-called " neutrality " of technical progress in the Hicks sense is a special case of holotheticity when $F_{(t)}[f(K, L)] = A(t)f(K, L)$.

4. It is important to note that the concept of holothetic technology is defined in terms of " a given type of technical progress ". Thus, a class of production functions may be holothetic under a certain type of technical progress T_1, but may not be holothetic under a different type of technical progress T_2. This point will be further discussed in the later section. Also see Sato (1980).

5. I owe this definition to P. J. Hammond.

6. It may be argued that assumptions A, B and C are too restrictive, for there may be many types of technical progress operating in an economy which do not satisfy these restrictions. Certainly it may be possible to construct a type of technical progress which is meaningful, yet does not satisfy the group properties. However, first we may say that all of the known types in the economic literature thus far do satisfy the above assumptions. Secondly, as can be seen later, the Lie group properties are the characteristics that are useful for *distinguishing* one production function from another. Furthermore, as also can be observed later, each production function possesses the holothetic property compatible with at least one type of technical progress having these restrictions (see Theorem 3). Hence, starting with any given family

of production functions, one can always derive at least one type of technical progress possessing these properties.

7. I owe this proof to P. J. Hammond.

REFERENCES

CAMPBELL, J. E. (1966) *Introductory Treatise on Lie's Theory* (New York: Chelsea).

EISENHART, L. P. (1933) *Continuous Groups of Transformations* (Princeton University Press).

JOHN, F. (1971) *Partial Differential Equations* (Springer-Verlag).

HOUTHAKKER, H. S. (1960), " Additive Preferences ", *Econometrica*, **28** (2), 244–257.

LIE, M. S. (1893) *Transformationsgruppen* (Vols. I, II, III).

KOLM, S. C. (1976), " Structures méta-homogènes des Productions et Préférences ", *Canadian Journa of Economics*.

LAU, L. (1972), " Profit Functions and Technologies with Multiple Inputs and Outputs ", *Review of Economics and Statistics*, **54**, 284–289.

SAMUELSON, P. A. (1965), " A Theory of Induced Innovations along Kennedy–Weizsäcker Lines ", *Review of Economics and Statistics*, 343–356.

SATO, R. (1970), " The Estimation of Biased Technical Progress and the Production Function ", *International Economic Review*, 179–208.

SATO, R. and BECKMANN, M. J. (1968), " Neutral Inventions and Production Functions ", *Review of Economic Studies*, 57–65.

SATO, R. (1977), " Analysis of Production Functions by Lie Theory of Transformation Groups: Classification of General CES Functions ", in *Resource Allocation and Division of Space*, Lecture Note Series in Mathematical Economics, No. 147 (New York: Springer).

SATO, R. (1980) *Theory of Technical Change and Economic Invariance: Application of Lie Groups* (Academic Press, forthcoming).

SHEPHARD, R. W. (1970) *Theory of Cost and Production Functions* (Princeton).

SOLOW, R. (1957), " Technological Change and Aggregate Production Function ", *Review of Economics and Statistics*, 312–320.

SOLOW, R. (1961), " Comment on Stigler ", in *Output, Input and Productivity Measurement*, 64–68 (Princeton: Income and Wealth Series).

STIGLER, G. (1961), " Economic Problems in Measuring Changes in Productivity ", in *Output, Input and Productivity*, 47–63 (Princeton: Income and Wealth Series).

WOLKOWITZ, B. (1970), " Homothetic Production Functions " (Ph.D. Dissertation, Brown University).

[15]

Oxford Economic Papers 39 (1987), 343–356

FACTOR PRICE VARIATION AND THE HICKSIAN HYPOTHESIS: A MICROECONOMIC MODEL

By RYUZO SATO* and RAMA RAMACHANDRAN

I. Introduction

IN THIS paper, we propose to construct a microeconomic model of a profit-maximizing firm which, faced with differential increases in input prices, could develop compensating cost reducing technologies. The problem hardly needs any introduction. More than fifty-years ago, Hicks succinctly stated the problem in an oft-quoted passage:

> "A change in the relative prices of the factors of production is itself a spur to invention, and to invention of a particular kind—directed to economizing the use of a factor which has become relatively expensive (1963, 2nd edition, p. 124).

One approach to the modelling of the process would be to consider a firm having production and research costs. Current research effort leads to increases in the efficiency of inputs and the decline of future production costs. The firm considers the discounted value of incremental profits from research induced costs reductions and determines the optimal level of current research expenditures. Such a study would parallel extensions of the theory of firm to incorporate non-production expenditures like selling costs.

Even though models are used to analyze the effects of patents and product competition on innovations, the theory of induced technical progress took, for historical reasons, a different route. Most of the theoretical models of biased technical progress are based on the Kennedy–Weisaker–Samuelson innovation possibility frontier which generally assumes cost minimization subject to constraints imposed by the frontier. The share of an input in costs is shown to have a decisive influence in determining optimal bias. If the industry is competitive and the frontier is exogenously given, then the cost of production is the total cost to the firm and the logic of minimizing costs is obvious. Also the share of input in costs is unambiguously defined. But if we assume a non-competitive market structure and research costs, then we must distinguish between production costs, total (production and research) costs, and total costs plus profits of the firm. Kamien and Schwartz (1969), in a profit maximizing model *with constant prices,* derived some traditional results by defining share of an input as the fraction of production costs. While the cost-minimization models may be generalizable to include market imperfections, research costs and input price increases, we submit that a profit-maximizing model is worth studying in itself.

*C. V. Starr, Professor of Economics, Graduate School of Business Administration, New York University, New York, N.Y.

Once we assume a non-competitive market structure, a very common assumption in the industrial organization literature on endogeneous technical progress, it is only natural to expect that the downward sloping demand curve facing the firm will play a role in determining its behaviour. This is clearly brought out in our model. It also makes the rate of growth of input prices a determinant of the degree of bias which again is a natural interpretation of the Hick's statement quoted above.

Governments and corporations spend considerable amount of resources in developing cost-reducing technologies. Recent excitement over the potential of robotics is an indication that such efforts will continue in the future. Currently, in theoretical and empirical literature on technological progress, one notices that, instead of a single overarching model, a number of paradigms, each developed to study a particular facet, coexist. In proposing a new model, our object is not to criticize or supersede any existing line of research but to propose the study of this complex problem from another angle which meshes with other extensions of the theory of the firm.

In an earlier paper (1978), we considered a monopolistic firm generating Hicks neutral technical progress, through research efforts, to compensate equiproportional increases in all input prices. We then set out to analyse, using the Maximum Principle, whether a monopolistic firm can have a steady-state where the increases in input prices are just compensated by increases in factor efficiency so that unit costs remain constant. Sufficient conditions for optimality and saddle-point stability were examined.[1] The insight gained by the discussion of the Hicks-neutral case enables us to extend the analysis to biased technical progress.[2] We now assume that factor prices are increasing at different rates and that the monopolistic firm through allocation of resources of research can determine the rate of augmentation of each factor. In Section II below, we consider the assumptions of the model in detail. In Section III we consider the existence of an optimal research policy, and of steady-states as also saddle-point stability.

II. Assumptions and model

1. We shall assume that the firm is a monopolist with an infinite time horizon and perfect foresight. There is a vast literature on the impact of market structure on research efforts; in this paper we consider only the limiting case where the firm can fully internalize the benefits from its research.

---

[1] This model was further extended in Sato (1981) to consider investments in two types of knowledge, basic and applied. An empirical study of the productivity of such investments was undertaken in Sato and Suzawa (1983).

[2] The technical difficulty in such an extension is that it now becomes a two state variable problem. As Pitchford (1977, p. 127) has pointed out, a large number of economic problems with two state variables have no known method of finding solutions.

2. The production function is linear homogeneous and can be written as

$$Y = F(A(t)X_1, B(t)X_2) \tag{1}$$

where X_1 and X_2 are two inputs. For example, they can be taken to be the conventional inputs, labour and capital, or X_1 can be considered as a composite non-energy input and X_2 as energy input. $A(t)$ and $B(t)$ are their levels of factor augmentation at time t.

3. Let P_1 and P_2 be the prices of the inputs X_1 and X_2. We assume that they increase at a constant proportionate rate ω_1 and ω_2.

$$P_1 = P_{01}e^{\omega_1 t} \qquad P_2 = P_{02}e^{\omega_2 t}. \tag{2}$$

4. The price of the product P is determined by the demand curve $P = P(Y)$.

5. We shall assume that the firm is in existence and that it finances all its research internally. Thus we assume away the problem of entry-and-exit. As we are confining ourselves to the study of an internal steady-state, this assumption does not affect the basic results of our paper.

6. The expenditure on research determines the rate of increase of $A(t)$ and $B(t)$ according to the two technical progress functions.[3] In empirical and industrial organization literature, there is a tradition of considering the proportion of sales revenue devoted to research as an index of the research intensity of the industry. We shall, therefore, express the research expenditures as proportions of total sales revenue, PY. Since $PY > 0$ by assumption 5, this particular formulation does not affect the results.

$$\frac{\dot{A}}{A} = h_1(\theta_1 PY) \qquad \frac{\dot{B}}{B} = h_2(\theta_2 PY) \qquad h_1' > 0 > h_i'' \tag{3}$$

where $\dot{A}$ and $\dot{B}$ are the time rates of change and h_i' and h_i'' are the first and second order derivatives with respect to $\theta_1 PY$.

7. Since the production function is linear homogeneous, it is well known that the cost functions can be written as:

$$C = YG\left(\frac{P_1}{A(t)}, \frac{P_2}{B(t)}\right) = Y\psi(g_1, g_2) \tag{4}$$

where

$$g_1 = \frac{A(t)}{P_1} = A(t)P_{01}^{-1}e^{-\omega_1 t} \quad \text{and} \quad g_2 = B(t)P_{02}^{-1}e^{-\omega_2 t}.$$

Further it can be easily shown that G is linear homogeneous in its

---

[3] It is not at all uncommon for corporations to have many research departments, each one dedicated to a particular problem. The two functions, h_1 and h_2, may be taken to correspond to two departments concerned with improving the productivity of the two inputs. If the firm is though as determining a research budget M before allocating it, then by substituting $M - \theta_1 PY$, say, for $\theta_2 PY$, we can obtain an innovation possibility frontier.

arguments and that ψ is homogeneous of degree -1 in g_1 and g_2.

$$g_1\frac{\partial\psi}{\partial g_1} + g_2\frac{\partial\psi}{\partial g_2} = -\psi.$$

The object of the firm is to maximize the discounted value of profit stream (revenue minus production and research costs):[4]

$$\underset{\theta_1, \theta_2, Y}{\text{Max}} \int_0^\infty e^{-\rho t}[(1 - \theta_1 - \theta_2)PY - Y\psi(g_1, g_2)] \, d\tau \tag{5}$$

subject to

$$\dot{g}_1 = [h_1(\theta_1 PY) - \omega_1]g_1$$
$$\dot{g}_2 = [h_2(\theta_2 PY) - \omega_2]g_2.$$

This problem is easily analyzed using the Maximum Principle of Pontryagin where we reduce it to the study of an autonomous Hamiltonian,

$$H = [(1 - \theta_1 - \theta_2)PY - Y\psi] + q_1[h_1(\theta_1 PY) - \omega_1]g_1$$
$$+ q_2[h_2(\theta_2 PY) - \omega_2]g_2. \tag{6}$$

Here θ_1, θ_2 and Y are control variables whose values are set at the level at which they maximize H. g_1 and g_2 are the state variable whose value at any instant of time is given. The rate at which g_1 and g_2 vary over time is given by the differential equations below. q_1 and q_2 are co-state variables and can be interpreted as shadow prices.

III. Analysis of the model

The value of Y which maximizes H, Y^*, is given by the first order condition $\partial H/\partial Y = 0$. As shown in Appendix A-1, this leads to the familiar condition that marginal revenue equals marginal costs.

$$P'Y^* + P(Y^*) = \psi(g_1, g_2). \tag{7}$$

An increase in g_i, $i = 1, 2$, is equivalent to an increase in the efficiency of one input relative to its price. Marginal costs will decrease leading to an increase in Y^* (Fig. 1). A result of some importance for subsequent analysis is that the total cost of production $C = Y^*\psi$ may increase or decrease, as g_i increases.

The expenditure on research is given by the equation

$$\theta_1 PY = \phi_1(q_1 g_1) \qquad \theta_2 PY = \phi_2(q_2 g_2). \tag{8}$$

---

[4] In general we have to define the inequality conditions that output and research expenditures are positive and that profit (revenue minus production and research costs) is non-negative. We are, however, concerned with the existence of an interior steady-state and hence assume that the discussion is confined to the region where these inequality conditions are satisfied.

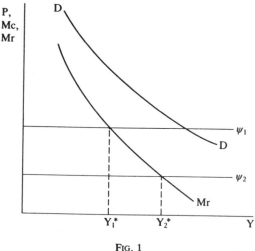

Fig. 1

It is shown in Appendix A-1 the ϕ_i is an increasing monotonic function of $q_i g_i$. From (3) we immediately notice that a constant rate of factor augmentation corresponds to a particular value of $q_i g_i$. In our earlier paper (1978) where we considered the Hicks-neutral progress only (for convenience this paper will be referred to as the Hicks-neutral model), we saw that the $\dot{g} = 0$ curve was a truncated hyperbola defined in that region of the state-space in which the inequality conditions corresponding to Footnote 4 are satisfied. Here we note that $\dot{g}_i = 0$ is also a truncated hyperbola.

Over time the values of the state and co-state variables will change according to the following equations.

$$\dot{q}_1 = (\rho - h_1 + \omega_1)q_1 + Y\frac{\partial \psi}{\partial g_1} \tag{9}$$

$$\dot{q}_2 = (\rho - h_2 + \omega_2)q_2 + Y\frac{\partial \psi}{\partial g_2} \tag{10}$$

$$\dot{g}_1 = [h_1(\theta_1 PY) - \omega_1]g_1 \tag{11}$$

$$\dot{g}_2 = [h_2(\theta_2 PY) - \omega_2]g_2. \tag{12}$$

The steady state, at which factor price increases are just compensated by development of factor saving technologies, is given by the values of g_1, g_2, q_1, q_2, at which the equations (9) to (12) are all equal to zero. At such a steady-state the unit cost of production is constant over time.

Now we must examine whether an optimal policy exists for this firm. Arrow and Kurz (1970) have shown that the sufficient condition for optimality is that the maximized Hamiltonian H^* obtained by substituting for $\theta_1, \theta_2,$ and Y, is concave in $g_1,$ and g_2. It turns out that certain restrictions on the various functions must be satisfied if H^* is to be concave. These conditions are mathematically derived in Appendix A-2. In the text we shall consider the economic implications of these restrictions.

One of the conditions for concavity is that

$$\frac{\partial^2 H^*}{\partial g_1^2} = -\frac{\partial Y^*}{\partial g_1}\frac{\partial \psi}{\partial g_1} - Y^*\frac{\partial^2 \psi}{\partial g_1^2} + \frac{\phi_1' q_1}{g_1} < 0. \qquad (13)$$
$$\qquad\qquad (-)\qquad\quad (?)\qquad (+)$$

An increase in g_1 is equivalent to an increase in the efficiency of the input relative to its price and the marginal cost ψ will decrease. This in turn will increase the instantaneous optimal output Y^*. Hence the product of the two partials in the first terms on the R.H.S. of (13) is negative and the term itself is positive. The sign of $\partial^2 \psi/\partial g_1^2$ is indeterminate unless further conditions are imposed.

In A-2 of the Appendix, it is shown that:

$$\frac{\partial^2 \psi}{\partial g_1^2} = \frac{D_1}{g_1^3}\left\{2 + \frac{\Pi_1}{\varepsilon_m} - \eta_1\right\} \qquad (14)$$

where $D_1 = AX_1/Y$ is the number of efficiency units of X_1 demanded for unit output, Π_1 is the share of X_1 in the total cost of production, η_1 is the elasticity of derived demand for X_1 and ε_m is the elasticity of the marginal revenue curve. (14) is positive if and only if $\eta_1 < 2 + \Pi_1/\varepsilon_m$. However, a sharper result is obtained by combining the first two terms of (13); as shown in Appendix A-2, the combined term equals $(D_1 Y^*/g_1^3)(\eta_1 - 2)$. A necessary condition for concavity is that $\eta_1 < 2$. This may be compared to the conditions in the Hicks neutral model that $(g/Y^*)(dY^*/dg) < 2$ where $g = Ae^{-wt}$ is the ratio of the level of factor augmentation to the common rate of price increase.

Concavity of the Hamiltonian further requires the $\partial^2 H^*/\partial g_2^2 < 0$ which in turn requires that $\eta_2 < 2$. Finally it is necessary that

$$\left(\frac{\partial^2 H}{\partial g_1^2}\right)\left(\frac{\partial^2 H}{\partial g_2^2}\right) - \left(\frac{\partial^2 H}{\partial g_1 \partial g_2}\right)^2 > 0.$$

This will be true if

$$\left(\frac{\partial^2 H}{\partial g_1^2}\right)\left(\frac{\partial^2 H}{\partial g_2^2}\right) > \left(\frac{\partial^2 H}{\partial g_1 \partial g_2}\right)^2. \qquad (15)$$

The expressions on L.H.S. of (15) are already evaluated. In A-2 of Appendix we show that

$$\frac{\partial^2 H}{\partial g_1 \partial g_2} = -\frac{Y^*}{\psi}\frac{\partial \psi}{\partial g_1}\frac{\partial \psi}{\partial g_2}\left[\sigma - \frac{1}{\varepsilon_m}\right] \qquad (16)$$

where σ is the elasticity of substitution of the production function. If $\sigma\varepsilon_m$ is close to unity, then the expression (16) is small and the inequality (15) will be satisfied.

Proposition 1: Necessary conditions for the concavity of the Hamiltonian are that the elasticity of derived demand of both imputs be less that two. Sufficiently conditions restricts the values of η_i, σ and ε_m so as to satisfy the inequalities:

$$\frac{\partial^2 H}{\partial g_i^2} < 0 \quad \text{and} \quad \left(\frac{\partial^2 H}{\partial g_1^2}\right)\left(\frac{\partial^2 H}{\partial g_2^2}\right) > \left(\frac{\partial^2 H}{\partial g_1 \partial g_2}\right)^2.$$

It is true that the concavity of the Hamiltonian is only the sufficient condition and the optimal policy may exist even if it is not satisfied. But the necessary conditions are even harder to identify.

Next we can consider whether a steady-state exists and, if so, whether it is unique? From (9), we see that $\dot{q}_1 = 0$ if only

$$(\rho - h_1 + \omega_1)q_1 = -Y\frac{\partial \psi}{\partial g_1}.$$

Further from (11) and $\dot{g} = 0$, we get

$$h_1 = \omega_1.$$

Combining and multiplying by g_1,

$$\rho q_1 g_1 = -Yg_1\frac{\partial \psi}{\partial g_1}. \tag{17}$$

Similarly

$$\rho g_2 q_2 = -Yg\frac{\partial \psi}{\partial g_2}. \tag{18}$$

Adding

$$\rho(q_1 g_1 + q_2 g_2) = Y\left[-g_1\frac{\partial \psi}{\partial g_1} - g_2\frac{\partial \psi}{\partial g_2}\right]$$

$$= Y\psi \tag{19}$$

as ψ is homogeneous of degree -1.

But $h_1(\phi_1(q_1 g_1)) = \omega_1$ and $h_2(\phi_2(q_2 g_2)) = \omega_2$. From monotonicity of the functions, we see that $q_1 g_1$ and $q_2 g_2$ must be constant. Just as in the Hicks-neutral model, $Y\psi$ is the same at different steady-states if there is more than one.

Proposition 2: The model can have unique or multiple steady-states at which unit cost of production remains constant over time. If there is a multiplicity of steady-states, then the firm has the same total cost of production at these different stationary points.

Consider a C.E.S. production function. The cost function can be written as[5]

$$C = Y[\Delta_1 g_1^{-(1-\sigma)} + \Delta_2 g_2^{-(1-\sigma)}]^{1/1-\sigma}$$
$$= Y\psi(g_1, g_2).$$

Let the inverse of the functions $h_i(\phi_i(q_i g_i))$ be k_i; $k_i(\omega_i) = q_i g_i$. Then from (17) and (18)

$$k_1(\omega_1) = \frac{1}{\rho} \psi^\sigma \Delta_1 g_1^{-(1-\sigma)} Y^*$$

$$k_2(\omega_2) = \frac{1}{\rho} \psi^\sigma \Delta_2 g_2^{-(1-\sigma)} Y^*$$

$$p'Y^* + P(Y) = \psi.$$

The above three equations in the three unknowns, g_1, g_2 and Y^* determine the steady-state. Depending on the demand curve and the values of the parameters, there may be more than one solution satisfying the three nonlinear equations and the inequality constraints corresponding to the interior solution; or there may be none.

Finally we turn to the question of stability of system in the neighbourhood of the steady-state. This can be determined by examining the characteristic roots of the Jacobian of the differential equations (9)–(12). If all roots are positive, then the system is unstable. If k roots are positive, then we can characterize the steady-state as a saddle point of type k (see Hale). In A-3 of the Appendix, it is shown that the characteristic equation can be written as

$$\left\{ -\lambda^2 + \rho\lambda + r_1\left(\rho + r_1 - \frac{g_1}{q_1} m_1\right) \right\}\left\{ -\lambda^2 + \rho\lambda + r_2\left(\rho + r_2 - \frac{g_2}{q_2} m_2\right) \right\}$$
$$- r_1 r_2 \frac{g_1 g_2}{q_1 q_2} N^2 = 0 \quad (20)$$

where

$$r_i = \frac{(h_i')^2}{h_i''} < 0, \qquad m_i = \frac{\partial q_i}{\partial g_i} = -\frac{\partial^2 H^*}{\partial g_i^2} > 0.$$

(due to concavity conditions on H^*), and $N = -\partial^2 H/\partial g_1 \partial g_2$. If, for a moment, we assume that $N = 0$, then the characteristic equation factorizes into the product of two quadratics and the characteristic root corresponding to each can be examined separately. Consider

$$f_1(\lambda) = -\lambda^2 + \rho\lambda + r_1\left(\rho + r_1 - \frac{g_1}{q_1} m_1\right). \quad (21)$$

[5] C.E.S. is self dual and the cost-function has the same form as production function. Also note that g_i is the reciprocal of the price of an efficiency unit of input.

If $(\rho + r_1 - (g_1/q_1)m_1) < 0$, then the term independent of λ is positive. Applying the Descartes' rule of sign to $f(\lambda)$ and $f(-\lambda)$, we see that there is one positive and one negative characteristic root corresponding to $f_1(\lambda) = 0$. If $(\rho + q_i - (g_1/q_1)m_1) > 0$, then both characteristic roots can be positive. But, as shown in A-3 of the Appendix,

$$\rho + r_1 - \frac{g_1}{q_1}m_1 = \frac{1}{q_1}\left[\frac{Y^*D_1}{g_1^2}(\eta_1 - 1)\right].$$ (22)

The L.H.S. will be negative if and only if $\eta_1 < 1$ which is more restrictive than the condition for concavity that $\eta_1 < 2$. This has a parallel to the Hicks-neutral model where the conditions are the $(g/y^*)(dY^*/dg)$ be less than two and one respectively for concavity and saddle-point stability.

An analysis of the other quadratic expression leads to parallel conclusion. The analysis so far assumes that $N = 0$. Now

$$N = -\frac{\partial^2 H}{\partial g_1 \, \partial g_2} = \frac{Y^*}{\psi}\frac{\partial \psi}{\partial g_1}\frac{\partial \psi}{g_2}\left[\sigma - \frac{1}{\varepsilon_m}\right].$$ (23)

We have already seen that this expression is bounded by the inequality (15). If we increase the value of N in (20) from zero to that given in (23), the characteristic roots will vary continuously (Lancaster, p. 225).[6] But the sign patterns possible are limited. As shown by Kurz (1968), these roots are real and symmetric around $\rho/2$. Hence, a minimum of two roots must be positive. The other two roots may both be positive, one negative and one positive, or both negative. If the model has a steady-state, then the rate of augmentation of each factor equals the rate of its price increase (see equations (11) and 12)). Note that, if there is multiplicity of steady-states, each of them satisfies this condition but for different values of θ_1, P and Y. Whether the firm will converge to this steady-state depends on the conditions discussed above. Thus, for a monopolistic firm with infinite time horizon, we can prove the Hicksian proposition.

Proposition 3: The rate of bias of endogenous technical progress generated by this firm will, in steady-state, equal the difference in the rates of growth of its input prices.

[6] If the characteristic equation is written as

$$\lambda^4 + a\lambda^3 + b\lambda^2 + c\lambda + d = 0$$

then Ferrari's method reduces this equation to

$$(\lambda^2 + \tfrac{1}{2}a\lambda + \tfrac{1}{2}\xi + s\lambda + \mu)(\lambda^2 + \tfrac{1}{2}a\lambda + \tfrac{1}{2}\xi - s\lambda - \mu) = 0,$$

where ξ is the root of the reduced cubic

$$\xi^3 - b\xi^2 + (ac - d)\xi + 4bd - a^2d - c^2 = 0.$$

IV. Conclusion

The theory of endogeneous technical progress assumes that increases in an input price will lead to the development of factor-saving technologies. Such developments may be undertaken by a public institution or by profit-maximizing firms. In this paper we seek the conditions under which a monopolistic firm may attain a steady-state where unit costs are constant. We see that a number of very special conditions have to be satisfied for the existence and stability of such a steady-state.

Assumptions of the model including full internalization of the benefits of research and diminishing returns to research expenditures, would normally be expected to lead to a robust dynamic equilibrium. Yet, in the direct extension of the theory of firm to include research efforts, additional conditions for optimality and stability had to be imposed. Only a future research programme can establish whether changes in any of the assumptions would relax or tighten these conditions.

N.Y. University, USA
Southern Methodist University, Dallas, USA.

APPENDIX

A-1 First order conditions

The first order condition

$$\frac{\partial H}{\partial \theta_i} = -PY + q_i h_i' g_i PY = 0 \qquad i = 1, 2$$

$$\frac{\partial H}{\partial Y} = (1 - \theta_1 - \theta_2)(P'Y + P) - \psi + q_1 g_1 h_1' \theta_1 (P'Y + P)$$

$$+ q_2 g_2 h_2' \theta_2 (P'Y + P) = 0.$$

This reduces to

$$q_i g_i h_i' = 1 \quad \text{or} \quad \theta_i PY = \emptyset_i(q_i g_i) \quad \text{since} \quad h_i' = h_i'(\theta_i PY) \quad \text{and} \quad P'Y + P = \psi(g_1, g_2).$$

The second order conditions are satisfied if $h_i'' < 0$ and $P''Y + 2P' < 0$ (marginal revenue curve slopes downwards to the right). Since

$$q_i g_i h_i'(\emptyset_i(q_i g_i)) = 1$$

$$\emptyset_i' = -\frac{h_i'}{h_i'' q_i g_i} = -\frac{(h_i')^2}{h_i''} > 0.$$

Also

$$\frac{\partial H}{\partial g_1} = (P'Y + P)\frac{\partial Y}{\partial g_1} - \frac{\partial \theta_1 PY}{\partial g_1} - \frac{\partial \theta_2 PY}{\partial g_1} - \psi \frac{\partial Y}{\partial g_1}$$

$$- Y\frac{\partial \psi}{\partial g_1} + q_1[h_1(\theta_1 PY) - \omega_1] + q_1 g_1 h_1' \frac{\partial \theta_1 PY}{\partial g_1}$$

$$+ q_2 g_2 h_2' \frac{\partial \theta_2 PY}{\partial g_1}.$$

Substituting for $q_i g_i h_i$ and ψ, we get

$$\dot{q}_1 = \rho q_1 - \frac{\partial H}{\partial g_1}$$

$$= (\rho - h_1 + \omega)q_1 + Y\frac{\partial \psi}{\partial g_1}.$$

Similarly $\dot{q}_2$ can be derived. $\dot{g}_1$ and $\dot{g}_2$ are given by definition.

A-2 Concavity conditions

Let H^* be the value of H obtained by substituting for θ_1, θ_2 and Y. Then

$$\frac{\partial^2 H^*}{\partial g_1^2} = -\frac{\partial Y^*}{\partial g_1}\frac{\partial \psi}{\partial g_1} - Y^*\frac{\partial^2 \psi}{\partial g_1^2} + q_1 h_1' \phi_1' q_1$$

$$= -\frac{\partial Y^*}{\partial g_1}\frac{\partial \psi}{\partial g_1} - Y^*\frac{\partial^2 \psi}{\partial g_1^2} + \frac{\phi_1' q_1}{g_1}$$

where $\phi_1' = \partial \phi_1/\partial(q_1 g_1)$. To determine the signs of the first term, differentiate the first order condition for Y^*:

$$(P''Y^* + 2P')\frac{\partial Y^*}{\partial g_1} = \frac{\partial \psi}{\partial g_1}$$

since

$$P''Y + 2P' < 0, \qquad \frac{\partial Y^*}{\partial g_1} \cdot \frac{\partial \psi}{\partial g_1} < 0.$$

Now, let $l_i = 1/g_i$ be the price of one efficiency unit of input i. Then $c(l_1, l_2) = \psi(g_1, g_2)$ is the unit cost function. Therefore, by Shepard-Hotelling lemma, $\partial c/\partial l_1 = D_1 = AX_1/Y$ is the number of efficiency units of input i demanded by the firm. This relation enables us to express the various conditions in terms of the elasticities of the marginal revenue curve and elasticity of derived demand for an input instead of what would otherwise be the elasticity of cost curves.

$$\frac{\partial \psi}{\partial g_1} = \frac{\partial c}{\partial l_1} \cdot \frac{dl_1}{dg_1} = -l_1^2 \frac{\partial c}{\partial l_1} = -l_1^2 D_1$$

$$\frac{\partial^2 \psi}{\partial g_1^2} = \frac{\partial}{\partial l_1}\left\{-l_1^2 \frac{\partial c}{\partial l_1}\right\}\frac{dl_1}{dg_1}$$

$$= -l_1^2\left\{-2l_1 D_1 - l_1^2 \frac{\partial D_1}{\partial l_1}\right\}$$

$$= l_1^3 D_1\left\{2 + \frac{l_1}{D_1}\frac{\partial D_1}{\partial l_1}\right\}.$$

Let η_1 be the elasticity of derived demand for AX_1. Then

$$-\eta_1 = \frac{\partial \log D_1 Y^*}{\partial \log l_1} = \frac{\partial \log D_1}{\partial \log l_1} + \frac{\partial \log Y^*}{\partial \log l_1}$$

$$= \frac{\partial \log D_1}{\partial \log l_1} + \frac{\partial \log Y^*}{\partial \log c} \cdot \frac{\partial \log c}{\partial \log l_1}$$

$$= \frac{\partial \log D_1}{\partial \log l_1} + \frac{\partial \log Y^*}{\partial \log mr} \cdot \frac{D_1 l_1}{c}$$

$$= \frac{d \log D_1}{d \log l_1} - \frac{\Pi_1}{\varepsilon_m}$$

where ε_m is the elasticity of the marginal revenue curve and Π_1 is the share of factor X_1 in total cost. Substituting

$$\frac{\partial^2\psi}{\partial g_1^2} = \frac{D_1}{g_1^3}\left\{2 + \frac{\Pi_1}{\varepsilon_m} - \eta_1\right\} \quad \text{as} \quad l_i = \frac{1}{g_i}.$$

Further

$$-\frac{\partial Y^*}{\partial g_1}\frac{\partial\psi}{\partial g_1} - Y^*\frac{\partial^2\psi}{\partial g_1^2} = -\frac{1}{P''Y^* + 2P'}\left(\frac{\partial\psi}{\partial g_1}\right)^2 - Y^*\frac{\partial^2\psi}{\partial g_1^2}$$

$$= -\left(\frac{\partial\psi}{\partial g_1}\right)\left[\frac{1}{\frac{\partial mr}{\partial Y^*}}\frac{\partial\psi}{\partial g_1} + \frac{Y^*D_1 l_1^3\left\{2 + \frac{\Pi_1}{\varepsilon_m} - \eta_1\right\}}{-l_1^2 D_1}\right]$$

$$= l_1^2 D_1 Y^*\left[\frac{mr}{Y^*\frac{\partial mr}{\partial Y^*}}\frac{-l_1^2 D_1}{c} - l_1\left\{2 + \frac{\Pi_1}{\varepsilon_m} - \eta_1\right\}\right]$$

$$= \frac{D_1 Y^*}{g_1^3}\left[\frac{\Pi_1}{\varepsilon_m} - \left\{2 + \frac{\Pi_1}{\varepsilon_m} - \eta_1\right\}\right]$$

$$= \frac{D_1 Y^*}{g_1^3}\{\eta_1 - 2\}.$$

Also

$$\frac{\partial^2 H}{\partial g_2\,\partial g_1} = \frac{\partial}{\partial g_2}\left(\frac{\partial H}{\partial g_1}\right)$$

$$= -\frac{\partial Y^*}{\partial g_2}\frac{\partial\psi}{\partial g_1} - Y^*\frac{\partial^2\psi}{\partial g_1\,\partial g_2}$$

$$= -\frac{1}{P''Y + P'}\cdot\frac{\partial\psi}{\partial g_2}\cdot\frac{\partial\psi}{\partial g_1} - Y^*\frac{\partial^2\psi}{\partial g_1\,\partial g_2} = \frac{\partial^2 H}{\partial g_1\,\partial g_2}$$

$$= -\frac{Y^*}{\psi}\cdot\frac{\partial\psi}{\partial g_2}\frac{\partial\psi}{\partial g_1}\left[\frac{\psi}{Y^*\frac{\partial mr}{\partial Y^*}} + \frac{\psi\frac{\partial^2\psi}{\partial g_1\,\partial g_2}}{\frac{\partial\psi}{\partial g_1}\frac{\partial\psi}{\partial g_2}}\right]$$

$$\sigma = \frac{c\frac{\partial^2 c}{\partial l_1\,\partial l_2}}{\frac{\partial c}{\partial l_1}\frac{\partial c}{\partial l_2}} = \frac{\psi\frac{1}{l_1^2 l_2^2}\frac{\partial^2\psi}{\partial g_1\,\partial g_2}}{\left(-\frac{1}{l_1^2}\right)\frac{\partial\psi}{\partial g_1}\left(-\frac{1}{l_2^2}\right)\frac{\partial\psi}{\partial g_2}}.$$

$$= \frac{\psi\frac{\partial^2\psi}{\partial g_1\,\partial g_2}}{\frac{\partial\psi}{\partial g_1}\frac{\partial\psi}{\partial g_2}}.$$

Hence

$$\frac{\partial^2 H}{\partial g_1\,\partial g_2} = -\frac{Y^*}{\psi}\frac{\partial\psi}{\partial g_1}\frac{\partial\psi}{\partial g_2}\left[\sigma - \frac{1}{\varepsilon_m}\right].$$

A-3. Stability

The stability in the neighbourhood of a steady-state can be determined by considering the characteristic roots of the Jacobian

$$\frac{\partial(\dot{q}_1, \dot{q}_2, \dot{g}_1, \dot{g}_2)}{\partial(q_1, q_2, g_1, g_2)}.$$

To evaluate the elements, consider

$$\frac{\partial \dot{q}_1}{\partial q_1} = (\rho - h_1 + \omega_1) - q_1 h_1' \frac{\partial \theta_1 PY}{\partial q_1}$$

$$= \rho - h_1 + \omega_1 + \frac{(h_1')^2}{h_1''}$$

$$= \rho - h_1 + \omega_1 + r_1 \text{ say}$$

$$\frac{\partial \dot{q}_1}{\partial g_1} = \frac{\partial}{\partial g_1} \left\{ \rho q_1 - \frac{\partial H^*}{\partial g_1} \right\} = -\frac{\partial^2 H^*}{\partial g_1^2} = m_1 \text{ say}$$

$$\frac{\partial \dot{q}_1}{\partial g_2} = \frac{\partial}{\partial g_2} \left\{ \rho q_1 - \frac{\partial H^*}{\partial g_1} \right\} = -\frac{\partial^2 H}{\partial g_1 \partial g_2} = N \text{ say.}$$

Other elements of the Jacobian matrix can be derived in a similar manner. Hence the Jacobian evaluated at steady state is:

$$\begin{bmatrix} \rho + r_1 & 0 & m_1 & N \\ 0 & \rho + r_2 & N & m_2 \\ -r_1 \dfrac{g_1}{q_1} & 0 & -r_1 & 0 \\ 0 & -r_2 \dfrac{g_2}{q_2} & 0 & -r_2 \end{bmatrix}$$

The characteristic equations can be written as:

$$\left\{ (\rho + r_1 - \lambda)(r_1 + \lambda) - r_1 m_1 \frac{g_1}{q_1} \right\} \left\{ (\rho + r_2 - \lambda)(r_2 + \lambda) - r_2 m_2 \frac{g_2}{q_2} \right\} - r_1 r_2 \frac{g_1 g_2}{q_1 q_2} N^2 = 0.$$

The expression in each of the brackets is:

$$f(\lambda) = -\lambda^2 + \rho \lambda + r_1 \left(\rho + r_1 - \frac{g_1}{q_1} m_1 \right).$$

Concentrating on this equation, the sign pattern of its roots are determined by that of the independent term (by Descartes' rule). But

$$\rho + r_1 - \frac{g_1}{q_1} m_1 = \frac{g_1}{q_1} \left[\rho \frac{q_1}{g_1} + r_1 \frac{q_1}{g_1} + \frac{\partial^2 H}{\partial g_1^2} \right] \quad \text{(by definition of } m_1)$$

$$= \frac{g_1}{q_1} \left[\frac{D_1 Y_1^*}{g_1^3} + \frac{r_1 q_1}{g_1} + \frac{D_1 Y^*}{g_1^3} (\eta_1 - 2) + \frac{\phi_1' q_1}{g_1} \right] \quad \text{(by (17) and (13))}$$

$$= \frac{g_1}{q_1} \left[\frac{D_1 Y^*}{g_1^3} (\eta_1 - 1) \right] \quad \text{(by definition of } r_1)$$

Hence, if the characteristic equation is the product of the two quadratics (if $N = 0$), then the sign pattern are determined by the value of η_1. If $N \neq 0$, the above expression can be reduced to a product of quadratics by the method of Ferrari but it is not possible to give a simple economic interpretation of the conditions. Note that N represents the cross effect on unit cost of change in both input prices.

REFERENCES

ARROW, K. J. and KURZ, M., *Public Investment, the Rate of Return and Optimal Fiscal Policy,* Johns Hopkins Press, Baltimore, 1970.

HALE, J. K., *Ordinary Differential Equations,* Academic Press, New York, 1969.

356   FACTOR PRICE VARIATION AND THE HICKSIAN HYPOTHESIS

HICKS, J. R., *The Theory of Wages,* McMillan, London, 1963.
KAMIEN, M. I. and SCHWARTZ, N. L., "Induced Factor Augmenting Technological Progress from a Microeconomic Viewpoint," *Econometrica,* 1969, 37, 668–684.
KURZ, M., "The General Instability of a Class of Competitive Growth Process," *Rev. Econ. Stud.,* 1968, 35, 155–174.
LANCASTER, P., *Theory of Matrices,* Academic Press, New York, 1969.
PITCHFORD, J. D., "Two State Variable Problems," in PITCHFORD, J. D. and TURNOVSKY, S. J., *Applications of Control Theory to Economic Analysis,* North Holland, Amsterdam, 1977.
SATO, R., *Theory of Technical Change and Economic Invariance: Applications of Lie Group,* Academic Press, New York, 1981.
SATO, R. and RAMACHANDRAN, R. V., "Factor Price Variation, Optimal Technical Progress and Economic Growth," Brown University Working Paper, 1978.
SATO, R. and SUZAWA, G. S., *Research and Productivity,* Auburn House, Boston, 1983.

Vol. 42 (1982), No. 1, pp. 1—22

Zeitschrift für
Nationalökonomie
Journal of Economics
© by Springer-Verlag 1982

A Theory of Endogenous Technical Progress: Dynamic Böhm-Bawerk Effect and Optimal R & D Policy

By

Ryuzo Sato, Providence, R. I., U. S. A., and
Takayuki Nôno, Fukuoka, Japan*

(Received May 18, 1981)

I. Introduction

1. Historians, political scientists, sociologists and economists will all agree that one of the major forces shaping human destiny has been technology and innovation. The discovery of cultivated grain is responsible for the agricultural surplus enabling the existence of urban society. The introduction of gun powder in Europe was a major factor in terminating the feudal regime. The printing machine helped Luther in the Reformation. The internal combustion machine is, of course, the basis for automobiles and airplanes. There are but a few examples from quite a long list[1]. However, these advances were considered exogenous, subject to chance, like "manna from heaven". Only in the last twenty years, economists, and other specialists engaged in the problems of less developed countries have begun viewing the technological progress as endogenous.

An important dimension of technical change is that it is the outcome of investment activities; society postpones a portion of present consumption for the benefit of increased consumption later. In the

---

* The substantial portion of this work was completed while Nôno was at Brown University as a Visiting Professor of Economics for the academic year 1979—1980. The authors gratefully acknowledge support from the National Science Foundation.

[1] See: Jacobs [1969], for a fascinating discussion. Mrs. Jacobs' original contribution is to explain the innovation process as an endogeneous factor; her methods are best described as belonging to historical research. See: M. Bloch [1961], for a brilliant exposition how material and technological factors shape human state of mind and consciousness. Also see: M. McLuhan [1969] for general analysis of the effect of the printed word.

0044-3158/82/0042/0001/$ 04.40

theory of the firm behavior, the firm postpones a fraction of present profits in the form of research and development (R & D) investment for the purpose of enjoying future cost saving benefits. Viewing technological change in an intertemporal context affords us many possibilities for understanding better the relationship between R & D and the efficiency increase in production of goods and services. Economists discovered long ago that a significant increase of productivity is largely due to R & D activities of the firm industry and economy as a whole. Quoting the conclusion drawn at the 1972 colloquium on R & D and economic growth-productivity sponsored by the National Science Foundation, Kamien and Schwartz [1975] write:

> "despite methodological difficulties and debates, all the evidence — at the level of the firm, industry and economy — indicates that the contribution of R & D to economic growth/productivity is positive, significant, and high. Estimates of rates of return range between 10 percent and 50 percent with a bias toward the higher values."

Perhaps the most dramatic evidence for the direct effect of R & D is found in agriculture. Evenson and Kislev [1975] report:

> „We have found that very systematic relationships exist between levels of research activity and economic performance."

The studies done by industrial organization specialists have shown that the R & D cost relation to output follows the same (*U*-shaped) pattern as the cost relation of other commodities (Scherer [1970], Schmookler [1966], Mansfield [1981]). This indicates that R & D can be viewed as one of the factors of production and that we may apply the "production function" approach to the theory of endogenous technical progress. We abstract from problems of management and engineering, labor relations and other factors. We recognize that much of the strength (and weakness) in the concept of production function lies in its being a "black box", and that the "black box" can include the creative process, assimilation and processing of information, sociology of science and scientific society, and other factors.

Basic vs. Applied Research

2. Review of the literature of technical progress and of production function in general shows that the present approach is unique in the following two respects[2]:

---

[2] There is a number of excellent surveys of the area, this is why we refrain from detailed bibliographical account. The surveys are: Kamien

(i) There are *two main categories of research: basic and applied.* Developments fall under the "applied" category. It is useful to think of basic knowledge obtained by basic research as an intermediate product in the production of technical knowledge by applied research. The combination of basic and applied research is responsible for productivity increase.

(ii) The production function depends not only on current research, but on a *stock* of technical knowledge accumulated by applied research done in several years. There exist *time lags* between research inputs and research outputs[3].

Holotheticity and Endogenous Technical Progress

3. In Sato [1980] it is shown that for any given production function there exists an infinite number of different types of technical change that can be transformed to the scale effcte — holotheticity. That is to say, there exists an infinite number of holothetic technical change expressible in terms of "neutral type" of technical progress. This suggests that we are *not* required to justify the existence of *endogenous* technical change for every *different* type of *exogenous* technical change. It suffices to concentrate just on a "neutral type" of technical progress. It turns out, however, that it is much more convenient to use the neutral type of technical progress which generally applies to the cost function rather than to the production function itself. In short, our purpose is that, *rather than taking the neutral type (applied to the cost function) as exogenous, we formulate a model of technical change which is generated endogenously by efficient allocation of resources.*

II. Formulation of the Model

Dynamic Böhm-Bawerk Effects

4. The process of accumulation of knowledge is *endogenous,* and should be determined by the firm so as to maximized long-run profits. The firm may change its stock of *basic and applied* knowledge by producing a *flow* of the two. Basic knowledge is an inter-

---

and Schwartz [1975], Nordhaus [1969], Scherer [1970], ch. 15 and others. See also Griliches [1980].

[3] The present analysis is a direct extension of Sato and Ramachandran [1978]. Time lags considered here are the so-called "transport lags" (Bate [1969]). Thus, this is an application of optimal control with transport lags.

mediate product in the production of new technical knowledge. Consider the celebrated example of productivity increase by a round-about production process of Böhm-Bawerk. A fisherman does not go to sea to catch fish by bare hands. He would rather use his labor first by making fishing nets and boates, which are intermediate products for the final output-fish, to catch it more efficiently. The idea behind our formulation is similar to this type of the Böhm-Bawerk process, except that we assume here a dynamic process of continuous delays between research inputs and research outcomes. Next we assume that the firm is a profit-maximizing monopolist[4], engaging in production (and sales) of the product and in R & D activities[5]. It buys capital (K) and labor (L) at given prices r and w respectively. The firm may increase the stock of basic knowledge (B) or applied knowledge (A) by employing specialized research workers a and research capital b. But there are time lags between inputs and outputs of this research activity. If we allow for continuous time lags, the flow of outputs appears as cumulative. Formally we write the cumulative effects as:

$$\dot{A}(t) = \int_{-\infty}^{t} G^1 [A(\tau), B(\tau), a_A(\tau), b_A(\tau)] W_1(t-\tau) \, d\tau - \nu A(t). \tag{1}$$

$$\dot{B}(t) = \int_{-\infty}^{t} G^2 [B(\tau), a_B(\tau), b_B(\tau)] W_2(t-\tau) \, d\tau - \mu B(t). \tag{2}$$

Looking at the second equation, we see that the potential flow of basic knowledge $\dot{B}$ without a time lag depends on the level of stock of basic knowledge itself B, the factor inputs a_B and b_B. Here, G^2 may be considered as a *production function* of the potential flow of basic knowledge, which represents the potential gross increase in B. Eq. (1) without a time lag is, on the other hand, the production function of applied knowledge which has a direct influence on productivity increase. Thus G^1 represents the potential gross increase in the stock of applied knowledge resulting from A, a_A and b_A and more importantly from the value of basic knowledge B. The fact that G^1 contains B but G^2 does *not* contain A shows the essential *asymmetric* property of technical change. *Basic knowledge B is "essential" for production of applied knowledge A.* Looking

---

[4] It is known that big firms only engage in research — the threshold is 5,000 workers. It is conceivable that such firms view a negatively sloped demand cure.

[5] This is the general framework adopted by Sato and Ramachandran [1978]. They, however, do not separate basic and applied research.

A Theory of Endogenous Technical Progress 5

at the extreme case in which the stock of basic knowledge is zero (a case which exists in principle, but not in practice), we find that the following conditions would hold:

$$\text{(i)} \quad G^1(A, 0, a_A, b_A) = 0$$

$$\text{(ii)} \quad \frac{\partial G^1(A, 0, a_A, b_A)}{\partial B} = +\infty \tag{3}$$

The first expression states that without basic knowledge, the production of applied knowledge is impossible. The assumption is quite realistic. Elementary language skills, and fundamental numerical skills fall under the category of basic knowledge. It is clear, for example, that a student with no knowledge of Russian could not possibly formulate an intelligent interpretation of the original works of Tolstoy. Similarly, a researcher with no basic knowledge of a certain computer language could not possibly produce useful programs written in that language.

The second expression states that the marginal productivity of the first unit of basic knowledge in the production of technical knowledge is extremely high. As an approximation, one may envision the change in applied knowledge that is brought about by mastering simple arithmetic. Regarding the effects of other variables on G^1 and G^2 we shall simply assume the positivity (nonnegativity) of the marginal products and the *concavity* of G^1 and G^2 with respect to their arguments. In summary, we assume that

$$\text{(i)} \quad \frac{\partial G^1}{\partial A} \geq 0, \ \frac{\partial G^1}{\partial B} > 0, \ \frac{\partial G^1}{\partial a_A} \geq 0, \ \frac{\partial G^1}{\partial b_A} \geq 0,$$

$$\text{(ii)} \quad \frac{\partial G^2}{\partial A} = 0, \ \frac{\partial G^2}{\partial B} \geq 0, \ \frac{\partial G^2}{\partial a_B} \geq 0, \ \frac{\partial G^2}{\partial b_B} \geq 0, \tag{4}$$

$$\text{(iii)} \quad G^1 \text{ and } G^2 \text{ are concave functions.}$$

Eqs. (1) and (2) allow for the existence of time lags between the inputs and increases in A and B. Because of time lags, the actual increase in A or B depends on the cumulative effect expressed by the integro-differential equation. We may call this as the *dynamic Böhm-Bawerk effect*, with W_i $(i=1, 2)$ being a weighting function which has the property

$$\int_{-\infty}^{t} W_i(t-\tau) \, d\tau = 1, \quad i=1, 2. \tag{5}$$

Then, Eq. (1) [or (2)] states that the realized gross increase in technical knowledge is a weighted average of past values of G^1 (or

6   R. Sato and T. Nôno:

G^2 for B). Both ν and μ ($\nu \geq 0$, $\mu \geq 0$) are depreciation factors in applied and basic knowledge respectively. It takes account of the fact that a part of the production effort of knowledge is aimed at renewing and transferring of knowledge. One may think on the beginning of the Middle Ages as a time where G^2 was near zero, and so the level of basic knowledge deteriorated.

The firm is faced with a discount rate ϱ, time series of expected prices of a and b, $P_a(t)$ and $P_b(t)$; r_t, w_t — the development of prices of capital and labor and $P_t(Y)$ — the demand function for the final output Y which is also subject to dynamic change. The firm may naturally expect the increasing scarcity of resource[6] to be reflected in knowledge, thus increasing its productivity and reducing its cost. We will see below that this indeed happens. Fig. 1 depicts the cumulative effects of investment in research and development of new technology. The results of the past investments appear continuously, with the investment of, say, five years ago yielding the highest effect. The form and shape of this curve depend on a particular type of weighting functions we employ. It is found that a gamma distribution function is particularly appealing, and useful for an empirical study (Sato and Suzawa [1980]).

Allocation of Resources

5. We assume that the firm produces the output (Y) from K and L using its neoclassical production function

$$Y(t) = F[A(t) K(t), A(t) L(t)]. \tag{6}$$

$A(t)$ is the level of factor augmentation at time t, and it is the measure of technical progress of the firm, that we have discussed before.

From the production function we can derive the total cost function

$$TC(Y, w, r, A) = \frac{1}{A(t)} \overline{TC}(Y, w, r) \tag{6'}$$

where $\overline{TC}(Y, w, r)$ is the minimum cost of producing Y given the production function with no factor augmentation. This property is valid for a general production function. We do not assume any

---

[6] Scarcity of oil follows from its being an exhaustible resource. Scarcity of food follows from growth of population, and constancy of fertile land. So far the Malthusian famine was averted by a rate of technological innovation in production of food which was equal to the rate of population growth. This agrees with the predictions of our model.

A Theory of Endogenous Technical Progress   7

homogeneity. Hence, we want to justify the indirect holotheticity and indirect neutrality with respect the cost function, as discussed before in Section 3[7].

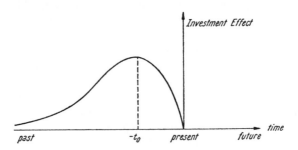

Fig. 1. Continuous Böhm-Bawerk effect

The firm's objective is to solve the maximization problem of the following type:

$$\max_{\substack{a_A(t),\, a_B(t)\\ b_A(t),\, b_B(t),\, Y(t)}} \int_0^\infty e^{-\rho t} \left[Y(t)\, P\left(Y(t)\right) - \overline{TC}\left(Y(t), \frac{w(t)}{A(t)}, \frac{r(t)}{A(t)}\right) \right. \tag{7}$$

$$\left. - P_a(t)\left(a_A(t) + a_B(t)\right) - P_b\left(b_A(t) + b_B(t)\right) \right] dt$$

subject to the constraints,

$$\dot{A}(t) = -\nu A(t) + \int_{-\infty}^{t} G^1 \left[A(\tau), B(\tau), a_A(\tau), b_A(\tau)\right] W_1(t-\tau)\, d\tau \tag{1}$$

$$\dot{B}(t) = -\mu B(t) + \int_{-\infty}^{t} G^2 \left[B(\tau), a_B(\tau), b_B(\tau)\right] W_2(t-\tau)\, d\tau \tag{2}$$

and the initial conditions.

The firm's problem is to choose a time path of output and a program of research and development which maximizes the present value of future profits. In conducting its research and development

---

[7] If F is a homogeneous function of degree one, the indirect neutrality $\dfrac{TC}{A(t)}$ coincides with the direct neutrality $Z = A(t) F$. A more general case must consider a non-uniform (biased) type of technical progress in (6) ($Y = F[A(t), K, B(t) L]$) in the context of endogenous technical change. This will enable one to analyze the implication of the *expanding* innovation frontier of Samuelson [1965]. A simple case of expanding innovation frontier where there is no distinction between basic and applied research is studied by Sato and Ramachandran [1978].

program the firm chooses the level of labor and capital inputs in the R & D process. In hiring inputs, there may be substantial interaction between firms. For example, the representative firm may hire researchers who have been already trained at another firm, or may purchase a device or process patented by another firm. It is assumed that these inputs are purchased in one competitive market. However, it may be that the firm recruits R & D inputs from two sources — (1) educational institutions and (2) other firms. As a first approximation, inputs into the production of basic knowledge a_B and b_B are probably hired more intensively in the educational sector, and applied inputs are most likely to be hired from other firms. Therefore, the wage and rental payments to basic and applied inputs is assumed to be the same. The validity of this assumption is an empirical question, and the assumption may easily be relaxed.

Additional Assumptions

6. In order to insure the existence of a long-run steady-state equilibrium, we shall make the following additional assumptions:

$$
\begin{aligned}
&\text{(i)} \quad P\left(Y\left(t\right)\right) = e^{\alpha t}\, \bar{P}\left(Y\left(t\right)\right) \\
&\text{(ii)} \quad r\left(t\right) \quad = e^{\beta t}\, \bar{r} \\
&\text{(iii)} \quad w\left(t\right) \quad = e^{\beta t}\, \bar{w} \quad\quad \varrho \geq \beta \geq \alpha \geq 0 \quad\quad\quad (8)\\
&\text{(iv)} \quad P_a\left(t\right) \quad = e^{\alpha t}\, \bar{P_a} \quad\quad \bar{P} > 0,\ \bar{r} > 0 \\
&\text{(v)} \quad P_b\left(t\right) \quad = e^{\alpha t}\, \bar{P_b} \quad\quad \bar{w} > 0,\ \bar{P_a} > 0,\ \bar{P_b} > 0.
\end{aligned}
$$

Here we assume that the commodity price $P\left(Y\right)$ is increasing at the same rate (α) as the prices of inputs in the R & D sector, while the wage rate and the return to capital both grow at the rate β.

Define a new state variable

$$g\left(t\right) = e^{-(\beta-\alpha)t}\, A\left(t\right). \tag{9}$$

Then we have by the homogeneity property

$$
\begin{aligned}
TC = \overline{TC}\left(Y, \tfrac{w}{A}, \tfrac{r}{A}\right) \\
= \tfrac{1}{A}\, \overline{TC}\left(Y, w, r\right) \\
= \tfrac{e^{\beta t}}{A}\, \overline{TC}\left(Y, \bar{w}, \bar{r}\right) \quad \text{(by homogeneity)}
\end{aligned}
$$

$$\therefore\ TC = e^{\alpha t}\, \tfrac{1}{g}\, C\left(Y\right),\ C\left(Y\right) = \overline{TC}\left(Y, \bar{w}, \bar{r}\right). \tag{10}$$

Also the total revenue function can be expressed as

$$Y(t) P(Y(t)) = e^{\alpha t} Y(t) \bar{P}(Y(t))$$

$$\therefore Y(t) P(Y(t)) = e^{\alpha t} R(Y(t)), \quad R(Y(t)) = Y(t) \bar{P}(Y(t)). \quad (11)$$

Eq. (9) obviously implies

$$\frac{\dot{A}}{A} = \frac{\dot{g}}{g} + (\beta - \alpha). \quad (9')$$

Using these new variables, our maximization problem of optimal endogenous technical change can be reformulated as:

$$\max_{\substack{a_A(t),\, a_B(t) \\ \{b_A(t),\, b_B(t),\, Y(t)\}}} \int_0^\infty e^{-\gamma t} \left[R(Y(t)) - \frac{1}{g(t)} C(Y(t)) - \bar{P}_a (a_A(t) + a_B(t)) \right.$$

$$\left. - \bar{P}_b (b_A(t) + b_B(t)) \right] dt \qquad (7')$$

subject to[8]

$$\dot{g}(t) = -(\beta - \alpha + \nu) g(t) + \int_{-\infty}^t e^{-(\beta-\alpha)t} G^1 [e^{(\beta-\alpha)\tau} \cdot g(\tau), B(\tau) \quad (1')$$

$$a_A(\tau), b_A(\tau)] W_1(t-\tau) d\tau,$$

$$\dot{B}(t) = -\mu B(t) + \int_{-\infty}^t G^2 [B(\tau), a_B(\tau), b_B(\tau)] W_2(t-\tau) d\tau \quad (2)$$

where

$$\gamma = \rho - \alpha > 0. \quad (12)$$

III. Solution of the Model

7. The model we have just formulated is formally similar to the optimal control problem of a system with transport (or continuous) lag, first studied by Bate [1969], and later applied to economic analysis by Sethe [1973, 1974], Pauwels [1977], Sethi and McGuire [1977], and others. In order to guarantee the sufficiency conditions for the optimal program we assume that the production functions G^1, G^2, $F(K, L)$ and the profit function are all concave

---

[8] Eq. (1') was derived from (1) and (9') by

$$e^{(\beta-\alpha)t} \dot{g}(t) + (\beta-\alpha) e^{(\beta-\alpha)t} g(t) = -\nu e^{(\beta-\alpha)t} g(t)$$

$$+ \int_{-\infty}^t G^1 [e^{(\beta-\alpha)\tau} \cdot g(\tau), B(\tau), a_A(\tau), b_A(\tau)] W_1(t-\tau) d\tau.$$

in such a way that the maximized Hamiltonian is concave in the state variables for each t. We may further assume that the maximized Hamiltonian is concave in the state variables for each given implicit price vector and for each t (Sethi [1974]).

We shall basically follow the transformation suggested by Sethi [1973] to derive solutions to this type of problems. Thus the *current-value Hamiltonian* is equal to

$$H [g (t), B (t), \lambda_1 (\tau \geq t), \lambda_2 (\tau \geq t), Y (t), a_A (t), b_A (t), a_B (t),$$
$$b_B (t)] = R (Y (t))$$

$$- \frac{1}{g (t)} C (Y (t)) - \bar{P}_a (a_A (t) + a_B (t)) - \bar{P}_b (b_A (t) + b_B (t))$$

$$- \lambda_1 (t) (\beta - \alpha + \nu) g (t) - \lambda_2 (t) \mu B (t)$$

$$+ \int_t^\infty e^{-\gamma (\tau - t)} \{ \lambda_1 (\tau) G^1 [e^{(\beta - \alpha) t} \cdot g (t), B (t), a_A (t), b_A (t)] e^{-(\beta - \alpha) \tau}$$

$$\cdot W_1 (\tau - t) + \lambda_2 (\tau) G^2 [B (t), a_B (t), b_B (t),] W_2 (\tau - t) \} d\tau,$$

i. e.,

$$H = R (Y (t)) - \frac{1}{g (t)} C (Y (t)) - \bar{P}_a (a^A (t) + a^B (t)) - \bar{P}_b (b^A (t) + b^B (t))$$

$$- \lambda_1 (t) (\beta - \alpha + \nu) g (t) - \lambda_2 (t) \mu B (t)$$

$$+ G^1 [e^{(\beta - \alpha) t} \cdot g (t), B (t), a_A (t), b_A (t)] \int_t^\infty e^{-(\beta - \alpha) \tau} \cdot \lambda_1 (\tau) e^{-\gamma (\tau - t)}$$

$$\cdot W_1 (\tau - t) d\tau + G^2 [B (t), a_B (t), b_B (t)] \int_t^\infty \lambda_2 (\tau) e^{-\gamma (\tau - t)} \qquad (13)$$

$$\cdot W_2 (\tau - t) d\tau.$$

The current value adjoint vector (λ_1, λ_2) of the implicit prices is given by

(i) $$\dot{\lambda}_1 (t) = (\gamma + \beta - \alpha + \nu) \lambda_1 (t) - \frac{1}{g^2 (t)} C (Y (t))$$

$$- e^{(\beta - \alpha) t} G_1^1 \cdot \int_t^\infty e^{-(\beta - \alpha) \tau} \cdot \lambda_1 (\tau) e^{-\gamma (\tau - t)} W_1 (\tau - t) d\tau,$$

$$(14)$$

(ii) $$\dot{\lambda}_2 (t) = (\gamma + \mu) \lambda_2 (t) - G^1_2 \cdot \int_t^\infty e^{-(\beta - \alpha) \tau} \cdot \lambda_1 (\tau) e^{-\gamma (\tau - t)} \cdot W_1 (\tau - t) d\tau$$

$$- G_2^2 \cdot \int_t^\infty \lambda_2 (\tau) e^{-\gamma (\tau - t)} \cdot W_2 (\tau - t) d\tau,$$

where $G^1 = G^1 [e^{(\beta - \alpha)} t \cdot g (t), B (t), a_A (t), b_A (t)] = G^1 (X_1, X_2, X_3, X_4)$
$G^2 = G^2 [B (t), a_B (t), b_B (t)] = G^2 (Y_2, Y_3, Y_4)$, and
$G_i^1 = \frac{\partial G^1}{\partial X_i} (i = 1, 2, 3, 4), \quad G_j^2 = \frac{\partial G^2}{\partial Y_j} (j = 2, 3, 4).$

A Theory of Endogenous Technical Progress   **11**

By the maximum principles similar to the one developed by Pontryagin, *et al.* [1962], we have,

(i) $\dfrac{\partial H}{\partial Y} = R\,(Y\,(t)) - \dfrac{1}{g}\,C_Y\,(Y\,(t)) = 0$

(ii) $\dfrac{\partial H}{\partial a_A} = -\bar{P} + G_3{}^1 \cdot \int\limits_t^\infty e^{-(\beta-\alpha)\tau} \cdot \lambda_1\,(\tau)\,e^{-\gamma\,(\tau-t)} \cdot W_1\,(\tau-t)\,d\tau = 0$

(iii) $\dfrac{\partial H}{\partial b_A} = -\bar{P}_b + G_4{}^1 \cdot \int\limits_t^\infty e^{-(\beta-\alpha)\tau} \cdot \lambda_1\,(\tau)\,e^{-\gamma\,(\tau-t)} \cdot W_1\,(\tau-t)\,d\tau = 0$

(iv) $\dfrac{\partial H}{\partial a_B} = -\bar{P}_a + G_3{}^2 \cdot \int\limits_t^\infty \lambda_2\,(\tau)\,e^{-\gamma\,(\tau-t)} \cdot W_2\,(\tau-t)\,d\tau = 0$ (15)

(v) $\dfrac{\partial H}{\partial b_B} = -\bar{P}_b + G_4{}^2 \cdot \int\limits_t^\infty \lambda_2\,(\tau)\,e^{-\gamma\,(\tau-t)} \cdot W_2\,(\tau-t)\,d\tau = 0.$

These equations give the optimality conditions for endogenous technical progress: The first is the familiar condition of the equality of the marginal revenue (R_Y) with the marginal cost $\left(\dfrac{C_Y}{g}\right)$: The remaining conditions state that *the ratios between the prices of the research factor inputs and their marginal products in creation of the basic and applied knowledge must be equal to their averages of the implicit prices,* i. e.,

$$\frac{\bar{P}_a}{G_3{}^1} = \int\limits_t^\infty e^{-(\beta-\alpha)\tau} \cdot \lambda_1\,(\tau)\,e^{-\gamma\,(\tau-t)} \cdot W_1\,(\tau-t)\,d\tau$$

$$\vdots$$

$$\frac{\bar{P}_b}{G_4{}^2} = \int\limits_t^\infty \lambda_2\,(\tau)\,e^{-\gamma\,(\tau-t)} \cdot W_2\,(\tau-t)\,d\tau.$$

Further Simplifications

8. Rather than pursuing the general line of analysis, we shall further simplify the model by assuming that *A (t) in the production of A is multiplicative and Ḃ (t) does not appear in the production of B.* In addition, we shall consider the case in which *a* and *b* are highly substitutable so that a linear combination of these two inputs can be treated as one aggregate input θ. Let a linear combination be represented by

$$\theta\,(t) = \bar{P}_a\,a\,(t) + \bar{P}_b\,b\,(t)$$

with the weights $\bar{P}_a$, $\bar{P}_b$ — (deflated) constant prices of a and b, respectively. Then we have $G^1 = G^1 (B_1, \theta_1)$ and $G^2 = G^2 (\theta_2)$ where $\theta_1 (t) = \bar{P}_a a_A (t) + \bar{P}_b b_A (t)$ and $\theta_2 (t) = \bar{P}_a a_B (t) + \bar{P}_b b_B (t)$. We may *alternatively* look at G^1 and G^2 as the potential production functions of the flows of A and B depending upon different research input factors θ_1 and θ_2 such as $\theta_1 = P_a a_A$ and $\theta_2 = P_b b_B$. In this case, the production of the flow of A does not require the second factor b, whereas production of the flow of B does not require the first factor a.

By these simplifications we can reduce the number of control variables from five (Y, a_A, a_B, b_A, b_B) to three (Y, θ_1, θ_2). At the same time the model is changed to one more convenient for estimation purposes[9]. It is often not possible to estimate empirically the quantities of research factor inputs, while the deflated expenditures for these input costs θ_1 and θ_2 are readily available. These simplifications do not destroy the essential property of the Böhm-Bawerk effects in the model by allowing $B (t)$ to remain in the production of technical knowledge in G^1. Hence, the production of basic knowledge is possible with research inputs only, while the production of applied knowledge requires not only research inputs but also the stock of basic knowledge[10].

Our problem of optimal control is now reduced to:

$$\max_{\{\theta_1(t), \theta_2(t), Y(t)\}} \int_0^\infty e^{-\gamma t} \left[R\ (Y(t)) - \frac{1}{g(t)} C\ (Y(t)) - \theta_1(t) - \theta_2(t) \right] dt \quad (16)$$

subject to

$$\dot{g}(t) = -(\beta - \alpha + \nu)\ g(t) + \int_{-\infty}^t g(\tau)\ G^1\ [B(\tau), \theta_1(\tau)] \cdot$$

$$\cdot e^{-(\beta - \alpha)(t - \tau)} \cdot W_1\ (t - \tau)\ d\tau, \quad (17)$$

$$\dot{B}(t) = -\mu B(t) + \int_{-\infty}^t G^2\ [\theta_2(\tau)]\ W_2\ (t - \tau)\ d\tau \quad \gamma = \rho - \alpha > 0. \quad (18)$$

---

[9] This model has been tested against U. S. data in a paper by Sato and Suzawa [1980].

[10] One should not take the words, basic and applied in a literary sense. Hence in the Böhm-Bawerk example we used earlier, the skill of fishing is applied or technical knowledge, while the skill of making nets and fishing boats is basic knowledge — basic for the purpose of fishing.

A Theory of Endogenous Technical Progress   13

The current value Hamiltonian for this is

$$H = R(Y) - \frac{1}{g} C(Y) - \theta_1 - \theta_2 - \lambda_1 (\beta - \alpha + \nu) g - \lambda_2 \mu B$$

$$+ g(t) G^1 [B(t), \theta_1(t)] \int_t^\infty \lambda_1(\tau) e^{-\gamma(\tau-t)} D_1(\tau-t) d\tau \quad (19)$$

$$+ G^2 [\theta_2(t)] \int_t^\infty \lambda_2(\tau) e^{-\gamma(\tau-t)} D_1(\tau-t) d\tau$$

where $D_1(t) = e^{-(\beta-\alpha)t} W_1(t)$, $D_2(t) = W_2(t)$.

IV. Analysis of the Solution

9. By redefining $G^1 = h$ and $G^2 = f$, the equations of motion for the above problem of optimal control are expressed by

$$\dot{g}(t) = -(\beta - \alpha + \nu) g(t) + \int_{-\infty}^t g(\tau) h[B(\tau), \theta_1(\tau)] D_1(t-\tau) d\tau \quad (17)$$

$$\dot{B}(t) = -\mu B(t) + \int_{-\infty}^t f[\theta_2(\tau)] D_2(t-\tau) d\tau \quad (18)$$

$$\dot{\lambda}_1(t) = (\gamma + \beta - \alpha + \nu) \lambda_1(t) - \frac{1}{g^2} C(Y(t))$$
$$- h[B(t), \theta_1(t)] \int_t^\infty \lambda_1(\tau) e^{-\gamma(\tau-t)} D_1(\tau-t) d\tau, \quad (20)$$

$$\dot{\lambda}_2(t) = (\gamma + \mu) \lambda_2(t) - g h_1[B(t), \theta_1(t)] \int_t^\infty \lambda_1(\tau) e^{-\gamma(\tau-t)} D_1(\tau-t) d\tau. \quad (21)$$

Next we present the following most important lemma:

Lemma (Behavior Near $t \to +\infty$):

When $t \doteq +\infty$, we have

(i) $\int_t^\infty \lambda_1(\tau) e^{-\gamma(\tau-t)} D_1(\tau-t) d\tau \doteq \omega_1 \lambda_1(t)$

where $\omega_1 = \int_0^\infty e^{-\gamma\sigma} D_1(\sigma) d\sigma$, $\tau-t = \sigma$

14 R. Sato and T. Nôno:

(ii) $\int_t^\infty \lambda_2(\tau) e^{-\gamma(\tau-t)} D_2(\tau-t) d\tau \doteq \omega_2 \lambda_2(t)$

where $\omega_2 = \int_0^\infty e^{-\gamma\sigma} D_2(\sigma) d\sigma$,

(iii) $\int_{-\infty}^t g(\tau) h[B(\tau), \theta_1(\tau)] D_1(t-\tau) d\tau \doteq \omega_3 g(t) h[B(t), \theta_1(t)]$,

where $\omega_3 = \int_0^\infty D_1(\sigma) d\sigma$, (22)

(iv) $\int_{-\infty}^t f[\theta_2(\tau)] D_2(t-\tau) d\tau \doteq \omega_4 f(\theta_2(t))$

where $\omega_4 = \int_0^\infty D_2(\sigma) d\sigma$,

and $\omega_1, \omega_2, \omega_3, \omega_4$ are constants > 0.

Proof: By setting

$\int_t^\infty \lambda_1(\tau) e^{-\gamma(\tau-t)} D_1(\tau-t) d\tau = \int_0^\infty \lambda_1(t+\sigma) e^{-\gamma\sigma} D_1(\sigma) d\sigma$, $\sigma = \tau - t$

and $t \doteq +\infty$ and

$$\lambda_1(t+\sigma) \doteq \lambda_1(t) \quad (\sigma > 0)$$

we obtain

$\int_0^\infty \lambda_1(t+\sigma) e^{-\gamma\sigma} D_1(\sigma) d\sigma \doteq \lambda_1(t) \int_0^\infty e^{-\gamma\sigma} D_1(\sigma) d\sigma = \omega_1 \lambda_1(t)$ (22-i)

where $\omega_1 = \int_0^\infty e^{-\gamma\sigma} D_1(\sigma) d\sigma$.

In the same way we get (22-ii). To prove (22-iii) we can show that by setting $\sigma = t - \tau$,

$$\int_{-\infty}^t g(\tau) h[B(\tau), \theta_1(\tau)] D_1(t-\tau) d\tau$$
$$= -\int_{-\infty}^0 g(t-\sigma) h[B(t-\sigma), \theta_1(t-\sigma)] \cdot D_1(\sigma) d\sigma$$
$$= \int_0^\infty g(t-\sigma) h[B(t-\sigma), \theta_1(t-\sigma)] D_1(\sigma) d\sigma.$$

When $t \doteq +\infty$, we can assume

$$g(t-\sigma) \doteq g(t), h[B(t-\sigma), \theta_1(t-\sigma)] = h[B(t), \theta_1(t)]$$

A Theory of Endogenous Technical Progress 15

for $t \doteq +\infty$ and for a rapidly decreasing $D_1(\sigma)$, $(\sigma > 0)$. Hence, we have

$$\int_{-\infty}^{t} g(\tau) h[B(\tau), \theta_1(\tau)] D_1(t-\tau) d\tau$$

$$\doteq g(t) h[B(t), \theta_1(t)] \int_{0}^{\infty} D_1(\sigma) d\sigma \qquad (22\text{-iii})$$

$$= \omega_3 g(t) h[B(t), \theta_1(t)], \quad \text{where } \omega_3 = \int_{0}^{\infty} D_1(\sigma) d\sigma.$$

In the same way we can show (22-iv).   Q. E. D.

In view of this lemma we now write the equations of motion in (17), (18), (20) and (21) *near* $t \doteq +\infty$ as,

(i) $\dot{g}(t) = -(\beta - \alpha + \nu) g(t) + \omega_3 g(t) h[B(t), \theta_1(t)]$

(ii) $\dot{B}(t) = -\mu B(t) + \omega_4 f[\theta_2(t)]$

(iii) $\dot{\lambda}_1(t) = (\gamma + \beta - \alpha + \nu) \lambda_1(t) - \dfrac{1}{g^2} C(Y(t))$ (23)
$\qquad - \omega_1 \lambda_1(t) h[B(t), \theta_1(t)]$

(iv) $\dot{\lambda}_2(t) = (\gamma + \mu) \lambda_2(t) - \omega_1 \lambda_1(t) g(t) h_1[B(t), \theta_1(t)]$

together with the following equilibrium conditions resulting from the maximum principle:

(i) $R'(Y) - \dfrac{C'(Y)}{g} = 0$

(ii) $\omega_1 \lambda_1(t) g(t) h_2[B(t), \theta_1(t)] = 1$ (24)

(iii) $\omega_2 \lambda_2(t) f'[\theta_2(t)] = 1$

where

(i) $\omega_1 = \int_{0}^{\infty} e^{-\gamma\sigma} D_1(\sigma) d\sigma$

(ii) $\omega_2 = \int_{0}^{\infty} e^{-\gamma\sigma} D_2(\sigma) d\sigma$

(iii) $\omega_3 \int_{0}^{\infty} D_1(\sigma) d\sigma$ (25)

(iv) $\omega_4 = \int_{0}^{\infty} D_2(\sigma) d\sigma$

In this formulation *when $\omega_1 = \omega_2 = \omega_3 = \omega_4 = 1$, the general model is reduced to the standard Pontryagin problem with no lags* (see Arrow and Kurz [1970], Samuelson [1972]). Having established optimal behavior near the steady-state position, we now want to study the optimal path near the equilibrium position as $\dot{g} = \dot{B} = \dot{\lambda}_1 = \dot{\lambda}_2 = 0$ at $t = +\infty$.

After complicated calculations (see Part V, Mathematical Appendix), we can write down the characteristic equations for this problem as

$$\det (J - XE) = (X + \mu) \, X \, (X - \gamma - (\omega_3 - \omega_1) \, h) \, (X - \gamma - \mu)$$

$$+ \frac{h_2^2}{h_{22}} (X + \mu) \, (X - \gamma - \mu) \left\{ (\omega_3 - \omega_1) \, X + \frac{\omega_3}{\lambda_1 g} \left(C - \frac{C'^2}{C'' - gR''} \right) \right\}$$

$$- \omega_1 \frac{\lambda_1}{\lambda_2} \, g \cdot \frac{f'^2}{f''} \left(\frac{h_{11} h_{22} - h_{12}^2}{h} \right) X \, (X - \gamma - (\omega_3 - \omega_1) \, h) \qquad (26)$$

$$- \omega_1 \frac{\lambda_1}{\lambda_2} g \frac{f'^2}{f''} \left\{ \left(h_1 - \frac{h_2 h_{21}}{h_{22}} \right)^2 + \frac{h_2^2 \, (h_{11} h_{22} - h_{12}^2)}{h_{22}^2} \right\}$$

$$\cdot \left\{ (\omega_3 - \omega_1) \, X + \frac{\omega_3}{\lambda_1 g^2} \left(C - \frac{C'^2}{C'' - gR''} \right) \right\} = 0,$$

where J = the Jacobian matrix near $t = +\infty$ and we normalize by $\omega_4 = 1$, $1 \geqq \omega_3 \geqq \omega_1 > 0$.

Optimal Behavior Near the Steady-State Position

10. It is not very easy to determine how the optimal behavior should look like for the case $\omega_3 > \omega_1$. As long as γ is sufficiently small we may assume that $\omega_3 - \omega_1 \doteqdot 0$ so that (26) becomes

$$F (X) = (X + \mu) \, X \, (X - \gamma) \, (X - \gamma - \mu) + a \, (X + \mu) \, (X - \gamma - \mu)$$

$$+ b \, X \, (X - \gamma) + c = 0 \qquad (27)$$

where

$$a = a_0 \sigma, \quad \sigma = C - \frac{C'^2}{C'' - gR''}, \quad a_0 = \frac{\omega_3}{\lambda_1 g} \frac{h_2^2}{h_{22}},$$

$$b = - \omega_1 \frac{\lambda_1}{\lambda_2} g \frac{f'^2}{f''} \cdot \frac{h_{11} h_{22} - h_{12}^2}{h_{22}},$$

$$c = c_0 \sigma, \quad c_0 = - \omega_1 \omega_3 \frac{1}{\lambda_2} \frac{f'^2}{f''} \left\{ \left(h_1 - \frac{h_2 h_{21}}{h_{22}} \right)^2 + \frac{h_2^2 (h_{11} h_{22} - h_{12}^2)}{h_{22}} \right\}.$$

We then have,

Theorem (Stable and Unstable Optimal Paths):

For sufficiently small value of γ. i. e., $\omega_3 - \omega_1 \doteq 0$, the optimal path is stable in the saddle point sense if:

$$\text{(i)} \quad 0 < \sigma < \sigma_2 \text{ or}$$
$$\text{(ii)} \quad \sigma_1 < \sigma \tag{28}$$

and it is unstable if:

$$\sigma_0 < \sigma < 0 \tag{29}$$

where $\sigma = C\,(Y) - \dfrac{C'\,(Y)^2}{C''\,(Y) - gR''\,(Y)}$

$\sigma_0 = $ the lower bound of $\sigma = \dfrac{\dfrac{\gamma^2}{4}\left(\dfrac{\gamma^2}{4} - b + \mu\,(\mu + \gamma)\right)}{\dfrac{a_0}{4}\gamma^2 + a_0\mu\,(\mu + \gamma) - c_0}$

$\sigma_1, \sigma_2 = $ real nonnegative roots of $\Delta\,(\sigma) = 0\ (\sigma_1 \geq \sigma_2)$,

$\Delta\,(\sigma) = a_0{}^2\sigma^2 + 2\,\{a_0\,(\mu\,(\mu + \gamma) - b) + 2\,(a_0 b - c_0)\}\,\sigma + (\mu\,(\mu + \gamma) - b)^2.$

Proof: See Part V, Mathematical Appendix.

Economic Interpretation and the Concluding Remark

11. Economic interpretation of this theorem is straightforward. Thus when σ is positive which means that from $\sigma = C - \dfrac{C'^2}{C'' - gR''}$, $\dfrac{C'^2}{C'' - gR''} > 0$ is sufficiently small compared with C. σ is most likely positive whenever the *profit function is strongly concave* so that $C'' - gR''$ is very large. This condition is almost identical with the condition derived by Sato and Ramachandran [1978] for a less complicated model of technical progress. When σ is negative, and bounded by σ_0, which means that the profit function is not very concave, there is a chance of unstable optimal paths. There may be even a possibility of oscillating optimal behavior. (See a comment at the end of the proof of the theorem, Section 12.)

For the case where $\omega_3 - \omega_1 > 0$, optimal behavior is similar to the one just described as long as ω_3 is not too different from ω_1. This will be true as long as the value of $\gamma = \varrho - \alpha \geq 0$, is sufficiently small. That is to say, as long as the discount rate ϱ and the inflation rate α are not too far apart.

It may be of some interest to consider briefly a case when the ω_i's are determined by a special type of density function, say the gamma function. Let $D_i (s)$ be given by

$$D_i (s; n_i, b_i) = \frac{a_i}{n_i! \, b_i{}^{n_i+1}} \, s^{n_i} \cdot e^{-\frac{s}{b_i}}, \tag{30}$$

$n_i = $ integer, $a_i = $ constant, $b_i = $ constant, $i = 1, 2$.

Then we have $\omega_1 = \dfrac{a_1}{(1+\gamma b_1)^{n_1+1}}$, $\omega_2 = \dfrac{a_2}{(1+\gamma b_2)^{n_2+1}}$, $\omega_3 = a_1$ and $\omega_4 = a_2$.

By normalization we may set $\omega_4 = 1 = a_2$ and assume $0 < a_1 \leq a_2$. In order to have $\omega_3 - \omega_1 \geq 0$ we set $s_2 > 0$ for $\gamma \geq 0$ and n_2 (integer ≥ -1). The lag structure generated by (30) has the basic property exhibiting a continuous Böhm-Bawerk effect as depicted in Fig. 1. In the case of the exponential distribution $(n_i = 0)$, ω_1 and ω_2 are simply equal to $\omega_1 = \dfrac{a_1}{(1+\gamma b_1)}$ and $\omega_2 = \dfrac{a_2}{(1+\gamma b_2)}$. On the other hand, as $b_i \to 0$ for $a_1 = a_2$ we have $\omega_1 = \omega_2 = \omega_3 = \omega_4$, the no lag case.

Substituting the specific forms of the ω_i's into the steady-state solution of the system, we can calculate how the equilibrium values of the system change as one of the basic parameters of the distribution function changes. In particular, we may be interested in the comparative dynamics of the system with respect to the mean $(b_i (n_i + 1))$ and variance $(b_i{}^2 (n_i + 1))$ of the gamma distribution. It is found that in general the sign pattern of the comparative statics is not definite, unless we impose additional restrictions on the production functions h and f and on the profit function. The reader may be interested in studying the case involving the Cobb-Douglas functions and the iso-elastic profit function (see Pauwels [1977]).

One basic and new feature of the present analysis is that using the lemma we have reduced the model of optimal technical progress with *continuous lags* to a model with *no lags*, but with the appropriate weights ω_i's. It is hoped that this type of new approach will also prove to be useful in other areas of economic analysis.

V. Mathematical Appendix

Proof of (26)

12. The characteristic equation of J is expressed as

$$|J - XE| =$$

$$
\begin{vmatrix}
-\omega_3 \dfrac{h_2{}^2}{h_{22}} - X & \omega_3 g \left(h_1 - \dfrac{h_2 h_{21}}{h_{22}} \right) & -\omega_3 \dfrac{g}{\lambda_1} \dfrac{h_2{}^2}{h_{22}} & 0 \\[2ex]
0 & -\mu - X & 0 & -\dfrac{\omega_4}{\lambda_2} \dfrac{f'^2}{f''} \\[2ex]
\dfrac{S}{g^3} + \omega_1 \dfrac{\lambda_1}{g} \dfrac{h_2{}^2}{h_{22}} & -\omega_1 \lambda_1 \left(h_1 - \dfrac{h_2 h_{21}}{h_{22}} \right) & \begin{array}{c} \gamma + (\omega_3 - \omega_1)\, h \\ + \omega_1 \dfrac{h_2{}^2}{h_{22}} - X \end{array} & 0 \\[3ex]
\begin{array}{c} -\omega_1 \lambda_1 \cdot \\ \cdot \left(h_1 - \dfrac{h_1 h_{21}}{h_{22}} \right) \end{array} & -\omega_1 \lambda_1 g \dfrac{h_{11} h_{22} - h_{12}{}^2}{h_{22}} & -\omega_1 g \left(h_1 - \dfrac{h_2 h_{12}}{h_{22}} \right) & \gamma + \mu - X
\end{vmatrix}
$$

where $S = 2C\,(Y) - \dfrac{C'\,(Y)^2}{C''\,(Y) - g R''\,(Y)}.$

Expanding the above we get

$$(X + \mu)\, (X\, (X - \gamma - (\omega_3 - \omega_1)\, h)\, (X - \gamma - \mu)$$

$$+ \omega_3 \frac{g}{\lambda_1} \cdot \frac{h_2{}^2}{h_{22}} (X + \mu)\, (X - \gamma - \mu)$$

$$\times \left(\frac{\lambda_1}{g} \left(1 - \frac{\omega_1}{\omega_3} \right) X + \frac{S}{g^3} - \frac{\lambda_1}{g} (\gamma + (\omega_3 - \omega_1)\, h) \right)$$

$$- \omega_1 \omega_4 \frac{\lambda_1}{\lambda_2} \cdot \frac{f'^2}{f''} \frac{h_{11} h_{22} - h_{12}{}^2}{h_{22}} X\, (X - \gamma - (\omega_3 - \omega_1)\, h)$$

$$- \omega_1 \omega_3 \omega_4 \frac{g^2}{\lambda_2} \frac{f'^2}{f''} \left\{ \left(h_1 - \frac{h_2 h_{21}}{h_{22}} \right) + \frac{h_2{}^2\, (h_{11} h_{22} - h_{12}{}^2)}{h_{22}{}^2} \right\}$$

$$\times \left\{ \frac{\lambda_1}{g} \left(1 - \frac{\omega_1}{\omega_3} \right) X + \frac{S}{g^3} - \frac{\lambda_1}{g} (\gamma + (\omega_3 - \omega_1)\, h) \right\} = 0$$

which is reduced to (45) setting $\omega_4 = \int_0^\infty D_2\,(\sigma)\, d\sigma = 1.$ Q. E. D.

Proof of Theorem

We know that $\Delta\,(\sigma) = 0$ has two positive (nonnegative) roots $\sigma_1 \geq \sigma_2 \geq 0$, since $\sigma_1 + \sigma_2 = -2\,\{a_0\,(\mu\,(\mu + \gamma) - b) + 2(a_0 b - c_0)\}/a_0{}^2 \geq 0,$

2*

and $\sigma_1\sigma_2 = (\mu\,(\mu+\gamma)-b)^2/a_0{}^2 \geqq 0$. Looking at cases in which $\sigma_1 \leq \sigma$ or $\sigma \leq \sigma_2$ and $\varDelta\,(\sigma)\geqq 0$, the two real roots Z_1 and Z_2 satisfy

$$Z_1 + Z_2 = -(a_0\sigma + b - \mu\,(\mu+\gamma))$$

$$Z_1 Z_2 = (-a_0\mu\,(\mu+\gamma)+c_0)\,\sigma$$

where $Z = X^2 - \gamma X$ and $-a_0\mu\,(\mu+\gamma)+c_0 > 0$. First, when we have $\sigma > 0$ which implies $Z_1 Z_2 > 0$ and $Z_1 + Z_2 > 0$ and $Z_1 \geq Z_2 > 0$, we conclude that $X = \frac{1}{2}\,(\gamma \pm \sqrt{\gamma^2 + 4Z_i})$ $i = 1, 2$. Hence, there are two positive roots and two negative roots when (28) is satisfied. Secondly, when σ is negative which implies $Z_1 Z_2 < 0$, i. e., $Z_2 < 0$, $Z_1 > 0$, we have

$$X = \frac{1}{2}\,(\gamma \pm \sqrt{\gamma^2 + 4\,Z_1}):\ \text{1 positive, 1 negative roots}$$

$$X = \frac{1}{2}\,(\gamma \pm \sqrt{\gamma^2 + 4\,Z_2}):\ \text{2 positive roots if } Z_2 > -\frac{\gamma^2}{4}.$$

This proves the second part of the assertoin as long as $0 > Z_2 > -\frac{\gamma^2}{4}$ which means that σ is greater than the lower bound σ_0. In passing it is noted that there is a possibility of complex roots: When $\sigma < \sigma_0$, we have one positive, one negative and two complex roots; when $\sigma_2 < \sigma < \sigma_1$, all of the roots are complex. This allows for a possibility of oscillatory optimal behavior.   Q. E. D.

References

K. J. Arrow and M. Kurz (1970): Public Investment, the Rate of Return and Optimal Fiscal Policy (Resources for the Future), Baltimore and London.

R. R. Bate (1969): The Optimal Control of Systems with Transport Lag, in: C. T. Leondes (ed.): Advances in Control Systems, Vol. 7, New York – London, pp. 165—224.

M. Bloch (1961): Feudal Society, Chicago.

R. E. Evenson and Y. Kislev (1975): Agricultural Research and Productivity, New Haven and London.

Z. Griliches (1980): Returns to Research and Development in the Private Sector, in: J. W. Kendricks and B. Vaccara (eds.): New Developments in Productivity Measurement and Analysis, Studies in Income and Wealth, Vol. 44, Chicago, pp. 419—454.

J. Jacobs (1969): The Economy of Cities, New York.

M. I. Kamien and N. L. Schwartz (1975): Market Structure and Innovation: A Survey, Journal of Economic Literature 13, pp. 1—37.

E. Mansfield (1968): The Economics of Technological Change, New York.

M. McLuhan (1969): The Gutenberg Galaxy: The Making of Typographic Man, New York.

W. D. Nordhaus (1969): Invention, Growth and Welfare, Cambridge, Mass.

W. Pauwels (1977): Optimal Dynamic Advertising Policies in the Presence of Continuously Distributed Time Lags, Journal of Optimization Theory and Applications 22, pp. 79—89.

L. S. Pontryagin et al. (1962): The Mathematical Theory of Optimal Processes, New York.

P. A. Samuelson (1965): A Theory of Induced Innovations Along Kennedy-Weizsäcker Lines, Review of Economics and Statistics 47, pp. 343—356.

P. A. Samuelson (1972): The General Saddlepoint Property of Optimal-Control Motions, Journal of Economic Theory 5, pp. 102—120.

R. Sato and R. Ramachandran (1978): A Contribution to the Microeconomic Analysis of Biased Technical Progress, Discussion Paper, Department of Economics, Brown University, Providence.

R. Sato (1980): The Impact of Technical Change on the Holotheticity of Production Functions, presented at the World Congress of the Econometric Society, Toronto, Canada, 1975, published in Review of Economic Studies 47, pp. 767—776.

R. Sato and G. Suzawa (1980): An Analysis of the Effect of Basic and Applied Research on Productivity Gains, Research Project Sponsored by NSF Division of Policy Research and Analysis, Brown University, Providence.

F. M. Scherer (1970): Industrial Market Structure and Economic Performance, Chicago.

J. Schmookler (1966): Invention and Economic Growth, Cambridge, Mass.

S. P. Sethi (1973): A Useful Transformation of Hamiltonians Occuring in Optimal Control Problems in Economic Analyses, SCIMA Journal of Management Science and Applied Cybernetics 2, pp. 1—17.

S. P. Sethi (1974): Sufficient Conditions for the Optimal Control of a Class of Systems with Continuous Lags, Journal of Optimization Theory and Applications 13, pp. 545—552.

22   R. Sato et al.: A Theory of Endogenous Technical Progress

S. P. Sethi and T. W. McGuire (1977): Optimal Skill Mix: An Application of the Maximum Principle for Systems with Retarded Controls, Journal of Optimization Theory and Applications *23*, pp. 245—275.

Addresses of authors: Ryuzo Sato, Professor of Economics, Brown University, Providence, R. I., U. S. A., and Takayuki Nôno, Professor of Mathematics, Fukuoka University of Education, Munakata-city, Fukuoka 811-41, Japan.

Printed in Austria

[17]

Suppl. 4, pp. 1—37 (1984)

Zeitschrift für
Nationalökonomie
Journal of Economics
© by Springer-Verlag 1984

Technical Progress, the Schumpeterian Hypothesis and Market Structure

By

Ryuzo Sato, Providence, Rhode Island, and Cambridge, Massachusetts, U. S. A., and **Shunichi Tsutsui**, Providence, Rhode Island, U. S. A.*

(Received December 6, 1983; revised version received May 22, 1984)

1. Introduction

The objective of this paper is to present a theoretical model which will enable us to derive what is called "the Schumpeterian hypothesis" (Schumpeter (1950)). "The Schumpeterian hypothesis" states that in industries where Research and Development (R & D) is performed, it is not always true that competitiveness in industries leads to a higher level of technological advancement than when industries are less competitive. As R. Nelson and S. Winter (1980) put it, it implies that "A market structure involving large firms with a considerable degree of market power is the price that society must pay for rapid technological advance." In relation to the Schumpeterian hypothesis, another question is why there are differences between the achieved level of technology and the number of firms among different industries. That is, a couple of firms may be enough to attain maximum level of technological progress in one industry, while more than 100 firms may be needed to do so in another industry. In effect, many studies have been done on the relationship between R & D and the number of firms for specific industries. Various methodologies have been applied to deal with the questions

---

* The paper was presented at the Bonn University — Harvard University Conference on Entrepreneurship, Bonn, West Germany, September, 1983. The authors wish to acknowledge useful comments on an earlier version by D. Bös, J. Meyer, A. Mas-Colell, M. Aoki, J. Stein, E. Streissler, N. Onozawa, H. Ryder, J. Rizzo, the referee of this journal, and the participants in the conference.

raised above, but what we should be aware of is that an R & D process is a dynamic process. In a timeless, static world, there is no incentive to invest in R & D because the benefits from R & D (viz., technical progress) occur only over time. From this point of view, the objective of our studies inevitably has to take into account time lapse.

So what is the meaning of the difference between statics and dynamics and moreover the implications of this difference for the competitive model? Perfect competition results in Pareto optimality in a static world, in which the maximum level of welfare is attainable in the sense of Pareto. The theoretical conclusion for perfect competition is so splendid that it has occupied an important position in economic theory for many years. If one observes several economic policies in the "real world", it may be fully understood that the proposition of Pareto optimality forms a motivation for these policies. That is to say, the achievement of perfect competition is considered a primary goal by policy makers. Surely, this argument may be true in a static world, but does it still hold even in a world where stock variables or given parameters may change over time? In response to this question, Schumpeter offered his now well-known hypothesis.

If we take an extensive view of our real world, we readily see that R & D is being performed in many industries. In particular, R & D plays an important role in manufacturing industries exhibiting sizable economies of scale. For instance, most of the high-tech and "future oriented" industries such as computer, semiconductor and the robotic industries manifest extremely fierce technological competition especially in the form of R & D. In industries such as these, where technological competition prevails, the present state of economic theory does not provide a sufficient theoretical criterion for evaluating whether a fully competitive world leads to the highest level of technical progress. Despite this lack of a firm theoretical background for assessing technological advancement in a competitive world, various arguments have been made on this issue. In particular, this problem has become more and more serious in the field of trade. Some argue that it is advisable to take a protectionist measure against entries of foreign competitors until domestic firms acquire at least a "take off" level of technology for the industry on the grounds that it takes some time for the firms to reap the fruits of R & D. Others argue that free competition is the best way for the domestic firms to quicken their technology level on the grounds that a protectionist measure might lead the domestic firms to lose some of their incentives to advance their technological level due to the lack of competitive stimulus. There exists ample evidence to justify both of these extremely divergent views. Examples for the former argument may be found in the Japanese automobile and computer industries both of which had been protected until recently, while our example for the latter argument may be found in the U. S. steel industry. As can be seen by these examples, it is quite clear that we need a new comprehensive theory of trade and industrial organization. Thus, the theories for industries with substantial R & D are very important in regards to trade and industrial organization. In fact, Krugman in his recent survey paper (1983) stresses the importance of technological competition in trade among industrial countries. What he says is that conventional theories of comparative advantage have difficulties in accounting for real world trade problems. He argues that theories of comparative advantage cannot explain the existence of intra-industry trade. The fact is that many manufactured goods are being traded among countries that produce *the same* manufactured goods, i. e., the trade of many manufactured goods is a two-way trade. These two-way traded goods are usually produced in industries engaging in substantial level of R & D. In this context, too, it is clear that we need a theoretical model explaining Schumpeter's hypothesis because a two-way trade of manufactured goods can be considered worldwide technological competition by many countries (each of which may be viewed as a single firm) in a "world" market. Therefore, as has been seen, a verification of Schumpeter's hypothesis is not only of theoretical interest but is also very important from a policy perspective.

This paper first develops a general model, which is largely due to R. Sato (1981) and Flaherty (1980). Next, a steady-state level of technology is derived for an N-firm (or N-country) industry engaging in technological competition. A discussion of the relationship between the achieved level of technology and the number of firms (or countries) follows. It is shown that the level of technology is related to demand structure. In the model's specification, the Schumpeterian world emerges. Then, it is shown that an interesting relationship exists between stabilities of the steady states and the technical progress functions.

2. Model

A general model is developed in this section. The general model takes into account two different types of R & D knowledge: applied knowledge and basic knowledge. Basic knowledge is an intermediate product in the production of new applied knowledge (or applied technology), while actual process innovations are taken to be "applied knowledge" (or applied technology). This classification follows the suggestions of R. Sato (1981), R. Sato and G. Suzawa (1983). For a detailed discussion and economic interpretation for applied and basic knowledge, see Sato (1981, pp. 83—85). In addition to this classification in knowledge for technologies, Sato takes into account "dynamic Böhm-Bawerk effects". This implies that accumulated knowledge in the past affects production of the present level of knowledge, and that there is a time lag between investment in R & D and actual innovation. Although the underlying model involves advanced mathematics, it can be reduced to a common optimal control problem near time $t \rightarrow +\infty$, (see Lemma in Sato's book (1981, p. 102)). In this paper, this lag structure is not explicitly taken into consideration. Moreover, it is assumed that basic knowledge (or basic technology) has as broad a meaning as possible. In particular, the concept of basic knowledge may be considered as the state of academic training and intellectual ability in a society. In addition, basic knowledge is first considered as an endogenous variable, but is later taken to be exogenous in order to focus on the stability properties of the model. Notice the terms "basic knowledge" and "basic technology", "applied knowledge" and "applied technology" are used interchangeably throughout the paper.

2.1 Industrial Demand Function

In the industry with which this paper is concerned, it is assumed that each firm produces a homogeneous and nonstorable manufactured good. Demand for the industry's output is assumed to be stationary over time. There are N firms (which alternatively may be viewed as N countries) in the industry.

The inverse demand function in the industry is $P(y_t^*)$ which has the following properties:

$$P(y_t^*) \tag{2.1}$$

is continuously differentiable with respect to y_t^*

$$P_1(y_t^*) < 0, \quad P_{11}(y_t^*) \geqslant 0 \tag{2.2}$$

$$2P_1(y_t^*) + y^* P_{11}(y_t^*) \leqslant 0 \tag{2.3}$$

$$y_t^* \triangleq \sum_{i=1}^{N} y_{it}, \tag{2.4}$$

where y_{it} is the output of the i-th firm in the industry at time t.

The Schumpeterian Hypothesis and Market Structure   5

Notice that numerical subscripts on P indicate partial derivatives with respect to the corresponding argument (s) (here y_t^*).

Condition (2.3) states that marginal revenue for the industry is decreasing with respect to y_t^*.

2.2 Formulation of Applied Knowledge and Basic Knowledge Functions

Following the suggestions of R. Sato (1981), the flows of applied knowledge development and basic knowledge development for the i-th firm may be written as:

$$\dot{C}_i(t) = -\nu C_i(t) + G_i^1 [C_i(t), B_i(t), \theta_{i1}(t)] \qquad (2.5 \text{ i})$$

$$(i = 1, \ldots, N)$$

$$\dot{B}_i(t) = -\mu B_i(t) + G_i^2 [\theta_{i2}(t)] \qquad (2.5 \text{ ii})$$

where ν and μ are positive constants indicating depreciation rates for both applied knowledge and basic knowledge. Here, $C_i(t)$, $\dot{C}_i(t)$, $B_i(t)$, $\dot{B}_i(t)$, $\theta_{i1}(t)$ and $\theta_{i2}(t)$ are defined as follows:

$C_i(t)$:   applied knowledge level held by i-th firm at time t.
$\dot{C}_i(t)$:   flow of $C_i(t)$.
$B_i(t)$:   basic knowledge level held by i-th firm at time t.
$\dot{B}_i(t)$:   flow of $B_i(t)$.
$\theta_{i1}(t)$:   flow investment in applied knowledge development for i-th firm at time t.
$\theta_{i2}(t)$:   flow investment in basic knowledge development for i-th firm at time t.

In addition, to facilitate the discussion, the following assumption is made.

[Assumption 1]

Applied knowledge production functions G_i^1 and basic knowledge production function G_i^2 have the same mathematical forms for all firms in the industry[1]. All that characterizes the differences among firms is that applied knowledge levels and basic knowledge levels can both vary among firms over time.

---

[1] To keep the notation simple, we will drop the subscripts "i" in the discussion below, but it is to be understood that we focus on the behavior of the representative firm in the industry.

Unlike the model that R. Sato develops in which there is only one firm (he deals with the perfect monopoly case), there exist N firms which engage in technological competition with each other in this paper. Furthermore, it is more convenient for our purposes to utilize the calculus of variations (as Flaherty does in her paper (1980)) than to employ Pontryagin's maximum principle in order to derive a set of motion equation for the system. In particular, when discussing stabilities of the system we have to evaluate characteristic roots of the system[2].

Properties of the applied knowledge production function G^1 and the basic knowledge production G^2 are extensively discussed by R. Sato in his book (1981), but in this paper, we focus on the properties of the *transformed* functions of G^1 and G^2 [3].

2.3 Cost Functions and Effective Marginal Costs

Cost functions are derived from the following minimization problem.

$$\text{Min}_{K_i(t),\, L_i(t)} \quad rK_i(t) + wL_i(t) \tag{A}$$

$$\text{s. t.} \quad y_{it} = Y(C_i(t) K_i(t), \; C_i(t) L_i(t)) \qquad (i = 1, \ldots, N)$$

where y_{it} is the output of the i-th firm, $K_i(t)$ and $L_i(t)$ are capital and labor used to produce output for the i-th firm, $C_i(t)$ is applied knowledge level held by the i-th firm, r and w are, respectively, rental rate for the capital and wage rate for labor in money terms. $Y(\cdot, \cdot)$ is a neoclassical production function with the usual properties in Eq. (A). The way applied knowledge affects capital and labor is called "neutral type" of technical progress. R. Sato discusses this case (1981, p. 85):

> "for any given production function there exists an infinite number of different tapes of technical change that can be transformed to the scale effect-holotheticity. That is to say, there exists an infinite number of holothetic technical changes expressible in terms of 'neutral type' of technical progress."

This justifies the formulation of the production function as $y_{it} = Y(C_i(t) K_i(t), \; C_i(t) L_i(t))$. From this production function, we

---

[2] If the calculus of variations is used instead of the maximum principle, then the matrix from which the characteristic roots are derived for the system preserve a convenient symmetric property thus facilitating evaluation of the characteristic roots.

[3] This point will be discussed more fully below in Section 2.4.

The Schumpeterian Hypothesis and Market Structure   7

can derive the total cost function:

$$\frac{1}{C_i(t)} \overline{TO}\,(y_{it},\, w,\, r) \quad (i=1,\ldots,N)$$

where $\overline{TO}$ is the minimum cost of producing y_{it}, given the production function Y with no applied knowledge. Moreover, linear homogeneity is assumed on the production function, and w and r are assumed to be constant over time. Hence, the total cost function is given by:

$$\frac{y_{it}}{C_i(t)} \overline{TO}\,(w,\, r) \quad (i=1,\ldots,N).$$

Since w and r are assumed to be constant over time, $\overline{TO}\,(w,\,r)$ is also constant. With this homogeneity property, marginal costs are constant and equal to $\overline{TO}\,(w,\,r)/C_i\,(t)$. Now we can define *effective* marginal costs.

Definition:

Effective marginal costs are $A_i\,(t) \triangleq \dfrac{\overline{TO}\,(w,r)}{C_i\,(t)}$ $(i=1,\ldots,N)$. Effective marginal costs are lower, the higher the rate of technical progress attributable to applied knowledge. Using effective marginal costs gives us the total cost function:

$$A_i\,(t)\,y_{it} \qquad (i=1,\ldots,N). \tag{2.5 iii}$$

2.4 Transformation from G^1 and G^2 Functions to S and T Functions

In 2.3, we defined effective marginal cost for the representative firm, $A_i\,(t)$. Eq. (2.5 i) is rewritten using their new variables.

$$\dot{A}_i\,(t) = \nu A_i\,(t) - G^1\left[\frac{\overline{TO}\,(w,r)}{A_i\,(t)},\, B_i\,(t),\, \theta_{i1}\,(t)\right]\frac{A_i{}^2\,(t)}{\overline{TO}\,(w,r)} \tag{2.5 i'}$$

$$\dot{B}_i\,(t) = -\mu B_i\,(t) + G^2\,[\theta_{i2}\,(t)]. \tag{2.5 ii}$$

where $\dot{A}_i\,(t)$ is time derivative of $A_i\,(t)$. Solving (2.5 i') and (2.5 ii) in terms of $\theta_{i1}\,(t)$ and $\theta_{i2}\,(t)$ yields

$$\theta_{i1}\,(t) = S\,(A_i\,(t),\, \dot{A}_i\,(t),\, B_i\,(t)) \tag{2.6 i}$$

$$\theta_{i2}\,(t) = T\,(B_i\,(t),\, \dot{B}_i\,(t)) \qquad (i=1,\ldots,N). \tag{2.5 ii}$$

Notice that since the functions G^1 and G^2 are the same for all firms, the functions S and T are also *the same* for all firms. Now we are ready to discuss the properties of S and T. In general, the S function has the following property:

$$S_2 \triangleq \frac{\partial S}{\partial \dot{A}_i} < 0 \quad (i = 1, \ldots, N). \tag{2.7}$$

This condition states that if any firm tries to decrease the rate of change in effective marginal cost, then the cost of applied knowledge development strictly increases for any given level of effective marginal cost and basic knowledge.

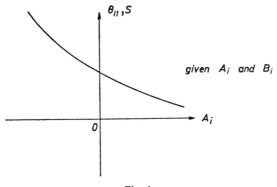

Fig. 1

The T function has the following property:

$$T_2 \triangleq \frac{\partial T}{\partial \dot{B}_i} > 0 \quad (i = 1, \ldots, N). \tag{2.8}$$

Similarly, this condition states that if any firm intends to increase the flow of its basic knowledge $B_i(t)$ it has to invest more.

$$S_3 \triangleq \frac{\partial S}{\partial B_i} < 0. \tag{2.9}$$

Condition (2.9) simply states that if the level of any firm's basic knowledge increases, then the cost of developing applied knowledge decreases for any given $A_i(t)$ and $\dot{A}_i(t)$. This statement makes sense economically, because it implies that if we have an advance in basic knowledge, then it becomes easier to develop applied knowledge.

$$T_1 \triangleq \frac{\partial T}{\partial B_i} \geqslant 0. \tag{2.10}$$

The Schumpeterian Hypothesis and Market Structure 9

Condition (2.10) states that if the level of any firm's basic knowledge rises, then the cost of increasing basic knowledge does not decrease for any given $\dot{B}_i(t)$.

$$S_1 \triangleq \frac{\partial S}{\partial A_i} \leqslant 0. \tag{2.11}$$

Condition (2.11) is similar to the condition (2.10). It states that if any firm's effective marginal cost decreases (or equivalently if the level of any firm's applied knowledge increases), then the cost of developing applied knowledge does not decrease for any given $\dot{A}_i(t)$, $\dot{B}_i(t)$.

$$S(A_i, \dot{A}_i, B_i) \geqslant 0, \quad T(B_i, \dot{B}_i) \geqq 0. \tag{2.12}$$

Condition (2.12) states that the cost of developing applied knowledge and basic knowledge is always positive over the relevant range.

$$A_{\min} < A_i < A_{\max}, \quad A_{\max} > A_{\min} \geqslant 0 \quad (i=1,\ldots,N). \tag{2.13}$$

Condition (2.13) states that any firm's effective marginal cost is assumed to be in the open interval $(A_{\min}, A_{\max})$.

$$B_{\min} < B_i < B_{\max}, \quad \infty \geqslant B_{\max} > B_{\min} \geqslant 0 \quad (i=1,\ldots,N). \tag{2.14}$$

This condition has the same meaning as (2.13).

$$S_{11} \triangleq \frac{\partial^2 S}{\partial A_1{}^2} \geqslant 0 \tag{2.15}$$

$$S_{22} \triangleq \frac{\partial^2 S}{\partial \dot{A}_i{}^2} \geqslant 0 \tag{2.16}$$

$$T_{11} \triangleq \frac{\partial^2 T}{\partial B_i{}^2} \geqslant 0 \tag{2.17}$$

$$T_{22} \triangleq \frac{\partial^2 T}{\partial \dot{B}_i{}^2} > 0 \tag{2.18}$$

$$S_{33} \triangleq \frac{\partial^2 S}{\partial B_i{}^2} \geqslant 0 \tag{2.19}$$

$$S_{12} \triangleq \frac{\partial^2 B}{\partial A_i \, \partial \dot{A}_i} = S_{21} \geqq 0 \tag{2.20}$$

$$T_{12} \triangleq \frac{\partial^2 T}{\partial B_i \, \partial \dot{B}_i} = T_{21} > 0. \tag{2.21}$$

The conditions (2.15) to (2.21) are nothing but extensions of conditions suggested by Flaherty (1980), and their meanings correspond to those in standard production theory, i. e., the properties of diminishing returns to scale in developing applied knowledge and basic knowledge.

Now we would like to consider a few more restrictive properties of S and T. For the purpose of more tractable results, R. Sato places a couple of specific conditions on G^1 function in (2.5 i) or (2.5 i'), i. e.,

$$G^1 [C_i (t), B_i (t), \theta_{i1} (t)] = G^{1*} [B_i (t), \theta_{i1} (t)] C_i (t) \qquad (2.22)$$

$$G^{1*} [B_i (t), \theta_{i1} (t)] \text{ is homogeneous of degree 1}$$
$$\text{in } B_i (t) \text{ and } \theta_{i1} (t). \qquad (2.22')$$

The condition (2.22) states that $C_i (t)$ enters the G^1 function multiplicatively. By this condition, Eq. (2.5 i') has the form of

$$\dot{A}_i (t) = \nu A_i (t) - G^{1*} [B_i (t), \theta_{i1} (t)] A_i (t) \qquad (2.5 \text{ i}'')$$

$$\dot{B}_i (t) = -\mu B_i (t) + G^2 [\theta_{i2} (t)]. \qquad (2.5 \text{ ii})$$

Together with the homogeneity condition (2.22), the S and T functions are expressed as follows.

$$\theta_{i1} (t) = S (A_i (t), \dot{A}_i (t), B_i (t))$$

$$= (B_i (t)) D \left(\frac{1}{B_i (t)} \left(\nu - \frac{\dot{A}_i (t)}{A_i (t)} \right) \right) \qquad (2.6 \text{ i}')$$

$$\theta_{i2} (t) = T (B_i (t), \dot{B}_i (t)) = F (\mu B_i (t) + \dot{B}_i (t)) \qquad (2.6 \text{ ii})$$

where $D' (\cdot) > 0$, $D'' (\cdot) \geqslant 0$, $F' (\cdot) > 0$, $F'' (\cdot) > 0$ and $D (\cdot) > 0$, $F (\cdot) > 0$. The expression (2.6 i') has the properties

$$S_1|_{\dot{A}=0} = 0, \quad S_{11}|_{\dot{A}=0} = 0, \quad S_{13}|_{\dot{A}=0} = 0. \qquad (2.23)$$

2.5 The Representative Firm's Maximization Problem

Each firm in this model is assumed to maximize its discounted present value of profits over an infinite time horizon, while investing in applied and basic knowledge, and it is assumed to behave noncooperatively taking the other $(N-1)$ firm's intertemporal decision vector as given. Thus, we specify an N-person, continuous time, stationary noncooperative game. The objective of each firm is to:

$$\text{Max} \int_0^\infty e^{-\rho t} [P (y_i^*) y_{it} - A_i (t) y_{it} - \theta_{i1} (t) - \theta_{i2} (t)] \, dt \qquad (2.24)$$

subject to $\theta_{i1}(t) = S(A_i(t), \dot{A}_i(t), B_i(t))$

$\theta_{i2}(t) = T(B_i(t), \dot{B}_i(t))$

given the other $(N-1)$ firms' intertemporal decision vector where ϱ is the firm's discount rate.

[Assumption 2]

It is assumed that there exists a feasible output and investment path for each firm in this game.

[Definition]

A noncooperative equilibrium path in this game is a set of all firms' outputs and investments paths which simultaneously solves all N firms' dynamic maximization problems. As Flaherty (1980) argues, a *steady-state* equilibrium path in this model is of particular interest because presumably this is the path that characterizes actual output and investment decisions in the "real world". In addition, she argues:

"It is inferred that if a particular steady state is locally stable then that steady state will be observed, whereas an unstable steady state will not."

Therefore, steady states of this dynamic game are derived and, then stability of steady states of this game is examined.

3. Steady-State Equilibria for the Dynamic Game

3.1 Determination of all Firms' Current Outputs

Each firm has to choose its output y_{it} at each moment of time so that it can maximize its profits before investment in applied knowledge and basic knowledge. This means that all firms behave as if their output decisions were equilibrium decisions for a static noncooperative game given their effective marginal costs $A_i(t)$, $\dot{A}_i(t)$ and their basic knowledge levels $B_i(t)$ $(i=1,\ldots,N)$. The condition for the uniqueness of their output decisions at equilibrium is assumed to be satisfied (see Rosen (1965)).

First Order Conditions

Each firm's current output decision is determined so as to:

$$\text{Max } P(y_t^*)\, y_{it} - A_i(t)\, y_{it} \qquad (i=1,\ldots,N) \qquad (3.1)$$

given the other firms' output decisions. Therefore, the first order condition for each firm is given by:

$$P_1(y_t^*)\, y_{it} + P(y_t^*) - A_i(t) = 0. \tag{3.2}$$

Our purpose is to express outputs in terms of $A_i(t)$s. Summing up Eqs. (3.2) from $i=1$ to N yields:

$$P_1(y_t^*)\, y_t^* + NP(y_t^*) - A^*(t) = 0 \tag{3.3}$$

where $y_t^* \underset{=}{\triangle} \sum_{i=1}^{N} y_{it}$, $A^*(t) \underset{=}{\triangle} \sum_{i=1}^{N} A_i(t)$.

As mentioned above, the uniqueness of all firms' output decisions is assumed. Thus, inverting Eq. (3.3), we can solve for y_t^* as a function of $A^*(t)$:

$$y_t^* \underset{=}{\triangle} H(A^*(t)). \tag{3.4}$$

Therefore, each firm's output decision at time t is given using (3.4) or

$$y_{it} = \frac{A_i(t) - P(y_t^*)}{P_1(y_t^*)} = \frac{A_i(t) - P(H(A^*(t)))}{P_1(H(A^*(t)))} \tag{3.5}$$

[Assumption 3]

All firms are assumed to produce positive outputs at each moment of time. In other words, profits before investments in R & D for all firms, $P(H(A^*(t))) - A_i(t)$, are always positive for given levels of the $A_i(t)$ s.

[Proposition 1]

$$dP(H(A^*(t)))/dA^*(t) > 0. \tag{i}$$

$$d^2 P(H(A^*(t)))/d^2 A^*(t) \geqslant 0. \tag{ii}$$

$$\partial P(H(A^*(t)))/\partial A_i(t) > 0. \tag{iii}$$

3.2 Formation of Each Firm's Dynamic Maximization

Now the current profits before investments in R & D of each firm may be expressed as a function of the current effective marginal costs of all firms:

$$\pi(A_i(t), \hat{A}_i(t)) \underset{=}{\triangle} [P(H(A^*(t))) - A_i(t)]\, y_{it}$$

$$= -\frac{(P(H(A^*(t))) - A_i(t))^2}{P_1(H(A^*(t)))} \quad (i=1,\ldots,N) \tag{3.6}$$

where $\hat{A}_i(t) \underset{=}{\triangle} \sum_{\substack{j \neq i \\ j=1}}^{N} A_j(t)$.

Therefore, each firm's present value of cash flow over time is given by:

$$\int_0^\infty e^{-\rho t} \left[\pi \left(A_i(t), \hat{A}_i(t) \right) - S \left(A_i(t), \dot{A}_i(t), B_i(t) \right) - T \left(B_i(t), \dot{B}_i(t) \right) \right] dt$$

$$(i = 1, \ldots, N). \tag{3.7}$$

Hence, each firm's objective is to choose time paths of $A_i(t)$, $B_i(t)$ given the corresponding time paths of the other $(N-1)$ firms so as to:

$$\underset{\{A_i(t)\}\{B_i(t)\}}{\text{Maximize}} \int_0^\infty e^{-\rho t} \left[\pi(A_i, \hat{A}_i) - S(A_i, \dot{A}_i, B_i) - T(B_i, \dot{B}_i) \right] dt \tag{3.8}$$

$$\text{given} \quad \{\hat{A}_i(t)\} \{\hat{B}_i(t)\} \qquad (i = 1, \ldots, N).$$

Note that from this part on, the time subscript will be suppressed (e. g., $A_i(t) \to A_i$, $B_i(t) \to B_i$, $y_{it} \to y_i$, etc.).

3.3 Motion Equations for the Model

From Eq. (3.8), we can derive a set of motion equations:

$$\pi_1(A_i, \hat{A}_i) - S_1(A_i, \dot{A}_i, B_i) = \varrho S_2(A_i, \dot{A}_i, B_i)$$

$$- \frac{d}{dt} \left(S_2(A_i, \dot{A}_i, B_i) \right) \quad (i = 1, \ldots, N) \tag{3.9}$$

$$- S_3(A_i, \dot{A}_i, B_i) - T_i(B_i, \dot{B}_i) = \varrho T_2(B_i, \dot{B}_i) - \frac{d}{dt} \left(T_2(B_i, \dot{B}_i) \right)$$

$$(i = 1, \ldots, N). \tag{3.10}$$

Eqs. (3.9) and (3.10) for all $i = 1, \ldots, N$ determine an industry equilibrium path along which every firm in the industry can maximize its over time cash flow (for the existence of an industry equilibrium path, see Friedman (1977)).

3.4 Steady States

As Flaherty shows, there exist not only symmetric steady states but also asymmetric steady states in models of this type. Here, symmetric steady states mean that at steady states all firms have the same levels of effective marginal costs and the same levels of basic knowledge, whereas asymmetric steady states mean that levels of

2*

effective marginal costs and levels of basic knowledge held by all firms in the industry vary. Since we are most interested in the relationship between the achieved levels of technologies and the number of firms in the industry, we restrict our analysis to a consideration of the more mathematically tractable symmetric steady states.

Symmetric steady states for effective marginal costs and basic knowledge are given by the following equations:

$$\pi_1 (A, (N-1) A) - S_1 (A, 0, B) = \varrho S_2 (A, 0, B) \qquad (3.11)$$

$$-S_3 (A, 0, B) - T_1 (B, 0) = \varrho T_2 (B, 0) \qquad (3.12)$$

where A is the level of effective marginal cost held by all firms at symmetric steady states and B is the level of basic knowledge held by all firms at symmetric steady-states. Before proceeding with the analysis, we specify the properties of π_1 and π_{11}:

$$\pi_1 < 0, \quad \pi_{11} > 0. \qquad (3.13)$$

These properties are easily derived by direct calculation of π with respect to the appropriate arguments.

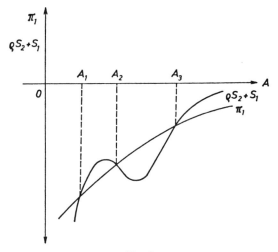

Fig. 2

Since $S_1 (A, 0, B)$ and $S_2 (A, 0, B)$ are negative (cf. (2.17), (2.11)), the graphs of the functions $\pi_1 (A, (N-1) A)$ and $(\varrho S_2 (A, 0, B) + S_1 (A, 0, B))$ are shown below (Fig. 2).

Since $S_3 (A, 0, B)$ is negative (cf. (2.9)) and $T_1 (B, 0)$ and $T_2 (B, 0)$ are positive (cf. (2.8), (2.10)), we can draw a corresponding picture of the equilibrium level of basic knowledge (Fig. 3).

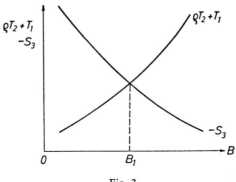

Fig. 3

Suppose that the functions S and T are given by (2.6 i′) and (2.6 ii′). Then Eqs. (3.11) and (3.12) are replaced with:

$$\pi_1 (A, (N-1) A) = -\varrho D' \left(\frac{1}{B} v\right) \frac{1}{A} \tag{3.14}$$

$$-D\left(\frac{1}{B} v\right) + D'\left(\frac{1}{B} v\right) v \frac{1}{B} = \varrho F' (B) + \mu F' (B). \tag{3.15}$$

Then the equilibrium values for basic knowledge and effective marginal cost may be drawn as below (Figs. 4 and 5).

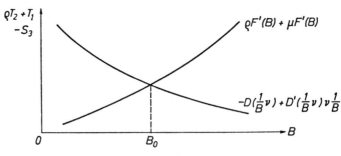

Fig. 4

The specification of S and T as (2.6 i′) and (2.6 ii′) has the following property: the level of *basic* knowledge is determined only by (3.15). This special property holds even in a general asymmetric steady-state case. That is:

$$\pi_1 (A_i, \hat{A}_i) = -\varrho D' \left(\frac{1}{B_i} v \right) \frac{1}{A_i} \quad (i=1, \ldots, N) \qquad (3.16)$$

$$-D \left(\frac{1}{B_i} v \right) + D' \left(\frac{1}{B_i} v \right) v \frac{1}{B_i} = (\varrho + \mu) F' (B_i) \qquad (3.17)$$

$$(i=1, \ldots, N).$$

The above specification of the S and T functions (cf. (2.6 i') and (2.6 ii') has an interesting and plausible economic interpretation. It implies that though steady-state levels of effective marginal costs may vary among N firms, steady-state levels of basic knowledge are the same for all N firms.

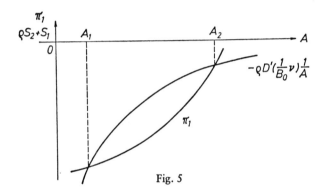

Fig. 5

[Theorem 1]

Under the specification of S and T as in (2.6 i') and (2.6 ii'), steady-state levels of basic knowledge held by all firms are unique and identical, and are independent of the number of firms, N.

3.5 Stability Around Steady States

To start with, the equations of motion (3.9) and (3.10) have to be linearized in the neighborhood of a steady state. These linearizations of the equations of motion are given by:

$$\pi_{11} A_i + \pi_{12} \hat{A}_i - S_{11} A_i - S_{12} \dot{A}_i - S_{13} B_i$$
$$= \varrho S_{21} A_i + \varrho S_{22} \dot{A}_i + \varrho S_{23} B_i - S_{21} \dot{A}_i - S_{22} \ddot{A}_i - S_{23} \dot{B}_i \qquad (3.18)$$
$$+ \text{const.}$$

$$-S_{31} A_i - S_{32} \dot{A}_i - S_{33} B_i - T_{11} B_i - T_{12} \dot{B}_i$$
$$= \varrho T_{21} B_i + \varrho T_{22} \dot{B}_i - T_{21} \dot{B}_i - T_{22} \ddot{B}_i + \text{const.} \qquad (3.19)$$

If we define new variables $X_i \underset{=}{\triangle} \dot{A}_i$, $Z_i \underset{=}{\triangle} \dot{B}_i$, and rearrange (3.18) and (3.19), we then have:

$$\dot{X}_i = \varrho X_i - \frac{S_{23}}{S_{22}} + Z_i \frac{\varrho S_{21} + S_{11} - \pi_{11}}{S_{22}} A_i - \frac{\pi_{12}}{S_{22}} \hat{A}_i$$

$$+ \frac{\varrho S_{23} + S_{33}}{S_{22}} B_i + \text{const.} \tag{3.20}$$

$$\dot{Z}_i = \frac{S_{32}}{T_{22}} X_i + \varrho Z_i + \frac{S_{31}}{T_{22}} A_i + \frac{\varrho T_{21} + T_{11} + S_{33}}{T_{22}} B_i + \text{const.} \tag{3.21}$$

or in the matrix form:

$$
\begin{bmatrix} \dot{X}_1 \\ \vdots \\ \dot{X}_N \\ \dot{Z}_1 \\ \vdots \\ \dot{Z}_N \\ \dot{A}_1 \\ \vdots \\ \dot{A}_N \\ \dot{B}_1 \\ \vdots \\ \dot{B}_N \end{bmatrix}
=
\begin{bmatrix} \varrho I_N & -\dfrac{S_{23}}{S_{22}} & R_1 & \dfrac{\varrho S_{23} + S_{13}}{S_{22}} \\ \dfrac{S_{23}}{T_{22}} & \varrho I_N & \dfrac{S_{31}}{T_{22}} & \dfrac{\varrho T_{21} + T_{11} + S_{33}}{T_{22}} \\ \multicolumn{2}{c}{} & \multicolumn{2}{c}{} \\ I_{2N} & & Q_{2N} & \end{bmatrix}
\begin{bmatrix} X_1 \\ \vdots \\ Z_N \\ \dot{Z}_1 \\ \vdots \\ Z_N \\ A_1 \\ \vdots \\ A_N \\ \dot{B}_1 \\ \vdots \\ \dot{B}_N \end{bmatrix}
+ \text{const.} \tag{3.22}
$$

where I_N and I_{2N} are, respectively, $(N \times N)$ and $(2N \times 2N)$ identity matrices, Q_{2N} is $(2N \times 2N)$ zero matrix. The $(N \times N)$ matrix R_1 is given by:

$$
R_1 \underset{=}{\triangle}
\begin{bmatrix}
\dfrac{\varrho S_{21} + S_{11} - \pi_{11}}{S_{22}}, & -\dfrac{\pi_{12}}{S_{22}}, & \cdots, & -\dfrac{\pi_{12}}{S_{22}} \\
-\dfrac{\pi_{12}}{S_{22}}, & \dfrac{\varrho S_{21} + S_{11} - \pi_{11}}{S_{22}}, & \cdots, & -\dfrac{\pi_{12}}{S_{22}} \\
& & \ddots & \\
\vdots & & \vdots & \\
-\dfrac{\pi_{12}}{S_{22}}, & \cdots\cdots, & & \dfrac{\varrho S_{21} + S_{11} - \pi_{11}}{S_{22}}
\end{bmatrix}
\tag{3.23}
$$

Therefore, the characteristic roots of this linearized system are derived by solving:

$$
\det \begin{vmatrix} \lambda\,(\varrho-\lambda)+R_1 & \dfrac{(\varrho-\lambda)\,S_{23}+S_1}{S_{22}} \\[2ex] \dfrac{\lambda S_{32}+S_{13}}{T_{22}} & \lambda\,(\varrho-\lambda)+\dfrac{\varrho\,T_{21}+T_{11}+S_{33}}{T_{22}} \end{vmatrix} = 0. \tag{3.24}
$$

In general, the evaluation of the characteristic roots (3.24) is very difficult unless we make further simplifications. So to examine stability properties of this system we ignore the effects of basic knowledge development. In other words, levels of basic knowledge are taken to be exogenous or regarded as parameters. Then, the equations of motion are given by:

$$
\pi_1\,(A_t,\dot{A}_t) = S_1\,(A_t,\dot{A}_t,B_t) + \varrho\,S_2\,(A_t,\dot{A}_t,B_t)
$$

$$
+ \frac{d}{dt}\,S_2\,(A_t,\dot{A}_t,B_t). \tag{3.25}
$$

Therefore, their linearization around steady states turns out to be:

$$
\pi_{11}\,A_t + \pi_{12}\,\hat{A}_t - S_{11}\,A_t - S_{12}\,\dot{A}_t
$$

$$
= \varrho\,S_{21}\,A_t + \varrho\,S_{22}\,\dot{A}_t - S_{21}\,\dot{A}_t - S_{22}\,\ddot{A}_t + \text{const.} \tag{3.26}
$$

The substitution $X_t \triangleq A_t$ yields

$$
\dot{X}_t = \varrho\,X_t + \frac{\varrho\,S_{21}+S_{11}-\pi_{11}}{S_{22}}\,A_t - \frac{\pi_{12}}{S_{22}}\,\hat{A}_t + \text{const.} \tag{3.27}
$$

or in matrix form:

$$
\begin{bmatrix} \dot{X}_1 \\ \vdots \\ \dot{X}_N \\ \dot{A}_1 \\ \vdots \\ \dot{A}_N \end{bmatrix} = \left[\begin{array}{c|c} \varrho I_N & R_1 \\ \hline I_N & Q_N \end{array} \right] \begin{bmatrix} X_1 \\ \vdots \\ X_N \\ A_1 \\ \vdots \\ A_N \end{bmatrix} \tag{3.28}
$$

This is a differential equation system which determines the time path of the model. We now study the stability conditions of the system.

[Theorem 2]

For a symmetric steady state to be locally stable, it is necessary that the slope of the marginal revenue function of new technology π_1 is strictly less than that of the marginal cost function $\varrho S_2 + S_1$.

As the proof of this requires several mathematical steps (lemmas), we present them in the Appendix. Theorem 2 provides us with a powerful criteria for determining whether steady states are locally stable or not. For example, the steady state A_2 in Fig. 3 and the steady state A_2 in Fig. 6 are locally unstable steady states.

4. The Schumpeterian Hypothesis and the Optimal Market Structure

A general model and the stability properties in the neighborhood of its steady state have been discussed in Sections 2 and 3. Here in Section 4, we intend to specify the optimal market structure by identifying the optimal number of firms consistent with the maximum efficacy and/or maximum output. In particular, as is argued in the introduction, our purpose there is to determine theoretically if the model presented can be used to explain the Schumpeterian hypothesis: Competition inhibits technological advancement. Let us briefly consider the possible market structures in any industry. To begin with, there are two extreme cases, one of which is the case of perfect competition, the other being the case of perfect monopoly. In general, the actual situation in the real world is considered between these two extremes, i. e., one of oligopoly. In the case of oligopoly, each firm's decision is based on how the other $N-1$ firms react when this particular firm changes its behavior. Mathematically, the representative i-th firm's objective is to:

$$\text{Maximize}_{y_i} P(y^*) y_i - A_i y_i.$$

Without information or conjecture of the other $(N-1)$ firms reaction for the i-th firms behavior $\left(\text{i. e., } \frac{\delta y_j}{\delta y_i}, j \neq i, j = 1, \ldots, N\right)$, it is impossible for the i-th firm to decide how much output it should produce to maximize its profits. The i-th firm may or may not consider that the other $(N-1)$ firms' reactions to its output decision are significant. However, we in general cannot specify forms for the other firms' reactions $\left(\frac{\delta y_j}{\delta y_i}, j \neq i, i, j = 1, \ldots, N\right)$ *a priori*. The concept of Nash equilibrium is used for an N-person game, because it is relatively easy to derive output decisions mathematically, since the concept of Nash equilibrium implies that the other $(N-1)$ firms' reactions do not change in response to the i-th firm's output decision $\left(\text{(i. e., } \frac{\delta y_j}{\delta y_i}=0, \; j\neq i, \; j=1,\ldots,N, \; i=1,\ldots,N\right)$.

As is well known in industrial organization theory, the Nash equilibrium has remarkable properties. Namely, Nash equilibrium for $N=1$ corresponds to a world of perfect monopoly, and a world of perfect competition for $N=\infty$. Clearly, then, it can be seen that in Nash equilibrium the number of firms in the industry can be one of the indices which measure the degree of competition. Of course, we can never say that there exists a finite number N_0 such that for any $N>N_0$ the industry is *perfectly competitive*[4]. All we can say is that if there are two numbers of firms N_1 and N_2 with $N_1>N_2$, the industry is more competitive at N_1 than at N_2 in Nash equilibrium. Using this reasoning, we consider in this section that the degree of market influence held by each firm in the industry is a decreasing function of the number of firms in the industry. Keeping this in mind we proceed with the analysis.

4.1 Specification of Industry Demand Functions

In order to derive sharper results, we consider two special forms of industry demand functions which are commonly used in economics.

(Case 1) *Linear Demand* $P(y^*)=a-by^*$, $a>0$ and $b>0$ are constants.

(Case 2) *Isoelastic Demand* $P(y^*)=\alpha(y^*)^{-\delta}$, $\alpha>0$ and $1\geqslant\delta>0$ are constants.

These specifications lead to the following:

(Case 1) *Linear Demand*

$$y^* = \frac{Na-A^*}{b(N+1)} \tag{4.1}$$

$$y_i = \frac{a+A^*-(N+1)A_i}{b(N+1)} \quad (i=1,\ldots,N) \tag{4.2}$$

$$\pi(A_i,\hat{A}_i) = \frac{(a+\hat{A}_i-NA_i)^2}{b(N+1)^2} \quad (i=1,\ldots,N). \tag{4.3}$$

---

[4] The concept of perfect competition used here and also in most of the studies in the industrial organization literature is somewhat different from that in the general equilibrium analysis. Here we simply refer to the number of firms $=+\infty$ but not necessarily to the situation where demand is infinitely elastic. We owe this observation to Mas-Colell.

The Schumpeterian Hypothesis and Market Structure   21

Eq. (4.1) gives total output in the industry, Eq. (4.2) gives output of i-th firm, and Eq. (4.3) is profits of i-th firm, given levels of effective marginal costs of all firms.

(Case 2) *Isoelastic Demand*

$$y^* = \left[\frac{\alpha (N-\delta)}{A^*} \right]^{1/\delta} \tag{4.4}$$

$$y_i = \frac{1}{\delta} \left[1 - \frac{(N-\delta) A_i}{A^*} \right] \left[\frac{\alpha (N-\delta)}{A^*} \right]^{1/\delta} \tag{4.5}$$

$$\pi (A_i, \hat{A}_i) = \frac{\alpha}{\delta} \left[1 - \frac{(N-\delta) A_i}{A_i + \hat{A}_i} \right]^2 \left[\frac{\alpha (N-\delta)}{A_i + \hat{A}_i} \right]^{(1-\delta)/\delta} \tag{4.6}$$

where

$$A^* \underset{=}{\underline{\Delta}} \sum_{i=1}^{N} A_i, \quad A_i \underset{=}{\underline{\Delta}} \sum_{\substack{j \neq i \\ j=1}}^{N} A_j \quad \text{and} \quad y^* = \sum_{i=1}^{N} y_i.$$

4.2 Marginal Revenue Curves π_1 at a Symmetric Steady State

Symmetric steady states occur at the intersection of $\pi_1 (A, (N-1) A)$ and $(\varrho S_2 (A, 0) + S_1 (A, 0))$. To derive these intersections, it is necessary to know the slope of the marginal revenue curve for technical progress $\pi_1 (A, (N-1) A)$.

(Case 1) *Linear Demand*

$$\pi_1 (A, (N-1) A) = \frac{2 N}{b (N+1)^2} (A-a). \tag{4.7}$$

(Case 2) *Isoelastic Demand*

$$\pi_1 (A, (N-1) A) = \alpha^{1/\delta} A^{-1/\delta} \left[\frac{(N-\delta)^{(1-\delta)/\delta} [-2 N^2 + 2 (1+\delta) N - (1+\delta)]}{N^{3+(1-\delta)/\delta}} \right]. \tag{4.8}$$

The π_1 curve for Case 1 is a linear function of a symmetric level of effective marginal cost A, while the π_1 curve for Case 2 is a hyperbolic function of A. Figs. 6a and 6b depict graphs of (4.7) and (4.8), respectively.

4.3 Effects of Number of Firms in the Industry on the Curves of Developing New Technology

Now that symmetric steady states of effective marginal costs are given by the introduction of the π_1 curve and the $\varrho S_2 + S_1$ curve,

22   R. Sato and Sh. Tsutsui:

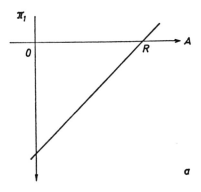

a

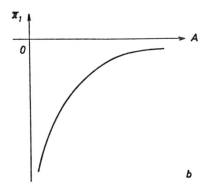

b

Fig. 6

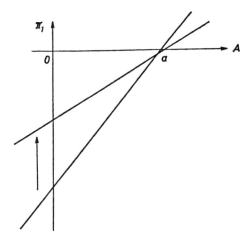

*The directions of
increase in N.*

Fig. 7

The Schumpeterian Hypothesis and Market Structure 23

and that the π_1 curve is a function of the number of firms in the industry, it remains to study the effects of the number of firms on the π_1 curves.

(Case 1) *Linear Demand*

The slope of the π_1 curve in this case is $2 N/b (N+1)^2$ (which is always positive) and the effect of the number of firms is:

$$\frac{\partial}{\partial N} \left(\frac{2 N}{b (N+1)^2} \right) = \frac{2 (1-N)}{b (N+1)^3} \leqslant 0 \text{ for } N > 1. \tag{4.9}$$

Eq. (4.9) states that as the number of firms increases, the slope of the π_1 decreases, as is demonstrated in Fig. 7.

The above result may be summarized in a theorem:

[Theorem 3] (Linear Demand)

The marginal revenue of producing an additional unit of new knowledge always rises as the number of firms in the industry increases, i. e., $\frac{\partial \pi_1}{\partial N} > 0$ for $N \geqslant 1$.

(Case 2) *Isoelastic Demand*

Case 2 is not as clear cut as Case 1. The sign of $\frac{\partial \pi_1}{\partial N}$ depends on the partial derivative of the term in the large bracket of (4.8) by calculating:

$$\frac{\partial}{\partial N} \left[\frac{(N-\delta)^{(1-\delta)/\delta} [-2 N^2 + 2 (1+\delta) N - (1+\delta)]}{N^{3+(1-\delta)/\delta}} \right] \text{ for } 0 < \delta \leqslant 1. \tag{4.10}$$

In view of the results presented in the Appendix (in particular, Lemma 8), we have the following interesting theorem for this case of isoelastic demand:

[Theorem 4] (Isoelastic Demand)

The marginal revenue of producing an additional unit of new knowledge always rises as the number in the industry increases beyond $N=3$, i. e., $\frac{\partial \pi_1}{\partial N} > 0$ for $N > 3$. If the number of the firms in the industry is less than four $(N < 4)$, the marginal revenue may increase or decrease as N rises, depending upon the elasticity of demand δ, i. e., $\frac{\partial \pi_1}{\partial N} \gtrless 0$ for $N=1, 2, 3$. This is illustrated in Fig. 8.

Example.

For $\delta=1$, $\delta=\frac{1}{2}$, the coefficients of (4.8) are given by Table 1.

Tabelle 1

δ	N			
	1	2	3	4
1	0	$-\frac{1}{8}$	$-\frac{4}{27}$	$-\frac{9}{64}$
$\frac{1}{2}$	$-\frac{1}{4}$	$-\frac{21}{64}$	$-\frac{105}{324}$	$-\frac{301}{1024}$

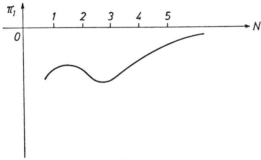

Fig. 8

The relationships between π_1 and N for the above examples are given in Fig. 9 a and 9 b.

These examples show that when $\delta=1$, the marginal revenue function achieves the maximum value at $N=3$ (oligopoly with three firms), and when $\delta=\frac{1}{2}$, at $N=2$ (duopoly).

4.4 Symmetric Steady States and the Number of Firms (or Schumpeterian World)

We shall now study how the steady-state conditions will be affected as the number of firms changes.

(Case 1) *Linear Demand*

If the demand function in the industry is linear, the relationship between steady states and the number of firms is simple, as demonstrated in the following graph:

The Schumpeterian Hypothesis and Market Structure   25

Fig. 10 illustrates the essence of the relationship between steady states and the number of firms. When the slope of π_1 is greater than or equal to that of $\varrho S_2 + S_1$, the steady-state level of effective marginal cost is inversely related to the number of firms. On the other hand, the

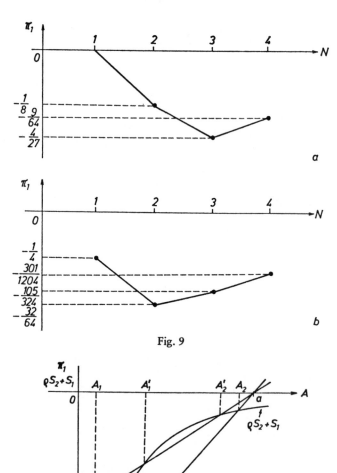

Fig. 9

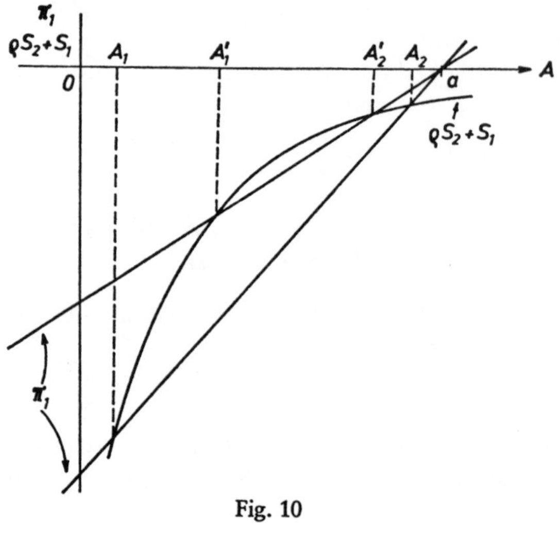

Fig. 10

steady-state level of effective marginal cost is positively related to the number of firms when the slope of π_1 is strictly less than that of $\varrho S_2 + S_1$. The shift of the steady-state level of effective marginal cost from A_2 to A_2' in Fig. 11 means that as the industry becomes more and more competitive, the achieved level of applied knowledge for all firms rises. On the other hand, the shift of the steady-state level of effective marginal cost from A_1 to A_1' reflects the fact that as the industry becomes more and more competitive, the achieved level of applied knowledge for all firms decreases. Using Theorem 2, we now establish Theorem 5.

[Theorem 5]

If the industry demand function is linear in y^*, then the stable symmetric steady state of effective marginal costs held by all firms increases as the number of firms increases.

The economic meaning of this theorem is that if market demand is linear, the maximum level of applied knowledge (or equivalently the smallest level of effective marginal cost) occurs at $N=1$ (perfect monopoly).

(Case 2) *Isoelastic Demand*

If the industry demand function is iso-elastic with respect to y^*, because of the result in Theorem 4, the relationship between the steady states and the number of firms is not so simple as in Case 1. We illustrate this by the following example:

Example (for $\delta = 1$)

For $\delta = 1$, the highest level of applied knowledge (or the smallest level of effective marginal cost) occurs at the stable symmetric steady state of a three-firm industry (see A_2' (at $N=3$) < A_2'' (at $N=4$) < A_2 (at $N=1$) in Fig. 11. This illustration leads to the following theorem.

[Theorem 6]

If the industry demand function is iso-elastic with respect to y^*, then the stable symmetric steady-state levels of effective marginal costs can attain their maximal values at $N=1$ or at $N=2$ or $N=3$, depending on the value of the elasticity of demand.

The proof of this important theorem depends on Theorem 2 and Theorem 4. Theorems 5 and 6 are consistent with Schumpeter's hypothesis. Each of these theorems implies that perfect competitiveness is far from the best market structure to promote technical progress. Nevertheless, Theorem 5 is substantially different from Theorem 6. In an industry with a linear market demand function, perfect monopoly (at $N=1$) leads to the greatest level of technical progress no matter what parametric values we assign to a downward sloping linear demand function, while in an industry with an

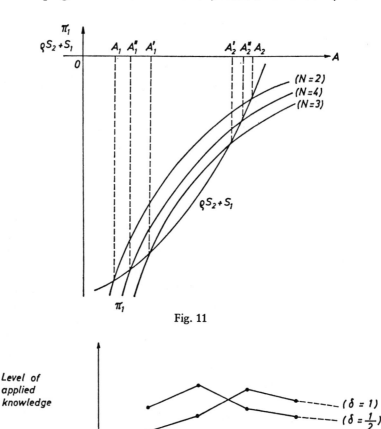

Fig. 11

Fig. 12

iso-elastic market demand function, perfect monopoly does not necessarily lead to the highest level of technical progress. The following graph (Fig. 12) demonstrates this.

At $\delta=1$, $N=3$ leads to maximal technical progress, at $\delta=\frac{1}{2}$, $N=2$ leads to maximal technical progress.

28   R. Sato and Sh. Tsutsui:

Demand Structure and the Schumpeterian Hypothesis

To derive Theorems 5 and 6 it was, of course, necessary to specify explicit forms for the industrial demand function. Generally speaking, though achieved levels of technical progress do depend on both technical production function (*S* and *T*) and industrial demand structures, the optimal number of firms to attain the maximum levels of technical progress depends only on industry demand structures in our model. Therefore, we have to stress the importance of industry demand structures with respect to technical progress, though it seems that this importance has not been fully understood. The fact that the optimal number of firms to promote technical progress is related to industry demand structures has a practical meaning.

First, let us consider the question: why does the number of firms differ in the same industry among different countries? For instance, in the U. S. and Japanese automobile industries there are four firms in the U. S., while there are eight firms in Japan.

In the computer industry, there is one dominant firm in the U. S. while there are five or six firms with almost equal market shares in Japan. Of course, firms market shares are not exactly equal as in the symmetric steady-states case we discuss in this paper. Still the question is why the industrial structures between the U. S. and Japan are so different. Theorems 5 and 6 seem to provide us with one of the clues to this question. That is to say, it may be that the differences in demand structure between the U. S. and Japan lead to the differences in industrial structure (i. e., in number of firms) between these countries. In particular, in the computer industry, the demand structure in the U. S. might exhibit linearity, while the demand structure in Japan might be better represented by a nonlinear (isoelastic) demand function. In relation to this, we hope that extensive empirical studies will be done. A second question concerns the welfare aspects of monopoly. Standard textbooks argue that an economy achieves the most socially desirable level of output in a perfectly competitive world. As has been seen, the theoretical background of this statement solely depends on the results of static general equilibrium framework.

One typical example concerning this statement is "Anti-trust Law", one purpose of which is to vitalize monopolistic industries by means of dividing monopoly into many smaller firms[5]. But as Theorem 5 and Theorem 6 argue, full competition is not always

---

[5] See, for example, the recent anti-trust decisions affecting AT & T.

the best in terms of the developments of technology. It should also be noted that Theorems 5 and 6 say nothing about the level of output. Thus, it seems appropriate to have two types of concepts about efficiency. One is about "output efficiency", and the other is about "technological efficiency". If we use these classifications, we think that the spirit of Anti-trust Law may be interpreted as promoting output efficiency. But as Theorem 5 and Theorem 6 suggest, it may not be always true that output efficiency is compatible with technical efficiency.

4.5 Output Efficiency and Technological Efficiency: Incompatibility

In the last subsection (4.4), we mentioned the incompatibility of output efficiency and technological efficiency. In other words, there exists a tradeoff relationship between them. In order to avoid the ambiguous conclusions, we consider a linear demand function. Total output in an industry is given by:

$$y^* = \frac{Na - A^*}{b(N+1)}. \tag{4.1}$$

At a symmetric steady state, we have

$$y^* = \frac{N(a-A)}{b(N+1)}. \tag{4.11}$$

Together with the technical production function S and the given level of basic knowledge, the steady-state level of effective marginal cost is determined by:

$$\frac{2N}{b(N+1)^2}(A-a) = \varrho S_1(A, 0, B) + S_2(A, 0, B). \tag{4.12}$$

The effect of the number of firms on the steady-state level of effective marginal cost is calculated by taking the derivative of (4.12) with respect to N:

$$\frac{2N}{b(N+1)^2}\frac{\partial A}{\partial N} + \frac{2(1-N)}{b(N+1)^3}(A-a) = (\varrho S_{21} + S_{11})\frac{\partial A}{\partial N}. \tag{4.13}$$

Rearranging (4.13) yields

$$\frac{\partial A}{\partial N} = \frac{\dfrac{2(1-N)}{b(N+1)^3}(A-a)}{\varrho S_{21} + S_{11} - \dfrac{2N}{b(N+1)^2}}. \tag{4.14}$$

Note that from locally stable condition, the denominator of (4.14) is positive and the two terms in the numerator are negative. Thus, the sign of $\frac{\partial A}{\partial N}$ is positive.

The effect of the number of firms on total output is given by:

$$\frac{\partial y^*}{\partial N} = -\frac{N}{b(N+1)}\frac{\partial A}{\partial N} + (a-A)\frac{1}{b(N+1)^2}. \tag{4.15}$$

Notice that in an industry with no investment in R & D, the effect of the number of firms on total output is given by:

$$\frac{\partial y^*}{\partial N} = (a-A)\frac{1}{b(N+1)^2}. \tag{4.16}$$

Substituting $\frac{\partial A}{\partial N}$ for (4.17) yields

$$\frac{\partial y^*}{\partial N} = \frac{(a-A)}{b(N+1)^2}\left[\frac{\varrho S_{21}+S_{11}-\dfrac{2N^2}{b(N+1)^2}}{\varrho S_{21}+S_{11}-\dfrac{2N}{b(N+1)^2}}\right]. \tag{4.17}$$

The sign of $\frac{\partial y^*}{\partial N}$ depends on the numerator in the last bracket of (4.17). Eq. (4.17) states that if the slope of ϱS_2+S_1 is nearly linear (or equivalently, $\varrho S_{21}+S_{11}$ is nearly constant in the relevant range of A), then the sign of $\frac{\partial y^*}{\partial N}$ tends to change from positive to negative, since the term $\frac{2N}{b(N+1)^2}$ decreases as N increases and the term $\frac{2N^2}{b(N+1)^2}$ increases as N increases. In particular, at $N=1$, both of these terms are identical to $\frac{1}{2b}$ This implies that at $N=1$, the sign of $\frac{\partial y^*}{\partial N}$ is positive at a stable steady state. Therefore, we can conclude that *perfect monopoly is not the best in terms of total output in the industry.* Then, the question would be how many firms would be needed to maximize the level of total output in the industry. In an industry with no investment in R & D, the relationship between total output and the number of firms is given by (4.16). Eq. (4.16) implies the $\frac{\partial y^*}{\partial N}$ is always positive for all positive integer N. Thus, the industry can attain maximal level of industry total output at $N=\infty$. This is consistent with the conventional argument that perfect competition (i. e., $N = \infty$) is the best to achieve the greatest industry output. However, once we take into account development of technologies, the result may become so different. The following example illustrates the difference clearly.

Example.

We use (2.6 i′) as the technical production function, and substitute into (4.17) to obtain

$$\frac{\partial y^*}{\partial N} = \frac{N(a-A)}{b(N+1)^2(a-2A)A}\left[\varrho D' \frac{b(N+1)^2}{2N^2} - A^2\right]$$

where $\dfrac{\partial A}{\partial N}$ for this example is:

$$\frac{\partial A}{\partial N} = \frac{(1-N)(A-a)A}{N(N+1)(a-2A)}.$$

Notice that $2A - a < 0$ from the condition of stability. If we define ξ_1 and ξ_2 as

$$\xi_1 \underline{\triangleq} - \varrho D'\left(\frac{1}{B}\nu\right)\frac{b(N+1)^2}{2N}$$

$$\xi_2 \underline{\triangleq} - \varrho D'\left(\frac{1}{B}\nu\right)\frac{b(N+1)^2}{2N} = \xi_1 \frac{1}{N}$$

then $\xi_1 < \xi_2 < 0$ for $N \geqslant 2$.

And we have

$$\frac{\partial \xi_1}{\varrho N} < 0, \qquad \frac{\partial \xi_2}{\partial N} > 0.$$

In Fig. 13 the intersection of ξ_1 and $A^2 - aA$, Q_0, gives the steady-state level of effective marginal cost, and Q_1 on the ξ_2 curve lies in the negative region of $-A^2$ wherefore the sign of $\frac{\partial y^*}{\partial N}$ is positive, while the intersection of ξ_1' and $A^2 - aA$, Q_0', gives another steady-state level of effective marginal cost, and Q_1' on the ξ_2' curve lies in the positive region of $-A^2$ wherefore the sign of $\frac{\partial y^*}{\partial N}$ is negative.

Fig. 14 is the graph of the relationship between total industry output and the number of firms.

This example shows that there exists a finite positive integer N_0 $(\geqslant 1)$ such that at N_0, the industry can attain maximal level of total industry output. This example establishes the following theorem.

[Theorem 7]

If the demand function is linear in the industry with investment in R & D, then the maximal level of total industry output can be attained at N_0 such that $1 < N_0 < \infty$.

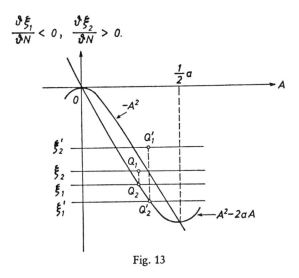

Fig. 13

This theorem is quite contrary to the standard argument that perfect competition is the best. Moreover, we should be aware that the optimal number of firms to attain the maximum level of tech-

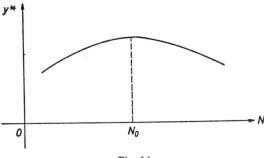

Fig. 14

nical progress is in general different from the optimal number of firms to attain the maximum level of total industry output. In addition, Theorem 7 states that even to maximize total industry output, perfect competition (for $N = \infty$) is not always good. Therefore, we can prove[6]

[Theorem 8]

If an industry engages in R & D, perfect competition is in general far from the best both for technical progress and for maximal level of total industry output.

Appendix

Proof of Theorem 2.

[Lemma 1]

As symmetric steady-states, the characteristic roots of (3.28) are:

$$\lambda_1 = \frac{\varrho + \sqrt{\varrho^2 + 4\,m_2}}{2}, \quad \lambda_i = \frac{\varrho + \sqrt{\varrho^2 + 4\,m_1}}{2}, \quad (i = 2, \ldots, N)$$

$$\lambda_{N+1} = \frac{\varrho - \sqrt{\varrho^2 + 4\,m_2}}{2}, \quad \lambda_j = \frac{\varrho - \sqrt{\varrho^2 + 4\,m_1}}{2}, \quad (j = N+2, \ldots, 2N)$$

where

$$m_1 \underset{=}{\triangle} \frac{\varrho S_{21} + S_{11} - \pi_{11} + \pi_{12}}{S_{22}}, \quad m_2 \underset{=}{\triangle} \frac{\varrho S_{21} + S_{11} - \pi_{11} - (N-1)\,\pi_{12}}{S_{22}}.$$

Proof: This is a continuous version of the model discussed by Fla-herty (1980) and thus follows from her results (see Flaherty (1980)).

We now need several additional lemmas to establish Theorem 2 in the text.

[Lemma 2]

If m_1 and m_2 are strictly positive at a symmetric steady state, then the steady-state is locally stable.

---

[6] In the present paper we have completely ignored the dynamic behavior of exit and entry. Our intention here is to explain why in the long run a limited number of firms can achieve higher efficiency in terms of technical progress and/or output production. The dynamic problem of exit and entry together with the optimal number of firms, which is endogenously determined, will receive separate and careful attention in our next paper.

Proof: Positivities of m_1 and m_2 imply that N characteristic roots are positive and the rest are negative; viz., a saddle-point property.   Q. E. D.

[Lemma 3]

If $\pi_{12} < 0$ and $m_1 > 0$, then $m_2 > 0$.

Proof: Obvious from the definitions of the characteristic roots in Lemma 1.   Q. E. D.

Remark: The condition $\pi_{12} < 0$ holds in most cases because $\pi_{12} < 0$ implies that the slopes of reaction functions for all firms in a static noncooperative game are negative. Therefore, throughout the paper, $\pi_{12} < 0$ is assumed.

[Lemma 4]

Under the condition of $\pi_{12} < 0$, if $m_1 > 0$ at a symmetric steady state, then the steady state is locally stable.

Proof: From Lemma 3, $m_2 > 0$. So Lemma 2 can be applied.
                                                        Q. E. D.

[Lemma 5]

If the slope of π_1 is not smaller than that of $\varrho S_2 + S_1$ at a symmetric steady state, then the steady state is locally unstable.

Proof:

$$\text{the slope of } \pi_1 = \frac{\partial}{\partial A} \left(\pi_1 \left(A, (N-1) A \right) \right) = \pi_{11} + (N-1) \pi_{12}$$

$$\text{the slope of } \varrho S_2 + S_1 = \frac{\partial}{\partial A} \left(\varrho S_2 + S_1 \right) = \varrho S_{21} + S_{11}$$

$$\pi_{11} + (N-1) \pi_{12} \geqslant \varrho S_{21} + S_{11} \quad \text{means}$$

$$\varrho S_{21} + S_{11} - \pi_{11} - (N-1) \pi_{12} \leqslant 0$$

$$\varrho S_{21} + S_{11} - \pi_{11} + \pi_{12} \leqslant N \pi_{12} < 0 \quad \text{since} \quad \pi_{12} < 0.$$

Moreover, $S_{22} > 0$ (see (2.16)), therefore both m_1 and m_2 turn out to be negative. This means that the characteristic roots of the system (3.28) are all positive real numbers or else have complex roots with positive real parts. Hence, a symmetric steady state in which π_1 has a greater slope than $\varrho S_2 + S_1$ is locally unstable.   Q. E. D.

Proof of Theorem 4.

The result of the partial differential presented in (4.10) in the text is given by

$$\left(\frac{N_{3+(1-\delta)/\delta}}{1}\right)^2 (N-\delta)^{(1-\delta)/\delta} N^{2+(1-\delta)/\delta} [2N^3 - (4\delta+6)N^2$$

$$+ (2\delta^2 + 7\delta + 5)N - (1+\delta)(1+2\delta)]. \tag{A}$$

The sign of (A) depends on the sign of the last bracket since $N>1$ and $0 \leqslant \delta < 1$ imply $(N-\delta) > 0$. So we define $g(N) = 2N^3 - (4\delta+6)N^2 + (2\delta^2 + 7\delta + 5)N - (1+\delta)(1+2\delta)$. Taking the derivative of $g(N)$ with respect to N yields:

$$g'(N) = \frac{\partial g}{\partial N} = 6N^2 - 2(4\delta-6)N + (2\delta^2 + 7\delta + 5). \tag{B}$$

This quadratic function of N has two positive roots. We define these two positive roots as X_1 and X_2 such that $X_1 < X_2$.

[Lemma 6]

The locations of X_1 and X_2 are as follows.

$$0 < X_1 < 1 \quad \text{for} \quad 0 < \delta < 1$$

$$1 < X_2 \leqslant 2 \quad \text{for} \quad 0 < \delta \leqslant \frac{9 - \sqrt{4}}{4}$$

$$2 < X_2 < 3 \quad \text{for} \quad \frac{9 - \sqrt{4}}{4} < \delta < 1.$$

Proof: Lemma 6 is derived by using the relationship between roots and coefficients in quadratic functions.   Q. E. D.

[Lemma 7]

The signs of $g(1)$ and $g(3)$ are positive for $0 < \delta < 1$, and the sign of $g(2)$ depends on δ. For $0 < \delta < \frac{5 - \sqrt{2}}{4}$, $g(2) > 0$, and for $\frac{5 - \sqrt{2}}{4} < \delta < 1$, $g(2) < 0$.

Proof: Direct calculations of $g(1)$, $g(2)$, $g(3)$ lead to this lemma.

The graphs of $g(N)$ are given below and follow from Lemma 7, from which we also obtain Lemma 8

[Lemma 8]

(i) $0 < \delta < \dfrac{5-\sqrt{2}}{4}$

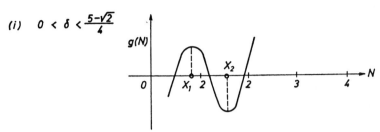

(ii) $\dfrac{5-\sqrt{2}}{4} < \delta < \dfrac{9-\sqrt{4}}{4}$

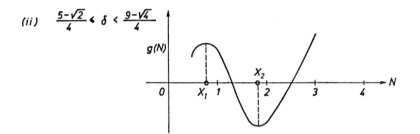

(iii) $\dfrac{9-\sqrt{4}}{4} < \delta < 1$

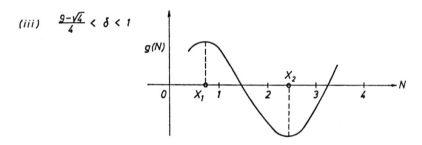

The coefficient of Eq. (4.18) first increases, then decreases, and finally increases as N rises.

References

P. Dasgupta and J. Stiglitz (1980 a): Uncertainty, Industrial Structure, and the Speed of R & D, Bell Journal of Economics *11*, pp. 1—28.

P. Dasgupta and J. Stiglitz (1980b): Industrial Structure and the Nature of Innovative Activity, Economic Journal *90*, pp. 266—293.

F. M. Fisher and P. Temin (1973): Returns to Scale in Research and Development: What Does the Schumpeterian Hypothesis Imply? Journal of Political Economy *81*, pp. 56—70.

M. T. Flaherty (1980): Industry Structure and Cost-Reducing Investment, Econometrica *48*, pp. 1187—1209.

J. W. Friedman (1977): Oligopoly and the Theory of Games, New York.

C. Futia (1980): Schumpeterian Competition, Quarterly Journal of Economics *94*, pp. 675—695.

M. Kamien and N. Schwartz (1975): Market Structure and Innovation, Journal of Economic Literature *13*, pp. 1—17.

P. Krugman (1983): New Theories of Trade Among Industrial Countries, American Economic Review *73*, Papers and Proceedings, pp. 343—347.

G. Lowry (1979): Market Structure and Innovation, Quarterly Journal of Economics *93*, pp. 395—410.

R. Nelson and S. Winter (1980): The Schumpeterian Tradeoff Revisited, American Economic Review *70*, pp. 114—132.

R. Nelson, S. Winter, and H. Schuette (1976): Technical Change in an Evolutionary Model, Quarterly Journal of Economics *90*, pp. 90—118.

J. Roberts and H. Sonnenschein (1977): On the Foundation of the Theory of Monopolistic Competition, Econometrica *45*, 101—113.

J. B. Rosen (1965): Existence and Uniqueness of Equilibrium Points for Concave *N*-Person Games, Econometrica *33*, pp. 520—534.

R. Sato (1981): Theory of Technical Change and Economic Invariance, New York.

R. Sato and G. Suzawa (1983): Research and Productivity, Endogenous Technical Progress, Boston, Mass.

J. A. Schumpeter (1939): The Theory of Economic Development, Cambridge, Mass.

J. A. Schumpeter (1950): Capitalism, Socialism, and Democracy, 3rd Edition, New York.

M. Spence (1976): Product Selection, Fixed Costs and Monopolistic Competition, Review of Economic Studies *43*, pp. 217—235.

Addresses of authors: Prof. Ryuzo Sato, Brown University, Department of Economics, Providence, RI 02912, U. S. A., and J. F. Kennedy School of Government, Harvard University, Cambridge, MA 02138, U. S. A.; Shunichi Tsutsui, Brown University, Department of Economics, Providence, RI 02912, U. S. A.

Printed in Austria

Journal of Economic Literature
Vol. XVIII (September 1980), pp. 1003–1024

Measuring the Impact of Technical Progress on the Demand for Intermediate Goods: A Survey

By

RYUZO SATO
Brown University

and

RAMA RAMACHANDRAN
Southern Methodist University

The authors acknowledge the financial support of the National Science Foundation (R&D assessment). The authors are also grateful to Thomas Woodward for his helpful comments on an earlier draft of this paper. We wish to thank Mark Perlman and his staff for their editorial assistance.

I. Introduction

MAN HAS always contemplated the nature of his relation to the material world that surrounds him. Animistic and polytheistic religions could be viewed as attempts to attribute a latent divine will to the perceived vagaries of nature; many rituals were initiated to propitiate the supernatural and to make nature more bountiful. As theological speculation led to the despiritualization of the universe and to the spread of monotheism, man claimed for himself a central role in the divine scheme. Molded in the image of God, he claimed to reside in the center of a universe created only for his benefit.

The developments of physical and biological sciences in the post-Copernican period, while destroying the anthropocentric view, gave man unparalleled control over himself and his material surroundings. As the first specie to inhabit the entire planet, he began to realize the limitations of natural resources at his disposal; it created what Gordon R. Taylor called a "crisis of responsibility" (1970, p. 294). The Malthusian view that growth of population would ultimately exceed our capacity to produce food was only an extreme version of pessimism shared by many classical economists. Both Marxian and non-Marxian optimists, on the contrary, argued that the development of scientific knowledge would permit circumvention of the limitations imposed by nature.

During the second half of the nineteenth century and through the first half of the twentieth century, the western world was able to escape the Malthusian trap because of spectacular developments in industrial and agricultural technology. Not surprisingly, most economic studies attributed a substantial portion of the growth in per capita income to technological progress, a conclusion most elegantly quantified by Robert Solow's seminal paper (1957). Writing in the middle of the 1960's, Lester B. Lave concluded that the classical economists erred so badly in their prediction because of their underestimation of the role of productivity growth (1966, p. 4).

The debate between technological optimists and pessimists was rekindled this past decade with the publication of a number of long-term global forecasts. Using varying degrees of intuitive assessments and quantitative forecasting, these studies tried to visualize the long-term future of mankind; while more sophisticated in their analytical techniques, they were in the tradition of the "magnificient dynamics" (William J. Baumol, 1959) of the classical economists. Herman Kahn and Anthony J. Wiener's book (1967), which was one of the earliest in this group, gave a fairly positive assessment. On the other hand, studies by system dynamists like Jay W. Forrester (1971) and Donella H. Meadows *et al.* (1972) drew emphatically negative conclusions. Reviewing this literature, S. Cole and I. Miles observed: "it is clear that despite the differences in views among participants in the global futures debate, and despite their very different policies prescriptions, there is agreement on one point: the rate and direction of technical change is crucial to the outcome, whatever global future is desired or predicted" (1978).

The general conclusion was that economic growth would ultimately be inhibited by the scarcity of some natural resources such as land, energy, clean air, or water. The rate of technical progress influenced the efficiency with which an economy utilized these limited resources or provided substitutes for them. In contrast to these discussions, the conventional analysis of technological change in growth economics was concerned with the study of its effects on the productivity and remuneration of primary inputs, capital and labor; this literature was recently analyzed in surveys by M. Ishaq Nadiri (1970) and Charles Kennedy and A. P. Thirlwall (1972).

Meanwhile a literature devoted to the analysis of efficiency of nonprimary inputs was growing under impetus from two sources. First, there was the controversy over the validity and usefulness of input-output analysis. Some kind of assumption about temporal stability of input-output coefficients was necessary to make the analysis interesting and operationally meaningful (Kenneth J. Arrow and Marvin Hoffenberg, 1959, pp. 15–16). The input-output economists assumed the validity of temporal stability in a static economy and attributed all variations to technological change. In essence, this implied denying the distinction between substitution and technological change. Anne P. Carter, in line with this tradition, denied the usefulness of trying to separate shift among "known" technological alternatives as compared to the development of a new one (1970, pp. 10–11). Arrow and Hoffenberg developed a causal analysis of the changes in input-output coefficients, an approach currently more popular in Europe. The RAS method originally suggested by Wassily W. Leontief (1941) and popularized by Richard Stone (1962) and Stone and J. A. C. Brown (1962), as well as the *ex ante* approach, sought to estimate a new input-output matrix from earlier ones using a computationally simple, but theoretically justifiable, rule of adjustment.

A second impetus was provided by attempts to generalize the traditional discussions of technical progress as affecting the productivity of two primary inputs to multifactor cases also incorporating intermediate goods.

The indices of total and partial productivity seem to draw from both the input-output literature and the growth-theoretic literature.

In this survey, we will concentrate on the literature on the measurement of technical progress as it affects the efficiency of intermediate goods. *Section* II discusses input-output analysis, while *Section* III reviews the production function approach. *Section* IV will discuss extension of the measures of total and partial productivity.

II. *Input-Output Analysis*

1. *Estimation of Structural Change by Variation in Input Requirements*

The method used by Beatrice N. Vaccara (1970) and Carter (1970) in their extensive analyses of structural change in the United States is to compute the change in elements of the direct input-output matrix or that of the Leontief Inverse Matrix. The former measures the amount of the input directly used in the production of a unit of a commodity, while the latter measures the amount of the input used directly and indirectly (through other intermediate products) in the production. Due to the linkage effects, the corresponding elements in the direct and Leontief Inverse Matrices may not change by the same amount. The ideal solution is to repeat the computations for elements of both matrices. But this is not practical because of the amount of computations involved.

Another step in the analysis is to compare the total and intermediate output required to produce a given final output with input-output tables of various years. Vaccara and Nancy Simon (1968), Vaccara (1970), and Carter (1970) use this approach. Vaccara and Simon try to split the change in the total output between

change due to final demand and change due to variations in the elements of the Leontief Inverse Matrix (1968). They notice that the division depends on whether they take the matrix for the beginning of the period under study or the matrix corresponding to the end point of time. They then average the two measures for technological change. G. Fromm, in his comment (1968), criticizes this averaging procedure. He argues that the two measures originally derived are the Paasche and Laspeyres indices and that the average is a meaningless hybrid. In Vaccara, the intermediate goods required to produce 1958 output are calculated with 1947, 1958, and 1961 coefficients, using both a direct and a Leontief inverse (1970).

Using the changes in intermediate requirements (necessary to produce a unit vector or subvector of final demand) as indices of the changes in input coefficients, Carter derives a number of important conclusions about the intermediate input requirements of various industries (1970). The demand by user industries for inputs from the general industry sector (consisting mainly of services, energy, and transportation) are increasing all the time; the general industry sector already absorbs half the nation's total employment. In the energy sector, the direct-plus-indirect coal requirements are decreasing, while that of petroleum and of electric and gas utilities are increasing.

Carter considers competition among basic materials. Before World War II, particular metals dominated specific product markets. This domination weakened in the postwar period. She notes (1970, p. 85):

Thus, there now seems to be a technological basis for greater substitutability as relative price conditions change. We are talking in terms of long-run substitutability. Shifts in materials use require outlays for design and retraining; hence, changes are geared to long-run price trends rather than short-term fluctuations.

In some areas—notably aircraft, aerospace, and instrumentation—technology has even reached the stage where materials are being designed "to order" through research and development. There is also research directed specifically towards the use of low-priced materials, which tend to blur even more the operational distinction between technological development and price substitution.

In these discussions Carter analyzes the changing requirements of various intermediate inputs to produce unit output. She sticks by her basic methodological position that substitution and technological change are indistinguishable. She does not distinguish between these two effects in the increasing demand for general outputs or for changes in the input requirements of various basic materials.

The study of the changing requirements for basic materials (confined to the 1947–58 period) shows that direct iron and steel purchases per unit of output tend to decrease in all industries, while input requirements of aluminum and plastic show a tendency to increase. Copper coefficients show mixed tendencies. Total—direct and indirect—requirements for basic materials generally follow these tendencies.

Carter raises the question of what relation these studies have to the modern production function approach. She argues that the measures she calculates take into consideration the shifting industrial specialization in relating primary factor requirements to final output (1970, pp. 147–50). The main argument is that the capital–labor ratios used by the production function approach measure only the ratios of direct labor to direct capital and the change in these ratios may differ from changes in the total (direct-*cum*-indirect) factor ratios. It is here necessary to remember that the input-output analysis used does not take into consideration the substitutability between primary and intermediate inputs or the substitutability between primary inputs in either the final

good or in the intermediate input producing sectors. The differences in the different rates of change of total and direct input ratios may arise from substitution as factor prices vary.

The next question considered is whether input requirements of specific materials to deliver 1961 final demand and two subsectors compared with 1958 and 1947 input-output structures reflect the price increases of these materials over the period. The conclusion Carter draws is that there is a slight tendency for substitution of relatively cheaper materials.

This leads to the question of whether the technology matrix of 1958 is superior for a reasonable range of factor prices. Carter analyzes this by setting up a linear programming problem to minimize the total factor requirement to produce the 1958 vector of outputs using either 1947 or 1958 technology in each industry (1970, p. 169). In only 14 out of 76 sectors are 1947 structures found to be superior to 1958 structures.

Of particular interest to our discussion is the choice of 1947 technologies attributed to the petroleum and iron mining industries. Carter explains that this is due to the exhaustion of superior reserves of these raw materials (1970, pp. 171–72). In the case of the steel industry, she claims that the new technology introduced between 1947 and 1958 was still not widely used, while most of the other preferences are due to special circumstances existing in 1947 or to changes in product mix in 1957.

These results are found to be valid for quite a variation in primary input prices. Carter draws the following conclusion from this analysis (1970, p. 175).

Had 1947 and 1958 structures been technological alternatives in 1947, 1958 structures should have been adopted in 1947. They were not adopted because they were not known in 1947. Our findings are presumptive evidence that 1947–1958 differences result from bona fide technological change rather than from simple substitution. The brief excursion into sensitivity analysis reinforces this impression. Structures of 1958 retain their superiority to those of 1947 over a wide range of changes in the relative price of labor to capital.

In analyzing the rates for scrapping old technology and for investing in new technology, Carter also tries to test the embodiment hypothesis that technical change is due to investment in new machinery (1970). The industries for which 1958 input-output structures were disadvantageous when compared to earlier structures showed low priority for retirement, while a few sectors like textile, construction, mining equipment, and various electrical and service machinery sectors placed high priority on replacing old machinery.

James Just uses a model (1974), similar in many respects to the one described above but without the programming element, to analyze the growth of energy demand in the United States with three new technological possibilities: (1) high-BTU coal gasification, (2) low-BTU coal gasification, and (3) gas turbine topping cycle. The essential principle is illustrated by a two-period model formulated as follows:

First consider the case of constant technology. Let technological coefficient matrix A apply to both periods. Let the vector of final demand Y consist of current demand Y^F and capital investment purchases Y^I and let C be the capital coefficient matrix. The problem is to find, for period 1, the total output X_1 and total final demand Y_1, given the total output for period 0, X_0, and noninvestment final demand for period 1, Y_1^F.

$$X_1 = (I - A)^{-1} Y_1 \qquad (1)$$
$$= (I - A)^{-1}(Y_1^F + Y_1^I).$$

If one gives an intuitive interpretation to $(I - A)$ as production leakage (that part of output not used as intermediate good for further production), then the above

equation is similar to the conventional multiplier.

$$Y_1^I = C(X_1 - X_0). \qquad (2)$$

This equation is a statement of the acceleration principle.

New technology is introduced by redefining C as follows: Let A_i and C_i be the technological coefficient vector and capital coefficient vector for industry i using current technology; let A_n and C_n be the corresponding vectors using new technology. If the new technology is expected to take over a fraction g of the total production of sector i and a fraction h of total new capacity of capital additions, then the new production matrices are defined as weighted average of the old and new matrices.

$$\overline{A}_i = (1 - g)A_i + gA_n \qquad (3)$$
$$\overline{C}_i = (1 - h)C_i + hC_n. \qquad (4)$$

$\overline{A}_i$ and $\overline{C}_i$ are substituted into A to give the technology of period 1. This model is used to project a series of five alternative 1985 scenarios involving various energy-use growth rates and different assumptions about technological alternatives.

Rudyard Istvan uses a more complex version of an input-output model to analyze the economic impact of projected technological changes up to 1980 and of major alternative utility investment strategies (1974). His model is a lagged dynamic input-output model.

Investment models without lag assume that investment becomes instantaneously productive. This assumption is very unrealistic in utility industries. Hence, Istvan introduces a set of lag operator matrices, $L_j, j = 0, \ldots, N$, where N is the maximum gestation period. The lag operator matrices are a function of incremental capital coefficients, which are empirically observable. He solves the model using an iterative procedure.

In two recent articles, Carter (1974;

1976) combines the analyses of Just and Istvan into a general equilibrium analysis to compute possible growth rates for the U.S. economy. The analytical framework for this approach is given by the equation:

$$(I - A)X - B\dot{X} = 0, \tag{5}$$

where X is a vector of total sectoral outputs and $\dot{X}$ is a vector of their time derivatives. A and B are current account and capital coefficient matrices; these are enhanced by a column and a row vector to include the household and to close the model. $[I - A]X$ now represents the output not utilized as intermediate good or for final consumption; the equation states that this should just equal the capital investment. If all sectors are to grow at the same rate (balanced growth with $\dot{X} = \lambda X$), then equations can be written as:

$$(I - A - \lambda B)X = 0, \tag{6}$$

where λ is the uniform or turnpike growth rate. The article gives computations of λ under various alternate technological and behavioral assumptions. The technological assumptions are:

(i) First, the input coefficients in the base year's flow coefficient matrix are replaced by coefficients for a projected 1980 input structure of the electric power sector estimated by Istvan. The capital coefficient matrix is also adjusted according to Istvan's estimates. These estimates result in the total capital coefficient of the electric power industry increasing from 3.2 to 4.8 and a 9 percent increase in real costs.

(ii) The second set of modifications convert the incremental requirements of fossil fuel in the electricity industry to gasified coal on the basis of Just's projections of the technological structure of the Hygas process of coal gasification.

(iii) The above assumptions are considered together with the assumption that base year energy flow coefficients increase by 40 percent.

(iv) The technological impacts of various pollution control methods are considered.

In calculating λ, different assumptions about individuals' consumption behavior are also considered. The basic conclusion of this paper is that taken individually changes in technology given above do not reduce the growth rate significantly, but collectively they are capable of reducing it from 3.5 percent to a low 2.1 percent.

2. Prediction of Structural Change by Estimation of Input-Output Coefficients

There are two separate approaches to the prediction of changes in input-output coefficients. The first approach, attributable to Leontief (1941), Stone (1962), and Stone and Brown (1962), assumes that input-output matrices change over time in a "biproportional" way. The other approach is to estimate trends in individual coefficients using statistical analysis.

In the Leontief–Stone approach, the input-output matrix for year $t + 1$ is related to the matrix for year t by the relation

$$A^{t+1} = R^t A^t S^t, \tag{7}$$

where A^t is known and R^t and S^t are diagonal matrices estimated from a single observation of the marginal totals for year $t + 1$, i.e., the total intermediate and final inputs and outputs of each sector. In that only one set of observations is required for the estimation of R^t and S^t, the method is similar to the estimation of static models and achieves economy of information. Michael Bacharach argues that it has other desirable properties (1970): (1) the new matrix is nonnegative; (2) it preserves the zero elements in the original matrix; (3) it can be shown that the new matrix is as near the original as it can be—minimizing a distance criterion function—while satisfying the given marginal constraints so that it assures some form of stability in the technology matrix; and (4) the existence of such a matrix can be shown under weak conditions and its uniqueness universally.

The relationship given above assumes that all elements of the ith row are multiplied by r^t_i, while all elements of jth column are multiplied by s_j. The explanation for these variations differed between Leontief (1941) and Stone and Brown (1962). Stone and Brown's explanation can be summarized as follows:

(i) First, the coefficient a^{t+1}_{ij} will be greater or less than a^t_{ij}, showing the relative change in the usefulness of that input relative to other inputs; this is called "absorption effect." The simplifying assumption of the RAS method, which makes it a practical computational procedure, is that all industries using input i vary their input per unit of output in the same proportion r_i. Let R be a diagonal matrix whose elements are the multipliers, r_i for all the rows of A.

(ii) Secondly, the proportion of primary inputs used in the production of each commodity will change, and this will affect the total amount of intermediate goods used in the production of commodity j. This is called the "fabrication effect." Again, the assumption in the RAS method is that all elements in the jth column change by the same proportion due to this effect. Thus, the method assumes double proportionality in the temporal variation of input coefficients. Let S be the diagonal matrix whose elements are the multipliers s_j for all columns of A.

(iii) The estimated input matrix for year $t + 1$, A^{t+1}, is then $R^tA^tS^t$. It is then assumed that over future years, the coefficients continue to change at the same proportionate rate so that $A^{t+2} = R^tA^{t+1}S^t$. R and S can be solved using a system of simultaneous equations or by an iterative procedure if final output and intermediate output for the year $t + 1$ is known in addition to A^t.

E. Fontela *et al.* report a method of estimating in which some elements of A^{t+1} are determined by *a priori* information (1970). This requires a modification of the

procedure for the solution used in the RAS method. The advantage claimed for this method is that it dispenses with the double proportionality assumption of RAS (1970, p. 338).

In updating the 1963 input-output matrix to 1967, Clopper Almon, Jr., *et al.* used direct estimation of cells whenever possible and then used the RAS method to balance the matrix (1974). They, however, did not use the RAS method to predict future changes in coefficients. They assumed that all coefficients in a row of the input matrix change by the same percentage and that these changes follow a logistic curve. From the *Annual Survey of Manufactures,* they estimated the intermediate use by 185 industries and by construction. They then calculated what this usage would have been had input-output coefficients been constant at their 1969 values from 1958 to 1971. A logistic curve was fitted to the ratio of actual to estimated use. By the closeness of the scatter of points around the logistic curve, they show also how the uniform trend assumption would have worked in the past. Almon *et al.* report that for most products, such as steel, which are sold largely to intermediate use, the fit is close (1974, p. 162). They list 18 industries including crude "Petroleum and Natural Gas" and "Petroleum Refining" among the industries whose coefficients show little or no change. Twenty-six industries including "Electric Utilities" have spectacular increases in coefficients, while 23 industries including "coal mining," "steel," "copper," and "water transportation" show considerable percentage decline in coefficients per year. This part of the analysis is a cross between the approaches adopted by Carter (1970) and the RAS method. The assumption that the logistic curve approaches an asymptote amounts to the belief that structural change will ultimately die off.

The first quantitative description of the

causes for changes in input-output coefficients, using time-series data, is by Arrow and Hoffenberg (1959). They had three models: (i) a fixed coefficient model; (ii) a tentative model to explain variation in input coefficients; and (iii) a final model.

The fixed coefficient model leads to an equation quite similar to the conventional demand equation in the input-output model but for the random term.

$$X_i = \sum_{j=1}^{n} a_{ij} X_j + f_i + \omega_i, \qquad (8)$$

where X represents the output of an industry, f the final demand, a_{ij} the input coefficients, and ω the random disturbance term.

In the tentative model, the assumption is that the input coefficients are influenced by the rate of change in output, since the efficiency in utilization of embodied inputs is affected by it. The vintage distribution of non-embodied inputs also affects efficiency and hence influences the input coefficients. A trend element is considered to represent the changes in product mix. This model is found unsatisfactory because of its failure to take into account some visible influences on these coefficients and because of infeasible data requirements.

The final model makes the input-output coefficients depend on a number of variables, which are thought to be relevant:

(i) real disposable income whose changes influence quality of output;

(ii) ratio of defense expenditure to GNP, a significant influence during World War II years;

(iii) trend variations attributable to technological and taste changes; and

(iv) learning effects represented by the ratio of the excess of output in any year over the highest previous peak to the output of the year.

These equations are estimated only for a small number of inputs. The limited information maximum likelihood method and linear programming methods of estimation are used but, while Arrow and Hoffenberg could reject the constant coefficient model, they could not give a satisfactory causal account of the changes in input coefficients (1959, pp. 117–33).

Henri Theil considers that the matrices R and S can easily take unrealistic values in empirical work (1966), a view challenged by Bacharach (1970). Theil approaches the problem through an analysis based on the observed behavior of prediction errors. His approach requires more statistical information in the form of input tables for different years.

It begins with the observation that the logarithmic prediction errors, defined as the logarithm of the ratio of predicted to actual demand, satisfy the cumulation rule. The rule can be interpreted as follows. Suppose we want to calculate the input-output relation in year $t + 3$ but know only the table for year t. Then the logarithmic prediction error in using the table of year t in year $t + 3$ is the sum of the logarithmic errors that would have occurred if we had used table t for year $t + 1$, table $t + 1$ for year $t + 2$, and table $t + 2$ for year $t + 3$. Whether Theil's approach leads to an improvement in prediction, on the average, depends on the statistical structure of errors. But Theil argues that it performs as well as the crude input-output forecasts (1966, p. 238). Theil seems more concerned with correcting forecasting errors from using an outdated table than in forecasting the table itself.

Per Sevaldson uses the annual input-output tables for Norway for the period 1949–60 to fit regression equations to the individual elements of these matrices (1970). These equations take two alternate forms, one form incorporating time trends. On the basis of an assumption regarding the statistical distribution of the trend coefficient, Sevaldson classifies the trends in input coefficients.

In another paper, Sevaldson sets out to

analyze whether the changes in input-output coefficients for Norway are due to substitution defined as cost adjustment in the production sectors (1976). If substitution is possible, each sector will choose (from the input vectors available) that vector which has the lowest coefficient sum. Sevaldson tested this hypothesis and concluded that there is little evidence to suggest cost adjustment and hence favors the argument that actual variations are due to technological progress.

A. J. Middelhoek considers that the use of marginal coefficients instead of average coefficients would permit the use of input-output tables for medium-range planning (1970). He argues that the marginal coefficients ensure stability of coefficients while retaining the simplicity of the conventional input-output analysis. Using the input-output tables of the Netherlands from 1950 to 1964 inclusive, he utilizes regression analysis to test whether average values differ significantly from marginal values. This is found to be true in two-thirds of the cases tested. To test the stability of marginal coefficients, he divides the period into two, 1950 to 1957 and 1956 to 1964 inclusive. He estimates the marginal coefficients separately for the two subperiods and tests whether the difference is significant. He concludes that in three-fourths of the cases, the marginal coefficients for the two periods do not differ significantly.

Among all these studies, the most ambitious in analyzing the causes of input-coefficient change is the study of Finnish wood and paper industries by O. Forssell (1972). Since only a limited number of input-output tables are available for Finland, he concentrates on studying those industries for which annual data can be obtained. He concludes that the three measures of technical development—degree of electrification, degree of mechanization, and time—are highly correlated among themselves. Among the factors that influence

the input coefficients most are these three—individually and collectively—as are also product mix and relative prices of inputs.

Iwao Ozaki tests the effects of technological change, as measured through changes in the input-output coefficients, using a combination of methods (1976). First, he fits a factor-limitational or Cobb-Douglas production function to measure returns to scale for capital and labor in 54 sectors defined by the input-output table. Then he estimates a Leontief-type index of structural change for subsectors of the economy. Ozaki considers six sectors: (i) new technology block, (ii) employment block, (iii) services block, (iv) public utility block, (v) metal block, and (vi) traditional-technology block.

The main conclusions he derives are: (i) most of the capital investment was in sectors with a limitational production function showing increasing returns to capital; (ii) increased employment occurred in sectors with a Cobb-Douglas production function showing increasing returns to scale; and (iii) structural change increased inputs into most sectors from the new technology block while decreasing input from the employment block.

The *ex ante* approach developed by the Battelle Memorial Institute uses engineering information on technical changes to predict variations in input-output coefficients (see W. H. Fisher and C. H. Chilton, 1972). It is used in France and Russia for perspective planning. The essential steps in this approach are: (1) definition of sectors; (2) making a tentative estimate of the coefficient to be used as a benchmark by the experts interviewed; (3) selection of one or two interviewers with a sound familiarity with the technological history of the industry and acquaintance with its business practices; (4) an interview between a Battelle investigator and an expert chosen for the industry where the interviewer explained the objectives of the research project and carried out a cell-by-cell scrutiny; and (5) suggestions by the experts as to the quantitative changes in input coefficients of the industry. In certain respects this approach is similar (at least in intent) to the engineering approach in production function analysis.

R. A. Buzunov explains the Russian method (1970), which is basically projecting the coefficient on the basis of direct technical information. Technical relationships, like the linear relationship between expenditure on ferrous rolled metal in tons and the freight capacity of trucks, are used in these estimates.

Henri Aujac explains the problems faced in applying input-output analysis to France in a period of rapid projected technological progress (1972). Until 1965, the input-output tables played a crucial role in French planning; but at the end period the planners began to lay accent on R&D to develop new products and new processes. It became necessary to forecast here and now the nomenclature that input-output analysis would be using in a decade or two. The author gives a short summary of the attempt to trace, at five-year intervals beginning with 1955 and going up to the end of this century, the probable stages of transition of these inventions to the marketing stage and thus develop a "dynamics of nomenclatures." We find this study mentioning much more explicitly than any of the others discussed in this survey the problems created by new products. The description of the method is sketchy, and we can only quote their own summary.

> By exploring the future of different chains by the same methods, it seems possible to define and date the "technological eras" for each industry, as well as "eras of transition," and to identify at each epoch what are the fields of the input-output table which have ceased to be representative and to anticipate the new descriptions characteristic of those fields, to analyse the effects of domination which technical progress recorded in one sector may have

on the economic and technical patterns of another. [Aujac, 1972, p. 416.]

The author hopes to formulate a more aggregative function interrelating different technological periods in the same way that a consumption function spans periods of taste changes; he states that, because of the complexity of formulating such a function, he is not in a position to report results.

III. Production Function Approach

This approach can be applied to study the technology of an individual industry or of an economy. In the latter case we assume the existence of an aggregate production function.

Among the industries related to raw materials, the U.S. electric power generation industry was an object of repeated studies using various techniques within the production function approach. The popularity of this industry stems from its importance in the economy. Its capital assets are far greater than the next largest industry, petroleum. The share of electricity in energy utilization of the country is constantly on the increase. Finally, the availability of data for this industry exceeds that of any other, since the industry is organized as a public utility.

Melvyn A. Fuss (1970; 1977), Ernst Berndt and David Wood (1974), and Berndt and M. S. Khaled (1979) use flexible functional forms to analyze the economy-wide technological progress and its impact on efficiency in the use of material and energy inputs.

1. Electric Power Generation Industry

In considering the various studies of electric power generation, this survey will emphasize the techniques used to measure technical progress. An early study of American industry by Ryutaro Komiya (1962) tries to estimate technical progress by considering the performance of each plant constructed between 1930 and 1956. The 235 plants constituting his sample are divided into four groups—technological epochs—according to year of construction. Each plant is assumed to incorporate the latest technology for the period, and its performance is observed only once, when new, so that its performance is not affected by use or depreciation over time. The plants are also classified into coal- and noncoal-using units. A production function is fitted, as described below, to each of these eight cells, and analysis of covariance is used to decide whether there are shifts in production functions that are to be attributed to technological change.

Komiya begins by using a multifactor Cobb-Douglas production function (1962). Since it is obvious that capital, labor, and fuel are essential inputs into the production process, the author of this study as well as of those considered below felt it essential to use at least a three-factor production function. Attempts to fit the multifactor Cobb-Douglas production function failed, probably due to multicollinearity, and he ended up using a set of limitational production functions.

Even with this model, Komiya failed to get a conclusive result for the labor equation. But for the other two inputs, his main conclusion is that economies of scale are more important than technical progress. "The result of the present study shows that in steam power generation the scale effect is a far more important factor in the process of technological progress than either factor substitution or pure technological change" (1962, p. 166).

Yoram Barzel studies economies of scale and technological change through input demand functions (1964). He fits the fuel and labor input functions to 220 plants constructed between 1941 and 1959 and the capital input function to 178 plants. While the capital input equation uses one observation per plant, the other input

equation is fitted to annual observations of each plant from its first year of full-time operation until any major change is undertaken or until 1960, whichever is earlier. The independent variables for fuel and labor input functions are six economic variables and thirteen dummy variables, the latter representing the thirteen years in the period in which plants began operation. The six economic variables are plant size, anticipated load factor, anticipated average input price ratio, two variables giving within-plant variation of the load factor and input price ratio, and age of plant. The capital equation is slightly different. The net result of Barzel's method is that technological progress appears as a shift in the intercept, while the slope is constant. In the case of the capital equation, the analysis is vitiated by the assumption about the price of capital, since changes in it will also influence the shift parameter. Barzel tries to separate it by running another regression with the dummy variables of the other two equations as proxies for change in quality of equipment. This *ad hoc* procedure has no satisfactory economic rationale and throws doubt on his conclusion that scale economies are more important than technical progress.

The study by Phoebus Dhrymes and Mordecai Kurz is significant for two reasons (1964). It represents the first attempt to formulate a nonhomothetic CES function and to apply it to empirical estimation. Secondly, it attempts to differentiate between scale economy and technological change by stratifying the sample according to size. Giora Hanoch discusses the relation between this production function and the production model given in his paper, which includes nonhomothetic CES (1975). The production function is originally written as:

$$Q = A\left(\sum_{i=1}^{n} a_i X_i^{\beta_i} \right)^{1/\gamma}, \qquad (9)$$

where Q is the output and X_i's are the inputs. In empirical work they reduce the number of inputs to three: capital, labor, and fuel. Assuming cost minimization, they derive a set of equations to which two-stage least squares techniques could be applied. The equation for labor, as derived from the nonhomothetic production function, fits badly, and the production function is modified to make a mix limitational–substitutional production function:

$$Q = \min[\, g(L), (\alpha_f F^{\beta_f} + \alpha_K K^{\beta_K})^{1/\gamma}\,], \quad (10)$$

where Q is output, L is labor, F is fuel, and K is capital.

The new labor function assumes that labor demand varies with the region in which the firm is located. The United States is divided into three regions. The main conclusions drawn are that the elasticity of substitution tends to fall with size, with one exception, but that technology influences elasticity only for larger plants. This is taken to imply that technical progress is not purely neutral, but the neutral components are also significant.

Malcolm Galatin is concerned with the measurement of capital and capacity when plants with machines of different vintage and fuel are used in production and when information is available only about input and output of plants and not of the individual machines (1968). He is also concerned with adjustment for the time the machine is hot but not connected (i.e., boiler hot but no generation of electricity). In retrospect this adjustment turned out to be insignificant. As a result of these deliberations, certain indices for fuel input and capacity utilization are derived for plants that have machines of the same size and vintage. Microeconomic considerations are used to show that only two regression equations give best linear unbiased estimations.

The conclusion of this analysis is that economies of scale exist for the full range of the sample, although its strength varies over the range. Over time technological change has acted to reduce fuel requirements for machines. Newly embodied technology is seen to be more efficient in reducing fuel requirements for coal-using plants than noncoal-using plants and for relatively smaller machines than for larger machines.

We shall now turn to the consideration of the three Ph.D. theses prepared at the University of California, Berkeley, under the guidance of Professor McFadden. They seek to estimate technical progress in the U.S. using various approaches. Alexander Belinfante aims at estimating embodied, disembodied, neutral, and nonneutral technical progress using a nonhomothetic (implicitly defined) production function (1969).

Beginning with an implicit definition of the production function (1969, p. 38):

$$F(Y, J, L, M, N, t) = 1, \quad (11)$$

where Y is output, t time, and J, L, M, N are variable inputs, Belinfante derives an equation to estimate the rate of disembodied technical progress and another to measure embodied technical progress. The parameters of the former are estimated by regressing against year-by-year performances of given plants into which no additional equipment is introduced so that there is no possibility of embodied technical progress. For estimating embodied technical progress, the sample consists of plants of different vintage at a given point of time.

Belinfante tries to estimate the bias in technical progress by estimating different regression equations with the logarithmic rate of change of factor proportions as the dependent variable (1969). The main conclusion from these exhaustive studies is that the rate of disembodied technical progress is quite small (though the two different methods of estimation give different estimates), while the rate of embodied technical progress is seen to be about

3 percent per year. A separate combined estimate put it at 2.64 percent, but the discrepancy is found to be statistically insignificant. The measures of non-neutrality are also not significantly different from zero.

Fuss presents a theoretical model to relate *ex ante* and *ex post* production functions and a statistical model for estimating these relationships (1970). He then applies it to the analysis of the electric power generation industry. The underlying idea of this approach is to use the generalized Leontief production function developed by W. E. Diewert (see Diewert [1974] for a short survey of the generalized Leontief production function and translog production function) and express the parameters in it as *ex ante* choice of technique.

The number of parameters is so large that it is impossible to estimate them. Therefore, Fuss undertakes an extensive analysis of the conditions in the electric industry to reduce the number of parameters to manageable levels (1970). The important assumptions made include the reduction of factors to four—structures, equipment, fuel, and labor—and treating the first two as constants in the *ex post* (short-run) case. The expected load is taken to be one, and constant interest and fuel prices are also assumed. Perfect foresight for future wages is assumed. The interplant variation of the matrix of technological coefficients is assumed to be confined to diagonal elements. The structure of this matrix shows whether the industry has putty-clay, putty-putty, or clay-clay technology.

Fuss concludes that putty-clay technology is an acceptable hypothesis for this industry; it is also seen that *ex ante* elasticities between pairs of factors are not equal to each other. *Ex ante* and *ex post* economies of scale are noticed, and embodied technical progress is factor saving and slightly biased towards fuel savings.

Before considering the third thesis prepared at Berkeley, it is useful to consider the paper presented by Scott E. Atkinson and Robert Halvorsen (1976). It uses the translog production function together with the duality theorems and is closely related to the method used by Fuss (1970). Atkinson and Halvorsen use a translog restricted profit function related to a translog production function, together with the assumption that the only variable inputs are the fuels. This approach, they claim, has the advantage of avoiding the measurement of the price of capital. Further, instead of measuring fuel input in terms of BTU's, it is disaggregated into coal, gas, and oil. Plants using two of these fuels in 1972 are considered in the statistical analysis. They conclude that both scale elasticities and embodied technical progress are overemphasized in earlier studies, while substitutability among fuels is underestimated.

The problems faced in using generalized Leontief and translog production functions are due to the large number of parameters to be estimated. Fuss treated this by trying to find economic rationales for reducing them, though some of his assumptions are extremely strong (1970). Atkinson and Halvorsen seem to have ignored it (1976). Their model requires estimation of 21 parameters, which considerably reduces the degrees of freedom, since their sample sizes for different fuel groups are 61, 31, and 17, respectively. In Table 1 of the 1975 revised version of the paper, they present the results of their oil–gas sample, which is the largest of the three. While R^2 is quite high for their restricted profit function, 15 out of 21 coefficients are insignificant (at critical value of 1.96). Their specific conclusions are, therefore, hard to accept as conclusive. The whole problem of using generalized Leontief production functions and translog production function compared to simpler but more specific formulations of production functions like nonhomothetic CES is succinctly discussed by Hanoch (1975, pp. 395–96). See also Sato (1974a; 1974b).

In the production function analysis, there are attempts to derive a production function from *ex ante* data obtained from engineering sources. The pioneering study is made by Hollis B. Chenery (1949; 1953) and is also used by Anne Grosse (1953) and Allen Ferguson (1953). Thomas G. Cowing uses it to estimate technical progress in the electric power generation industry (1970).

His model assumes fixed proportions *ex post* while assuming substitutability between capital and fuel. Capital is measured with a hedonic index based on characteristics, capacity, efficiency, vintage, and relative factor prices. The nominal price of capital is written as:

$$K = C^I(z, E, v) \cdot H(P_I), \qquad (12)$$

where K is the nominal price of one machine, z size, E efficiency, v vintage, and P_I is vector of input prices faced by machine producers. In model A, Cowing uses the following form for C^I:

$$C^I(z, E, v) = AE^\gamma z^{1-\alpha} + BE^\gamma z^\beta e^{-\delta v}. \qquad (13)$$

The firm is assumed to minimize the discounted present value of costs—capital costs as above and current costs—for each plant.

The rates of capital and fuel augmenting technical progress are found to be 15 percent and 2 percent respectively. The value of α is found to be 3.9, while there are *a priori* reasons for considering it to be less than one. This led to the formulation of a more general model where

$$C^I = AE^\gamma z^{1-\alpha} e^{-\epsilon v} + BE^\xi z^\beta e^{-\delta v}. \qquad (14)$$

Unfortunately, this model is underidentified without restrictions on parameters. The empirical analysis of model A suggested the restriction $\gamma = \xi$. Further, ϵ is set to be equal to zero.

No other industry has achieved the de-gree of detailed and complex analysis of technical progress as the electric power generation industry. This is due partly to its significance in the corporate sector and partly to the availability of data.

Another study that deserves mention is the attempt by T. Osborne to use a multifactor nonhomothetic CES to study substitutability between intermediate and primary output in the manufacturing sector (1975). The production function is fitted to nineteen industries using time-series data based on the Census-of-Manufacture (C.O.M.) four-digit level of aggregation. The C.O.M. dollar figures for material inputs are divided by an index number of input prices computed for each industry using one to six materials. The more general CES production functions, based on Sato (1970; 1975), gave better fit than the conventional ones with the same elasticity of substitution between all inputs.

2. *Economy-Wide Studies*

There are very few studies using aggregate multifactor production functions for the economy to estimate technical change. Berndt and Wood (1975) and Fuss (1977) considered Hicks neutral technical change, but the main thrust of these papers is to use flexible functional forms to estimate other characteristics of the technology. Only Berndt and Khaled give a detailed analysis of technological change (1979).

Berndt and Khaled (1979) use a generalized Box-Cox (GBC) functional form to estimate biased technical progress in U.S. economy. They recognize that different flexible functional forms like a generalized Leontief could give substantially differing empirical results, although they all claim to be second-order approximations of an arbitrary cost function. The GBS has the advantage that other well-known functional forms are special or limiting cases of GBS. They adopt the representation:

$$C = \left\{ \frac{2}{\lambda} \sum_i \sum_j \beta_{ij} P_i^{\lambda/2} P_j^{\lambda/2} \right\}^{1/\lambda}$$

$$\cdot Y^{\beta(Y,P)} e^{T(t,P)}, \tag{15}$$

where

$$\beta(Y, P) = \beta + \frac{\theta}{2} \ln Y$$

$$+ \sum_i \phi_i \ln P_i$$

$$T(t, P) = t(\tau + \sum_i \tau_i \ln P_i)$$

and Y is output and P_i are the prices of input capital (K), labor (L), energy (E), other intermediate materials (M) and t is time. The production function is homothetic if $\phi_i = 0$ for all i and homogeneous of degree $1/\beta$ if, in addition, $\theta = 0$. Finally, technical progress is Hicks-neutral at a constant exponential rate τ if $\tau_i = 0$. They use the data from Berndt and Wood (1975) to fit the production function and derive a number of results.

First, they test whether restrictions on the production function and on the form of technical progress are admissible. The homotheticity restriction is decisively rejected. Neutrality of technical progress is only marginally rejected if the production function is taken to be non-homothetic. The interesting observation is that the sample likelihood function has different plateaus; and a *chi*-square test does not have the power to reject a specification among the many plateaus that form one level of the likelihood function.

Brandt and Khaled then argue that this inability to distinguish between a constant returns to scale production function with neutral technical progress and a homogeneous production function with zero technical progress is the source of controversy over the role of returns to scale and technical progress in explaining residual productivity (1979). They suggest that the solution to this indeterminacy is to specify nonhomothetic production with nonneutral technical progress.

Sato and Ramachandran have shown that there is a homothetic production function that corresponds to any homogeneous production function with Hicks neutral technical progress (1974). The empirical results derived by Berndt and Khaled (1979) are easily explained by this theorem. Sato has further extended this theorem to correspondences between nonhomothetic production functions and nonneutral technical progress (1974b). In the light of this extension it is not clear that the more general production function would resolve the inability to separate the two factors.

Berndt and Khaled also argue that there is a bias in technical progress (1979). Technical change is, on the one hand, capital and energy using, while, on the other hand, it is labor and intermediate-good saving. Considering the price changes of these inputs from 1967–71, they point out that the results are consistent with the induced innovation hypothesis.

Finally, they estimate the Allen partial elasticity between various inputs. They conclude that the elasticities between different inputs vary substantially and that these estimates are robust.

Berndt and Khaled recognize that the various flexible forms of the production function can give differing empirical estimates. What is not clear is that the adoption of an even more general form suggested by them would give conclusive answers. D. Guilkey and Ramachandran (1976) fitted a nonhomothetic CES production function developed by Sato (1974a) to the data in Berndt and Wood (1975). Using the composite commodity extension proposed by Sato (1970), they tested the null hypothesis that various elasticities of substitution are equal and could not reject it. Berndt and Khaled's assertion (1979) about the robustness of their elasticity estimates are also at variance with the earlier simulation results derived by T. Krishna Kumar and James H. Gapinski (1974).

IV. *Measures of Total Factor Productivity*

1. *Indices of Structural Change of the Economy*

A study of the changes in the industrial structure of the United States led Leontief to formulate an index of structural change (1941). If the index is negative, then it implies that the economy is capable of producing the same output with a lower amount of input. If the definition of technical change is broadened to include all changes in factor productivity, then this is a measure of technical change. Lave argued that the complexity of the index and the unavailability of data made the index unattractive (1966, p. 21). The latter criticism is surprising in view of the vast amount of empirical work on input-output tables. It seems more reasonable to assume that the limited interest on the material problem was the main factor behind this neglect. Evsey D. Domar argued for a wider use of the index, though he had some criticisms of it (1969, pp. 44–45).

Following Domar (1961), the Leontief index can be formulated as follows. Let a_{ik}^t, $t = 0,1$, be the input coefficient and let x_{ik}^t, $t = 0,1$, be the value of input i used in the production of commodity k in period t. Then, the industrial change index $\bar{a}_{ik} = (a_{ik}^1 - a_{ik}^0)/(a_{ik}^1 + a_{ik}^0)/2$. When the individual $\bar{a}_{ik}$'s are aggregated over an industry or over the economy, each of these indices are weighted according to the average value of the inputs in the two periods, $(x_{ik}^1 + x_{ik}^0)/2$. Thus in the case of an individual industry, the index is:

$$\bar{I}_k = \frac{\sum_i \frac{x_{ik}^1 + x_{ik}^0}{2} \cdot 2\left(\frac{a_{ik}^1 - a_{ik}^0}{a_{ik}^1 + a_{ik}^0}\right)}{\sum_i \frac{x_{ik}^1 + x_{ik}^0}{2}}. \quad (16)$$

For the economy as a whole, the summation should be both over i and k, in which case the denominator will be the average value of all commodities produced in the two periods.

Domar analyzes this model extensively for invariance under different degrees of aggregation of industries (1961; 1967). In his 1961 paper, he compares it to the indices of residual productivity derived from the production function approach. He first points out that, in the case of a single industry, and in the case of two industries, neither using the output of the other as an input, the index of residual productivity agrees with the Leontief index (1961, pp. 727–28). In the case of one industry using the output of the other industry as an input, the two indices differ. Domar develops a model in which he relates the Leontief index to the indices of residual productivity based on the Cobb-Douglas production function. He considers two outputs Y and M (our notations); Y is produced with capital (K), labor (L), and raw materials (M). The entire output of M is used for production of Y.

Through simple mathematical manipulations, Domar shows that (1961, pp. 728–29):

$$I = \bar{A}_1 + O_M\bar{A}_2 = I_1 + O_M I_2, \quad (17)$$

where $O_M = M/Y$ (Domar takes the initial ratio and is not concerned with possible changes in the relative prices of M and Y); $\bar{A}_1$ and $\bar{A}_2$ are the residual productivity indices for the two industries separately; I_1 and I_2 are the Leontief indices for both industries separately; and I is the Leontief index for the two industries after aggregation. Since the residual index for the two industries together is given by $\bar{A}_1 + O_M\bar{A}_2$ (as can be easily shown), the Leontief index agrees with the conventional residual index in this case.

If, instead of integrating the two industries into one, the two Leontief indices are calculated separately and combined as suggested by Leontief, then

$$I = \frac{YI_1 + MI_2}{Y + M}$$

$$< I_1 + \frac{M}{Y}I_2 \qquad (18)$$

$$= I_1 + O_M I_2.$$

To quote Domar (1961, p. 729):

Thus Leontief's index is not invariant to the degree of integration. His method disregards the fact that an input-output relationship among industries produces a Residual, or an index of structural change, whose relative rate of growth is larger than the conventionally weighted sum of the *A*'s or *I*'s of the individual industries.

Spencer Star argues that this difference in relative growth is necessary to reconcile the estimates of the residual using net output at the industry level with that estimated using the value-added concept at the economy-wide level (1974). Charles R. Hulten (1978) shows that the index suggested by Domar (1961) is the rate of change of social production possibility curve, assuming primary inputs to be constant.

In his 1967 paper, Domar returns to this issue in the context of comparing the various indices of industrial activity, particularly the ones used to compare the United States and the Soviet Union. He defines an index *B* as:

$$B = \frac{\sum_{i=1}^{n} \sum_{j=1}^{m} y_{ij}(X_{ij} - X_j)}{\sum_{i=1}^{m} y_i'}, \qquad (19)$$

where

X_{ij} = the rate of growth of the material input from industry *i* to industry *j*;

X_j = the rate of growth of output of industry *j*;

y_{ij} = the value of output of industry *i* used by industry *j*, $1 \leq i, j \leq m$, $i \neq j$;

y_i' = value added by industry *i*;

m = the number of domestic industries;

n = number of all industries including imports.

Domar (1967, p. 179) points out that this index is a variant of Leontief's index of structural change, which arises from savings (if $B < 0$) on material inputs. On their difference he states in the footnote (1967, p. 179*n*):

The numerator of *B* . . . is identical with Leontief's, but in the denominator he used $\sum_1^n \sum_1^m y_{ij}$ instead of the correct (for his purpose) $\sum_1^m y_{iF}$ [where y_{iF} = the value of the final output of industry *i*].

This is equivalent to the statement that had Leontief used *Y* instead of $Y + M$ in the denominator of *I*, (equation [18]) then $I = I_1 + O_M I_2$.

As noted earlier, the Leontief measure is not widely used in empirical studies.

2. Indices of Total Productivity in Individual Industries

In the previous section we considered indices on the efficiency of raw material usage based on input-output analysis. Now we turn to the analysis of the indices of total productivity based on the studies by Robert Solow (1957), John W. Kendrick (1961), and others, but altered to include raw materials. The advantage of this approach in measuring technical change taking place in an industry producing or consuming raw materials is its extreme simplicity. The computational efforts are much less than in fitting a production function.

We find that one of the pioneering studies on technical change in a raw material producing industry is Donald N. McCloskey's study of the British Pig Iron Industry (1968). He follows Solow's method of measuring total productivity (1957). If Q is the output of pig iron, C is the input of coke, O of ore, K of capital, and L of labor, and S the share of the factor, then the rate of change of total productivity A is measured by:

$$\frac{\Delta A}{A} = \frac{\Delta Q}{Q} - \left(S_c \frac{\Delta C}{C} + S_o \frac{\Delta O}{O} \right.$$
$$\left. + S_k \frac{\Delta K}{K} + S_l \frac{\Delta L}{L} \right). \qquad (20)$$

This paper recommends itself to the attention of a researcher in the field, not so much for a modified application of the Divisia index, but for its careful attention to the various problems that could arise in adopting this technique to an industry case. He carefully analyzes the assumptions underlying its adaptation: (1) The first is that capital, like labor, is freely variable. He argues that the variation in the number of blast furnaces from year to year can be taken as evidence of this. (2) Secondly, he considers the possible influence of economies of scale. He argues that only pecuniary economies or diseconomies of scale could produce spurious productivity and that they are absent for the industry under consideration. (3) He argues that while the Hicks neutral form of technical change may not represent the true shift in the production function, it still measures the proportionate change in output attributable to the shift. (4) Further the assumption of perfect competition is justifiable; he points out that if this assumption is not true, then the true measure of total productivity is obtained by substituting the elasticity of output with respect to each input for factor share in the equation. After making some simplifying assumptions, he tests the difference between the two measures and argues that it is negligible. (5) He argues that a different measure of capital such as surface area of blast furnaces does not affect the results. (6) Finally, he argues that accounting for the quality of iron ore does not affect the results. The importance of such a careful analysis of the assumptions is brought out by G. S. Maddala (1965). He argues that the increase in the productivity of the coal industry in the United States as frequently estimated is solely due to increased horsepower per worker; his arguments are based on fitting production functions to cross-sectional data.

3. *Measures of Partial Productivity*

Changes in the partial productivity of one input are occasionally used as a measure of the technical efficiency with which it is used. If the input has a natural unit, there is no difficulty in measuring partial productivity. Frequently, as in the case of energy, the input consists of physically heterogeneous commodities; then any error in the construction of the composite input index will bias the productivity measure.

Ralph Turvey and A. R. Nobay argue that measuring energy consumption in terms of coal-equivalence or thermal content can bias the measures of partial productivity (1965). They argue that to measure coal-equivalence of gas and electricity is to measure the secondary fuels in terms of fuel inputs required to produce them. Thus, if coal is the only primary source of energy, the share of gas and electricity in the energy market in terms of coal-equivalence would be an indirect way of stating the fraction of coal output used to produce these sources of energy. Since coal is not the only primary source of energy, it only tells how much coal would be used if these primary sources were substituted for by coal—a measure of doubtful usefulness. It also ignores secondary costs like controllability, cleanliness, and capital costs of equipment required in using a fuel.

They argue that the relevant conversion factors are either the marginal rate of transformation in production or the marginal rates of substitution in their consumption. But due to the absence of data, the only possible measure is price or average revenue.

Berndt and Wood are concerned with the interpretation of the energy-GNP ratio (1974). They measure energy in thermal units and consider a production function:

$$Y = F(K,L,E,M), \qquad (21)$$

where Y is gross output, K capital, L labor, E energy, and M other raw material inputs. If the production function is homothetic, the cost function can be written as the product of two functions, one of which involves only output and the other the prices of inputs. They now define value-added as follows:

$$P_v V = P_k K + P_l L. \qquad (22)$$

Following Arrow (1972), they argue that a value-added concept has meaning only if the production function takes a special nested form:

$$\begin{aligned} Y &= F(K,L,E,M) \\ &= F_1[B(K,L),E,M] \\ &= F_2(V,E,M), \end{aligned} \qquad (23)$$

where B is a function of K and L only (1974, p. 25). For this to hold, it is necessary and sufficient that technological substitution between K and L be independent of the levels of E and M. Quoting Berndt and Laurits R. Christensen (1973), Berndt and Wood argue that the necessary and sufficient condition for weak separability is that the Allen partial elasticity of substitution between E and K equal that between E and L and that between E and V. (Similarly for elasticities between M and K, L, or V).

Finally, quoting L. J. Lau (1972), Berndt and Wood (1974, p. 25) argue that, subject to certain regularity conditions, these assumptions lead to a new cost function.

$$\begin{aligned} G &= H(Y) \, J(P_K,P_L,P_E,P_M) \\ &= H(Y) \, J_1[Q(P_K,P_L),P_E,P_M] \\ &= H(Y) \, J_2(P_V,P_E,P_M). \end{aligned} \qquad (24)$$

Now using the Hotelling–Shepard Lemma,

$$\frac{E}{V} = \frac{\partial J_2 / \partial P_E}{\partial J_2 / \partial P_V}. \qquad (25)$$

This is the familiar energy-GNP ratio. Even if all the assumptions implied in its derivation hold true, it can vary due to changes in price ratios; on the other hand, technological change that is Hicks-neutral will not affect the ratio.

They conclude that the study of the elasticity of substitution between the various inputs and testing of the existence of relations among them is a necessary prelude both to the interpretation of such indices as the energy-GNP ratio and to addressing policy issues on the effect of prices and taxes on these indices.

Conclusion

Only very recently have economists become conscious of the constraints to growth from nonprimary inputs. The impact of technical progress on these constraints is currently analyzed using either input-output analysis or production functions.

Input-output analysts, like Carter (1970, pp. 10–11), argue that movements along a production frontier and movements of the frontier can never be separated and take every change in the coefficient to be an indication of technical change. An alternate approach, which can be traced to Leontief (1941) and Arrow and Hoffenberg (1959), sets out to analyze the causative factors for coefficient change. This approach seems to be more popular outside the United States.

The production functions give a more detailed structure to the technology. The problem still faced in the use of this approach is to introduce it in such a manner that it is possible to handle more than two inputs simultaneously, to differentiate between scale elasticity and technical progress, and to measure substitutability between inputs accurately. In spite of many studies using aggregate production functions with two primary inputs, few attempts have been made to measure technical progress using a multifactor production function. Considering that the interest in this problem became visible only recently, this paucity of literature is not surprising. Hopefully we can look forward to a more productive period in analysis of the impact of technological change on the scarcity of material inputs.

REFERENCES

ALMON, CLOPPER, JR., ET AL. *1985: Inter-industry forecasts of the American economy.* Lexington, Mass.: Lexington Books, 1974.

ARROW, KENNETH J. "The Measurement of Real Value Added," Stanford University Institute for Mathematical Studies in the Social Science, Technical Report, No. 69, 1972.

———, ET AL. "Capital Labor Substitution and Economic Efficiency," *Rev. Econ. Statist.,* August 1961, *43*(3), pp. 225–50.

——— AND HOFFENBERG, MARVIN. *A time series analysis of interindustry demands.* Amsterdam: North-Holland, 1959.

ATKINSON, SCOTT E. AND HALVORSEN, ROBERT. "Interfuel Substitution in Steam Electric Power Generation," *J. Polit. Econ.,* Oct. 1976, *84*(5), pp. 959–78.

AUJAC, HENRI. "New Approaches in French National Economy: Input-Output Tables and Technological Forecasting," in *Input-output techniques.* Edited by ANDREW BRÓDY AND ANNE P. CARTER. Amsterdam: North-Holland, 1972, pp. 406–17.

BACHARACH, MICHAEL. *Biproportional matrices and input-output change.* Cambridge: Cambridge University Press, 1970.

BARZEL, YORAM. "The Production Function and Technical Change in the Steam-Power Industry," *J. Polit. Econ.,* April 1964, *72*(2), pp. 133–50.

BAUMOL, WILLIAM J. *Economic dynamics: An introduction.* Second edition. New York: Macmillan, 1959.

BELINFANTE, ALEXANDER. *Technical change in the steam-electric power generating industry.* Ph.D. Thesis, University of California, Berkeley, 1969.

BERNDT, ERNST R. AND CHRISTENSEN, LAURITS R. "The Translog Function and the Substitution of Equipment, Structures, and Labor in U.S. Manufacturing, 1929–68," *J. Econometrica,* March 1973, *1*(1), pp. 81–113.

——— AND KHALED, M. S. "Econometric Productivity Measurements and Choice among Flexible

Functional Firms," *J. Polit. Econ.,* Dec. 1979, *87*(6), pp. 1220–45.

——— AND WOOD, DAVID O. "An Economic Interpretation of Energy-GNP Ratio," in *Energy: Demand, conservation, and institutional problems.* Edited by MICHAEL S. MACRAKIS. Cambridge, Mass.: MIT Press, 1974, pp. 21–30.

——— AND WOOD, DAVID O. "Technology, Prices, and Derived Demand for Energy," *Rev. Econ. Statist.,* August 1975, *57*(3), pp. 259–68.

BUZUNOV, R. A. "Technical Economic Projection of Coefficients of Direct Material Inputs," in *Applications of input-output analysis:* Published in honor of WASSILY LEONTIEF, edited by ANNE P. CARTER AND ANDREW BRÓDY. Amsterdam: North-Holland, 1970, pp. 322–30.

CARTER, ANNE P. *Structural change in the American economy,* Cambridge, Mass.: Harvard University Press, 1970.

———. "Energy, Environment, and Economic Growth," *Bell J. Econ. Manage. Sci.,* Autumn 1974, *5*(2), pp. 578–92.

———, ed. *Energy and the environment: A structural Analysis.* Hanover, N.H.: University Press of New England for Brandeis University Press, 1976.

CHENERY, HOLLIS B. "Engineering Production Functions," *Quart. J. Econ.,* Nov. 1949, *63*(4), pp. 507–31.

———. "Process and Production Functions from Engineering Data," in *Studies in the structure of the American economy.* By WASSILY LEONTIEF et al., New York: Oxford University Press, 1953, pp. 297–325.

CHRISTENSEN, LAURITS R., JORGENSEN, DALE W. AND LAU, LAWRENCE J. "Transcendental Logarithmic Production Frontiers," *Rev. Econ. Statist.,* Feb. 1973, *55*(1), pp. 28–45.

COLE, S. AND MILES, I. "Assumptions and Methods: Population, Economic Development, Modelling and Technical Change," in *World futures: The great debate.* Edited by CHRISTOPHER FREEMAN AND MARIE JAHODA. New York: Universe Books, 1978.

COWING, THOMAS G. *Technical change in steam-electric generation: An engineering approach.* Ph.D. Thesis, University of California, Berkeley, 1970.

DHRYMES, PHOEBUS J. AND KURZ, MORDECAI. "Technology and Scale in Electricity Generation," *Econometrica,* July 1964, *32*(3), pp. 287–315.

DIEWERT, W. E. "Applications of Duality Theory," in *Frontiers of quantitative economics.* Vol. II. Edited by MICHAEL D. INTRILIGATOR AND DAVID KENDRICK. Amsterdam: North-Holland, 1974, pp. 106–71.

DOMAR, EVSEY D. "On the Measurement of Technical Change," *Econ. J.,* Dec. 1961, *71*(284), pp. 709–29.

———. "An Index-Number Tournament," *Quart. J. Econ.,* May 1967, *81*(2), pp. 169–88.

———. "Theory of Innovation: Discussion," *Amer. Econ. Rev.,* May 1969, *59*(2), pp. 44–46.

EVANS, WILMOTH D. AND HOFFENBERG, MARVIN. "The Interindustry Relations Study for 1947," *Rev. Econ. Statist.,* May 1952, *34*(2), pp. 97–142.

FERGUSON, ALLEN R. "Commercial Air Transportation in the United States," in *Studies in the structure of the American economy.* Edited by WASSILY LEONTIEF *et al.* New York: Oxford University Press, 1953, pp. 421–47.

FISHER, W. H. AND CHILTON, C. H. "Developing Ex-Ante Input-Output Flow Capital Coefficients," in *input-output techniques.* Edited by ANDREW BRÓDY AND ANNE P. CARTER. Amsterdam: North-Holland, 1972, pp. 393–405.

FONTELA, E., ET AL. "Forecasting Technical Coefficients and Changes in Relative Prices," in *Applications of input-output analysis.* Edited by ANNE P. CARTER AND ANDREW·BRÓDY. Amsterdam: North-Holland, 1970, pp. 331–45.

FORRESTER, JAY W. *World dynamics.* Cambridge, Mass.: Wright-Allen, 1971.

FROMM, GARY. "Factors Affecting the Postwar Industrial Composition of Real Product: Comment," in *The industrial composition of income and products.* Edited by JOHN W. KENDRICK. New York: National Bureau of Economic Research; distributed by Columbia University Press, 1968, pp. 59–66.

FORSSELL, OSMO. "Explaining Changes in Input-Output Coefficients of Finland," in *Input-output techniques.* Edited by ANDREW BRÓDY and ANNE P. CARTER. Amsterdam: North-Holland, 1972, pp. 343–69.

FUSS, MELVYN A. *The time structure of technology: An empirical analysis of the putty-clay hypothesis.* Ph.D. Thesis, University of California, Berkeley, 1970.

———. "The Demand for Energy in Canadian Manufacturing: An Example of the Estimation of Production Structures with Many Inputs," *J. Econometrics,* Jan. 1977, *5*(1), pp. 89–116.

———. "The Structure of Technology over Time: A Model of Testing the 'Putty-Clay' Hypothesis," *Econometrica,* Nov. 1977, *45*(8), pp. 1797–1821.

GALATIN, MALCOLM. *Economies of scale and technological change in thermal power generation.* Amsterdam: North-Holland, 1968.

GEORGESCU-ROEGEN, NICHOLAS. "Energy and Economic Myths," *Southern Econ. J.,* Jan. 1975, *41*(3), pp. 347–81.

GRABOWSKI, HENRY G. "The Determinants of Industrial Research and Development: A Study of the Chemical, Drug, and Petroleum Industries," *J. Polit. Econ.,* March–April 1968, *76*(2), pp. 292–306.

GROSSE, ANNE P. "The Technological Structure of the Cotton Textile Industry," in *Studies of the structure of the American economy.* Edited by WASSILY LEONTIEF *et al.* New York: Oxford University Press, 1953, pp. 360–420.

GUILKEY, D. AND RAMACHANDRAN, R. V. "A Note on Technology and the Demand for Energy," Department of Economics, Southern Methodist University, 1976.

HANOCH, GIORA. "Production and Demand Models with Direct or Indirect Implicit Additivity," *Econometrica,* May 1975, *43*(3), pp. 395–419.

HULTEN, CHARLES R. "Growth Accounting with Intermediate Inputs," *Rev. Econ. Stud.,* Oct. 1978, *45*(3), pp. 511–18.

INTRILIGATOR, MICHAEL. D. AND KENDRICK, DAVID A., eds. *Frontiers on quantitative economics.* Vol. II. Amsterdam: North-Holland, 1974.

ISTVAN, RUDYARD. "Interindustry Impacts of Alternate Utility Investment Strategies," in *Energy: Demand, conservation, and institutional problems.* By MICHAEL M. MACRAKIS. Cambridge, Mass.: MIT Press, 1974, pp. 129–40.

JUST, JAMES E. "Impacts of New Energy Technology Using Generalized Input-Output Analysis," in *Energy: Demand, conservation, and institutional problems.* Edited by MICHAEL M. MACRAKIS. Cambridge, Mass.: MIT Press, 1974, pp. 113–28.

KAHN, HERMAN AND WIENER, ANTHONY J. *The year 2000.* New York and London: Macmillian, 1967.

KENDRICK, JOHN W. *Productivity trends in United States.* Princeton, N.J.: Princeton University Press, 1961.

KENNEDY, CHARLES AND THIRLWALL, A. P. "Technical Progress: A Survey," *Econ. J.,* March 1972, *82*(325), pp. 11–72.

KOMIYA, RYUTARO. "Technological Progress and the Production Function in the United States Steam Power Industry," *Rev. Econ. Statist.,* May 1962, *44*(2), pp. 156–66.

KUMAR, T. KRISHNA AND GAPINSKI, JAMES H. "Nonlinear Estimation of CES Production Parameters: A Monte Carlo Study," *Rev. Econ. Statist.,* Nov. 1974, *56*(4), pp. 563–67.

LAU, L. J. "Duality and the Structure of Cost Functions," Stanford University, Department of Economics, 1972.

LAVE, LESTER B. *Technological change: Its conception and measurement.* Englewood Cliffs, N.J.: Prentice-Hall, 1966.

LEONTIEF, WASSILY W. *The structure of the American economy, 1919–1929.* Cambridge, Mass.: Harvard University Press, 1941.

———, ET AL. *Studies in the structure of the Ameri-*

can economy. New York: Oxford University Press, 1953.

MADDALA, G. S. "Productivity and Technological Change in the Bituminous Coal Industry, 1919–54," *J. Polit. Econ.,* August 1965, *73*(4), pp. 352–65.

McCLOSKEY, DONALD N. "Productivity Change in British Pig Iron, 1870–1939," *Quart. J. Econ.,* May 1968, *82*(2), pp. 281–96.

MEADOWS, DONELLA H., ET AL., *The limits to growth.* New York: Universe Books, 1972.

MIDDELHOEK, A. J. "Test of the Marginal Stability of Input-Output Coefficients," in *Applications of input-output analysis.* Edited by ANNE P. CARTER AND ANDREW BRÓDY. Amsterdam: North-Holland, 1970, pp. 261–79.

NADIRI, M. ISHAQ. "Some Approaches to the Theory and Measurement of Total Factor Productivity: A Survey," *J. Econ. Lit.,* Dec. 1970, *8*(4), pp. 1137–77.

OSBORNE, T. "Factor Substitution and Scale Effects." University of New York at Albany, Working Paper, 1975.

OZAKI, IWAO. "The Effects of Technological Change on Economic Growth of Japan, 1955–1970," in *Advances in input-output analysis.* Edited by KAREN R. POLENSKE AND JIRI V. SKOLA. Cambridge, Mass.: Ballinger, 1976, pp. 93–111.

SATO, RYUZO. "The Estimation of Biased Technical Progress and the Production Function," *Int. Econ. Rev.,* June 1970, *11*(2), pp. 179–208.

———. "On the Class of Separable Non-Homothetic CES Functions," *Econ. Stud. Quart.,* April 1974[a], *25*(1), pp. 42–55.

———. "The Impact of Technological Change Under Homothetic and Holothetic Production Functions," Brown University, Discussion Paper, 1974b; presented in the 1975 World Congress of the Econometric Society, Toronto, Canada.

——— AND BECKMANN, MARTIN J. "Neutral Inventions and Production Functions," *Rev. Econ. Stud.,* Jan. 1968, *35*(1), pp. 57–65.

——— AND RAMACHANDRAN, R. V. "Models of Optimal Endogenous Technical Progress, Scale Effect and Duality of Production Functions." Paper read at North American Econometric Conference, 1974.

SEVALDSON, PER. "The Stability of Input-Output Coefficients," in A. Bródy and A. P. Carter,

Applications of input-output analysis. Edited by ANNE P. CARTER AND ANDREW BRÓDY. Amsterdam: North-Holland, 1970, pp. 207–37.

———. "Price Changes as Causes of Variations in Input-Output Coefficients," in *Advances in input-output analysis.* Edited by KAREN R. POLENSKE AND JIRI V. SKOLKA. Cambridge, Mass.: Ballinger, 1976, pp. 113–33.

SOLOW, ROBERT M. "Technical Change and the Aggregate Production Function," *Rev. Econ. Statist.,* August 1957, *39*(3), pp. 312–20.

STÄGLIN, REINER AND WESSELS, HANS. "Intertemporal Analysis of Structural Change in the German Economy," in *Input-output techniques.* Edited by ANDREW BRÓDY AND ANNE P. CARTER. Amsterdam: North-Holland, 1972, pp. 370–92.

STAR, SPENCER. "Accounting for Growth of Output," *Amer. Econ. Rev.,* March 1974, *64*(1), pp. 123–35.

STONE, RICHARD. "Multiple Classifications in Social Accounting," *Bulletin de l'Institut International de Statistique,* 1962, *39*(3), pp. 215–33.

——— AND BROWN, J. A. C. "A Long-Term Growth Model for the British Economy," in *Europe's future in figures.* Edited by ROBERT C. GEARY. Amsterdam: North-Holland, 1962, pp. 287–310.

TAYLOR, GORDON R. *The doomsday book.* New York: World Publishing, 1970.

THEIL, HENRI. *Applied economic forecasting.* Amsterdam: North-Holland; Chicago: Rand McNally, 1966.

TURVEY, RALPH AND NOBAY, A. R. "On Measuring Energy Consumption," *Econ. J.,* Dec. 1965, *75*(300), pp. 787–93.

VACCARA, BEATRICE N. "Changes Over Time in Input-Output Coefficients for the United States," in *Applications of input-output analysis.* Edited by ANNE P. CARTER AND ANDREW BRÓDY. Amsterdam: North-Holland, 1970, pp. 238–60.

——— AND SIMON, NANCY W. "Factors Affecting the Post-War Industrial Composition of Real Product," in *The industrial composition of income and product.* Edited by JOHN W. KENDRICK. New York: National Bureau of Economic Research; distributed by Columbia University Press, 1968, pp. 19–58.

VALAVANIS-VAIL, STEFAN. "An Econometric Model of Growth, U.S.A., 1869–1953," *Amer. Econ. Rev.,* 1955, *45*, pp. 208–21.

ZELLNER, A. AND REVANKAR, N. S. "Generalized Production Functions," *Rev. Econ. Stud.,* April 1969, *36*(106), pp. 241–50.

Name index

Economists of the Twentieth Century

Monetarism and Macroeconomic
Policy
Thomas Mayer

Studies in Fiscal Federalism
Wallace E. Oates

The World Economy in Perspective
Essays in International Trade and European
Integration
Herbert Giersch

Towards a New Economics
Critical Essays on Ecology, Distribution and
Other Themes
Kenneth E. Boulding

Studies in Positive and Normative
Economics
Martin J. Bailey

The Collected Essays of Richard E.
Quandt (2 volumes)
Richard E. Quandt

International Trade Theory and Policy
Selected Essays of W. Max Corden
W. Max Corden

Organization and Technology in Capitalist
Development
William Lazonick

Studies in Human Capital
Collected Essays of Jacob Mincer, Volume 1
Jacob Mincer

Studies in Labor Supply
Collected Essays of Jacob Mincer, Volume 2
Jacob Mincer

Macroeconomics and Economic Policy
The Selected Essays of Assar Lindbeck,
Volume I
Assar Lindbeck

The Welfare State
The Selected Essays of Assar Lindbeck,
Volume II
Assar Lindbeck

Classical Economics, Public Expenditure
and Growth
Walter Eltis

Money, Interest Rates and Inflation
Frederic S. Mishkin

The Public Choice Approach to Politics
Dennis C. Mueller

The Liberal Economic Order
Volume I Essays on International Economics
Volume II Money, Cycles and Related Themes
Gottfried Haberler
Edited by Anthony Y.C. Koo

Economic Growth and Business Cycles
Prices and the Process of Cyclical Development
Paolo Sylos Labini

International Adjustment, Money and
Trade
Theory and Measurement for Economic Policy,
Volume I
Herbert G. Grubel

International Capital and Service Flows
Theory and Measurement for Economic Policy,
Volume II
Herbert G. Grubel

Unintended Effects of Government
Policies
Theory and Measurement for Economic Policy,
Volume III
Herbert G. Grubel

The Economics of Competitive Enterprise
Selected Essays of P.W.S. Andrews
Edited by Frederic S. Lee
and Peter E. Earl

The Repressed Economy
Causes, Consequences, Reform
Deepak Lal

Economic Theory and Market Socialism
Selected Essays of Oskar Lange
Edited by Tadeusz Kowalik

Trade, Development and Political
Economy
Selected Essays of Ronald Findlay
Ronald Findlay

General Equilibrium Theory
The Collected Essays of Takashi Negishi,
Volume I
Takashi Negishi

The History of Economics
The Collected Essays of Takashi Negishi,
Volume II
Takashi Negishi

Studies in Econometric Theory
The Collected Essays of Takeshi Amemiya
Takeshi Amemiya

Capitalism, Socialism and Post-
Keynesianism
Selected Essays of G.C. Harcourt
G.C. Harcourt

Time Series Analysis and
Macroeconometric Modelling
The Collected Papers of Kenneth F. Wallis
Kenneth F. Wallis

Foundations of Modern Econometrics
The Selected Essays of Ragnar Frisch
(2 volumes)
Edited by Olav Bjerkholt

Growth, the Environment and the
Distribution of Incomes
Essays by a Sceptical Optimist
Wilfred Beckerman

The Economics of Environmental
Regulation
Wallace E. Oates

Econometrics, Macroeconomics and
Economic Policy
Selected Papers of Carl F. Christ
Carl F. Christ

Strategic Approaches to the International
Economy
Selected Essays of Koichi Hamada
Koichi Hamada

Economic Analysis and Political Ideology
The Selected Essays of Karl Brunner,
Volume One
Edited by Thomas Lys

Growth Theory and Technical Change
The Selected Essays of Ryuzo Sato
Volume One
Ryuzo Sato

Employment, Labor Unions and Wages
The Collected Essays of Orley Ashenfelter
Volume One
Edited by Kevin F. Hallock

Education, Training and Discrimination
The Collected Essays of Orley Ashenfelter
Volume Two
Edited by Kevin F. Hallock

Economic Institutions and the Demand and
Supply of Labor
The Collected Essays of Orley Ashenfelter
Volume Three
Edited by Kevin F. Hallock

Economic Controversies Volume One
Microeconomics, Industrial Organization and
Related Themes
Julian L. Simon

Economic Controversies Volume Two
Population Economics, Natural Resources and
Related Themes
Julian L. Simon

Microeconomics, Growth and Political
Economy
The Selected Essays of Richard G. Lipsey
Volume One
Richard G. Lipsey

Macroeconomic Theory and Policy
The Selected Essays of Richard G. Lipsey
Volume Two
Richard G. Lipsey

Economic Theory and Public Decisions
The Selected Essays of Robert Dorfman
Robert Dorfman

Bayesian Analysis in Econometrics and
Statistics
The Zellner View and Papers
Arnold Zellner

Monetary Theory and Monetary Policy
The Selected Essays of Karl Brunner,
Volume Two
Edited by Thomas Lys